ASP.NET Core 2.0
MVC & Razor Pages
for Beginners

How to Build a Video Course Website

Overview

I would like to welcome you to *ASP.NET Core 2.0 MVC & Razor Pages for Beginners*. This book will guide you through creating your very first MVC and Razor Page applications. To get the most from this book, you should have a basic understanding of HTML and be familiar with the C# language.

ASP.NET Core is a new framework from Microsoft. It has been designed from the ground up to be fast and flexible and to work across multiple platforms. ASP.NET Core is the framework to use for your future ASP.NET applications.

The first application you build will evolve into a basic MVC application, starting with an empty template. You will add the necessary pieces one at a time to get a good understanding of how things fit together. The focus is on installing and configuring middleware, services, and other frameworks. Styling with CSS is not a priority in this application; you'll learn more about that in the second application you build.

You will install middleware to create a processing pipeline, and then look at the MVC framework. If you already are familiar with MVC or Web API from previous versions of ASP.NET, you will notice some similarities.

There still are model classes, which are used as data carriers between the controller and its views. There are, however, many new features that you will learn, such as Tag Helpers and view components. You will also work with Entity Framework to store and retrieve data, implement authentication with ASP.NET Identity framework, install CSS libraries such as Bootstrap, and install JavaScript libraries such as JQuery. Note that dependency injection now is a first-class design pattern.

The second solution you will create will contain three projects: one for the database and services (referenced from the other two projects), one MVC project for the user UI, and one Razor Page project for the administrator UI. Pre-existing MVC and Razor Page templates will be used for the two UI projects, and an empty template will be used for the database project.

You will modify the database support installed by the templates to instead target the database created by the database project. Only minor modifications will be made to the authentication and routing provided by the templates.

By the end of this book you will be able to create simple ASP.NET Core 2.0 applications on your own, which can create, edit, delete, and view data in a database.

All applications you will build revolve around video data and playing videos. In one application, you will be able to add and edit video titles, and in another, you will build a more sophisticated customer portal, where users can view the course videos that they have access to.

Setup

In this book, you will be using C#, HTML, and Razor with Visual Studio 2017 version 15.3.5 or later that you have access to. You can even use Visual Studio Community 2017, which you can download for free from www.visualstudio.com/downloads.

You can develop ASP.NET Core 2.0 applications on Mac OS X and Linux, but then you are restricted to the ASP.NET Core libraries that don't depend on .NET Framework, which requires Windows.

The applications in this book will be built using ASP.NET 2.0 without .NET Framework.

You will install additional libraries using NuGet packages when necessary, throughout the book.

The complete code for all applications is available on GitHub with a commit for each task.

The first application: https://github.com/csharpschool/AspNetVideoCore

The second application: https://github.com/csharpschool/VideoOnDemandCore2

Book Version

The current version of this book: 1.0

Errata: https://github.com/csharpschool/VideoOnDemandCore2/issues

Contact: csharpschoolonline@gmail.com

Other Books by the Author

The author has written other books and produced video courses that you might find helpful.

Below is a list of the most recent books by the author. The books are available on Amazon.

ASP.NET Core 2.0 – MVC & Razor Pages

ASP.NET Core 1.1 – Building a Website

ASP.NET Core 1.1 – Building a Web API

ASP.NET MVC 5 – Building a Website

C# for Beginners

Video Courses Produced by the Author

MVC 5 – How to Build a Membership Website (video course)

This is a comprehensive video course on how to build a membership site using ASP.NET MVC 5. The course has more than **24 hours** of video.

In this video course you will learn how to build a membership website from scratch. You will create the database using Entity Framework code-first, scaffold an Administrator UI, and build a front-end UI using HTML5, CSS3, Bootstrap, JavaScript, C#, and MVC 5. Prerequisites for this course are: a good knowledge of the C# language and basic knowledge of MVC 5, HTML5, CSS3, Bootstrap, and JavaScript.

You can watch this video course on Udemy at this URL:
www.udemy.com/building-a-mvc-5-membership-website

Store Secret Data in .NET Core Web App with Azure Key Vault (video course)

In this Udemy course you will learn how to store sensitive data in a secure manner. First you will learn how to store data securely in a file called *secrets.json* with the User Manager. The file is stored locally on your machine, outside the project's folder structure. It is therefore not checked into your code repository. Then you will learn how to use Azure Web App Settings to store key-value pairs for a specific web application. The third and final way to secure your sensitive data is using Azure Key Vault, secured with Azure Active Directory in the cloud.

The course is taught using an ASP.NET Core 1.1 Web API solution in Visual Studio 2015.

You really need to know this if you are a serious developer.

You can watch this video course on Udemy at this URL:
www.udemy.com/store-secret-data-in-net-core-web-app-with-azure-key-vault

Source Code

The source code accompanying this book is shared under the MIT License and can be downloaded on GitHub, with a commit for each task.

The first application: https://github.com/csharpschool/AspNetVideoCore

The second application: https://github.com/csharpschool/VideoOnDemandCore2

Disclaimer – Who Is This Book for?

It's important to mention that this book is not meant to be a *get-to-know-it-all* book; it's more on the practical and tactical side, where you will learn as you progress through the exercises and build real applications in the process. Because I personally dislike having to read hundreds upon hundreds of pages of irrelevant fluff (filler material) not necessary for the tasks at hand, and also view it as a disservice to the readers, I will assume that we are of the same mind on this, and therefore I will include only important information pertinent for the tasks at hand, thus making the book both shorter and more condensed and also saving you time and effort in the process. Don't get me wrong: I will describe the important things in great detail, leaving out only the things that are not directly relevant to your first experience with ASP.NET Core 2.0 web applications. The goal is for you to have created one working MVC application and one Razor Page application upon finishing this book. You can always look into details at a later time when you have a few projects under your belt. *If you prefer encyclopedic books describing everything in minute detail with short examples, and value a book by how many pages it has, rather than its content, then this book is NOT for you.*

The examples in this book are presented using the free Visual Studio 2017 (version 15.3.5) Community version and ASP.NET Core 2.0. You can download Visual Studio 2017 (version 15.3.5) here: www.visualstudio.com/downloads

Rights

About the Author

Jonas started a company back in 1994 focusing on teaching Microsoft Office and the Microsoft operating systems. While still studying at the University of Skovde in 1995, he wrote his first book about Widows 95, as well as a number of course materials.

In the year 2000, after working as a Microsoft Office developer consultant for a couple of years, he wrote his second book about Visual Basic 6.0.

From 2000 to 2004, he worked as a Microsoft instructor with two of the largest educational companies in Sweden teaching Visual Basic 6.0. When Visual Basic.NET and C# were released, he started teaching those languages, as well as the .NET Framework. He was also involved in teaching classes at all levels, from beginner to advanced developers.

In 2005, Jonas shifted his career toward consulting once again, working hands-on with the languages and framework he taught.

Jonas wrote his third book, *C# Programming*, aimed at beginner to intermediate developers in 2013, and in 2015 his fourth book, *C# for Beginners – The Tactical Guide*, was published. Shortly thereafter his fifth book, *ASP.NET MVC 5 – Building a Website: The Tactical Guidebook*, was published. In 2017 he wrote three more books: *ASP.NET Core 1.1 Web Applications*, *ASP.NET Core 1.1 Web API*, and *ASP.NET Core 2.0 Web Applications*.

Jonas has also produced a 24h+ video course titled *Building an ASP.NET MVC 5 Membership Website* (www.udemy.com/building-a-mvc-5-membership-website), showing in great detail how to build a membership website.

And a course on how to secure sensitive data in web applications titled *Store Secret Data in a .NET Core Web App with Azure Key Vault* is also available on Udemy.

All the books and video courses have been specifically written with the student in mind.

Part 1:
ASP.NET Core 2.0 MVC
Your First Application

1. Your First ASP.NET Core Application

If you haven't already installed Visual Studio 2017 version 15.3.5 version or later, you can download a free copy here: www.visualstudio.com/downloads.

Now that you have Visual Studio 2017 installed on your computer, it's time to create your first solution and project.

1. Open Visual Studio 2017 and select **File-New-Project** in the main menu to create a new solution.
2. Click on the **Web** tab and then select **ASP.NET Core Web Application** in the template list (see image below).
    a. Name the project *AspNetCoreVideo* in the **Name** field.
    b. Select a folder for the solution in the **Location** field.
    c. Name the solution *AspNetVideoCore* in the **Solution name** field.
    d. Make sure that the **Create directory for solution** checkbox is checked.
    e. Learning how to use GitHub is not part of this course, so if you are unfamiliar with GitHub, you should make sure that the **Create new Git repository** checkbox is unchecked.
    f. Click the **OK** button.
3. In the project template dialog:
    a. Select **.NET Core** and **ASP.NET Core 2.0** in the two drop-downs.
    b. Select **Empty** in the template list.
    c. Click the **OK** button in the wizard dialog.
4. When the solution has been created in the folder you selected, it will contain all the files in the *AspNetVideoCore* project.
5. Press Ctrl+F5 on the keyboard, or select **Debug-Start Without Debugging** in the main menu, to run the application in the browser.
6. Note that the application only can do one thing right now, and that is to display the text *Hello World!* Later in this, and the next, module you will learn why that is, and how you can change that behavior.

For now, just note that the application is running on *localhost:55554* (the port number might be different on your machine).

If you right click on the IIS icon in the system tray, you can see that ISS is hosting the *AspNetCoreVideo* application.

The Project Layout and the File System

There is a direct correlation between the files in the solution folder and what is displayed in the Solution Explorer in Visual Studio. To demonstrate this, you will add a file to the file structure in the File Explorer and see it show up in the Solution Explorer in real-time.

1. Right click on the **AspNetVideoCore** solution node in the Solution Explorer and select **Open Folder in File Explorer**.
2. When the File Explorer has opened, you can see that the solution file *AspNetCoreVideo.sln* is in that folder, along with the project folder with the same name.
3. Double click on the project folder in the File Explorer to open it.

4. Right click in the File Explorer window and select **New-Text Document** and press **Enter** on the keyboard.
5. A new file with the name *New Text File* should have been created in the folder.
6. Now look in the Solution Explorer in Visual Studio; the same file should be available there.
7. Double click the icon for the *New Text File* document in the Solution Explorer in Visual Studio, to open it.
8. Write the text *Some text from Visual Studio* in the document and save it.
9. Now switch back to the File Explorer and open the file. It should contain the text you added.
10. Change the text to *Some text from Notepad* using the text editor (not in Visual Studio) and save the file.
11. Switch back to Visual Studio and click the **Yes** button in the dialog. The altered text should now be displayed in Visual Studio.

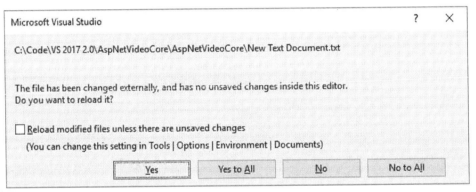

12. Close the text document in Visual Studio and in the text editor.
13. Right click on the file in the Solution Explorer in Visual Studio and select **Delete** to remove the file permanently.
14. Go to the File Explorer and verify that the file was deleted from the folder structure.

As you can see, the files in the project are in sync with the files in the file system, in real-time.

Important Files

There are a couple of files that you need to be aware of in ASP.NET Core 2.0, and these have changed from the 1.0 version.

The **Properties** folder in the Solution Explorer contains a file called *launchSettings.json*, which contains all the settings needed to launch the application. It contains IIS settings, as well as project settings, such as environment variables and the application URL.

One major change from ASP.NET Core 1.0 is that the *project.json* file no longer exists; instead the installed NuGet packages are listed in the *.csproj* file. It can be opened and edited directly from Visual Studio (which is another change) or its content can be changed using the NuGet Package Manager.

To open the *.csproj* file, you simply right click on the project node in the Solution Explorer and select **Edit AspNetVideoCore.csproj** (substitute *AspNetVideoCore* with the name of the project you are in).

You can add NuGet packages by adding **PackageReference** nodes to the file *.csproj,* or by opening the NuGet Package Manager. Right click on the **project node** or the **References** node, and select **Manage NuGet Packages** to open the NuGet Manager.

One change from the ASP.NET Core 1.1 version is that there now only is one main NuGet package called **Microsoft.AspNetCore.All** that is installed when the project is created. It contains references to the most frequently used NuGet packages, the ones that you had to add separately in the 1.1 version.

Open the *.csproj* file and the NuGet manager side by side and compare them. As you can see, the same package is listed in the dialog and in the file.

```
11 □   <ItemGroup>
12 □      <PackageReference
13 ➡        Include="Microsoft.AspNetCore.All"
14           Version="2.0.0" />
15      </ItemGroup>
```

You will be adding more NuGet packages (frameworks) as you build the projects.

Compiling the Solution

It is important to know that ASP.NET will monitor the file system and recompile the application when files are changed and saved. Because ASP.NET monitors the file system and recompiles the code, you can use any text editor you like, such as Visual Studio Code, when building your applications. You are no longer bound to Visual Studio; all you need to do is to get the application running in the web server (IIS). Let's illustrate it with an example.

1. Start the application without debugging (Ctrl+F5) to get it running in IIS, if it isn't already open in a browser.
2. Open the *Startup.cs* file with Notepad (or any text editor) outside of Visual Studio. This file is responsible for configuring your application when it starts.
3. Locate the line of code with the string *Hello World*. This line of code is responsible for responding to every HTTP request in your application.
   ```
   await context.Response.WriteAsync("Hello World!");
   ```
4. Change the text to *Hello, from My World!* and save the file.
   ```
   await context.Response.WriteAsync("Hello, from My World!");
   ```
5. Refresh the application in the browser. Do not build the solution in Visual Studio before refreshing the page.
6. The text should change from *Hello World!* To *Hello, from My World!*
   The reason this works is because ASP.NET monitors the file system and recompiles the application when changes are made to a file.

You can create cross-platform applications using ASP.NET Core 2.0, but this requires the *.NET Core* template. As of this writing, this template has limitations compared with the *.NET Framework* template. This is because .NET Framework contains features that are relying on the Windows operating system. In a few years' time, this gap will probably not be as significant, as the .NET Core platform evolves. So, if you don't need the added features in .NET Framework, then use the *.NET Core* template, as it is much leaner and cross-platform ready.

The Startup.cs File

Gone are the days when the *web.config* file ruled the configuration universe. Now the *Startup.cs* file contains a **Startup** class, which ASP.NET will look for by convention. The application and its configuration sources are configured in that class.

The **Configure** and **ConfigureServices** methods in the **Startup** class handle most of the application configuration. The HTTP processing pipeline is created in the **Configure** method, located at the end of the class. The pipeline defines how the application responds to requests; by default, the only thing it can do is to print *Hello World!* to the browser.

If you want to change this behavior, you will have to add additional code to the pipeline in this method. If you for instance want to handle route requests in an ASP.NET MVC application, you have to modify the pipeline.

In the **Configure** method, you set up the HTTP request pipeline (the middleware) that is called when the application starts. In the second part of this book, you will add an object-to-object mapper called AutoMapper to this method. AutoMapper transforms objects from one type to another.

The **ConfigureServices** method is where you set up the services, such as MVC. You can also register your own services and make them ready for Dependency Injection (DI); for instance, the service that you implement using the **IMessageService** interface at the beginning of the book.

You will learn more about how to configure your application in the next chapter.

For now, all you need to know about dependency injection is that, instead of creating instances of a class explicitly, they can be handed to a component when asked for. This makes your application loosely coupled and flexible.

Adding a Configuration Service

Let's say that the hard-coded string *Hello, from My World* is a string that shouldn't be hardcoded, and you want to read it from a configuration source. The source is irrelevant; it could be a JSON file, a database, a web service, or some other source. To solve this, you could implement a configuration service that fetches the value when asked.

Let's implement this scenario in your application

1. Right click on the project folder and select **Add-New Item**.
2. Search for *JSON* in the dialog's search field.
3. Select the **ASP.NET Configuration File** template.
4. Make sure the name of the file is *appsettings.json*. The file could be named anything, but *appsettings* is convention for this type of configuration file.
5. Click the **Add** button.
6. As you can see, a default connection string is already in the file. Remove the connection string property and add the following key-value pair: *"Message":"Hello, from configuration"*. This is the file content after you have changed it.
   ```
   {
        "Message": "Hello, from configuration"
   }
   ```
7. To read configuration information from the *appsettings.json* file, you have to add a constructor to the **Startup** class. You can do that by typing *ctor* and hitting the **Tab** key twice in the class.
   ```
   public class Startup
   {
        public Startup()
        {
        }
        . . .
   }
   ```
8. You need to create an instance of the **ConfigurationBuilder** class called **builder** in the constructor, and chain on the **SetBasePath** method with the application's current directory as an argument. Without specifying the base path, the application will not know where to search for files.
   ```
   var builder = new ConfigurationBuilder()
        .SetBasePath(Directory.GetCurrentDirectory());
   ```

9. To get access to the classes used in the previous step, you have to resolve the following two namespaces by adding **using** statements for them.
```
using Microsoft.Extensions.Configuration;
using System.IO;
```

10. To read the JSON *appsettings.json* file you need to chain on the **AddJsonFile** method, with *appsettings.json* as an argument, to the **builder** object. If you need to include more files, you can chain on the method multiple times.
```
var builder = new ConfigurationBuilder()
    .SetBasePath(Directory.GetCurrentDirectory())
    .AddJsonFile("appsettings.json");
```

11. Add a property called **Configuration**, of type **IConfiguration**, to the **Startup** class.
```
public IConfiguration Configuration { get; set; }
```

12. Now, you need to build the configuration structure from the **ConfigurationBuilder** object, and store it in the **Configuration** property. You do this by calling the **Build** method on the **builder** variable in the constructor.
```
Configuration = builder.Build();
```

13. To replace the hardcoded text *Hello, from My World!* with the value stored in the **Message** property in the *appsettings.json* file, you have to index into the **Configuration** property. Store the value in a variable in the **Configure** method above the **WriteAsync** method call.
```
var message = Configuration["Message"];
```

14. Now, replace the hardcoded text with the variable.
```
await context.Response.WriteAsync(message);
```

15. Save all the files and go to the browser. Refresh the application to see the new message.

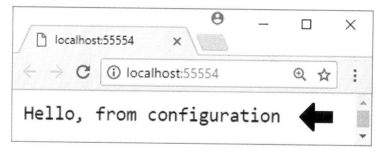

The **Startup** class's code, so far:

```
public class Startup
{
    public IConfiguration Configuration { get; set; }

    public Startup()
    {
        var builder = new ConfigurationBuilder()
            .SetBasePath(Directory.GetCurrentDirectory())
            .AddJsonFile("appsettings.json"); ;

        Configuration = builder.Build();
    }

    public void ConfigureServices(IServiceCollection services)
    {
    }

    public void Configure(IApplicationBuilder app,
    IHostingEnvironment env)
    {
        if (env.IsDevelopment())
        {
            app.UseDeveloperExceptionPage();
        }

        app.Run(async (context) =>
        {
            var message = Configuration["Message"];
            await context.Response.WriteAsync(message);
        });
    }
}
```

Creating a Service

Instead of using one specific source to fetch data, you can use services to fetch data from different sources, depending on the circumstance. This mean that you, through the use of configuration, can use different data sources according to the need at hand.

You might want to fetch data from a JSON file when building the service, and later switch to another implementation of that service, to fetch real data.

To achieve this, you create an interface that the service classes implement, and then use that interface when serving up the instances. Because the service classes implement the same interface, instances from them are interchangeable.

To get access to the services from the **Configure** method in the **Startup** class, or any other constructor, model, Razor Page, or view, you must use dependency injection. That is, pass in the interface as a parameter to the method.

You must register the service interface, and the desired service class, with the **services** collection in the **ConfigureServices** method, in the **Startup** class. This determines which class will be used to create the instance, when dependency injection is used to pass in an instance of a class implementing the interface.

In the upcoming example, you will inject a service class into the **Configure** method, but it works just as well with regular classes that you want to inject into a constructor, model, Razor Page, or view, using dependency injection. The same type of registration that you did in the **ConfigureServices** method could be applied to this scenario, but you wouldn't have to implement it as a service.

You might ask how the **IApplicationBuilder** parameter gets populated in the **Configure** method, when no configuration has been added for it in the **ConfigureServices** method. The answer is that certain service objects will be served up for interfaces automatically by ASP.NET; one of those interfaces is the **IApplicationBuilder**. Another is the **IHosting-Environment** service, which handles different environments, such as development, staging, and production.

Example

Let's implement an example where you create two service classes that retrieve data in two different ways. The first will simply return a hardcoded string (you can pretend that the data is fetched from a database or a web service if you like), and the second class will return the value from the **Message** property that you added to the *appsettings.json* file.

You will begin by adding an interface called **IMessageService**, which will define a method called **GetMessage**, which returns a string.

Then you will implement that interface in a service class called **HardcodedMessage-Service**, which will return a hardcoded string. After implementing the class, you will add configuration for it and the interface in the **ConfigureServices** method and test the functionality.

Then you will implement another class called **ConfigurationMessageService**, which reads from the *application.json* file and returns the value from its **Message** property. To use the new service class, you must change the configuration. Then you will refresh the application in the browser to make sure that the configuration value is returned.

Adding the IMessageService Interface

1. Right click on the project node in the Solution Explorer and select **Add-New Folder**.
2. Name the folder *Services*.
3. Right click on the *Services* folder and select **Add-New Item**.
4. Select the **Interface** template, name the interface **IMessageService**, and click the **Add** button.
5. Add the **public** access modifier to the interface (make it public).
6. Add a method called **GetMessage**, which returns a **string** to the interface. It should not take any parameters.
7. Save the file.

The complete code for the interface:

```
public interface IMessageService
{
    string GetMessage();
}
```

Adding the HardcodedMessageService Class

1. Right click on the *Services* folder and select **Add-Class**.
2. Name the class **HardcodedMessageService** and click the **Add** button.
3. Implement the **IMessageService** interface in the class by clicking on the light bulb icon that appears when you hover over the interface name when you have added it to the class. Select **Implement interface** in the menu that appears.
4. Remove the code line with the **throw** statement and return the string *Hardcoded message from a service.*
5. Save all files by pressing Ctrl+Shift+S on the keyboard.

The complete code for the **HardcodedMessageService** class:

```
public class HardCodedMessageService : IMessageService
{
    public string GetMessage()
    {
        return "Hardcoded message from a service.";
    }
}
```

Configure and Use the HardcodedMessageService Class
1. Open the *Startup.cs* file.
2. Locate the **ConfigureServices** method.
3. To create instances that can be swapped for the **IMessageService** interface when dependency injection is used, you must add a definition for it to the **services** collection. In this example, you want ASP.NET to swap out the interface with an instance of the **HardcodedMessageService** class. Add the definition by calling the **AddSingleton** method on the **services** object, specifying the interface as the first type and the class as the second type.
```
services.AddSingleton<IMessageService, HardcodedMessageService>();
```

4. You need to add a **using** statement to the *Services* folder.
```
using AspNetVideoCore.Services;
```

5. Now you can use dependency injection to access the **IMessageService** from the **Configure** method.
```
public void Configure(IApplicationBuilder app, IHostingEnvironment env, IMessageService msg)
{
    ...
}
```

6. Remove the line that declares the **message** variable from the **Run** block.
7. Replace the **message** variable name in the **WriteAsync** method with a call to the **GetMessage** method on the **msg** object, which will contain an instance of the **HardcodedMessageService** class.
```
await context.Response.WriteAsync(msg.GetMessage());
```

8. Save all files, switch to the browser, and refresh the application. The message *Hardcoded message from a service* should appear.

The complete code for the **ConfigureServices** method:

```
public void ConfigureServices(IServiceCollection services)
{
    services.AddSingleton<IMessageService, HardcodedMessageService>();
}
```

The complete code for the **Configure** method:

```
public void Configure(IApplicationBuilder app, IHostingEnvironment env,
IMessageService msg)
{
    if (env.IsDevelopment())
    {
        app.UseDeveloperExceptionPage();
    }

    app.Run(async (context) =>
    {
        await context.Response.WriteAsync(msg.GetMessage());
    });
}
```

When adding a service to the service collection, you can choose between several **Add** methods. Here's a rundown of the most commonly used.

Singleton creates a single instance that is used throughout the application. It creates the instance when the first dependency-injected object is created.

Scoped services are lifetime services, created once per request within the scope. It is equivalent to **Singleton** in the current scope. In other words, the same instance is reused within the same HTTP request.

Transient services are created each time they are requested and won't be reused. This lifetime works best for lightweight, stateless services.

Add and Use the ConfigurationMessageService Class

1. Right click on the *Services* folder and select **Add-Class**.
2. Name the class **ConfigurationMessageService** and click the **Add** button.
3. Implement the **IMessageService** interface in the class.
4. Add a constructor to the class (you can use the *ctor* code snippet).
5. Inject the **IConfiguration** interface into the constructor and name it **configuration**.
6. Save the **configuration** object in a private class-level variable called **_configuration**. You can let Visual Studio create the variable for you by writing the variable name in the method, clicking the light bulb icon, and selecting **Generate field...**

   ```
   private IConfiguration _configuration;

   public ConfigurationMessageService(IConfiguration configuration)
   {
       _configuration = configuration;
   }
   ```

7. You need to add a using statement to the **Microsoft.Extensions.Configuration** namespace.

   ```
   using Microsoft.Extensions.Configuration;
   ```

8. Remove the **throw** statement from the **GetMessage** method and return the string from the **Message** property stored in the *appsettings.json* file. You achieve this by indexing into the **Configuration** object.

   ```
   return _configuration["Message"];
   ```

9. Open the *Startup.cs* file and locate the **ConfigureServices** method.
10. Change the **HardcodedMessageService** type to the **ConfigurationMessageService** type in the **AddSingleton** method call.

    ```
    services.AddSingleton<IMessageService,
    ConfigurationMessageService>();
    ```

11. Add another call to the **AddSingleton** method <u>above</u> the previous **AddSingleton** method call. This time use the existing **Configuration** object and pass it to the method's provider using a Lambda expression. This is another way to use the

Add methods when you already have an object. You must add this line of code to prepare the **configuration** object for dependency injection.
`services.AddSingleton(provider => Configuration);`

12. Save all files by pressing Ctrl+Shift+S on the keyboard.
13. Switch to the browser and refresh the application.
14. You should now see the message *Hello, from configuration*, from the *appsettings.json* file.

The complete code for the **ConfigurationMessageService** class:

```
public class ConfigurationMessageService : IMessageService
{
    private IConfiguration _configuration;

    public ConfigurationMessageService(IConfiguration configuration)
    {
        _configuration = configuration;
    }

    public string GetMessage()
    {
        return _configuration["Message"];
    }
}
```

The complete code for the **ConfigureServices** method:

```
public void ConfigureServices(IServiceCollection services)
{
    services.AddSingleton(provider => Configuration);
    services.AddSingleton<IMessageService,
        ConfigurationMessageService>();
}
```

Summary

In this chapter, you created your first ASP.NET application and added only the necessary pieces to get it up and running. Throughout the first part of this book you will add new functionality using services and middleware.

You also added a configuration file, and created and registered a service to make it available through dependency injection in other parts of the application.

In the next chapter, you will learn about middleware.

2. Middleware

In this chapter, you will add middleware that handles HTTP requests, like how the application behaves if there is an error. One key aspect of the middleware is to perform user authentication and authorization.

By the end of this chapter you will have built a middleware pipeline for a MVC application.

How Does Middleware Work?

Let's have a look at how middleware works and what it is used for.

When an HTTP request comes to the server, it is the middleware components that handle that request.

Each piece of middleware in ASP.NET is an object with a very limited, specific, and focused role. This means that you will have to add many middleware components for an application to work properly.

The following example illustrates what can happen when an HTTP POST request to a URL, ending with *reviews*, reaches the server.

Logging is a separate middleware component that you might want to use to log information about every incoming HTTP request. It can see every piece of data, such as the headers, the query string, cookies, and access tokens. Not only can it read data from the request, it can also change information about it, and/or stop processing the request.

The most likely scenario with a logger is that it will log information and pass the processing onto the next middleware component in the pipeline.

This mean that middleware is a series of components executed in order.

The next middleware component might be an authorizer that can look at access tokens or cookies to determine if the request will proceed. If the request doesn't have the correct credentials, the authorizer middleware component can respond with an HTTP error code or redirect the user to a login page.

If the request is authorized, it will be passed to the next middleware component, which might be a routing component. The router will look at the URL to determine where to go next, by looking in the application for something that can respond. This could be a method on a class returning a JSON, XML, or HTML page for instance. If it can't find anything that can respond, the component could throw a *404 Not Found* error.

Let's say that it found an HTML page to respond; then the pipeline starts to call all the middleware components in reverse order, passing along the HTML. When the response ultimately reaches the first component, which is the logger in our example, it might log the time the request took and then allow the response to go back over the network to the client's browser.

This is what middleware is, a way to configure how the application should behave. A series of components that handle specific, narrow tasks, such as handle errors, serve up static files and send HTTP requests to the MVC framework. This will make it possible for you to build the example video application.

This book will not go into the nitty-gritty of middleware – only the basics that you need to build a MVC application.

IApplicationBuilder

The **IApplicationBuilder** interface injected into the **Startup** class's **Configure** method is used when setting up the middleware pipeline.

```
public void Configure(IApplicationBuilder app, IHostingEnvironment env,
IMessageService msg)
{
    if (env.IsDevelopment()) app.UseDeveloperExceptionPage();

    app.Run(async (context) =>
    {
        await context.Response.WriteAsync(msg.GetMessage());
    });
}
```

To add middleware, you call extension methods on the **app** parameter, which contains the dependency-injected object for the **IApplicationBuilder** interface. Two middleware components are already defined in the **Configure** method.

The **UseDeveloperExceptionPage** middleware component will display a pretty error page to the developer, but not the user; you can see that it is encapsulated inside an if-block that checks if the environment variable is set to the development environment.

The **UseDeveloperExceptionPage** middleware component then calls the **Run** middleware component that is used to process every response. **Run** is not frequently used because it is a terminal piece of middleware, which means that it is the end of the pipeline. No middleware component added after the **Run** component will execute, because **Run** doesn't call into any other middleware components.

```
app.Run(async (context) =>
{
    await context.Response.WriteAsync(msg.GetMessage());
});
```

By using the **context** object passed into the **Run** method, you can find out anything about the request through its **Request** object –the header information, for instance. It will also have access to a **Response** object, which currently is used to print out a string.

In the previous chapter, you called the **GetMessage** method on the message service in the **Run** method.

Most middleware components will be added by calling a method beginning with **Use** on the **app** object, such as **app.UseDeveloperExceptionPage**.

As you can see, there are several middleware components available out of the box using the **app** object. You can add more middleware components by installing NuGet packages containing middleware.

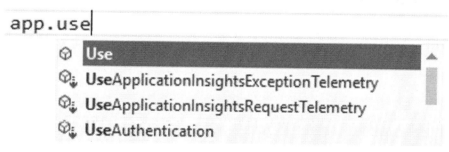

Handling Exceptions

Let's have a look at how exception messages are handled by the pipeline. As previously mentioned the **app.UseDeveloperExceptionPage** middleware is in place to help the developer with any exceptions that might occur. To test this behavior, you can add a **throw** statement at the top of the **Run**-block and refresh the application in the browser.

1. Open the *Startup.cs* file and locate the **Run** middleware in the **Configure** method.

2. Add a **throw** statement that returns the string *Fake Exception!* to the **Run**-block.

```
app.Run(async (context) =>
{
    throw new Exception("Fake Exception!");
    await context.Response.WriteAsync(msg.GetMessage());
});
```

3. Add a **using** statement for the **System** namespace to access the **Exception** class.

```
using System;
```

4. If you haven't already started the application, press Ctrl+F5 to start it without debugging. Otherwise switch to the browser and refresh the application.

5. A pretty error message will be displayed. Note that this message will be displayed only when in development mode. On this page, you can read detailed information about the error, query strings, cookie information, and header content.

Now let's see what happens if you change the environment variable to *Production* and refresh the page.

1. Select **Project-*AspNetVideoCore* Properties** in the main menu.
2. Click on the **Debug** tab on the left side of the dialog.
3. Change the **ASPNETCORE_ENVIRONMENT** property to *Production*.
4. Save all files (Ctrl+Shift+S).
5. Refresh the application in the browser.
6. Now you will get an HTTP *500 Error- This page isn't working* error, which is what a regular user would see. If you don't see this message, then you have to manually build the project with Ctrl+F5.

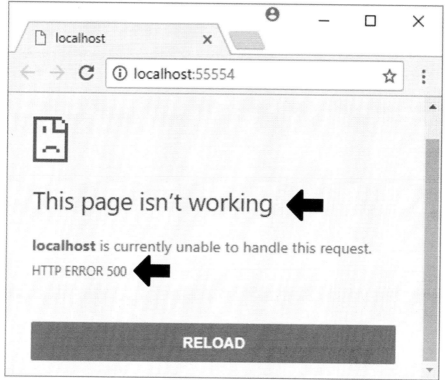

7. Switch back to Visual Studio and change back the **ASPNETCORE_ENVIRONMENT** property to *Development*.
8. Save all files.
9. Refresh the application in the browser; you should now be back to the pretty error page.

Now let's see what happens if we comment out the **app.UseDeveloperExceptionPage** middleware.

1. Open the *Setup.cs* file and locate the **Configure** method.
2. Comment out the call to the **app.UseDeveloperExceptionPage** middleware.
   ```
   //app.UseDeveloperExceptionPage();
   ```
3. Save the file.
4. Refresh the application in the browser.
5. The plain HTTP 500 error should be displayed because you no longer are loading the middleware that produces the pretty error message.

6. Uncomment the code again and save the file.
7. Refresh the browser one last time to make sure that the pretty error message is displayed.
8. Remove the **throw** statement from the **Run**-block and save the file.
   ```
   throw new Exception("Fake Exception!");
   ```

You can use the **IHostingEnvironment** object, passed in through dependency injection, to find out information about the environment. You have already used an if statement to determine if the environment variable is set to *Development*, if it is, a pretty error page will be displayed. You can also use it to find out the absolute path to the *wwwroot* directory in the project with the **WebRootPath** property.

Serving Up Static Files

A feature that nearly all web applications need is the ability to serve up static files, such as JSON, CSS, and HTML files. To allow ASP.NET to serve up files, you must add a new middleware component that is called with the **UseStaticFiles** method, located in the **Microsoft .AspNetCore.StaticFiles** NuGet package, which is installed with the default **Microsoft .AspNetCore.All** NuGet package.

Without the **UseStaticFiles** middleware component, the application will display the message from the **Run** middleware.

Let's add an HTML file to the *wwwroot* folder and see what happens, and why. Static files must be added to the *wwwroot* folder for ASP.NET to find them.

1. Right click on the *wwwroot* folder and select **Add-New Item**.
2. Search for the **HTML Page** template and select it.
3. Name the file *index.html* and click the **Add** button.
4. Add the text *An HTML Page* to the **<title>** tag, and *Hello, from index.html* in the **<body>** tag.
5. Save all files and navigate to the */index.html* page in the browser.
6. The message *Hello, from configuration* is displayed, which probably isn't what you expected.

The reason why the message *Hello, from configuration* is displayed is that there currently is no middleware that can serve up the static file. Instead the message in the **Run** middleware, which is accessible, will be displayed.

Let's fix this by adding a new middleware located in the **Microsoft.AspNetCore.StaticFiles** NuGet package, which is installed by deafult.

When the **UseStaticFiles** method is called on the **app** object, ASP.NET will look in the *wwwroot* folder for the desired file. If a suitable file is found, the next piece of middleware will not be called.

1. Open the *Startup.cs* file and locate the **Configure** method.
2. Add a call to the **UseStaticFiles** method on the **app** object <u>above</u> the **Run** middleware.
   ```
   app.UseStaticFiles();
   ```
3. Save all the files and start the application with F5.

4. Navigate to the *index.html* file. The message *Hello, from index.html* should be displayed.

The complete code for the **Configure** method:

```
public void Configure(IApplicationBuilder app, IHostingEnvironment env,
IMessageService msg)
{
    if (env.IsDevelopment())
    {
        app.UseDeveloperExceptionPage();
    }

    app.UseStaticFiles();

    app.Run(async (context) =>
    {
        await context.Response.WriteAsync(msg.GetMessage());
    });
}
```

Setting Up ASP.NET MVC

The last thing you will do in this chapter is to set up the ASP.NET MVC middleware and add a simple controller to test that it works.

The NuGet **Microsoft.AspNetCore.Mvc** package, which is installed by default, contains the MVC middleware that you will add to the HTTP pipeline and the MVC service that you will add to the services collection.

You will add a controller class with an **Index** action method that can be requested from the browser. In ASP.NET MVC, static HTML files, such as *index.html*, are not used. Instead views are usually used to serve up the HTML, JavaScript, and CSS content to the user. You will learn more about MVC in the next chapter. For now, let's look at a simple example.

1. Add a controller that can respond to the HTTP requests coming in to the application pipeline. The convention is to add controller classes to a folder named *Controllers*. Right click on the project node and select **Add-New Folder** and name it *Controllers*.

2. Right click on the *Controllers* folder and select **Add-Class**.

3. Name the class **HomeController** (the convention for a default controller) and click the **Add** button. The class doesn't have to inherit from any other class.
    ```
    public class HomeController
    {
    }
    ```

4. Add a **public** method named **Index** that returns a **string**, to the **HomeController** class. Return the string *Hello, from the controller!* in the method.
    ```
    public string Index()
    {
        return "Hello, from the controller!";
    }
    ```

5. Save all files and run the application (F5). Navigate to the index.html page. Note that the *index.html* file still is being served up to the user, displaying the text *Hello, from index.html*. This is because you haven't yet added the MVC service and middleware.

6. Stop the application in Visual Studio.

7. Delete the *index.html* file you added to the *wwwroot* folder; you won't be needing it anymore since you want the controller to respond instead. You can do this either from the Solution Explorer or a File Explorer window in Windows.

8. Open the *Startup.cs* file and locate the **Configure** method.

9. Add the MVC middleware after the **UseFileServer** middleware method call, by calling the **UseMvcWithDefaultRoute** method. Adding it before the **UseFileServer** middleware would give the application a different behavior.
    ```
    app.UseMvcWithDefaultRoute();
    ```

10. Save all files and run the application (F5). You will be greeted by an exception message telling you that the necessary MVC service hasn't been added.

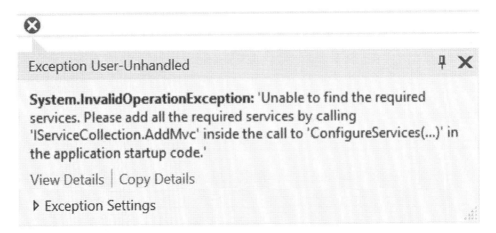

11. Open the **Startup** class and locate the **ConfigureServices** method.

12. Add the MVC services to the **services** collection at the top of the method. This will give ASP.NET everything it needs to run a MVC application.

```
public void ConfigureServices(IServiceCollection services)
{
    services.AddMvc();
    ...
}
```

13. Comment out or delete the **UseStaticFiles** method call.

```
app.UseStaticFiles();
```

14. Save all files and run the application (F5). Now the message *Hello, from the controller!* will be displayed in the browser. This means that MVC is installed and working correctly. In the next chapter, you will implement a more sophisticated controller.

The complete code in the **ConfigureServices** method:

```
public void ConfigureServices(IServiceCollection services)
{
    services.AddMvc();
    services.AddSingleton(provider => Configuration);
    services.AddSingleton<IMessageService,
        ConfigurationMessageService>();
}
```

The complete code in the **Configure** method:

```
public void Configure(IApplicationBuilder app, IHostingEnvironment env,
IMessageService msg)
{
    if (env.IsDevelopment())
    {
        app.UseDeveloperExceptionPage();
    }

    app.UseMvcWithDefaultRoute();

    app.Run(async (context) =>
    {
        await context.Response.WriteAsync(msg.GetMessage());
    });
}
```

Summary

In this chapter, you learned how to configure middleware in the **Configure** method of the **Startup** class.

The application now has several middleware components, including a developer error page and MVC. The MVC middleware can forward a request to an action method in a controller class to serve up content.

In the next chapter, you will learn more about controllers, and that you can use many different controllers in the same application, and how to route the HTTP requests to the appropriate one.

You will also create controller actions that return HTML, instead of just a string, as in the previous example.

3. MVC Controllers

In this chapter, you will learn about MVC, which is a popular design pattern for the user interface layer in applications, where *M* stands for Model, *V* stands for View, and *C* stands for Controller. In larger applications, MVC is typically combined with other design patterns, like data access and messaging patterns, to create a full application stack. This book will focus on the MVC fundamentals.

The controller is responsible for handling any HTTP requests that come to the application. It could be a user browsing to the */videos* URL of the application. The controller's responsibility is then to gather and combine all the necessary data and package it in model objects, which act as data carriers to the views.

The model is sent to the view, which uses the data when it's rendered into HTML. The HTML is then sent back to the client browser as an HTML response.

The MVC pattern creates a separation of concerns between the model, view, and controller. The sole responsibility of the controller is to handle the request and to build a model. The model's responsibility is to transport data and logic between the controller and the view, and the view is responsible for transforming that data into HTML.

For this to work, there must be a way to send HTTP requests to the correct controller. That is the purpose of ASP.NET MVC routing.

The **controller** handles the request and fills the model with data

The **model** carries the data and logic to the view

The **view** renders HTML using the **model** data, and sends the HTML as a HTTP response to the user's browser

1. The user sends an HTTP request to the server by typing in a URL.
2. The controller on the server handles the request by fetching data and creating a model object.
3. The model object is sent to the view.
4. The view uses the data to render HTML.
5. The view is sent back to the user's browser in an HTTP response.

Routing

The ASP.NET middleware you implemented in the previous chapter must be able to route incoming HTTP requests to a controller, since you are building an ASP.NET Core MVC application. The decision to send the request to a controller action is determined by the URL, and the configuration information you provide.

It is possible to define multiple routes. ASP.NET will evaluate them in the order they have been added. You can also combine convention-based routing with attribute routing if you need. Attribute routing is especially useful in edge cases where convention-based routing is hard to use.

One way to provide the routing configuration is to use convention-based routing in the **Startup** class. With this type of configuration, you tell ASP.NET how to find the controller's name, action's name, and possibly parameter values in the URL. The controller is a C# class, and an action is a public method in a controller class. A parameter can be any value that can be represented as a string, such as an integer or a GUID.

The configuration can be done with a Lambda expression, as an inline method:

```
app.UseMvc(routes =>
{
    routes.MapRoute(
        name: "default",
        template: "{controller=Home}/{action=Index}/{id?}");
});
```

ASP.NET looks at the route template to determine how to pull apart the URL. If the URL contains */Home*, it will locate the **HomeController** class by convention, because the name begins with *Home*. If the URL contains */Home/Index*, ASP.NET will look for a public action method called **Index** inside the **HomeController** class. If the URL contains */Home/Index/ 123*, ASP.NET will look for a public action method called **Index** with an **Id** parameter inside the **HomeController** class. The *Id* is optional when defined with a question mark after its name. The controller and action names can also be omitted, because they have default values in the **Route** template.

Another way to implement routing is to use attribute routing, where you assign attributes to the controller class and its action methods. The metadata in those attributes tell ASP.NET when to call a specific controller and action.

Attribute routing requires a **using** statement to the **Microsoft.AspNetCore.Mvc** namespace.

```
[Route("[controller]/[action]")]
public class HomeController
{
}
```

Convention-Based Routing

In the previous chapter, you created a C# controller class named **HomeController**. A controller doesn't have to inherit from any other class when returning basic data such as strings. You also implemented routing using the **UseMvcWithDefaultRoute** method, which comes with built-in support for default routing for the **HomeController**. When building an application with multiple controllers, you want to use convention-based routing, or attribute routing to let ASP.NET know how to handle the incoming HTTP requests.

Let's implement the default route explicitly, first with a method and then with a Lambda expression. To set this up you replace the **UseMvcWithDefaultRoute** method with the **UseMvc** method in the **Startup** class. In the **UseMvc** method, you then either call a method or add a Lambda expression for an inline method.

Implement Routing

1. Open the **Startup** class and locate the **Configure** method.
2. Replace the **UseMvcWithDefaultRoute** method with the **UseMvc** method and add a Lambda expression with the default route template.
   ```
   app.UseMvc(routes =>
   {
       routes.MapRoute(
           name: "default",
           template: "{controller=Home}/{action=Index}/{id?}");
   });
   ```

3. Save the file and refresh the application in the browser. As you can see, the **Index** action was reached with the explicit URL */home/index*.

4. Now change to a URL without the action's name, and only the controller's name (*/Home*). You should still get the message from the action method, because you specified the **Index** action method as the default action in the routing template.

5. Now call the root URL. A root URL is a URL with only the localhost and the port specified (*http://localhost:xxxxx*). This should also call the **Index** action because both *Home* and *Index* are declared as default values for the controller and the action in the routing template.

Adding Another Controller

Now that you have implemented default routing, it's time to add another controller and see how you can reach that controller.

1. Right click on the **Controllers** folder and select **Add-Class**.

2. Name the controller **EmployeeController** and click the **Add** button.
```
public class EmployeeController
{
}
```

3. Add an action method called **Name** that returns a string to the controller. Return your name from the method.
```
public string Name()
{
    return "Jonas";
}
```

4. Add another action method called **Country** that also returns a string. Return your country of residence from the method.

5. Save the file and switch to the browser. Try with the root URL first. This should take you to */Home/Index* as defined in the default route.

6. Change the URL to */Employee/Name*; this should display your name in the browser. In my case *Jonas*.

7. Change the URL to */Employee/Country*; this should display your country of residence in the browser. In my case *Sweden*.

8. Change the URL to */Employee*. ASP.NET passes the request on to the **Run** middleware, which returns the string *Hello from configuration*, using the **ConfigurationMessageService** that you implemented earlier. The reason is that the **EmployeeController** class has no action method called **Index**, which is the

name defined as the default action in the default route you added earlier to the **Startup** class.

9. Add a new method called **Index** that returns the string *Hello from Employee* to the **EmployeeController** class.
10. Save the file and refresh the application in the browser, or use the */Employee* URL. Now the text *Hello from Employee* should be displayed.

The complete code for the **EmployeeController** class:

```
public class EmployeeController
{
    public string Name()
    {
        return "Jonas";
    }

    public string Country()
    {
        return "Sweden";
    }

    public string Index()
    {
        return "Hello from Employee";
    }
}
```

Attribute Routing

Let's implement an example of attribute routing, using the **EmployeeController** and its actions.

1. Open the **EmployeeController** class.
2. If you want the controller to respond to */Employee* with attribute routing, you add the **Route** attribute above the controller class, specifying *employee* as its parameter value. You will have to bring in the **Microsoft.AspNetCore.Mvc** namespace for the **Route** attribute to be available.
    ```
    [Route("employee")]
    public class EmployeeController
    ```

3. Save the file and navigate to the */Employee* URL. An exception is displayed in the browser. The reason for this exception is that ASP.NET can't determine which of the three actions is the default action.

4. To solve this, you can specify the **Route** attribute for each of the action methods, and use an empty string for the default action. Let's make the **Index** action the default action, and name the routes for the other action methods the same as the methods.

```
[Route("")]
public string Index()
{
      return "Hello from Employee";
}

[Route("name")]
public string Name()
{
      return "Jonas";
}

[Route("country")]
public string Country()
{
      return "Sweden";
}
```

5. Save the file and refresh the application in the browser. Make sure that the URL ends with */Employee*. You should see the message *Hello from Employee* in the browser.

6. Navigate to the other actions by tagging on the route name of the specific actions to the */Employee* URL, for instance */Employee/Name*. You should be able to navigate to them and see their information.

7. Let's clean up the controller and make its route more reusable. Instead of using a hardcoded value for the controller's route, you can use the **[controller]** token that represents the name of the controller class (*Employee* in this case). This makes it easier if you need to rename the controller for some reason.
```
[Route("[controller]")]
public class EmployeeController
```

8. You can do the same for the action methods, but use the **[action]** token instead. ASP.NET will then replace the token with the action's name. Keep the empty **Route** attribute on the **Index** action and add the **[action]** token to a second **Route** attribute so that it has two routes; this will make it possible to use either the base route */Employees* or the */Employees/Index* route to reach the **Index** action.
```
[Route("")]
[Route("[action]")]
public string Index()
{
    return "Hello from Employee";
}

[Route("[action]")]
public string Name()
{
    return "Jonas";
}
```

9. Save the file and refresh the application in the browser. Make sure that the URL ends with */Employee/Name*. You should see your name in the browser. Test the other URLs as well, to make sure that they work properly.

10. You can also use literals in the route. Let's say that you want the route for the **EmployeeController** to be *Company/Employee*; you could then prepend the controller's route with *Company/*.
```
[Route("company/[controller]")]
public class EmployeeController
```

11. Save the file and refresh the application in the browser. Make sure that the URL ends with */Employee/Name*. You will not see your name in the browser; instead ASP.NET displays the text from the **Run** middleware. The reason for this is that

there isn't a route to */Employee/Name* anymore; it has changed to */Company/Employee/Name*. Change the URL in the browser to */Company/Employee/Name*. You should now see your name again.

12. If you don't want a default route in your controller, you can clean it up even more by removing all the action attributes and changing the controller route to include the **[action]** token. This means that you no longer can go to */Company/Employee* and reach the **Index** action; you will have to give an explicit URL in the browser to reach each action.
```
[Route("company/[controller]/[action]")]
public class EmployeeController
```

13. Remove all the **Route** attributes from the action methods and change the controller's **Route** attribute to include the **[action]** token. Save the file and refresh the browser with the URL */Company/Employee/Name*. You should now see your name.

14. Now navigate to the */Company/Employee* URL. You should see the message from the **Run** middleware because ASP.NET couldn't find any default action in the **EmployeeController**. Remember, you must give a specific URL with an action specified.

The complete code in the **EmployeeController** class:

```
[Route("company/[controller]/[action]")]
public class EmployeeController
{
    public string Name() { return "Jonas"; }

    public string Country() { return "Sweden"; }

    public string Index() { return "Hello from Employee"; }
}
```

IActionResult

The controller actions that you have seen so far have all returned strings. When working with actions, you rarely return strings. Most of the time you use the **IActionResult** return type, which can return many types of data, such as objects and views. To gain access to **IActionResult** or derivations thereof, the controller class must inherit the **Controller** class.

There are more specific implementations of that interface, for instance the **ContentResult** class, which can be used to return simple content such as strings. Using a more specific return type can be beneficial when unit testing, because you get a specific data type to test against.

Another return type is **ObjectType**, which often is used in Web API applications because it turns the result into an object that can be sent over HTTP. JSON is the default return type, making the result easy to use from JavaScript on the client. The data carrier can be configured to deliver the data in other formats, such as XML.

A specific data type helps the controller decide what to do with the data returned from an action. The controller itself does not do anything with the data, and does not write anything into the response. It is the framework that acts on that decision, and transforms the data into something that can be sent over HTTP. That separation of letting the controller decide what should be returned, and the framework doing the actual transformation, gives you flexibility and makes the controller easier to test.

Implementing ContentResult

Let's change the **Name** action to return a **ContentResult**.

1. Open the **EmployeeController** class.
2. Have the **EmployeeController** class inherit the **Controller** class.
   ```
   public class EmployeeController : Controller
   ```

3. Change the **Name** action's return type to **ContentResult**.
   ```
   public ContentResult Name()
   ```

4. Change the **return** statement to return a content object by calling the **Content** method, and pass in the string to it.
   ```
   public ContentResult Name()
   {
       return Content("Jonas");
   }
   ```

5. Save all files, open the browser, and navigate to the *Company/Employees/Name* URL.

6. Your name should be returned to the browser, same as before.

Using a Model Class and ObjectResult

Using a model class, you can send objects with data and logic to the browser. By convention, model classes should be stored in a folder called **Models**, but in larger applications it's not uncommon to store models in a separate project, which is referenced from the application. A model is a POCO (*Plain Old CLR Object* or *Plain Old C# Object*) class that can have attributes specifying how the browser should behave when using it, such as checking the length of a string or displaying data with a certain control.

Let's add a **Video** model class that holds data about a video, such as a unique id and a title. Typically you don't hardcode a model into a controller action; the objects are usually fetched from a data source such as a database (which you will do in another chapter).

1. Right click on the project node in the Solution Explorer and select **Add-New Folder**.

2. Name the folder *Models*.

3. Right click on the *Models* folder and select **Add-Class**.

4. Name the class **Video** and click the **Add** button.

5. Add an **int** property called **Id**. This will be the unique id when it is used as an entity in the database later.

6. Add a **string** property called **Title**. Let's keep it simple for now; you will add more properties later.
   ```
   public class Video
   {
       public int Id { get; set; }
       public string Title { get; set; }
   }
   ```

7. Open the **HomeController** class and inherit the **Controller** class.
   ```
   public class HomeController : Controller
   ```

8. You need to add a **using** statement to the **Mvc** namespace to get access to the **Controller** class.
   ```
   using Microsoft.AspNetCore.Mvc;
   ```

9. Instead of returning a string from the **Index** action, you will change the return type to **ObjectResult**.

```
public ObjectResult Index()
```

10. You need to add a **using** statement to the **Models** namespace to get access to the **Video** class.
```
using AspNetVideoCore.Models;
```

11. Create an instance of the **Video** model class and store it in a variable called **model**. Assign values to its properties when you instantiate it.
```
var model = new Video { Id = 1, Title = "Shreck" };
```

12. Return an instance of the **ObjectResult** class passing in the **model** object as its parameter.
```
return new ObjectResult(model);
```

13. Save all the files.

14. Browse to the root URL or /Home. As you can see, the object has been sent to the client as a JSON object.

The complete code for the **HomeController** class:

```
public class HomeController : Controller
{
    public ObjectResult Index()
    {
        var model = new Video { Id = 1, Title = "Shreck" };
        return new ObjectResult(model);
    }
}
```

Introduction to Views

The most popular way to render a view from an ASP.NET Core MVC application is to use the Razor view engine. To render the view, a **ViewResult** is returned from the controller action using the **View** method. It carries with it the name of the view in the filesystem, and a model object if needed.

The framework receives that information and produces the HTML that is sent to the browser.

Let's implement a view for the **Index** action and pass in a **Video** object as its model.

1. Open the **HomeController** class.
2. Change the return type of the **Index** action to **ViewResult**.
   ```
   public ViewResult Index()
   ```
3. Call the **View** method and pass in the **model** object that you created earlier.
   ```
   return View(model);
   ```
4. Save the file and refresh the application in the browser.
5. By convention ASP.NET will look for a view with the same name as the action that produced the result. It will look in two places, both subfolders, to a folder called *Views*: the first is a folder with the same name as the controller class, the second a folder named *Shared*. In this case, there is no view for the **Index** action, so an exception will be thrown.

6. To fix this you must add a view called **Index**. Right click on the project node in the Solution Explorer and select **Add-New Folder**.

7. Name the folder *Views*.

8. Right click on the *Views* folder and select **Add-New Folder**; name it *Home*.

9. Right click on the *Home* folder and select **Add-New Item**.

10. Select the **MVC View Page** template and click the **Add** button (it should be named *Index* by default).

11. Delete everything in the *Index.cshtml* view that was added.

12. Type *html* and press the **Tab** key on the keyboard to insert a skeleton for the view.

13. Add the text *Video* to the <title> element.
    `<title>Video</title>`

14. Although you can use the passed-in model and have it inferred from the actual object, it is in most cases better to explicitly specify it to gain access to IntelliSense and pre-compilation errors. You specify the model using the **@model** directive at the top of the view. Note that it should be declared with a lowercase *m*.
    `@model AspNetVideoCore.Models.Video`

15. To display the value from the **Title** property in the <body> element, you use the **@Model** object (note the capital letter *M*, and that it is prefixed with the @-sign to specify that it is Razor syntax). The IntelliSense will show all properties available in the model object passed to the view.
    `<body>@Model.Title</body>`

16. Save the **Index** view and refresh the application in the browser. You should now see the video title in the browser and the text *Video* in the browser tab.

A View with a Data Collection

Now that you know how to display one video, it's time to display a collection of videos. To achieve this, you'll first have to create the video collection and then pass it to the view displaying the data. In the view, you'll use a Razor **foreach** loop to display the data as HTML.

1. Open the **HomeController** class.
2. Add a **using** statement to the **System.Collections.Generic** namespace to gain access to the **List** collection.
   ```
   using System.Collections.Generic;
   ```

3. Replace the single **Video** object with a list of **Video** objects.
   ```
   var model = new List<Video>
   {
       new Video { Id = 1, Title = "Shreck" },
       new Video { Id = 2, Title = "Despicable Me" },
       new Video { Id = 3, Title = "Megamind" }
   };
   ```

4. Switch to the browser and navigate to */Home/Index*, or start the application without debugging (Ctrl+F5), if it's not already started.
5. An error message will appear, telling you that you are sending in a collection (list) of **Video** objects to the **Index** view, when it is designed for a single **Video** object.

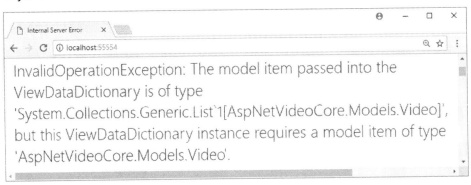

6. To solve this, you will have to change the **@model** directive in the **Index** view. You can use the **IEnumerable** interface, which is a nice abstraction to many different collections.
   ```
   @model IEnumerable<AspNetVideoCore.Models.Video>
   ```

7. When you change the **@model** directive, the **@Model** object no longer is a single instance of the **Video** class; you therefore must implement a loop to display the data in the model. Remove the **@Model.Title** property and add a table by typing *table* in the <body> element and press the **Tab** key.

```
<table>
    <tr>
        <td></td>
    </tr>
</table>
```

8. Add a **foreach** loop around the <tr> element with Razor to loop over the **Model** object. Using Razor makes it possible to mix C# and HTML. Note that you don't add the @-sign when already inside Razor code, but you use it when in HTML. Use the loop variable to add the **Id** and **Title** properties to the table row. The **video** variable in the loop doesn't have an @-sign because the **foreach** loop has one. When the **video** variable is used in HTML, however, the @-sign must be used.

```
@foreach (var video in Model)
{
    <tr>
        <td>@video.Id</td>
        <td>@video.Title</td>
    </tr>
}
```

9. Save all files, switch to the browser, and refresh the application. The three films should now be displayed.

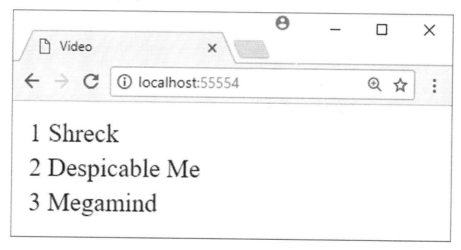

The full code for the **Index** action:

```
public ViewResult Index()
{
    var model = new List<Video>
    {
        new Video { Id = 1, Title = "Shreck" },
        new Video { Id = 2, Title = "Despicable Me" },
        new Video { Id = 3, Title = "Megamind" }
    };
    return View(model);
}
```

The full markup for the **Index** view:

```
@model IEnumerable<AspNetCoreVideo.Models.Video>

<html xmlns="http://www.w3.org/1999/xhtml">
<head>
    <title>Video</title>
</head>
<body>
    <table>
        @foreach (var video in Model)
        {
        <tr>
            <td>@video.Id</td>
            <td>@video.Title</td>
        </tr>
        }
    </table>
</body>
</html>
```

Adding a Data Service

Hardcoding data in a controller is not good practice. Instead you want to take advantage of dependency injection to make data available in a constructor, using a service component, like the **Message** service you added earlier.

One big benefit of implementing a service is that its interface can be used to implement different components. In this book you will implement one for Mock data and one for a SQL Server database.

In this section, you will implement a **MockVideoData** component that implements an interface called **IVideoData**.

The data will be implemented as a **List<Video>**. Note that a **List** collection isn't thread safe, and should be used with caution in web applications; but this code is for experimental purposes, and the component will only ever be accessed by one user at a time.

To begin with, the interface will only define one method, called **GetAll**, which will return an **IEnumerable<Video>** collection.

1. Right click on the *Services* folder and select **Add-New Item**.
2. Select the **Interface** template, name it **IVideoData**, and click the **Add** button.
3. Add the **public** access modifier to the interface to make it publicly available.
   ```
   public interface IVideoData
   {
   }
   ```
4. Add a **using** statement to the **Models** namespace to get access to the **Video** class.
   ```
   using AspNetVideoCore.Models;
   ```
5. Add a method called **GetAll** that returns an **IEnumerable<Video>** collection.
   ```
   IEnumerable<Video> GetAll();
   ```
6. Right click on the *Services* folder and select **Add-Class**.
7. Name the class **MockVideoData** and click the **Add** button.
8. Add a **using** statement to the **Models** namespace to get access to the **Video** class.
   ```
   using AspNetVideoCore.Models;
   ```
9. Implement the **IVideoData** interface in the class.
   ```
   public class MockVideoData : IVideoData
   {
       public IEnumerable<Video> GetAll()
       {
           throw new NotImplementedException();
       }
   }
   ```
10. Add a private field called **_videos** of type **IEnumerable<Video>** to the class. This field will hold the video data, loaded from a constructor.
    ```
    private IEnumerable<Video> _videos;
    ```

11. Add a constructor below the **_videos** field in the class. You can use the *ctor* snippet and hit the **Tab** key.
```
public MockVideoData()
{
}
```

12. Open the **HomeController** class and copy the video list, then paste it into the **MockVideoData** constructor. Remove the **var** keyword and rename the **model** variable **_videos** to assign the list to the field you just added.
```
_videos = new List<Video>
{
    new Video { Id = 1, Title = "Shreck" },
    new Video { Id = 2, Title = "Despicable Me" },
    new Video { Id = 3, Title = "Megamind" }
};
```

13. Remove the **throw** statement in the **GetAll** method and return the **_videos** list.
```
public IEnumerable<Video> GetAll()
{
    return _videos;
}
```

14. Now that the service is complete, you must add it to the **services** collection in the **Startup** class's **ConfigureServices** method. Previously you registered the **IMessageService** interface with the services collection using the **AddSingleton** method; this would ensure that only one instance of the defined class would exist. Let's use another method this time. Register the **IVideoData** interface using the **AddScoped** method; this will ensure that one object is created for each HTTP request. The HTTP request can then flow through many services that share the same instance of the **MockVideoData** class.
```
services.AddScoped<IVideoData, MockVideoData>();
```

15. Open the **HomeController** class and a **using** statement to the **Services** namespace.
```
using AspNetVideoCore.Services;
```

16. Add a private field of type **IVideoData** called **_videos** on class level. This field will hold the data fetched from the service.
```
private IVideoData _videos;
```

17. Add a constructor to the **HomeController** class and inject the **IVideoData** interface into it. Name the parameter **videos**. Assign the **videos** parameter to

the **_videos** field, inside the constructor. This will make the video service available throughout the controller.

```
public HomeController(IVideoData videos)
{
    _videos = videos;
}
```

18. Replace the hardcoded **List<Video>** collection assigned to the **model** variable in the **Index** action, with a call to the **GetAll** method on the service.
```
var model = _videos.GetAll();
```

19. Save all the files.

20. Switch to the browser and refresh the application. You should now see the list of videos.

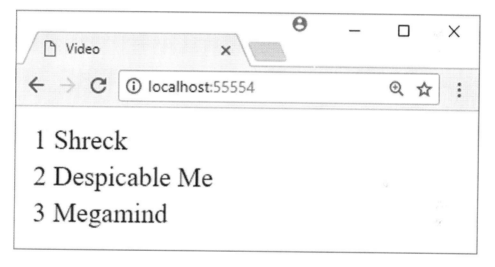

The complete code for the **IVideoData** interface:

```
public interface IVideoData {
    IEnumerable<Video> GetAll();
}
```

The complete code for the **MockVideoData** class:

```
public class MockVideoData : IVideoData
{
    private List<Video> _videos;
```

```
    public MockVideoData()
    {
        _videos = new List<Video>
        {
            new Video { Id = 1, Genre = Models.Genres.Romance,
                Title = "Shreck" },
            new Video { Id = 2, Genre = Models.Genres.Comedy,
                Title = "Despicable Me" },
            new Video { Id = 3, Genre = Models.Genres.Action,
                Title = "Megamind" }
        };
    }

    public IEnumerable<Video> GetAll() { return _videos; }
}
```

The complete code for the **ConfigureServices** method in the **Startup** class:

```
public void ConfigureServices(IServiceCollection services)
{
    services.AddMvc();
    services.AddSingleton(provider => Configuration);
    services.AddSingleton<IMessageService,
        ConfigurationMessageService>();
    services.AddScoped<IVideoData, MockVideoData>();
}
```

The complete code for the **HomeController** class:

```
public class HomeController : Controller
{
    private IVideoData _videos;
    public HomeController(IVideoData videos)
    {
        _videos = videos;
    }

    public ViewResult Index()
    {
        var model = _videos.GetAll();

        return View(model);
    }
}
```

Summary

In this chapter, you learned about the MVC (Model-View-Controller) design pattern, and how the controller receives an HTTP request, gathers data from various sources, and creates a model, which is then processed into HTML by the view, along with its own markup.

You will continue to use MVC throughout the book and create Razor Views and more sophisticated views and models that can be used to view and edit data.

4. Models

In this chapter, you will learn more about different types of model classes in the MVC framework and how to use them.

Up until now, you have used the **Video** class as a model for the **Index** view. In simple solutions that might be fine, but in more complex solutions, you need to use entity models and view models. Sometimes you even make a more granular distinction between the models, using Data Transfer Objects (DTOs) with the view models.

An entity model is typically used to define a table in a database. A view model is used to transport data from the controller to the view, but sometimes the view model needs to contain objects, and that's where the DTOs come into play. Some might argue that DTOs are view models, and in some scenarios they are.

You will create a new folder called *Entities* and move the **Video** class to that folder. The reason for moving the file is that the **Video** class later will be used to define a table in a SQL Server database. A class used to define a database table is referred to as an entity. You will also add a new folder named *ViewModels*, which will hold the view models created throughout the first part of the book.

Important to note is that the view model typically contains other data than the entity model, although some properties are the same. One example is when a video is being added in a **Create** view. The view model needs some properties from the entity model, but could also need other information that is not stored in the **Video** entity and must be fetched from another database table, or an **enum**.

A view model is never used to directly update the database. To update the database the data from the view model is added to an entity model, which then in turn updates the database table.

Let's look at an example where an **enum** is used to display the genre a video belongs to. For simplicity, a video can only belong to one genre.

View Model Example

First you need to add an *Entities* folder and a *ViewModels* folder to the folder structure.

Changing the Folder Structure

1. Create a new folder called *Entities* in the project.
2. Move the *Video.cs* file from the *Models* folder to the *Entities* folder, using drag-and-drop.
3. Open the **Video** class and change the **Models** namespace to **Entities**.
   ```
   namespace AspNetVideoCore.Entities
   ```

4. Open the **MockVideoData** class and change the **using** statement from **Models** namespace to **Entities**.
5. Open the **IVideoData** interface and change the **using** statement from **Models** namespace to **Entities**.
6. Open the **Index** view and change the **Models** namespace to **Entities** for the **@model** directive.
7. Open the **HomeController** class and remove any unused **using** statements.

Adding the View Model

1. Add a new folder called *ViewModels* to the project.
2. Add a class called **Genres** to the *Models* folder.
3. Replace the **class** keyword with the **enum** keyword and add some genres.
   ```
   public enum Genres
   {
       None,
       Animated,
       Horror,
       Comedy,
       Romance,
       Action
   }
   ```

4. Open the **Video** class and add an **int** property called **GenreId** to the class. This will hold the **enum** value for the video's genre.
   ```
   public class Video
   {
       public int Id { get; set; }
       public string Title { get; set; }
       public int GenreId { get; set; }
   }
   ```

5. Open the **MockVideoData** class and add a genre id for each video.
    ```
    new Video { Id = 3, GenreId = 2, Title = "Megamind" }
    ```
6. Add a class called **VideoViewModel** to the *ViewModel* folder.
7. The view model will contain the **Id** and **Title** properties, but you don't want to display the genre id; it would be nicer to display the actual genre. To achieve this, you add a **string** property called **Genre** to the **VideoViewModel** class, but not to the **Video** class.
    ```
    public class VideoViewModel
    {
        public int Id { get; set; }
        public string Title { get; set; }
        public string Genre { get; set; }
    }
    ```

Using the View Model

Now that the view model has been created, you need to send it to the view as its model. This requires some changes to the **HomeController** class and the **Index** view. You need to fetch the video from the **_videos** collection using its id, and then convert the genre id to the name for the corresponding value in the **Genres enum**.

When the view model has been assigned values from the entity object and the **enum** name, it is sent to the view with the **View** method.

1. Open the **HomeController** class.
2. Add a **using** statement to the **System.Linq** namespace to get access to the **Select** method and the **System** namespace to get access to the **Enum** class. Also, add a **using** statement to the **ViewModels** and **Models** namespaces to get access to the genre **enum** and the view model you added.
    ```
    using AspNetVideoCore.Models;
    using AspNetVideoCore.ViewModels;
    using System;
    using System.Linq;
    ```
3. Use the LINQ **Select** method in the **Index** action to convert each video into a **VideoViewModel** object, and store it in the **model** field. Use the **Enum.GetName** method to fetch the genre corresponding to the video's genre id.

```
public ViewResult Index()
{
    var model = _videos.GetAll().Select(video =>
        new VideoViewModel
        {
            Id = video.Id,
            Title = video.Title,
            Genre = Enum.GetName(typeof(Genres), video.GenreId)
        });
    return View(model);
}
```

4. Open the **Index** view and change the **@model** directive to an
   IEnumerable<VideoViewModel>.
   ```
   @model IEnumerable<AspNetVideoCore.ViewModels.VideoViewModel>
   ```

5. Add a new <td> for the genre.
   ```
   <td>@video.Genre</td>
   ```

6. Switch to the browser and refresh the application. As you can see, the genres are
   now displayed beside each of the video titles.

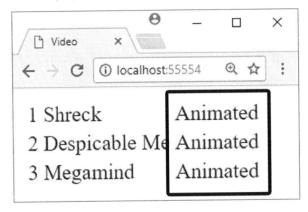

Adding a Details View

Now that you know how to use the **VideoViewModel** to send data to the **Index** view, it is
time to add a new view to the **Views** folder.

The **Details** view will display a single video in the browser, based on the id sent to the
Details action you will add next.

1. Add a new public action method called **Details** to the **HomeController**. It should have an **int** parameter named **id**, which will match a video id from the URL or the request data. The return type should be **IActionResult**, which makes it possible to return different types of data.
   ```
   public IActionResult Details(int id)
   {
   }
   ```

2. To fetch the video matching the passed-in id, you must add a new method called **Get** to the **IVideoData** interface. The method should have an **int** parameter called **id** and return a video object.
   ```
   Video Get(int id);
   ```

3. Now you need to implement that method in the **MockVideoData** class, and have it return the video matching the **id** parameter value. Use LINQ to fetch the video with the **FirstOrDefault** method.
   ```
   public Video Get(int id)
   {
       return _videos.FirstOrDefault(v => v.Id.Equals(id));
   }
   ```

4. Add a **using** statement to the **System.Linq** namespace.
   ```
   using System.Linq;
   ```

5. Add a variable called **model** to the **Details** action in the **HomeController** class. Call the **Get** method to fetch the videos matching the passed-in id and assign them to the **model** variable.
   ```
   var model = _videos.Get(id);
   ```

6. To test the **Get** method, return the **model** variable using an **ObjectResult** instance.
   ```
   return new ObjectResult(model);
   ```

7. Save all files and switch to the browser. Navigate to the */Home/Details/2* URL. The video matching the id 2 should be displayed.

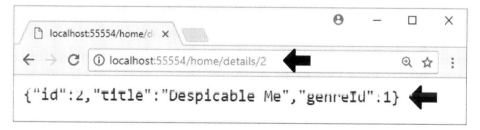

8. Change the **return** statement in the **Details** action to return the **View** method and pass in an instance of the **VideoViewModel** class filled with data from the **model** variable.
    ```
    return View(new VideoViewModel
        {
            Id = model.Id,
            Title = model.Title,
            Genre = Enum.GetName(typeof(Genres), model.GenreId)
        }
    );
    ```

9. Add a new **MVC View Page** file called *Details.cshtml* to the *Views/Home* folder in the Solution Explorer.

10. Delete all content in the **Details** view.

11. Type *html* and hit **Tab** to add the HTML skeleton to the view.

12. Add the **@model** directive for a single **VideoViewModel** to the view. This enables the view to display information about one video.
    ```
    @model AspNetVideoCore.ViewModels.VideoViewModel
    ```

13. Add the text *Video* to the <title> element.

14. Add a <div> element inside the <body> element for each property.
    ```
    <div>Id: @Model.Id</div>
    <div>Title: @Model.Title</div>
    <div>Genre: @Model.Genre</div>
    ```

15. Save all the files and switch to the browser and refresh. You should see the data for the video matching the id in the URL.

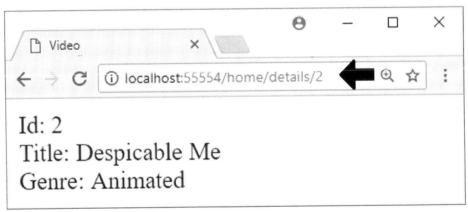

16. Change the id in the URL and make sure that the correct film is displayed.

17. Change to an id that doesn't exist. An error should be displayed in the browser. The reason for the error is that the **Get** method will return **null** if the video doesn't exist, and the view can't handle **null** values for the model.

18. One way to solve this is to redirect to another action; in this case the **Index** action is appropriate. Add an if-statement above the previous **return** statement, which checks if the **model** is **null**; if it is, redirect to the **Index** action. Implementing this check will ensure that the action won't show the error message, and instead display the video list.
```
if (model == null)
    return RedirectToAction("Index");
```

19. Switch to the browser and refresh. The **Index** view should be displayed.

20. Let's add a link to the **Index** view in the **Details** view, for easy navigation back to the root. You can use a traditional HTML <a> tag, or you can use the Razor **ActionLink** HTML helper method. There is a new, third way to add a link, using Tag Helpers. You will explore Tag Helpers shortly.
```
@Html.ActionLink("Home", "Index")
```

21. Switch to the browser and navigate to */Home/Details/2* URL. The view should have a link with the text *Home*. Click the link to get back to the **Index** view.

22. Now open the **Index** view and add links for the video ids. To achieve this, you must pass in an anonymous object as an extra parameter, and add an id property to that object.
```
<td>@Html.ActionLink(video.Id.ToString(), "Details",
    new { id = video.Id })</td>
```

23. Switch to the browser and go to the root (/). Click one of the links to view the details for that video.

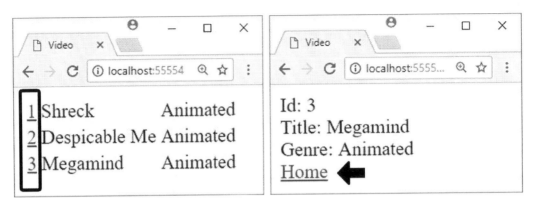

The complete markup for the **Index** view:

```
@model IEnumerable<AspNetVideoCore.ViewModels.VideoViewModel>

<html xmlns="http://www.w3.org/1999/xhtml">
<head>
    <title>Video</title>
</head>

<body>
    <table>
        @foreach (var video in Model)
        {
            <tr>
            <td>@Html.ActionLink(video.Id.ToString(), "Details",
                    new { id = video.Id })</td>
            <td>@video.Title</td>
            <td>@video.Genre</td>
            </tr>
        }
    </table>
</body>
</html>
```

The complete markup for the **Details** view:

```
@model AspNetVideoCore.ViewModels.VideoViewModel

<html xmlns="http://www.w3.org/1999/xhtml">
<head>
    <title>Video</title>
</head>
```

```
<body>
    <div>Id: @Model.Id</div>
    <div>Title: @Model.Title</div>
    <div>Genre: @Model.Genre</div>
    @Html.ActionLink("Home", "Index")
</body>
</html>
```

The complete markup for the **Details** action:

```
public IActionResult Details(int id)
{
    var model = _videos.Get(id);

    if (model == null) return RedirectToAction("Index");

    return View(new VideoViewModel
    {
        Id = model.Id,
        Title = model.Title,
        Genre = Enum.GetName(typeof(Genres), model.GenreId)
    });
}
```

Adding a Create View

When creating a new record in the data source with a **Create** view, you have to implement two action methods. The first is a method using HTTP GET to render the **Create** view in the browser, filling select lists and other controls that need data. The second method is an HTTP POST method that receives data from the client through an HTTP POST request.

The post from the client can be done in several ways, for instance with JavaScript or a form post. In this example, you will use a form post to call back to the server when the user clicks a **Submit** button.

The HTTP POST action method can fetch data from several places in the posted data: the header, the query string, and the body of the request. The data is then matched against properties in a model object, which is a parameter of the action method. The action can also handle simple types such as **int** and **string**, without them being encapsulated in a model object.

There is a naming convention that you need to be aware of, to properly match posted form data with properties in model objects and other parameters. The rule states that the element names in the form data must match the property names to be matched.

The default behavior of a view using an **enum** is to display it as a text field. This is not the best way to display a selected item in a list of values. In this section, you will remove the **Video** class's **GenreId** property, and add a new property of the **enum** type **Genres** called **Genre**. This makes it easier to work with **enum** data, especially when working with a SQL Server database entity model.

You will also add the **enum** as a property to a new view model called **VideoEditView-Model**, which can be used both when creating a new video and when editing one.

Refactoring the Application

1. Open the **Video** class.
2. Delete the **GenreId** property.
3. Add a using statement to the **Models** namespace where the **Genre** enumeration is located.
   ```
   using AspNetVideoCore.Models;
   ```

4. Add a new property of type **Genres** and name it **Genre**. This property will hold the current genre for the video.
   ```
   public Genres Genre { get; set; }
   ```

5. Open the **MockVideoData** class.
6. Replace the **GenreId** property with the **Genre** property and assign its value from the **enum** directly.
   ```
   new Video { Id = 1, Genre = Models.Genres.Comedy, Title = "Shreck"
   },
   ```

7. Open the **HomeController** class.
8. Locate the **Index** action and change the assignment of the **Genre** string in the **VideoViewModel** object to use the value stored in the **Genre** property of the **Video** object. You can use the **ToString** method to fetch the name of the **enum** value.
   ```
   Genre = video.Genre.ToString()
   ```

9. Repeat step 7 for the **Details** action method but use the **model** variable instead of the **video** parameter.

10. Switch to the browser and refresh the application. It should look and work the same as before.

The complete code for the **Video** class, after the changes:

```
public class Video
{
    public int Id { get; set; }
    public string Title { get; set; }
    public Genres Genre { get; set; }
}
```

The complete code for the **MockVideoData** constructor, after the changes:

```
public MockVideoData()
{
    _videos = new List<Video>
    {
        new Video { Id = 1, Genre = Models.Genres.Animated,
            Title = "Shreck" },
        new Video { Id = 2, Genre = Models.Genres.Animated,
            Title = "Despicable Me" },
        new Video { Id = 3, Genre = Models.Genres.Animated,
            Title = "Megamind" }
    };
}
```

The complete **HomeController** class after the changes:

```
public class HomeController : Controller
{
    private IVideoData _videos;
    public HomeController(IVideoData videos)
    {
        _videos = videos;
    }

    public ViewResult Index()
    {
        var model = _videos.GetAll().Select(video =>
            new VideoViewModel
            {
                Id = video.Id,
                Title = video.Title,
                Genre = video.Genre.ToString()
```

```
            });

        return View(model);
    }

    public IActionResult Details(int id)
    {
        var model = _videos.Get(id);

        if (model == null) return RedirectToAction("Index");

        return View(new VideoViewModel
        {
            Id = model.Id,
            Title = model.Title,
            Genre = model.Genre.ToString()
        });
    }
}
```

Adding the HTTP GET Create Action and the Create View

The HTTP GET **Create** action method renders the **Create** view to the browser, displaying the necessary controls to create a new video and to post the form to the server.

1. Open the **HomeController** class.
2. Add a new action method called **Create**, with the return type **IActionResult**. Return the **View** method.
   ```
   public IActionResult Create()
   {
       return View();
   }
   ```
3. Add a **MVC View Page** to the *Views/Home* folder in the Solution Explorer and name it *Create.cshtml*.
4. Delete all the content in the view.
5. Add a **@using** statement to the *Models* folder, to get access to the **enum** definition for the select list.
   ```
   @using AspNetVideoCore.Models
   ```
6. Add an **@model** directive with the **Video** class as the view model.
   ```
   @model AspNetVideoCore.Entities.Video
   ```

7. To be able to use Tag Helpers, which is the new way to add ASP.NET specific markup to views, you have to add a **@addTagHelper** directive to the view, or a shared file. You will learn more about Tag Helpers later.
`@addTagHelper *`, `Microsoft.AspNetCore.Mvc.TagHelpers`

8. Add an <h2> heading with the text *Create Video*.

9. Add a <form> element and use the **asp-action** Tag Helper to specify the action to post to when the **Submit** button is clicked. Make the form post to the server by assigning **post** to the **method** attribute.
```
<form asp-action="Create" method="post">
```

10. Add a table with two rows to the form, one for the **Title** and one for the **Genre enum**.

11. Use the **asp-for** Tag Helper to specify which property the controls should bind to. Add a <label> and an <input> element for the **Title** property.
```
<tr>
    <td><label asp-for="Title"></label></td>
    <td><input asp-for="Title"/></td>
</tr>
```

12. Use the same Tag Helper when you add the <label> and <select> elements for the **Genre enum**. To list the **enum** items, you must add the **asp-items** Tag Helper to the <select> element and call the **GetEnumSelectList** method on the **Html** class.
```
<tr>
    <td><label asp-for="Genre"></label></td>
    <td><select asp-for="Genre"
        asp-items="Html.GetEnumSelectList<Genres>()"></select>
    </td>
</tr>
```

13. Add a **submit** button with the text *Create* to the form.
```
<input type="submit" value="Create" />
```

14. Add an anchor tag with the text *Back to List* below the form. Use the **asp-action** Tag Helper to specify that the link should navigate to the **Index** action.
```
<a asp-action="Index">Back to List</a>
```

15. Save all files and switch to the browser. Navigate to the */Home/Create* URL. You should see a form with a text field, a drop-down with all genres listed, a **Submit** button, and a link leading back to the **Index** view. The **Submit** button won't work yet, because you haven't added the required action method.

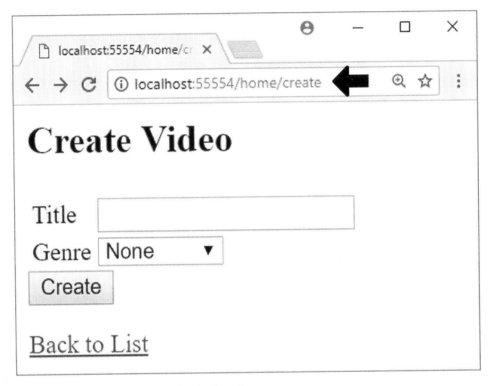

16. Click the link to navigate to the **Index** view.

The complete code for the HTTP GET **Create** action:

```
public IActionResult Create()
{
    return View();
}
```

The complete markup for the **Create** view:

```
@using AspNetVideoCore.Models
@model AspNetVideoCore.Entities.Video
@addTagHelper *, Microsoft.AspNetCore.Mvc.TagHelpers

<h2>Create Video</h2>
<form asp-action="Create" method="post">
    <table>
        <tr>
            <td><label asp-for="Title"></label></td>
            <td><input asp-for="Title" /></td>
```

```
        </tr>
        <tr>
            <td><label asp-for="Genre"></label></td>
            <td><select asp-for="Genre"
                asp-items="Html.GetEnumSelectList<Genres>()"></select>
            </td>
        </tr>
    </table>

    <input type="submit" value="Create" />
</form>

<div>
    <a asp-action="Index">Back to List</a>
</div>
```

Adding the VideoEditViewModel Class

This view model will be used when the controller receives a post from a video's **Edit** or **Create** view.

1. Create a new class called **VideoEditViewModel** in the *ViewModels* folder.
2. Add an **int** property named **Id** and a **string** property named **Title**.
3. Add a **using** statement to the **Models** namespace to get access to the **Genre** enumeration.
   using AspNetVideoCore.Models;

4. Add a property called **Genre** of type **Genres**. This property will contain the genre selected in the form when the **submit** button is clicked, and a post is made back to the controller on the server.
   public Genres Genre { get; set; }

The complete code for the **VideoEditViewModel** class:

```
public class VideoEditViewModel
{
    public int Id { get; set; }
    public string Title { get; set; }
    public Genres Genre { get; set; }
}
```

Adding the HTTP POST Create Action

A <form> element is used when a user should enter data in a view. There are a few steps that are performed when a user posts data. The first you already know: the user sends an HTTP request to the HTTP GET action in the controller, which fetches the necessary data after which the view is rendered.

To handle the form's post back to the server, an HTTP POST version of the action method is called with the form values. The names of the form controls are matched against the model properties or parameters available in the action's parameter list.

The POST action then uses that data to create, update, or delete data in the data source.

When passing data from the view to the action, MVC will, by default, match all properties in the form with properties in the model. This can be risky, especially if you use an entity class as the model. In many scenarios, you don't want to receive all data the form sends to the action. So how do you tell MVC to use only the values of interest? You create a separate view model, like you did in the previous section.

Let's implement the HTTP POST **Create** action in the **HomeController** class.

1. Open the **HomeController** class.
2. Add a new action method called **Create** that takes the **VideoEditViewModel** as a parameter named **model**.
   ```
   public IActionResult Create(VideoEditViewModel model) {
       return View();
   }
   ```
3. Save all files and switch to the browser. Navigate to the /Home/Create URL. You should see an error message telling you that multiple actions were found with the same name.

4. To fix this, you need to decorate the GET action with the **[HttpGet]** attribute, and the POST action with the **[HttpPost]** attribute. This will tell ASP.NET which method to call when the view is rendered and which method to call by the client when posting data.

```
[HttpGet]
public IActionResult Create()
{
    return View();
}

[HttpPost]
public IActionResult Create(VideoEditViewModel model)
{
    return View();
}
```

5. Place a breakpoint on the **return** statement in the POST action.
6. Save all files and start the application <u>with</u> debugging (F5). Navigate to the */Home/Create* URL. The **Create** view should be displayed again.
7. Fill out the form and click the **Create** button. The execution should halt at the breakpoint, proving that the **Create** button posts to the server. Inspect the content in the **model** object; it should contain the values you entered in the form.

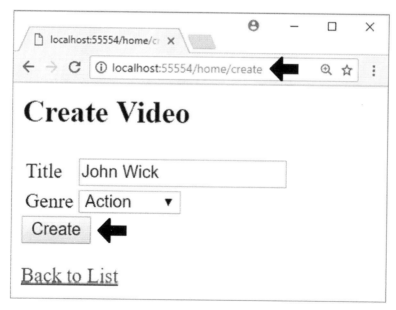

```
[HttpPost]
public IActionResult Create(
    VideoEditViewModel model)
{
    return View();
}
```

model	{AspNetVideoCore
Genre	Action
Id	0
Title	"John Wick"

8. Stop the application in Visual Studio.

9. Add a **using** statement to the **Entities** namespace to get access to the **Video** entity class.
   ```
   using AspNetVideoCore.Entities;
   ```

10. Because the purpose of the **Create** method is to add a new video to the data source, you will have to create an instance of the **Video** class and assign values to it from the **model** object properties. Note that you don't have to assign the **Id** property. The video doesn't exist in the data source yet, and therefore doesn't have an id.
    ```
    var video = new Video
    {
        Title = model.Title,
        Genre = model.Genre
    };
    ```

11. Because you have implemented the **IVideoData** Interface as a service that is injected into the constructor, you have to add an **Add** method to it, and **implement** it in the **MockVideoData** class. This will make it possible to call the **Add** method on the **_videos** variable to add a new video. Let's implement it one step at a time. Begin by opening the **IVideoData** Interface.

12. Add a new **void** method called **Add** that takes a **Video** parameter called **newVideo**.
    ```
    void Add(Video newVideo);
    ```

13. Add the method to the **MockVideoData** class. You can use the light bulb button if you hover over the interface name.

14. Remove the **throw** statement from the method.

15. Because the data source is a collection that is unable to generate new ids, you have to create a new id for the video object. You can fake an id by using LINQs **Max** method to fetch the highest id and add 1 to it. This id is <u>only</u> used for demo purposes and should never be used in a production application where the id is created automatically by the database.

```
newVideo.Id = _videos.Max(v => v.Id) + 1;
```

16. To add the new video to the **_videos** collection, you must change its data type to **List**. You can't add values to an **IEnumerable** collection. To preserve the values between HTTP requests, you will later change the scope of the **IVideoData** service in the **Startup** class.

```
private List<Video> _videos;
```

17. Make a call to the **Add** method on the **_videos** collection, to add the new video in the **Add** method you created in the **MockVideoData** class.

```
public void Add(Video newVideo)
{
    newVideo.Id = _videos.Max(v => v.Id) + 1;
    _videos.Add(newVideo);
}
```

18. Open the **HomeController** class and call the **Add** method you just created, from the HTTP POST **Create** action, and pass in the **video** object to it.

```
_videos.Add(video);
```

19. To prevent the user from submitting the Create form multiple times by refreshing the page, you must replace the **View** method with a call to the **RedirectToAction** method and redirect them to another view, like the **Details** view. Because the **Details** view has an **id** parameter you must pass in the name of the view, and the video id wrapped in an anonymous object.

```
return RedirectToAction("Details", new { id = video.Id });
```

20. Open the **Startup** class and locate the **ConfigureServices** method. Change the scope of the **IVideoData** service to singleton by calling the **AddSingleton** method instead of the **AddScoped** that is currently used. You do this to preserve the data between HTTP requests.

```
services.AddSingleton<IVideoData, MockVideoData>();
```

21. Save all the files and navigate to the */Home/Create* URL. Fill out the form and click the **Create** button. Instead of remaining on the **Create** view, you are

redirected to the **Details** view, which displays the added video. Note that the URL changed to */Home/Details/4* with the redirect.

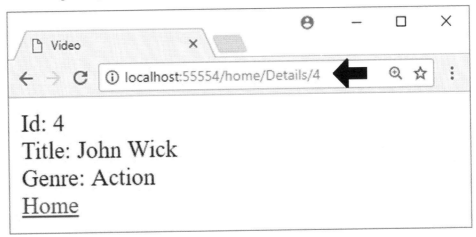

The complete code for the **IVideoData** interface:

```
public interface IVideoData
{
    IEnumerable<Video> GetAll();
    Video Get(int id);
    void Add(Video newVideo);
}
```

The complete code for the **Add** method in the **MockVideoData** class:

```
public void Add(Video newVideo)
{
    newVideo.Id = _videos.Max(v => v.Id) + 1;
    _videos.Add(newVideo);
}
```

The complete code for the **Create** actions:

```
[HttpGet]
public IActionResult Create()
{
    return View();
}
```

```
[HttpPost]
public IActionResult Create(VideoEditViewModel model)
{
    var video = new Video
    {
        Title = model.Title,
        Genre = model.Genre
    };

    _videos.Add(video);

    return RedirectToAction("Details", new { id = video.Id });
}
```

The complete code for the **ConfigureServices** method in the **Startup** class:

```
public void ConfigureServices(IServiceCollection services)
{
    services.AddMvc();
    services.AddSingleton(provider => Configuration);
    services.AddSingleton<IMessageService,
        ConfigurationMessageService>();
    services.AddSingleton<IVideoData, MockVideoData>();
}
```

Data Annotations

Data annotations are attributes you add to properties in a model, to enforce rules about them. You can specify that a field is required or must have a maximum number of characters. The text displayed in a label is normally the property name, but that can be overridden with the [Display] attribute.

Many data annotations can be found in the **System.ComponentModel.DataAnnotations** namespace. You can specify one annotation per code line, or multiple annotations as a comma-separated list inside a set of square brackets.

```
[Required]
[MaxLength(80)]
```

Or

```
[Required, MaxLength(80)]
```

Below is a list of commonly used data annotations.

Name	Purpose
MinLength / MaxLength	Enforces length of strings
Range	Enforces min and max for numbers
RegularExpression	Makes a string match a pattern
Display	Sets the label text for a property
DataType	Determines how the output control will be rendered in the browser, for instance password or email
Required	The model value is mandatory
Compare	Compares the values of two input controls, often used for password validation

Preparing the Create View for Validation

To validate the annotations in the browser, the view must be altered to display possible errors. You usually do this by adding a <span> or a <div> element decorated with the **asp-validation-for** Tag Helper, specifying which property it displays errors for. You can also add a validation summary that displays all errors as an unordered list inside a <div> element decorated with the **asp-validation-summary** Tag Helper.

Adding Validation to the Create View

Let's add both types of validation to the **Create** view to see what it looks like.

1. Open the **Create** view.
2. Add a validation summary <div> at the top of the form.
   ```
   <form asp-action="Create" method="post">
       <div asp-validation-summary="All"></div>
   ```

3. Add validation to the **Title** property. Add a <span> decorated with the **asp-validation-for** Tag Helper inside a <td> element below the **Title** <input>.
   ```
   <td><span asp-validation-for="Title"></span></td>
   ```

4. Repeat step 3 for the **Genre** property.

The complete **Create** view after the changes:

```
@using AspNetVideoCore.Models
@model AspNetVideoCore.Entities.Video
@addTagHelper *, Microsoft.AspNetCore.Mvc.TagHelpers

<h2>Create Video</h2>
<form asp-action="Create" method="post">
    <div asp-validation-summary="All"></div>
    <table>
        <tr>
            <td><label asp-for="Title"></label></td>
            <td><input asp-for="Title" /></td>
            <td><span asp-validation-for="Title"></span></td>
        </tr>
        <tr>
            <td><label asp-for="Genre"></label></td>
            <td><select asp-for="Genre"
                asp-items="Html.GetEnumSelectList<Genres>()"></select>
            </td>
            <td><span asp-validation-for="Genre"></span></td>
        </tr>
    </table>

    <input type="submit" value="Create" />
</form>

<div>
    <a asp-action="Index">Back to List</a>
</div>
```

Validating the Model on the Server

Since no JavaScript validation libraries have been added to the application, you must validate the model on the server. To enforce model validation in the HTTP POST **Create** action, you must check if the model is valid before taking any action. If the model is valid, the video will be added to the data source, otherwise it will re-render the view so that the user can change the values and resubmit.

The **ModelState** object's **IsValid** property can be used in the HTTP POST action to check if the model is valid. Surround the code that creates and adds the video to the data source with an if-statement that checks the **IsValid** property value. Return the view below the if-block if the model state is invalid.

1. Open the **HomeController** class.
2. Add an if-block that checks the model state; it should surround all the code inside the HTTP POST **Create** action.
   ```
   if (ModelState.IsValid)
   {
       ...
   }
   ```
3. Return the view below the if-block.
   ```
   return View();
   ```

The complete code for the HTTP POST **Create** action:

```
[HttpPost]
public IActionResult Create(VideoEditViewModel model)
{
    if (ModelState.IsValid)
    {
        var video = new Video
        {
            Title = model.Title,
            Genre = model.Genre
        };

        _videos.Add(video);

        return RedirectToAction("Details", new { id = video.Id });
    }

    return View();
}
```

Adding Data Annotations in the Video Entity and VideoEditViewModel Class

Data annotations added to an entity class can affect both the controls in a view and the database table it represents.

In the project you are building, the **Video** entity is used as the view model for the **Create** view. To enforce some rules on that model, you add attributes to its properties that restrict or enhance them.

Let's implement some annotations in the **Video** entity model that alter how the controls in the view are rendered, and later restrict the database columns.

1. Open the **Video** entity model.
2. Add a **using** statement to the **DataAnnotations** namespace to get access to the data annotation attributes.
   ```
   using System.ComponentModel.DataAnnotations;
   ```
3. Add the **Required** annotation to the **Title** property. This will restrict the value in the database table to non-**null** values, and force the user to enter a value in the control, for the **model** object to be valid.
   ```
   [Required]
   public string Title { get; set; }
   ```
4. Open the **VideoEditViewModel** and repeat step 2 and 3.
5. Save all files and switch to the browser. Navigate to the */Home/Create* URL.
6. Click the **Create** button without entering a title. The validation message should appear beside the input field.

7. Add the **MinLength** annotation, with a min length of 3, to the **Title** property in both the **Video** and **VideoEditViewModel** classes.
   ```
   [Required, MinLength(3)]
   ```
8. Save all files and switch to the browser. Navigate to the */Home/Create* URL.

9. Enter 2 characters in the **Title** input field and click the **Create** button. The validation message should tell you that too few characters have been entered in the input field.

10. Enter at least 3 characters in the **Title** input field and click the **Create** button. The video should be successfully added to the data source.

11. Add the **MaxLength** annotation, with a max length of 80, to the **Title** property in both the **Video** and **VideoEditViewModel** classes. This will ensure that the **Title** property can have at most 80 characters when saved to the data source, and that the input control only will accept that many characters.

12. You can use the **Display** annotation to change the label text for a property. Let's change the text for the **Genre** property to *Film Genre*. Add the **Display** attribute to the **Genre** property in the **Video** class. Set its **Name** parameter to the text *Film Genre*. You only have to add the attribute to the **Video** model, since it only is applied to labels in a view.
    ```
    [Display(Name ="Film Genre")]
    ```

13. Save all files and switch to the browser. Navigate to the */Home/Create* URL. The label for the **Genre** select list should display the text *Film Genre*.

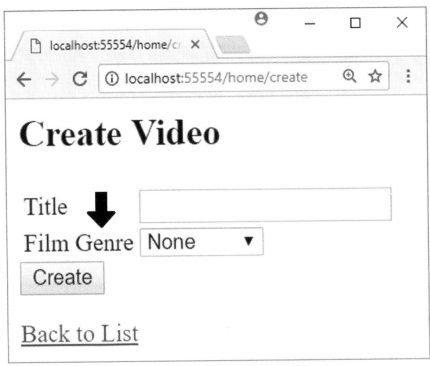

14. Let's try the **DataType** annotation next. Add it to the **Title** property in the **Video** class and select the **Password** type. This should display the entered text as password characters, typically dots or asterisks. Specifying a data type in the model can change its control's appearance on some devices, and can even change the layout of the keyboard displayed on the device screen, when the control has focus.
    [DataType(DataType.Password)]

15. Save all files and switch to the browser. Navigate to the */Home/Create* URL. Enter text in the **Title** input field. It should be displayed as password characters.

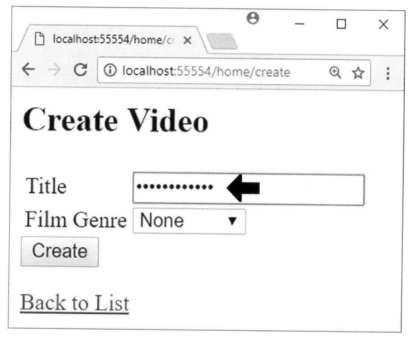

16. Remove the **Password** annotation and save the file.

Summary

In this chapter, you learned about different models that can be used with MVC, and how data annotations can be used to influence the labels and input controls, created with HTML and Tag Helpers in the view.

You also implemented validation checks on the server and displayed validation messages on the client.

5. Entity Framework

In this chapter, you will set up Entity Framework (EF) and get familiar with how it works. To work with EF, you must install the proper services, either manually in the *.csproj* file or by using the NuGet manager.

When the services have been installed and configured in the **Startup** class, you need to add a data context class that inherits from the **DbContext** class. This class will be the context that you use to interact with the database. To add a table to the database, the table's entity class must be added as a **DbSet** property in the context class.

When the services are installed and configured in the **Startup** class, you create the first migration by using the Package Manager Console and the **Add-Migration** command. When the initial migration has been added, the database can be generated with the **Update-Database** command.

If you make any changes to the database, like adding or changing columns or tables, then you must execute the **Add-Migration** and **Update-Database** commands again for the application to work properly.

In previous versions you had to install Entity Framework NuGet packages to create and use a database. In ASP.NET Core 2.0 those NuGet packages are installed as part of the **Microsoft.AspNetCore.All** NuGet package.

The setup for User Secrets has been incorporated into the new **BuildWebHost** method in the *Program.cs* file, which means that you no longer have to add any configuration for it in the **Startup** class. You can use User Secrets to store sensitive data locally in a file called *secrets.json*, which is stored outside the solution folder structure and is never committed to the source code repository, if you use that. You will store the connection string to the database securely in the *secrets.json* file.

Adding the VideoDbContext Class

Now that the NuGet packages have been installed, you can add a class called **VideoDb-Context** that inherits form the **DbContext** class. This class will be your connection to the database. It defines the entity classes as **DbSet** properties, which are mirrored as tables in the database.

For the **AddDbContext** method to be able to add the context to the services collection, the **VideoDbContext** must have a constructor with a **DbContextOptions<VideoDbContext>** parameter, which passes the parameter object to its base constructor. The **OnModelCreating** method must be overridden to enable Entity Framework to build the entity model for the database.

1. Add a new folder called *Data* to the project.
2. Add a class called **VideoDbContext** to the *Data* folder in the Solution Explorer.
3. Inherit the **DbContext** class in the **VideoDbContext** class. The **DbContext** class is in the **Microsoft.EntityFrameworkCore** namespace.
   ```
   public class VideoDbContext : DbContext { }
   ```
4. Add a **DbSet** property for the **Video** class in the **VideoDbContext** class. the **Video** class is in the **AspNetVideoCore.Entities** namespace.
   ```
   public DbSet<Video> Videos { get; set; }
   ```
5. Add the constructor with a **DbContextOptions<VideoDbContext>** parameter.
   ```
   public VideoDbContext(DbContextOptions<VideoDbContext> options)
   : base(options) { }
   ```
6. Override the **OnModelCreating** method.
   ```
   protected override void OnModelCreating(ModelBuilder builder)
   {
       base.OnModelCreating(builder);
   }
   ```
7. Save all the files.

The complete code for the **VideoDbContext** class:

```
public class VideoDbContext : DbContext
{
    public DbSet<Video> Videos { get; set; }

    public VideoDbContext(DbContextOptions<VideoDbContext> options)
        : base(options)
    {
    }

    protected override void OnModelCreating(ModelBuilder builder)
    {
        base.OnModelCreating(builder);
    }
}
```

Configuration in the Startup Class

Before the initial migration can be applied, you have to configure Entity Framework to use the **VideoDbContext**, and read the connection string from the *secrets.json* file. Using the *secrets.json* file has two purposes: It stores the connection string in a safe place that is not checked into source control. It also renders the *appsettings.json* obsolete for storing secret or sensitive data, which is a good thing, since it is checked into source control.

1. Right click on the project node in the Solution Explorer and select **Manage User Secrets**.

2. Add the following connection string property. Note that the database name is **VideoCoreDb**. The connection string should be on one row in the file.
   ```
   "ConnectionStrings": {
       "DefaultConnection": "Server=(localdb)\\mssqllocaldb;
           Database=VideoCoreDb;Trusted_Connection=True;
           MultipleActiveResultSets=true"
   }
   ```

3. Open the **Startup** class and locate the constructor.

4. Add the **optional: true** parameter value temporarily to the **AddJsonFile** method for the *appsettings.json* file if the file is missing from the project.
   ```
   .AddJsonFile("appsettings.json", optional: true);
   ```

5. To be able to check the environment the **IHostingEnvironment** interface must be injected into the constructor.
   ```
   IHostingEnvironment env
   ```

6. Add an if-statement, checking if the development environment is active, and use the **AddUserSecrets** method to add it to the **builder** object. Add it above the **Build** method call.
   ```
   if (env.IsDevelopment())
       builder.AddUserSecrets<Startup>();
   ```

7. Locate the **ConfigureServices** method and fetch the connection string from the *secrets.json* file using the **Configuration** object. Store the connection string in a variable called **conn**.
   ```
   var conn = Configuration.GetConnectionString("DefaultConnection");
   ```

8. Use the **AddDbContext** method on the **services** collection to add the database context and the EF services at the beginning of the **ConfigureServices** method. Call the **UseSqlServer** method on the **options** action in its constructor to specify that you want to use a SQL Server database provider. The **UseSqlServer** method

is in the **Microsoft.EntityFrameworkCore** namespace and the **VideoDbContext** class is in the **AspNetVideoCore.Data** namespace. Note that **DefaultConnection** is the name of the property you added to the *secrets.json* file.

```
services.AddDbContext<VideoDbContext>(options =>
    options.UseSqlServer(conn));
```

The complete code for the *secrets.json* file:

```
{
    "ConnectionStrings": {
        "DefaultConnection": "Server=(localdb)\\mssqllocaldb;
            Database=VideoCoreDb;Trusted_Connection=True;
            MultipleActiveResultSets=true"
    }
}
```

*Note that the **DefaultConnection** property value should be one line of code.*

The complete code for the **Startup** class's constructor:

```
public Startup(IHostingEnvironment env)
{
    var builder = new ConfigurationBuilder()
        .SetBasePath(Directory.GetCurrentDirectory())
        .AddJsonFile("appsettings.json");
        //.AddJsonFile("appsettings.json", optional: true);

    if (env.IsDevelopment())
        builder.AddUserSecrets<Startup>();

    Configuration = builder.Build();
}
```

The complete code for the **Startup** class's **ConfigureServices** method:

```
public void ConfigureServices(IServiceCollection services)
{
    var conn = Configuration.GetConnectionString("DefaultConnection");
    services.AddDbContext<VideoDbContext>(options =>
        options.UseSqlServer(conn));

    services.AddMvc();
    services.AddSingleton(provider => Configuration);
    services.AddSingleton<IMessageService,
        ConfigurationMessageService>();
    services.AddSingleton<IVideoData, MockVideoData>();
}
```

Adding the Initial Migration and Creating the Database

To add the initial migration and create the database, you execute the **Add-Migration** and **Update-Database** commands in the Package Manager Console (**View-Other Windows-Package Manager Console**).

When the **Add-Migration** command has been successfully executed, a new folder called *Migrations* will appear in the project. The current and all future migrations will be stored in this folder.

If you encounter the error message **No parameterless constructor was found on 'VideoDbContext': Either add a parameterless constructor to 'VideoDbContext' or add an implementation of 'IDbContextFactory<VideoDbContext>' in the same assembly as 'VideoDbContext',** then check that your connection string in *secrets.json* is correct and that it is being loaded in the **Startup** class, before doing any other troubleshooting.

1. Open the package Manager Console.
2. Type in the command *add-migration Initial* and press **Enter**. Note the *Migrations* folder, and the migration files in it.
3. Execute the command *update-database* in the Package Manager Console to create the database.
4. Open the **SQL Server Object Explorer** from the **View** menu.
5. Expand the **MSSQLLocalDb** node, and then the **Databases** node. If the **VideoCoreDb** database isn't visible, right click on the **Databases** node and select **Refresh**.

6. Expand the **VideoCoreDb** node, and then the **Tables** node. You should now see the **Videos** table in the **VideoCoreDb** database that you just created.

7. Expand the **Videos** table and then the **Columns** node. You should now see the columns in the table. Note that they match the properties in the **Video** entity class, and that they have the restrictions from the attributes you added to its properties.

8. Right click on the **Videos** table and select **View Data**. This will open the table in edit mode. Add a genre id from the **Genres** enum (it is zero based) and a title. Press **Enter** to commit the value to the database. Add a few more videos if you like.

Id	Genre	Title
1	1	Megamind
2	1	Despicable Me
4	1	Shreck
5	5	John Wick

Adding the SqlVideoData Service Component

To use the database in the application, you can implement the **IVideoData** interface in a new service component class. Then, you change the service registration in the **Configure-Services** method in the **Startup** class to create instances of the new component.

Implementing the SqlVideoData Service Component Class

Let's begin by implementing the **SqlVideoData** class that will communicate with the database through the **VideoDbContext**.

1. Add a class called **SqlVideoData** to the *Services* folder.
2. Open the **Startup** class and change the service registration for the **IVideoData** interface to create instances of the **SqlVideoData** class. Also, change the method from **AddSingleton** to **AddScoped** for the service to work with Entity Framework.
   ```
   services.AddScoped<IVideoData, SqlVideoData>();
   ```
3. Add a private field called **_db** to the **SqlVideoData** class. This variable will hold the context needed to communicate with the database. Add a **using** statement to the **VideoDbContext** in the **AspNetVideoCore.Data** namespace.
   ```
   private VideoDbContext _db;
   ```
4. Add a constructor that is injected with an instance of the **VideoDbContext** class; name the parameter **db**. Assign the injected object in the **db** parameter to the **_db** variable.
   ```
   public SqlVideoData(VideoDbContext db)
   {
       _db = db;
   }
   ```
5. Implement the **IVideoData** interface. You can use the light bulb button when hovering over the interface name.
   ```
   public class SqlVideoData : IVideoData
   ```
6. Replace the **throw** statement in the **Add** method with a call to the **Add** method on the **_db** context and pass in the **video** object to the method. Then call the **SaveChanges** method on the **_db** context to persist the changes in the database.
   ```
   public void Add(Video video)
   {
       _db.Add(video);
       _db.SaveChanges();
   }
   ```

7. Replace the **throw** statement in the **Get** method with a call to the **Find** method on the **_db** context to fetch the video matching the id passed-in to the method. Return the fetched video.
```
public Video Get(int id)
{
    return _db.Find<Video>(id);
}
```

8. Replace the **throw** statement in the **GetAll** method with a **return** statement that returns all the videos in the **Videos** table.
```
public IEnumerable<Video> GetAll()
{
    return _db.Videos;
}
```

9. Save all the files and navigate to the root URL (/Home). The list of videos from the database should be displayed.

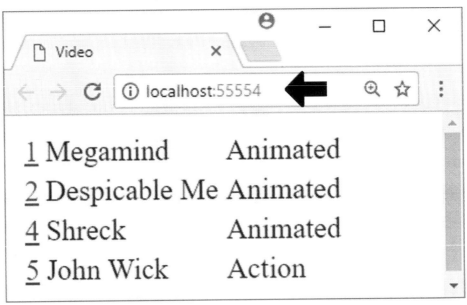

10. Add a new video by navigating to the /Home/Create URL and fill out the form. When you click the **Create** button in the form, the **Details** view should display the new video.

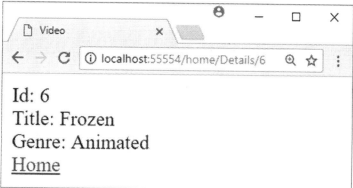

11. Click the **Home** link and make sure that the video is in the list.

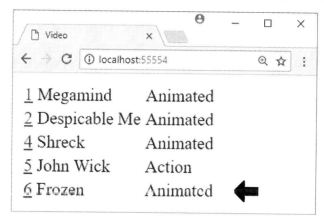

12. Open the **Video** table in the SQL Server Object Explorer and verify that the video is in the table.

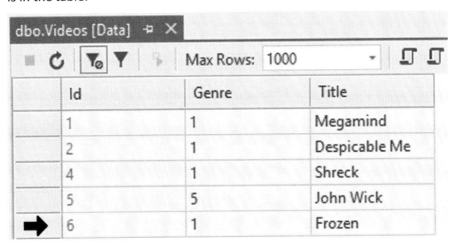

The complete code in the **SqlVideoData** class:

```
public class SqlVideoData : IVideoData
{
    private VideoDbContext _db;

    public SqlVideoData(VideoDbContext db)
    {
        _db = db;
    }

    public void Add(Video newVideo)
    {
        _db.Add(newVideo);
        _db.SaveChanges();
    }

    public Video Get(int id)
    {
        return _db.Find<Video>(id);
    }

    public IEnumerable<Video> GetAll()
    {
        return _db.Videos;
    }
}
```

The complete code in the **ConfigureServices** method:

```
public void ConfigureServices(IServiceCollection services)
{
    var conn = Configuration.GetConnectionString("DefaultConnection");
    services.AddDbContext<VideoDbContext>(options =>
        options.UseSqlServer(conn));

    services.AddMvc();
    services.AddSingleton(provider => Configuration);
    services.AddSingleton<IMessageService,
        ConfigurationMessageService>();

    services.AddScoped<IVideoData, SqlVideoData>();
}
```

Summary

In this chapter, you installed the Entity Framework and User Secrets services in the **Setup** class.

You also added a **DbContext** class that communicates with the database, and a new service component class that implements the **IVideoData** Interface, as a separation between the **DbContext** and the application.

Finally, you added a new video to the database using the **Create** view, and verified that it had been added to the database.

6. Razor Views

In this chapter, you will learn about different views that can be used for layout, to include namespaces, and to render partial content in a view.

Layout Views

The _Layout.cshtml_ Razor view gives the application more structure and makes it easier to display data that should be visible on every page, such as a navigation bar and a footer. You avoid duplication using this view. The underscore at the beginning of the name is not required, but it is a convention that is commonly used among developers. It signifies that the view shouldn't be rendered as a view result with the **View** method from a controller action.

The normal views, like the **Index** view, are rendered inside the **_Layout** view. This means that they don't have any knowledge about the navigation and the footer; they only need to render what the action tells them to render.

If you look inside the views you have created, they have some code in common, such as the <html>, <head>, and <body> elements. Because the markup is the same for all the views, it could be moved to the **_Layout** view.

Shared views, like **_Layout**, are placed in a folder called _Shared_ inside the _Views_ folder. These views are available anywhere in the application. The layout view doesn't have to be named **_Layout**; you can even have multiple layout views in the application if you like.

The **_Layout** view is a Razor view, which means that you can use C# inside the view, like you can in any other view. It should also have a method called **@RenderBody**, which is responsible for rendering the different content views the user navigates to, such as the **Index** and the **Details** views.

There is an object called **@ViewBag** in the **_Layout** view. It is a dynamic object that you can use to send data from the server to the view.

Another method that can be used in the **_Layout** view is the **@RenderSection**. This method can be used to render specific sections of HTML from the content view in the **_Layout** view. There is an asynchronous version of this method that you can use if you want that type of behavior.

Adding the _Layout View

1. Add a new folder called *Shared* to the *Views* folder.
2. Add a **MVC View Layout Page** called **_Layout** to the *Shared* folder using the **New Item** dialog.
3. Add a <footer> element at the bottom of the <body> element.
4. Add a call to the **@RenderSection** method to the <footer> element and pass in the name of the section that could be in any of the views. If you want the section to be optional, then pass in **false** for the second parameter. Name the section *footer* and pass in **false**.
   ```
   <footer>@RenderSection("footer", false)</footer>
   ```

The complete markup for the **_Layout** view:

```
<!DOCTYPE html>

<html>
<head>
    <meta name="viewport" content="width=device-width" />
    <title>@ViewBag.Title</title>
</head>
<body>
    <div>
        @RenderBody()
    </div>
    <footer>
        @RenderSection("footer", false)
    </footer>
</body>
</html>
```

Altering the Content Views

Now that the **_Layout** view has been added, you need to remove the markup shared among the content views.

Open the **Index** view and remove the <head> and <body> elements, and do the same for the other views in the *Home* folder. You can use the Ctrl+E, D keyboard command to format the HTML.

Since you removed the <title> element from the view, you can add it to the **ViewBag** object as a property called **Title**. Assign the name of the view to the property. Since the **ViewBag** is placed inside a C# block, it doesn't need the @-sign.

You can also use the **Layout** property in the C# block to tell the MVC framework which layout view to use with the view. The layout view must be specified with an explicit path, beginning with the tilde (~) sign.

The usual C# rules apply inside C# blocks, such as ending code lines with a semicolon.

1. Open the **Index** view and remove all the <html>, <head>, and <body> elements, but leave the table and the **@model** directive.

```
@model IEnumerable<AspNetCoreVideo.ViewModels.VideoViewModel>

<table>
    @foreach (var video in Model)
    {
        <tr>
            <td>@Html.ActionLink(video.Id.ToString(), "Details",
                new { id = video.Id })</td>
            <td>@video.Title</td>
            <td>@video.Genre</td>
        </tr>
    }
</table>
```

2. Add a C# block below the **@model** directive.

```
@{
}
```

3. Add a **Title** property to the **ViewBag** inside the C# block and assign a title to it (*Home*, in this case).

4. Add the **Layout** property inside the C# block and assign the explicit path to the *_Layout.cshtml* file.

```
@{
    ViewBag.Title = "Home";
    Layout = "~/Views/Shared/_Layout.cshtml";
}
```

5. Add a **@section** block named **footer** at the end of the **Index** view and place a
   <div> element with the text *This is the Index footer* inside it.
   `@section footer{ <div>This is the Index footer</div> }`

6. Repeat steps 1-4 for all the views in the *Views/Home* folder but change the Title
   property from *Home* to *Details* and *Create* respectively.

7. Save all the files and switch to the browser. Navigate to the **Index** view (/). You
   should be able to see the footer text below the video list. This verifies that the
   layout view is used to render the **Index** view.

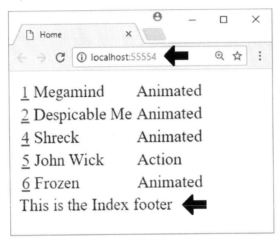

The complete code in the **Index** view, after removing the elements:

```
@model IEnumerable<AspNetCoreVideo.ViewModels.VideoViewModel>

@{
    ViewBag.Title = "Home";
    Layout = "~/Views/Shared/_Layout.cshtml";
}

<table>
    @foreach (var video in Model)
    {
        <tr>
            <td>@Html.ActionLink(video.Id.ToString(), "Details",
                new { id = video.Id })</td>
            <td>@video.Title</td>
            <td>@video.Genre</td>
        </tr>
    }
```

```
</table>

@section{
    <div>This is the Index footer</div>
}
```

The complete code in the **Details** view, after removing the elements:

```
@model AspNetCoreVideo.ViewModels.VideoViewModel

@{
    ViewBag.Title = "Details";
    Layout = "~/Views/Shared/_Layout.cshtml";
}

<div>Id: @Model.Id</div>
<div>Title: @Model.Title</div>
<div>Genre: @Model.Genre</div>

@Html.ActionLink("Home", "Index")
```

The complete code in the **Create** view, after removing the elements:

```
@using AspNetCoreVideo.Models
@model AspNetCoreVideo.Entities.Video
@addTagHelper *, Microsoft.AspNetCore.Mvc.TagHelpers

@{
    ViewBag.Title = "Create";
    Layout = "~/Views/Shared/_Layout.cshtml";
}

<h2>Create Video</h2>
<form asp-action="Create">
    <div asp-validation-summary="All"></div>
    <table>
        <tr>
            <td><label asp-for="Title"></label></td>
            <td><input asp-for="Title" /></td>
            <td><span asp-validation-for="Title"></span></td>
        </tr>
        <tr>
            <td><label asp-for="Genre"></label></td>
            <td><select asp-for="Genre" asp-items=
```

```
                "Html.GetEnumSelectList<Genres>()"></select></td>
            <td><span asp-validation-for="Genre"></span></td>
        </tr>
    </table>
    <input type="submit" value="Create" />
</form>

<div>
    <a asp-action="Index">Back to List</a>
</div>
```

The _ViewStart file

The Razor view engine has a convention that looks for a file called _ViewStart.cshtml. This file is executed before any other views, but it has no HTML output. One purpose it has is to remove duplicate code from code blocks in the views, like the **Layout** declaration. Instead of declaring the location of the **_Layout** view in each view, it can be placed inside the **_ViewStart** view. It is possible to override the settings in the **_ViewStart** view by adding the **Layout** declaration in individual views.

If you place this view directly in the *Views* folder, it will be available to all views. Placing it in another folder inside the *Views* folder makes it available to the views in that folder.

You can assign **null** to the **Layout** property in a specific view to stop any layout view from being used with the view.

Let's create the **_ViewStart** view in the *Views* folder, and add the **Layout** declaration in it.

1. Add a **MVC View Start Page** to the *Views* folder (use the **New Item** dialog). It is important that you name it **_ViewStart**, to adhere to MVC conventions.
2. Cut out the **_Layout** view path from the **Index** view.
3. Replace the current value for the **Layout** property in **_ViewStart** with the path you copied.

```
@{
    Layout = "~/Views/Shared/_Layout.cshtml";
}
```

4. Remove the **Layout** property from all the views in the *Views/Home* folder.
5. Save all the files and navigate to the root (/). You should still see the text *This is the Index footer* rendered by the **_Layout** view.

The _ViewImports file

The Razor view engine has a convention that looks for a file called *_ViewImports.cshtml*. This file is executed before any other views, but it has no HTML output. You can use this file to add **using** statements that will be used by all the views; this removes code duplication and cleans up the views.

So, if you know that many views will use the same namespaces, then add them to the *_ViewImports.cshtml* file. Add the file to the *Views* folder.

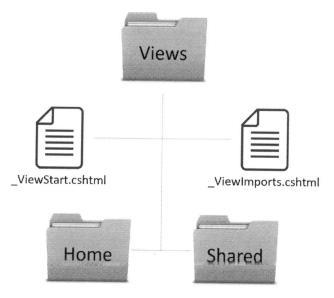

1. Add a **MVC View Imports Page** file named _ViewImports.cshtml_ to the _Views_ folder.
2. Open the **Create** view and cut out the **@using** and **@addTagHelper** rows.
3. Open the **_ViewImports** view and paste in the code.
4. Add a **using** statement to the **AspNetCoreVideo.Entities** namespace.
5. Save the **_ViewImports** view.
6. Open the **Create** view and remove the namespace path in the **@model** directive. The view should be able to find the **Video** model from the **using** statement in the **_ViewImports** view.
   ```
   @model Video
   ```
7. Open the **Index** view and cut out the **AspNetCoreVideo.ViewModels** namespace path from the **@model** directive and add it as a **using** statement to the **_ViewImports** view and save it. Leave only the class name in the **@model** directive.
   ```
   @model IEnumerable<VideoViewModel>
   ```
8. Open the **Details** view and delete the **AspNetCoreVideo.ViewModels** namespace path. Leave only the class name in the **@model** directive.
   ```
   @model VideoViewModel
   ```
9. Save all the files and navigate to the different views in the browser, to verify that the application still works as before.

The complete code in the **_ViewImports** file:

```
@using AspNetCoreVideo.Models
@using AspNetCoreVideo.Entities
@using AspNetCoreVideo.ViewModels
@addTagHelper *, Microsoft.AspNetCore.Mvc.TagHelpers
```

Tag Helpers

Tag Helpers are new to ASP.NET Core, and can in many instances replace the old HTML helpers. The Tag Helpers blend in with the HTML as they appear to be HTML attributes or HTML elements.

You have already used Tag Helpers in the **Create** form. There you added the **asp-for** and **asp-validation-for** among others. They blend in much better than the alternatives: **Label-For**, **TextBoxFor**, **EditorFor**, and other HTML helpers that are used in previous versions of ASP.NET. You can still use Razor HTML Helpers in ASP.NET Core, and they have one benefit over Tag Helpers; they are tightly coupled to the model. This means that you get Intelli-Sense and can rename properties more easily. In a Tag Helper, the property is added as a string value.

To use the Tag Helpers, you need to add a **@addTagHelper** directive to the **_ViewImports** view, or in specific views where you want to use them. The first parameter, the asterisk, specifies that all Tag Helpers in that namespace should be available. You can change this to a specific Tag Helper if you don't want to import all helpers.

```
@addTagHelper *, Microsoft.AspNetCore.Mvc.TagHelpers
```

Let's add a link calling the **Create** action from the **Index** view using Tag Helpers, so that you don't have to type in the URL to the **Create** view in the browser. Let's also replace the **ActionLink** HTML helper for the **Id** property, with a Tag Helper that opens the **Details** view and has the description *Details*.

Altering the Index View

1. Open the **Index** view.
2. Add an anchor tag (<a>) between the </table> tag and the **@section** block. Add the text *Create* to the anchor tag.
3. Use the **asp-action** Tag Helper to specify which action in the **Home** controller you want the link to call. You can add the **asp-controller** Tag Helper if you want to navigate to a controller that the view doesn't belong to.
   ```
   <a asp-action="Create">Create</a>
   ```
4. Save the file and navigate to the **Index** view in the browser. You should see a link with the text *Create*. When you click the link, the **Create** view should appear.
5. Click the *Back to List* link to get back to the **Index** view.
6. Place a breakpoint inside the HTTP GET **Create** action in the **HomeController** class, and start the application <u>with</u> debugging (F5).
7. Click the **Create** link again. The execution should halt at the breakpoint. This demonstrates that the **Action** was called by the Tag Helper.
8. Remove the breakpoint and stop the application in Visual Studio.
9. Remove the **ActionLink** for the **Id** property.
10. Add an anchor tag that opens the **Details** view using the **asp-action** Tag Helper, and the **asp-route-id** Tag Helper to pass in the video id.
    ```
    <td>
        <a asp-action="Details" asp-route-id="@video.Id">Details</a>
    </td>
    ```

11. Start the application without debugging (Ctrl+F5). You should now see *Details* links. Click one to verify that the **Details** view for that video is displayed.

The complete markup for the **Index** view:

```
@model IEnumerable<VideoViewModel>

@{
    ViewBag.Title = "Home";
}

<table>
    @foreach (var video in Model)
    {
        <tr>
            <td><a asp-action="Details"
                asp-route-id="@video.Id">Details</a></td>
            <td>@video.Title</td>
            <td>@video.Genre</td>
        </tr>
    }
</table>

<a asp-action="Create">Create</a>

@section footer{
    <div>This is the Index footer</div>
}
```

Adding an Edit View and Its Actions

There are two more views needed to complete the CRUD operations, the **Edit** and **Delete** views. Let's add the **Edit** view by copying the **Create** view and modify the form. Then let's refactor the **IVideoData** interface, and the classes implementing it. Instead of saving data directly when a video is added or edited, this refactoring will make it possible to add or edit multiple videos before saving the changes to the database.

1. Copy the **Create** view and paste it into the *Home* folder. Rename the view *Edit*.
2. Visual Studio sometimes gets confused when a view is copied, pasted, and renamed. To avoid confusion, close the **Edit** view and open it again.
3. Change the title to *Edit* followed by the video title.
   ```
   ViewBag.Title = $"Edit {Model.Title}";
   ```
4. Do the same for the view's heading; use the value from the **ViewBag**.
   ```
   <h2>@ViewBag.Title</h2>
   ```
5. Change the **asp-action** Tag Helper to call an action named **Edit**; you will add the action to the **HomeController** class later. Also specify that the form should use the **post** method; it is safer than using the default **get** method when posting a form.
   ```
   <form asp-action="Edit" method="post">
   ```
6. Change the **submit** button's text to *Edit*.
   ```
   <input type="submit" value="Edit" />
   ```
7. Open the **Index** view and add a link to the **Edit** view, like you did in the **Details** view. You can copy and change the **Details** anchor tag you added earlier. Move the links after the **Genre** table cell to make the form a little more pleasing to the eye.
   ```
   <tr>
       <td>@video.Title</td>
       <td>@video.Genre</td>
       <td><a asp-action="Details"
           asp-route-id="@video.Id">Details</a></td>
       <td><a asp-action="Edit"
           asp-route-id="@video.Id">Edit</a></td>
   </tr>
   ```
8. To make the **Edit** link and view work, you have to add HTTP GET and HTTP POST **Edit** actions to the **HomeController** class. Let's start with the HTTP GET action. Copy the HTTP GET **Details** action and paste it into the class. Rename it **Edit** and

111

add the **HttpGet** attribute to it. This will make it possible to open the **Edit** view with the link you added in the **Index** view.

```
[HttpGet]
public IActionResult Edit(int id)
{
    ...
}
```

9.   Rename the **model** variable **video**.

10. Replace the **return** statement with one that returns the **video** object to the view.

```
return View(video);
```

11. Add an HTTP POST **Edit** action that has an **id** parameter of type **int** and a **VideoEditViewModel** parameter called **model**. Add the **HttpPost** attribute to the action.

```
[HttpPost]
public IActionResult Edit(int id, VideoEditViewModel model)
{
    ...
}
```

12. Fetch the video matching the passed-in **id** and store it in a variable called **video**.

```
var video = _videos.Get(id);
```

13. Add an if-statement that checks if the model state is invalid, or the video object is null. If any of them are **true**, then return the view with the model.

```
if (video == null || !ModelState.IsValid)
    return View(model);
```

14. Assign the **Title** and **Genre** values from the model to the **video** object you fetched. Entity Framework will keep track of changes to the video objects.

```
video.Title = model.Title;
video.Genre = model.Genre;
```

15. Call the **Commit** method on the **_Video** object. This method does not exist yet, but you will add it to the **IVideoData** service classes shortly. After you have refactored the **IVideoData** service, the method will work, and save any changes to the database. Since Entity Framework keeps track of any changes to the **DbContext**, you don't have to send in the video object to the **Commit** method.

```
_videos.Commit();
```

16. Add a redirect to the **Details** view.

```
return RedirectToAction("Details", new { id = video.Id });
```

The complete code for the HTTP GET **Edit** action:

```
[HttpGet]
public IActionResult Edit(int id)
{
    var video = _videos.Get(id);

    if (video == null) return RedirectToAction("Index");

    return View(video);
}
```

The complete code for the HTTP POST **Edit** action:

```
[HttpPost]
public IActionResult Edit(int id, VideoEditViewModel model)
{
    var video = _videos.Get(id);

    if (video == null || !ModelState.IsValid) return View(model);

    video.Title = model.Title;
    video.Genre = model.Genre;

    _videos.Commit();

    return RedirectToAction("Details", new { id = video.Id });
}
```

Refactoring the IVideoData Service

The idea is that you should be able to do multiple changes and add new videos before committing the changes to the database. To achieve this, you must move the **SaveChanges** method call to a separate method called **Commit**. Whenever changes should be persisted to the database, the **Commit** method must be called.

1. Open the **IVideoData** interface.
2. Add a definition for a method called **Commit** that returns an **int**. The **int** value will in some instances reflect the number of records that were affected by the commit.
   `int Commit();`

3. Open the **MockVideoData** class and add a **Commit** method that returns 0. You must add the method even though it isn't necessary for the mock data. The

mock data is instantly saved when in memory. The interface demands that the **Commit** method is implemented.

```
public int Commit()
{
    return 0;
}
```

4. Open the **SqlVideoData** class and add a **Commit** method that return the results from the call to the **SaveChanges** method.

```
public int Commit()
{
    return _db.SaveChanges();
}
```

5. Remove the call to the **SaveChanges** method from the **Add** method.

```
public void Add(Video video)
{
    _db.Add(video);
}
```

6. Open the **HomeController** and verify that the **Commit** method doesn't have a red squiggly line and therefore is working properly.

7. Call the **Commit** method in the **Create** action, below the call to the **Add** method. This is necessary since you refactored out the call to the **SaveChanges** method from the **Add** method in the **SqlVideoData** service.

8. Save all files and navigate to the root URL. The new **Edit** links should appear to the right of the videos in the listing, beside the **Details** links.

9. Click the **Edit** link for one of the videos to open the new **Edit** view.
10. Make some changes to the video and click the **Edit** button.

11. The **Details** view for the video is displayed. Click the **Home** link to get back to the video list in the **Index** view.

12. The **Index** view should reflect the changes you made to the video.

The complete code in the **IVideoData** interface:

```
public interface IVideoData
{
    IEnumerable<Video> GetAll();
    Video Get(int id);
    void Add(Video newVideo);
    int Commit();
}
```

The complete code in the **SqlVideoData** class:

```
public class SqlVideoData : IVideoData
{
    private VideoDbContext _db;

    public SqlVideoData(VideoDbContext db)
    {
        _db = db;
    }
```

```
    public void Add(Video newVideo)
    {
        _db.Add(newVideo);
    }

    public int Commit()
    {
        return _db.SaveChanges();
    }

    public Video Get(int id)
    {
        return _db.Find<Video>(id);
    }

    public IEnumerable<Video> GetAll()
    {
        return _db.Videos;
    }
}
```

Partial Views

A partial view has two main purposes. The first is to render a portion of a view; the other is to enable the reuse of markup to clean up the code in a view.

To render a partial view, you can use either the synchronous **@Html.Partial** method or the asynchronous **@Html.PartialAsync** method. Both methods take two parameters, where the first is the name of the partial view and the second is an optional model object.

Note that partial views always use data from the parent view model.

The following example would render a partial view called **_Video** that receives a video object from the parent view's model. The first code line is synchronous while the second is asynchronous; you choose which one you want to use.

```
@Html.Partial("_Video", video);
```

```
@await Html.PartialAsync("_Video", video);
```

Let's create a partial view called **_Video** to clean up the **Index** view. It will display the videos as panels, and get rid of that ugly table in the process.

1. Add a new **MVC View Page** called **_Video** to the *Home* folder.
2. Delete all code inside the view.
3. Add the **VideoViewModel** class as its model.
   `@model VideoViewModel`
4. Add a <section> element in the partial view.
5. Add an <h3> element inside the <section> element and add the video title to it using the **@Model** object.
   `<h3>@Model.Title</h3>`
6. Add a <div> element below the <h3> element and add the video genre to it using the **@Model** object.
   `<div>@Model.Genre</div>`
7. Add another <div> element below the previous <div> element.
8. Copy the **Details** and **Edit** links from the **Index** view and paste them into the newest <div> element. Change the **asp-route-id** Tag Helper to fetch its value from the **@Model** object.

```
<div>
    <a asp-action="Details" asp-route-id="@Model.Id">Details</a>
    <a asp-action="Edit" asp-route-id="@Model.Id">Edit</a>
</div>
```

9. Open the **Index** view and replace the <table> element and all its content with a **foreach** loop that renders the partial view. The **foreach** loop is the same as the one in the <table> element, so you can copy it before removing the <table> element.

```
@foreach (var video in Model)
{
    @Html.Partial("_Video", video);
}
```

10. Place the remaining anchor tag inside a <div> element to make it easier to style.

```
<div>
    <a asp-action="Create">Create</a>
</div>
```

11. Remove the **@section footer** block. You will display other information at the bottom of the page using a View Component in the next section.
12. Save all the files and navigate to the root URL in the browser. The videos should now be stacked vertically as cards. They might not look pretty, but you can make them look great with CSS styling.

The complete code for the partial view:

```
@model VideoViewModel

<section>
    <h3>@Model.Title</h3>

    <div>@Model.Genre</div>
    <div>
        <a asp-action="Details" asp-route-id="@Model.Id">Details</a>
        <a asp-action="Edit" asp-route-id="@Model.Id">Edit</a>
    </div>
</section>
```

The complete code for the **Index** view:

```
@model IEnumerable<VideoViewModel>

@{ ViewBag.Title = "Home"; }

@foreach (var video in Model)
{
    @Html.Partial("_Video", video);
}

<div>
    <a asp-action="Create">Create</a>
</div>
```

View Components

A View Component is almost a complete MVC abstraction. It is a partial view that has its own model, which it gets from a method called **Invoke** in a controller-like class. A View Component's model is independent from the current view's model. You should not use a regular partial view, with a model, from the **_Layout** view, since it has no model and it is difficult to get one into it. Use a View Component to render partial content in the **_Layout** view.

In previous versions of MVC, you use **@Html.ActionHelper** to execute a child action. In this version of MVC it has been replaced with the View Component.

You can look at a View Component as having a controller that you never route to.

View Component views are always placed in a folder called *Components* inside the *Views* folder. If you place the folder in the *Views/Shared* folder, the view can be used from any view. Each View Component has a subfolder in the *Components* folder with the same name as the View Component.

Adding a View Component for the IMessageService Service

Let's implement a View Component that uses the **IMessageService** service to display the configuration message in every view.

1. Create a new folder called *ViewComponents* under the project node. This folder will hold the necessary files for View Components to work.
2. Add a class called **Message** to the folder and inherit the **ViewComponent** class. Add a **using** statement to the **Microsoft.AspNetCore.Mvc** namespace to get access to the **ViewComponent** class.
   ```
   public class Message : ViewComponent { }
   ```
3. Add a constructor and inject the **IMessageService** interface to it, name the parameter **message**, and store it in a private class-level variable called **_message**. Add a **using** statement to the **Services** namespace to get access to the **IMessageService** class.
   ```
   private IMessageService _message;

   public Message(IMessageService message)
   {
       _message = message;
   }
   ```

4. Add a public method called **Invoke** that returns an **IViewComponentResult**.
```
public IViewComponentResult Invoke()
{
}
```

5. Add a variable called **model** to the **Invoke** method, which stores the result from the **_message.GetMessage** method call.
```
var model = _message.GetMessage();
```

6. Return the **model** with the **View** method. Because the model is a string, the **View** method gets confused and thinks it is the name of the view to render. To fix this you pass in the name of the view as the first parameter and the **model** object as its second parameter.
```
return View("Default", model);
```

7. Create a new folder called *Components* inside the *Views/Shared* folder.
8. Add a folder called *Message* inside the *Components* folder.
9. Add a **MVC View Page** called *Default* in the *Message* folder.
10. Delete all code in the view.
11. Add an **@model** directive of type **string**.
```
@model string
```

12. Add a <section> element with a <small> element inside it. Add the **@Model** value to the <small> element.
```
<section>
    <small>@Model</small>
</section>
```

13. Open the **_Layout** view and call the **InvokeAsync** method on the **Component** property inside the <footer> element. Pass in the name of the View Component as a parameter. Remember to use **@await** when calling an asynchronous method.
```
<footer>
    @RenderSection("footer", false)
    @await Component.InvokeAsync("Message")
</footer>
```

14. Save all the files.
15. Navigate to all the views, one at a time, to verify that the message from the configuration file (*Hello from configuration*) is displayed in each of their footers.

The complete code for the **Message** View Component:

```
public class Message : ViewComponent
{
    private IMessageService _message;

    public Message(IMessageService message)
    {
        _message = message;
    }

    public IViewComponentResult Invoke()
    {
        var model = _message.GetMessage();
        return View("Default", model);
    }
}
```

The complete markup for the **Default** view:

```
@model string

<section>
    <small>@Model</small>
</section>
```

The complete code for the **_Layout** view:

```
<!DOCTYPE html>

<html>
<head>
    <meta name="viewport" content="width=device-width" />
    <title>@ViewBag.Title</title>
</head>
<body>
    <div>
        @RenderBody()
    </div>
    <footer>
        @RenderSection("footer", false)
        @await Component.InvokeAsync("Message")
    </footer>
</body>
</html>
```

Summary

In this chapter, you worked with layout views and partial views. You also used new features, such as Tag Helpers, View Components, and the **_ViewStart** and **_ViewImport** views.

Using these features allows you to reuse code and decompose a large view into smaller, more maintainable, pieces. They give you the ability to write maintainable and reusable code.

7. Forms Authentication

In this chapter, you will learn about ASP.NET Identity and how you can use it to implement registration and login in your application. You will add the authentication from scratch to learn how all the pieces fit together.

ASP.NET Identity is a framework that you need to install either with the NuGet Manager or by adding it manually in the *.csproj* file. It can handle several types of authentication, but in this chapter, you will focus on Forms Authentication.

The first thing you need to add is a **User** entity class that inherits from an identity base class, which gives you access to properties such as **Username**, **PasswordHash**, and **Email**. You can add as many properties to the **User** class as your application needs, but in this chapter, you will only use some of the inherited properties.

The **User** class needs to be plugged into a class called **UserStore**, provided by the **Identity** framework. It is used when creating and validating a user that then is sent to a database; Entity Framework is supported out of the box. You can implement your own **UserStore**, for a different database provider.

The **User** class needs to be plugged into an **IdentityDb** class that handles all communication with an Entity Framework-supported database, through an Entity Framework **DbContext**. The way this is done is by making your existing **VideoDbContext** inherit from the **IdentityDbContext** class instead of the current **DbContext** class.

The **UserStore** and the **IdentityDbContext** work together to store user information and validate against the hashed passwords in the database.

Another class involved in the process is the **SignInManager**, which will sign in a user once the password has been validated. It can also be used to sign out already logged in users. A cookie is used to handle Forms Authentication sign-in and sign-out. The cookie is then sent with every subsequent request from the browser, so that the user can be identified.

The last piece is the Identity Middleware that needs to be configured to read the cookie and verify the user.

The **[Authorize]** attribute can be applied to a controller to restrict user access; a user must be signed in and verified to have access to the actions in that controller.

The **[AllowAnonymous]** attribute can be applied to actions to allow any visitor access to that action, even if they aren't registered or signed in.

You can use parameters with the **[Authorize]** attribute to restrict the access even beyond being logged in, which is its default behavior. You can, for instance, add the **Roles** parameter to specify one or more roles that the user must be in to gain access.

You can also place the **[Authorize]** attribute on specific actions, instead of on the controller class, to restrict access to specific actions.

Adding the Authorize and AlowAnonymous Attributes

Let's start by adding the **[Authorize]** attribute to the **HomeController** class, to grant access only to logged in users. Let's also add the **[AllowAnonymous]** attribute to the **Index** action, so that any visitor can see the video list.

1. Open the **HomeController** class and add the **[Authorize]** attribute to it. The **[Authorize]** attribute is located in the **Microsoft.AspNetCore.Authorization** namespace.
    ```
    [Authorize]
    public class HomeController : Controller
    {
        ...
    }
    ```

2. Add the **[AllowAnonymous]** attribute to the **Index** action.

```
[AllowAnonymous]
public ViewResult Index()
{
    ...
}
```

3. Save all files and navigate to the root URL in the browser. As you can see, the **[AllowAnonymous]** attribute lets you see the video list in the **Index** view.

4. Click the **Edit** link to edit a video. Instead of being greeted by the **Edit** view, an error message is displayed. This confirms that the **[Authorize]** attribute is working. You are not logged in, and are therefore not allowed to use the **Edit** form.

Configuring the Identity Framework

Once you have changed the inheritance on the **VideoDbContext** from the current **DbContext** to the **IdentityDbContext**, the Identity services can be configured in the **ConfigureServices** method, and in the Identity middleware installed in the **Configure** method, in the **Startup** class.

The services that need to be configured are the **UserStore** and **SignInManager**.

1. Add the **User** entity class to the **Entities** folder and inherit from the **IdentityUser** class to gain access to its user properties. Add a **using** statement to the **Microsoft.AspNetCore.Identity** namespace to get access to the **IdentityUser** class. It's in the **User** class that you can add your own user properties, specific to your application; it could be any property related to the user. Below is a list of all the properties the **IdentityUser** class will bring

```
public class User : IdentityUser { }
```

2. Open the **VideoDbContext** and make it inherit the **IdentityDbContext** class instead of EFs default **DbContext**. You can specify the type of user it should store, which in this case is the **User** entity class you just added. The **IdentityDbContext** class is located in the **Microsoft.AspNetCore.Identity.EntityFrameworkCore** namespace.
```
public class VideoDbContext : IdentityDbContext<User>
{
    ...
}
```

3. Open the **Startup** class and add **using** statements to the **Entities** and **Identity** namespaces to get access to the **User** and **IdentityRole** classes, and then locate the **ConfigureServices** method.
```
using AspNetVideoCore.Entities;
using Microsoft.AspNetCore.Identity;
```

4. Add the **Identity** service to the **services** collection by calling the **AddIdentity** method. The method takes two generic type parameters: the first is the user you want it to use (the **User** entity class you just added) and the second is the identity role you want it to use (use the built-in **IdentityRole** class). You can inherit the **IdentityRole** class to another class if you want to implement your own identity role behavior. Add the service above the **AddMvc** method call.
```
services.AddIdentity<User, IdentityRole>();
```

5. You must also install the **Entity Framework Stores** services that handle creation and validation of users against the database. You need to provide the **VideoDbContext** to it, so that it knows which context to use when communicating with the database. You can use the fluent API to call the **AddEntityFrameworkStores** method on the **AddIdentity** method.
```
services.AddIdentity<User, IdentityRole>()
    .AddEntityFrameworkStores<VideoDbContext>();
```

6. Next you need to install the middleware components in the **Configure** method. The location of the middleware is important. If you place it too late in the pipeline, it will never be executed. Place it above the MVC middleware to make it available to the MVC framework.
```
app.UseAuthentication();
```

7. Build the application with Ctrl+Shift+B to make sure that it builds correctly.

The complete **User** class:

```
public class User : IdentityUser
{
}
```

The properties in the **IdentityUser** class:

```
public class IdentityUser<TKey> where TKey : IEquatable<TKey>
{
    public IdentityUser();
    public IdentityUser(string userName);
    public virtual DateTimeOffset? LockoutEnd { get; set; }
    public virtual bool TwoFactorEnabled { get; set; }
    public virtual bool PhoneNumberConfirmed { get; set; }
    public virtual string PhoneNumber { get; set; }
    public virtual string ConcurrencyStamp { get; set; }
    public virtual string SecurityStamp { get; set; }
    public virtual string PasswordHash { get; set; }
    public virtual bool EmailConfirmed { get; set; }
    public virtual string NormalizedEmail { get; set; }
    public virtual string Email { get; set; }
    public virtual string NormalizedUserName { get; set; }
    public virtual string UserName { get; set; }
    public virtual TKey Id { get; set; }
    public virtual bool LockoutEnabled { get; set; }
    public virtual int AccessFailedCount { get; set; }
    public override string ToString();
}
```

Creating the AspNet Identity Database Tables

Now that the configuration is out of the way, it is time to create a new migration that adds the necessary *AspNet* identity tables to the database.

1. Open the Package Manager Console and execute the following command to create the necessary migration file: add-migration IdentityTables

2. Execute the following command to create the identity tables in the database: update-database

3. Open the SQL Server Object Explorer and drill down to the tables in your **VideoDb** database.

User Registration

Now that all the configuration and database table creation is done, it is time to focus on how a user can register with the site.

If you run the application as it stands right now, the **Identity** middleware will redirect to the */Account/Login* URL, which doesn't exist yet. Instead, the next piece of middleware handles the request, and the message *Hello from configuration* will be displayed in the browser.

To display a **Login** view, you must add an **AccountController** class with a **Login** action. And to log in, the user needs to register. You therefore must implement a **Register** view, and a **Register** action in the **AccountController** class.

1. Add a class named **AccountController** to the *Controllers* folder and let it inherit the **Controllers** class located in the **Microsoft.AspNetCore.Mvc** namespace.
   ```
   public class AccountController : Controller
   {
   }
   ```

2. Add an HTTP GET **Register** action to the class. The view doesn't have to receive a model with data, because the user will supply all the registration information in the view.

```
[HttpGet]
public IActionResult Register()
{
    return View();
}
```

3. Add a class called **RegisterViewModel** in the *ViewModels* folder. This will be the view model for the **Register** view.

4. Add a **using** statement to the **System.ComponentModel.DataAnnotations** namespace to get access to the necessary data annotation attributes.

5. Add a **string** property called **Username** that is required and has a maximum of 255 characters. The length is determined by the max number of characters that the **AspNetUser** table can store for a username.

```
[Required, MaxLength(255)]
public string Username { get; set; }
```

6. Add a **string** property called **Password** that is required and has the **Password** data type.

```
[Required, DataType(DataType.Password)]
public string Password { get; set; }
```

7. Add a **string** property called **ConfirmPassword** that has the **Password** data type and uses the **Compare** attribute to compare its value with the **Password** property. You can use the C# **nameof** operator to specify the compare property, instead of using a string literal.

```
[DataType(DataType.Password), Compare(nameof(Password))]
public string ConfirmPassword { get; set; }
```

8. Add a new folder called *Account* inside the *Views* folder. This folder will hold all the views related to the **Account** controller.

9. Add a **MVC View Page** view called **Register** to the *Account* folder.

10. Delete all the content in the view.

11. Add an **@model** directive for the **RegisterViewModel** class.
```
@model RegisterViewModel
```

12. Use the **ViewBag** to add the *Register* to the **Title** property.
```
@{ ViewBag.Title = "Register"; }
```

131

13. Add an <h1> heading with the text *Register*.
14. Add a <form> that posts to the **Register** action in the **Account** controller. Use Tag Helpers to create the form.

```
<form method="post" asp-controller="Account"
 asp-action="Register"></form>
```

15. Add a validation summary that only displays errors related to the model.

```
<div asp-validation-summary="ModelOnly"></div>
```

16. Add a <div> that holds a <label> and an <input> for the **Username** model property and a <span> for the validation.

```
<div>
    <label asp-for="Username"></label>
    <input asp-for="Username" />
    <span asp-validation-for="Username"></span>
</div>
```

17. Repeat step 16 for the **Password** and **ConfirmPassword** properties in the model.
18. Add a **submit** button inside a <div> to the form. Assign the text *Register* to the **value** attribute.

```
<div>
    <input type="submit" value="Register" />
</div>
```

19. Open the **AccountController** class.
20. Add a using statement to the **ViewModels** namespace to get access to the **RegisterViewModel** class.

```
using AspNetVideoCore.ViewModels;
```

21. Add an HTTP POST **Register** action that will be called by the form when the **submit** button is clicked. It should return an **IActionResult** and take a **RegisterViewModel** parameter called **model**. The action must be asynchronous to **await** the result from the **UserManager** and **SignInManager**, which you will inject into the controller later.

```
[HttpPost]
public async Task<IActionResult> Register(RegisterViewModel model)
{
}
```

22. The first thing to do in any HTTP POST action is to check if the model state is valid; if it's not, then the view should be re-rendered.

```
if (!ModelState.IsValid) return View();
```

23. Add a using statement to the Entities and Identity namespaces to get access to the **User**, **UserManager**, and **SignInManager** classes.

24. Create a new instance of the **User** entity class and assign its **Username** property value from the passed-in model, below the if-statement.
```
var user = new User { UserName = model.Username };
```

25. To work with the user entity, you need to bring in the **UserManager** and the **SignInManager** via the constructor, using dependency injection. Add a constructor to the controller and inject the two classes mentioned above.
```
private UserManager<User> _userManager;
private SignInManager<User> _signInManager;

public AccountController(UserManager<User> userManager,
SignInManager<User> signInManager)
{
    _userManager = userManager;
    _signInManager = signInManager;
}
```

26. Next you want to use the **UserManager** in the HTTP POST **Register** action to create a new user. Save the result in a variable called **result**.
```
var result = await _userManager.CreateAsync(user, model.Password);
```

27. If the user was created successfully you want to sign in that user automatically. Use the **Succeeded** property on the **result** variable to check if the user was created successfully, and the **SignInAsync** method on the **SignInManager** to sign in the user. The second parameter of the method determines if the cookie should be persisted beyond the session or not.
```
if (result.Succeeded)
{
    await _signInManager.SignInAsync(user, false);
    return RedirectToAction("Index", "Home");
}
```

28. If the user wasn't created, you want to add the errors to the **ModelState** object, so that they are sent to the client as model errors, displayed in the validation summary.
```
else
{
    foreach (var error in result.Errors)
        ModelState.AddModelError("", error.Description);
}
```

29. Return the view below the else-block.
    ```
    return View();
    ```

30. Save all the files and navigate to the /Account/Register URL. The **Register** View
    should be displayed. Fill out the form with a three-letter password and click the
    Register button. The validation summary should display the errors that were
    looped into the **ModelState** object, in the **Register** action method.

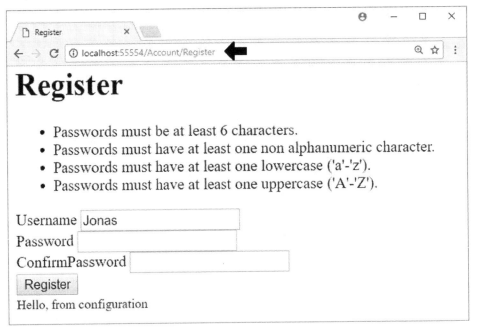

31. Fill out the form (with correct information this time). You should be redirected to
    the **Index** view through the **RedirectToAction** method in the **Register** action.

32. View the data in the **AspNetUsers** table in the SQL Server Object Explorer to
    verify that the user was registered.

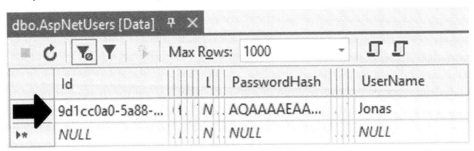

The complete code for the **RegisterViewModel** class:

```
public class RegisterViewModel
{
    [Required, MaxLength(255)]
    public string Username { get; set; }
    [Required, DataType(DataType.Password)]
    public string Password { get; set; }
    [DataType(DataType.Password), Compare(nameof(Password))]
    public string ConfirmPassword { get; set; }
}
```

The complete code for the **AccountController** class:

```
public class AccountController : Controller
{
    private UserManager<User> _userManager;
    private SignInManager<User> _signInManager;

    public AccountController(UserManager<User> userManager,
    SignInManager<User> signInManager)
    {
        _userManager = userManager;
        _signInManager = signInManager;
    }

    [HttpGet]
    public IActionResult Register()
    {
        return View();
    }

    [HttpPost]
    public async Task<IActionResult> Register(RegisterViewModel model)
    {
        if (!ModelState.IsValid) return View();

        var user = new User { UserName = model.Username };

        var result = await _userManager.CreateAsync(user,
            model.Password);

        if (result.Succeeded)
        [
            await _signInManager.SignInAsync(user, false);
```

```
                return RedirectToAction("Index", "Home");
            }
            else
            {
                foreach (var error in result.Errors)
                    ModelState.AddModelError("", error.Description);
            }

            return View();
        }
}
```

The complete code for the **Register** view:

```
@model RegisterViewModel

@{ ViewBag.Title = "Register"; }

<h1>Register</h1>

<form method="post" asp-controller="Account" asp-action="Register">
    <div asp-validation-summary="ModelOnly"></div>

    <div>
        <label asp-for="Username"></label>
        <input asp-for="Username" />
        <span asp-validation-for="Username"></span>
    </div>

    <div>
        <label asp-for="Password"></label>
        <input asp-for="Password" />
        <span asp-validation-for="Password"></span>
    </div>

    <div>
        <label asp-for="ConfirmPassword"></label>
        <input asp-for="ConfirmPassword" />
        <span asp-validation-for="ConfirmPassword"></span>
    </div>

    <div>
        <input type="submit" value="Register" />
    </div>
</form>
```

Login and Logout

In this section, you will implement login and logout in your application. The links will be added to a partial view called **_LoginLinks** that you will add to the *Views/Shared* folder. The partial view will then be rendered from the **_Layout** view using the **@Partial** or **@PartialAsync** method.

When an anonymous user arrives at the site, **Login** and **Register** links should be available. When a user has logged in or registered, the username and a **Logout** link should be visible.

You must also create a new view called **Login** in the *Views/Account* folder, a view that the **Login** link opens by calling a **Login** action in the **Account** controller.

To work with users and sign-in information in views, you inject the **SignInManager** and **UserManager**, similar to the way you use dependency injection in methods and constructors in classes.

When an anonymous user clicks a restricted link, like the **Edit** link, a **ReturnUrl** parameter is sent with the URL, so that the user will end up on that view when a successful login has been made. When creating the **LoginViewModel** you must add a property for the return URL, so that the application can redirect to it. Below is an example URL with the **ReturnUrl** parameter.

http://localhost:51457/Account/Login?**ReturnUrl=%2FHome%2FEdit%2F1**

Adding the _Login Partial View

This partial view will contain the **Login** and **Register** links that will be visible when an anonymous user visits the site, and a **Logout** link and the username when the user is logged in.

1. Add a **MVC View Page** called **_LoginLinks** to the *Views/Shared* folder.
2. Delete all the code in the view.
3. Add a **using** statement to the **Microsoft.AspNetCore.Identity** namespace to get access to the **SignInManager** and **UserManager**.
   ```
   @using Microsoft.AspNetCore.Identity
   ```
4. Inject the **SignInManager** and **UserManager** to the view, below the **using** statement.
   ```
   @inject SignInManager<User> SignInManager
   @inject UserManager<User> UserManager
   ```

5. Add if/else-blocks that check if the user is signed in, using the **IsSignedIn** method on the **SignInManager** passing it the **User** object.

```
@if (SignInManager.IsSignedIn(User))
{
    // Signed in user
}
else
{
    // Anonymous user
}
```

6. Add a <div> that displays the username to the *Signed in user*-block. Use the **User** object's **Identity** property.

```
<div>@User.Identity.Name</div>
```

7. Add a form to the *Signed in user*-block that posts to the */Account/Logout* action when a **submit** button is clicked.

```
<form method="post" asp-controller="Account" asp-action="Logout">
    <input type="submit" value="Logout" />
</form>
```

8. Add two anchor tags to the *Anonymous user* block that navigates to the **Login** and **Register** actions in the **Account** controller.

```
<a asp-controller="Account" asp-action="Login">Login</a>
<a asp-controller="Account" asp-action="Register">Register</a>
```

9. Open the **_Layout** view and add a <div> above the **@RenderBody** method in the <body> element.

10. Call the **@Html.PartialAsync** method to render the **_LoginLinks** partial view in the <div>.

```
<div>
    @await Html.PartialAsync("_LoginLinks")
</div>
```

11. Start the application without debugging (Ctrl+F5). Because you were signed in when registering, the username and a **Logout** button should be visible. Later when you have implemented the **Logout** action, the **Login** and **Register** links should be visible at the top of the view when logged out.

The complete code for the **_LoginLinks** partial view:

```
@using Microsoft.AspNetCore.Identity
@inject SignInManager<User> SignInManager
@inject UserManager<User> UserManager

@if (SignInManager.IsSignedIn(User))
{
    // Signed in user
    <div>@User.Identity.Name</div>
    <form method="post" asp-controller="Account" asp-action="Logout">
        <input type="submit" value="Logout" />
    </form>
}
else
{
    // Anonymous user
    <a asp-controller="Account" asp-action="Login">Login</a>
    <a asp-controller="Account" asp-action="Register">Register</a>
}
```

The complete code for the **_Layout** view:

```
<!DOCTYPE html>

<html>
<head>
    <meta name="viewport" content="width=device-width" />
    <title>@ViewBag.Title</title>
</head>
```

```
<body>
    <div>
        <div>
            @await Html.PartialAsync("_LoginLinks")
        </div>
        @RenderBody()
    </div>
    <footer>
        @RenderSection("footer", false)
        @await Component.InvokeAsync("Message")
    </footer>
</body>
</html>
```

Adding the Logout Action

The **SignOutAsync** method on the **SignInManager** must be called to log out a user when the **Logout** button is clicked. The **Logout** action in the **Account** controller must be asynchronous because the **SignOutAsync** method is asynchronous.

1. Open the **AccountController** class.
2. Add an **async** HTTP POST action called **Logout** that returns a **Task<IActionResult>**. This action will be called when the **Logout** link is clicked.
   ```
   [HttpPost]
   public async Task<IActionResult> Logout() { }
   ```

3. Call the **SignOutAsync** method on the **_signInManager** object inside the **Logout** action.
   ```
   await _signInManager.SignOutAsync();
   ```

4. Because the user is logging out, you want the user to end up on a safe view after the logout process has completed. Add a redirect to the **Index** action in the **Home** controller.
   ```
   return RedirectToAction("Index", "Home");
   ```

The complete code for the **Logout** action:

```
[HttpPost]
public async Task<IActionResult> Logout()
{
    await _signInManager.SignOutAsync();
    return RedirectToAction("Index", "Home");
}
```

Adding the LoginViewModel Class

This model is responsible for passing the login information provided by the user, and the **ReturnUrl** URL parameter value, to the HTTP POST **Login** action.

The model needs four properties: **Username**, **Password**, **RememberMe**, and **ReturnUrl**. The **RememberMe** property determines if the cookie should be a session cookie or if a more persistent cookie should be used.

1. Add a new class called **LoginViewModel** to the *ViewModels* folder.
2. Add a using statement to the **DataAnnotations** namespace to get access to the data annotation attributes.
   `using System.ComponentModel.DataAnnotations;`
3. Add three **string** properties called **Username**, **Password**, and **ReturnUrl**, and a **bool** property called **RememberMe**.
4. Add the **Required** attribute to the **Username** property.
   `[Required]`
5. Add the **DataType.Password** and **Required** attributes to the **Password** property.
   `[DataType(DataType.Password), Required]`
6. Use the **Display** attribute to change the label text to *Remember Me* for the **ReturnUrl** property.
   `[Display(Name = "Remember Me")]`

The complete code for the **LoginViewModel** class:

```
public class LoginViewModel
{
    [Required]
    public string Username { get; set; }
    [DataType(DataType.Password), Required]
    public string Password { get; set; }
    public string ReturnUrl { get; set; }
    [Display(Name = "Remember Me")]
    public bool RememberMe { get; set; }
}
```

Adding the HTTP GET Login Action

This action will be called when the user clicks the **Login** link. You will need to create an instance of the **LoginViewModel** and assign the return URL, passed into the action, to its **ReturnUrl** property. Then pass the model to the view.

1. Open the **AccountController** class.
2. Add an HTTP GET action called **Login** that takes a string parameter called **returnUrl** and returns an **IActionResult**.
    ```
    [HttpGet]
    public IActionResult Login(string returnUrl ="")
    {
    }
    ```
3. Create an instance of the **LoginViewModel** and assign the return URL passed into the action to its **ReturnUrl** property.
    ```
    var model = new LoginViewModel { ReturnUrl = returnUrl };
    ```
4. Return the model with the view.
    ```
    return View(model);
    ```

The complete code for the HTTP GET **Login** action:

```
[HttpGet]
public IActionResult Login(string returnUrl ="")
{
    var model = new LoginViewModel { ReturnUrl = returnUrl };
    return View(model);
}
```

Adding the HTTP POST Login Action

The HTTP POST **Login** action will be called when the user clicks the **Login** button in the **Login** view. The view's login form will send the user data to this action; it therefore must have a **LoginViewModel** as a parameter. The action must be asynchronous because the **PasswordSignInAsync** method provided by the **SignInManager** is asynchronous.

1. Open the **AccountController** class.
2. Add an **async** HTTP POST action called **Login** that takes an instance of the **LoginViewModel** as a parameter and returns a **Task<IActionResult>**.
    ```
    [HttpPost]
    public async Task<IActionResult> Login(LoginViewModel model)
    {
    }
    ```

3. The first thing to do in any HTTP POST action is to check if the model state is valid; if it's not, then the view should be re-rendered.
```
if (!ModelState.IsValid) return View(model);
```

4. Sign in the user by calling the **PasswordSignInAsync** method, passing in the username, password, and remember me values. Store the result in a variable called **result**. The last parameter determines if the user should be locked out, if providing wrong credentials.
```
var result = await
_signInManager.PasswordSignInAsync(model.Username, model.Password,
model.RememberMe, false);
```

5. Add an if-statement checking if the sign-in succeeded.
```
if (result.Succeeded)
{
}
```

6. Add another if-statement, inside the previous one, that checks that the URL isn't null or empty and that it is a local URL. It is important to check if it is a local URL, for security reasons. If you don't do that your application is vulnerable to attacks.
```
if (!string.IsNullOrEmpty(model.ReturnUrl) &&
Url.IsLocalUrl(model.ReturnUrl))
{
}
else
{
}
```

7. If the return URL exists and is safe, then redirect to it in the if-block.
```
return Redirect(model.ReturnUrl);
```

8. If the URL is empty or isn't local, then redirect to the **Index** action in the **Home** controller.
```
return RedirectToAction("Index", "Home");
```

9. Add a **ModelState** error and return the view with the model below it. Place the code below the if-statement, to be certain that it only is called if the login is unsuccessful.
```
ModelState.AddModelError("", "Login failed");
return View(model);
```

The complete code for the HTTP POST **Login** action:

```
[HttpPost]
public async Task<IActionResult> Login(LoginViewModel model)
{
    if (!ModelState.IsValid) return View();

    var result = await _signInManager.PasswordSignInAsync(
        model.Username, model.Password, model.RememberMe, false);

    if (result.Succeeded)
    {
        if (!string.IsNullOrEmpty(model.ReturnUrl) &&
            Url.IsLocalUrl(model.ReturnUrl))
        {
            return Redirect(model.ReturnUrl);
        }
        else
        {
            return RedirectToAction("Index", "Home");
        }
    }

    ModelState.AddModelError("", "Login failed");
    return View(model);
}
```

Adding the Login View

You need to add a view called **Login** to the **Account** folder, to enable visitors to log in.

1. Add a **MVC View Page** view called **Login** to the *Views/Account* folder.
2. Delete all the content in the view.
3. Add an **@model** directive for the **LoginViewModel** class.
   `@model LoginViewModel`

4. Use the **ViewBag** to add a title with the text *Login*.
   `@{ ViewBag.Title = "Login"; }`

5. Add an <h2> heading with the text *Login*.
6. Add a <form> that posts to the **Login** action in the **Account** controller. Use Tag Helpers to create the form, and to return the return URL.
   ```
   <form method="post" asp-controller="Account" asp-action="Login"
    asp-route-returnurl="@Model.ReturnUrl"></form>
   ```

7. Add a validation summary that only displays errors related to the model.
   ```
   <div asp-validation-summary="ModelOnly"></div>
   ```

8. Add a <div> that holds a <label> and an <input> for the **Username** model property, and a <span> for the validation.
   ```
   <div>
       <label asp-for="Username"></label>
       <input asp-for="Username" />
       <span asp-validation-for="Username"></span>
   </div>
   ```

9. Repeat step 8 for the **Password** and **RememberMe** properties in the model.

10. Add a **submit** button with the text **Login** to the form; place it inside a <div>.
    ```
    <div>
        <input type="submit" value="Login" />
    </div>
    ```

11. Start the application without debugging (Ctrl+F5). Log out if you are signed in.

12. Click the **Edit** link for one of the videos. The **Login** view should be displayed because you are an anonymous user. Note the **ReturnUrl** parameter in the URL.

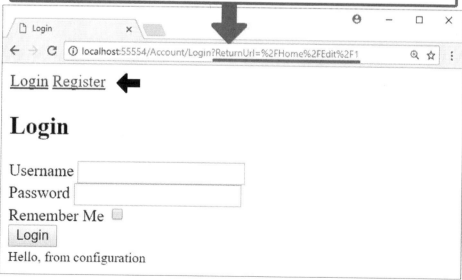

13. Log in as a registered user. The **Edit** view, for the video you tried to edit before, should open. Note the username and the **Logout** button at the top of the view.

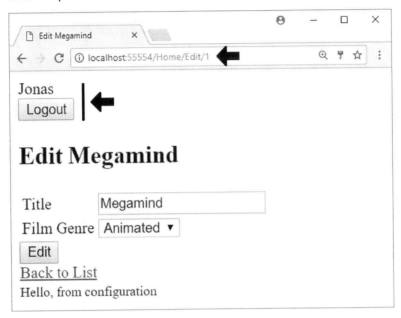

14. Click the **Logout** button to log out the current user. You should be taken to the **Index** view. Note the **Login** and **Register** links at the top of the view.

The complete markup for the **Login** view:

```
@model LoginViewModel

@{
    ViewBag.Title = "Login";
}

<h2>Login</h2>

<form method="post" asp-controller="Account" asp-action="Login"
        asp-route-returnurl="@Model.ReturnUrl">
    <div asp-validation-summary="ModelOnly"></div>

    <div>
        <label asp-for="Username"></label>
        <input asp-for="Username" />
        <span asp-validation-for="Username"></span>
    </div>
```

```
<div>
    <label asp-for="Password"></label>
    <input asp-for="Password" />
    <span asp-validation-for="Password"></span>
</div>

<div>
    <label asp-for="RememberMe"></label>
    <input asp-for="RememberMe" />
    <span asp-validation-for="RememberMe"></span>
</div>

<div>
    <input type="submit" value="Login" />
</div>
</form>
```

Summary

In this chapter, you used ASP.NET Identity to secure your application, implementing registration and login from scratch.

The first thing you did was to add a **User** entity class that inherited the **IdentityUser** base class. This gave you access to properties such as **Username**, **PasswordHash**, and **Email**.

Then you plugged the **User** entity into a **UserStore** and an **IdentityDb** class. This made it possible to create and validate a user, which then was stored in the database.

The **UserManager** and **SignInManager** were then used to implement registration and login for users, with a cookie that handles the Forms Authentication.

The **[Authorize]** and **[AllowAnonymous]** attributes were used to restrict user access to controller actions.

You also added views to register, log in, and log out a user.

In the next chapter, you will use front-end frameworks to style the application.

8. Front-End Frameworks

In this chapter, you will learn how to install front-end libraries using Bower. The two types of libraries you will install are for styling and client-side validation.

Bootstrap: This is the most popular library for styling and responsive design. You will use some Bootstrap CSS classes to style the video list and the navigation links. You can find out more about Bootstrap on their site: http://getBootstrap.com.

JQuery: You will use JQuery and JQuery Validation to perform client-side validation. This will make sure that the user input is conforming to the validation rules before the data is sent to the server action. Some validation rules are added by the framework; others you have added yourself to the entity and view model classes as attributes. Examples of validation rules are: password restrictions set by the framework (can be changed), and the **Required, MaxLength,** and **DataType** attributes.

Installing Bower and the Frameworks

Bower is the preferred way to install front-end frameworks in ASP.NET Core 2.0. When the libraries have been installed, they must be referenced from the **_Layout** view for global access, or in individual views for local access. You can use the environment tag to specify the environment the libraries should be accessible from. You usually want the un-minified libraries in the **Development** environment for easy debugging, and the minified versions in the **Staging** and **Production** environments for faster load times.

Many times, you can achieve even faster load times if you use Content Delivery Networks (CDNs), servers that have cached versions of the libraries that can be called. You can find information about the Microsoft's CDNs at:
https://docs.microsoft.com/en-us/aspnet/ajax/cdn/overview.

Four attributes are used to check that the JavaScript libraries have been installed: **asp-fallback-test-class, asp-fallback-test-property, asp-fallback-test-value,** and **asp-fallback-test.**

Two of the attributes are used to load an alternative source if the JavaScript libraries haven't been installed: **asp-fallback-src** and **asp-fallback-href.**

1. Open the **Startup** class and add the Static Files middleware by calling the **app.UseStaticFiles** method above the **UseMvc** method call in the **Configure** method to enable loading of CSS and JavaScript files.
   ```
   app.UseStaticFiles();
   ```

2. Add a **Bower Configuration File** to the project node. It's important that it is named *bower.json*. You can search for *bower* in the **New Item** dialog.

3. Install Bootstrap by using the **Manage Bower Packages** guide, or by typing it directly into the *dependencies* section of the *bower.json* file. Bootstrap has a dependency on JQuery, so that library will be automatically installed.
   ```
   "Bootstrap": "3.3.7"
   ```

4. Install the **JQuery-Validation** and **JQuery-Validation-Unobtrusive** libraries using Bower.
   ```
   "jquery-validation": "1.17.0",
   "jquery-validation-unobtrusive": "3.2.6"
   ```

5. Expand the *Dependencies/Bower* node in the Solution Explorer to verify that the libraries have been installed.

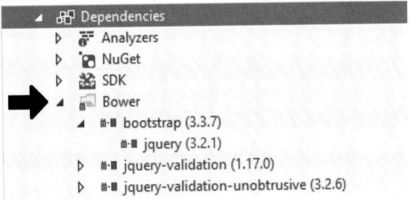

6. Expand the *wwwroot* node in the Solution Explorer. It should now have a folder named *lib*, under which the installed libraries reside.

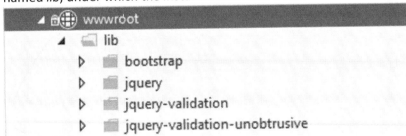

7. Open the **_Layout** view and add two <environment> Tag Helpers below the
   <title> element inside the <head> element. The first should only include the
   Development environment, and the second should exclude the **Development**
   environment. You can change environment in the project settings. In these two
   Tag Helpers, you specify CSS libraries you want to load when the view loads.

   ```
   <environment include="Development">
   </environment>
   <environment exclude="Development">
   </environment>
   ```

8. Add the un-minified Bootstrap library to the **Development** environment and the
   CDN version with a fallback for any other environments.

   ```
   <environment include="Development">
       <link href="~/lib/Bootstrap/dist/css/Bootstrap.css"
           rel="stylesheet" />
   </environment>
   <environment exclude="Development">
       <link rel="stylesheet" href="https://ajax.aspnetcdn.com/ajax/
       Bootstrap/3.3.7/css/Bootstrap.min.css"
       asp-fallback-href="~/lib/Bootstrap/dist/css/Bootstrap.min.css"
       asp-fallback-test-class="sr-only"
       asp-fallback-test-property="position"
       asp-fallback-test-value="absolute" />
   </environment>
   ```

9. Repeat step 6 at the bottom of the <body> element. In these two Tag Helpers,
   you specify JavaScript libraries you want to load when the HTML has finished
   loading.

10. Add the *Bootstrap.js, jquery.js, jquery.validation.js,* and
    jquery.validation.unobtrusive.js libraries and their CDN scripts to the
    <environment> Tag Helper you added in the <body> element.

    ```
    <environment include="Development">
        <script src="~/lib/jquery/dist/jquery.js"></script>
        <script src="~/lib/jquery-validation/dist/jquery.validate.js">
        </script>
        <script src="~/lib/jquery-validation-unobtrusive/jquery.
        validate.unobtrusive.js"></script>
    </environment>
    <environment exclude="Development">
    <script src="https://ajax.aspnetcdn.com/ajax/jquery/
    jquery-3.2.1.min.js"
    asp-fallback-src="~/lib/jquery/dist/jquery.js"
    asp-fallback-test="window.jQuery"></script>
    ```

```
<script src="http://ajax.aspnetcdn.com/ajax/jquery.validate/1.16.0/
   jquery.validate.min.js"
  asp-fallback-src="~/lib/jquery-validation/dist/jquery.validate.js"
  asp-fallback-test="window.jQuery && window.jQuery.validator">
</script>

<script src="http://ajax.aspnetcdn.com/ajax/mvc/5.2.3/jquery.
   validate.unobtrusive.min.js"
  asp-fallback-src="~/lib/jquery-validation-unobtrusive/jquery.
     validate.unobtrusive.js"
  asp-fallback-test="window.jQuery && window.jQuery.validator &&
     window.jQuery.validator.unobtrusive"></script>
</environment>
```

The complete dependency list in the *bower.json* file:

```
"dependencies": {
    "Bootstrap": "3.3.7",
    "jquery-validation": "1.17.0",
    "jquery-validation-unobtrusive": "3.2.6"
}
```

Styling with Bootstrap

Let's add a navigation bar in the **_Layout** view, and style it and the video list in the **Index** view, using Bootstrap.

The navigation bar for an anonymous user:

The navigation bar for a logged in user:

Adding a Navigation Bar

1. Open the **_Layout** view.
2. Add a <nav> element at the top of the <body> element and decorate it with the **navbar** and **navbar-default** Bootstrap classes, to create the navigation bar placeholder.
    ```
    <nav class="navbar navbar-default">
    </nav>
    ```
3. Add a <div> inside the <nav> that will act as the navigation bar container. Add the **container-fluid** Bootstrap class to it, to make it stretch across the whole screen.
    ```
    <div class="container-fluid">
    </div>
    ```
4. Add a <div> inside the fluid container <div>; it will act as the navigation bar header. Add the **navbar-header** Bootstrap class to it.
    ```
    <div class="navbar-header">
    </div>
    ```
5. Add an anchor tag to the navigation bar header. This link will take the user back to the application root (the **Index** view) if clicked. Add the Bootstrap class **navbar-brand** and the text *Video Application* to it.
    ```
    <a class="navbar-brand" href="/">Video Application</a>
    ```

6. Cut out the <div> containing the call to the **_LoginLinks** partial view and paste it below the navbar brand <div>. Add the Bootstrap classes **navbar**, **nabar-nav**, and **pull-right** to the <div> to turn the links into buttons and right align them in the navigation bar.

```
<div class="nav navbar-nav pull-right">
    @await Html.PartialAsync("_LoginLinks")
</div>
```

7. Open the **_LoginLinks** partial view.

8. Cut out the Razor expression that fetches the user's name, and paste it at the top of the form. Delete the <div>.

```
<form method="post" asp-controller="Account" asp-action="Logout">
    @User.Identity.Name
    <input type="submit" value="Logout" />
</form>
```

9. Add the Bootstrap classes **navbar-btn**, **btn**, and **btn-danger** to the **submit** button to style it.

```
<input type="submit" value="Logout" class="navbar-btn btn btn-danger"
/>
```

10. Add the Bootstrap classes **btn**, **btn-xs**, **btn-default**, and **navbar-btn** to the <a> elements to turn the links into buttons.

11. Add 10px left and bottom margin to the **Create** button in the **Index** view.

```
<div style="margin-left:10px;margin-bottom:10px;">
    <a class="btn btn-success" asp-action="Create">Create</a>
</div>
```

12. Save all files and start the application without debugging (Ctrl+F5). A navigation bar with the brand name and the links should be visible at the top of the view.

The complete markup for the **_LoginLinks** partial view:

```
@using Microsoft.AspNetCore.Identity

@inject SignInManager<User> SignInManager
@inject UserManager<User> UserManager

@if (SignInManager.IsSignedIn(User))
{
    // Signed in user
    <form method="post" asp-controller="Account" asp-action="Logout">
        @User.Identity.Name
```

154

```
        <input type="submit" value="Logout"
            class="navbar-btn btn btn-danger"/>
    </form>
}
else
{
    // Anonymous user
    <a asp-controller="Account" asp-action="Login"
        class="btn btn-xs btn-default navbar-btn">Login</a>
    <a asp-controller="Account" asp-action="Register"
        class="btn btn-xs btn-default navbar-btn">Register</a>
}
```

The navigation bar markup in the **_Layout** view:

```
<nav class="navbar navbar-default">
    <div class="container-fluid">
        <div class="navbar-header">
            <a class="navbar-brand" href="/">Video Application</a>
        </div>

        <div class="nav navbar-nav pull-right">
            @await Html.PartialAsync("_LoginLinks")
        </div>
    </div>
</nav>
```

Styling the Index View

Let's make the video list a bit more appealing by adding Bootstrap classes to make them appear like panels. The image below shows the end result.

1. Open the **Index** view.
2. Add the Bootstrap classes **btn** and **btn-success** to the **Create** link in the **Index** view. This should turn the button green, with the default Bootstrap theme.
   ```
   <a class="btn btn-success" asp-action="Create">Create</a>
   ```
3. Open the **_Video** view.
4. Add the **panel** and **panel-primary** Bootstrap classes to the <section> element, to turn it into a panel with blue heading background.
   ```
   <section class="panel panel-primary">
   ```
5. Replace the <h3> heading with a <div> decorated with the **panel-heading** Bootstrap class, for the title.

```
<div class="panel-heading">@Model.Title</div>
```

6. Move the ending </div> for the genre, below the ending </div> for the anchor tags. Add the **panel-body** Bootstrap class to the <div> surrounding the genre and anchor tags. Add the **btn** and **btn-default** Bootstrap classes to the anchor tags to turn them into buttons.

```
<div class="panel-body">
    @Model.Genre
    <div>
        <a class="btn btn-default" asp-action="Details"
           asp-route-id="@Model.Id">Details</a>
        <a class="btn btn-default" asp-action="Edit"
           asp-route-id="@Model.Id">Edit</a>
    </div>
</div>
```

7. Save all files and start the application without debugging (Ctrl+F5). The videos should be displayed in panels.

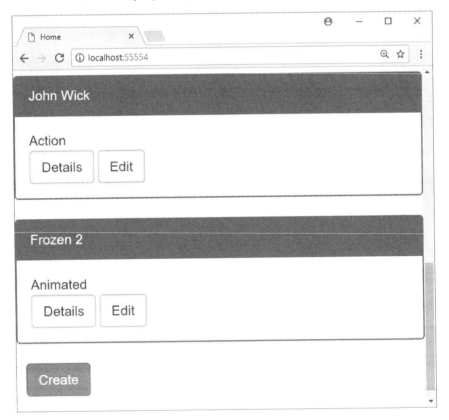

The complete markup for the **_Video** view:

```
@model VideoViewModel

<section class="panel panel-primary">
    <div class="panel-heading">@Model.Title</div>
    <div class="panel-body">
        @Model.Genre
        <div>
            <a class="btn btn-default" asp-action="Details"
                asp-route-id="@Model.Id">Details</a>
            <a class="btn btn-default" asp-action="Edit"
                asp-route-id="@Model.Id">Edit</a>
        </div>
    </div>
</section>
```

Adding Client-Side Validation

To take advantage of client-side validation, you only have to add the **jquery, jquery. validate**, and **jquery.validate.unobtrusive** JavaScript libraries. You have already added the libraries in a previous section, so now you only have to check that the validation works.

Pay attention to the URL field in the browser as you click the **Login**, **Edit**, and **Create** buttons when you try to enter invalid data (you can for instance leave one of the text fields empty). The URL should not refresh, because no round-trip is made to the server.

1. Run the application without debugging (Ctrl+F5).
2. Click the **Edit** button in the **Index** view; this should display the **Login** view. If you're already logged in then click the **Logout** button and repeat this step.
3. Leave the **Username** field empty and click the **Login** button. Pay attention to the URL; it should not refresh. An error message should be displayed in the form.

4. Log in with correct credentials.
5. Clear the **Title** field and click the **Edit** button. Pay attention to the URL; it should not refresh. Two error messages should be displayed, one for the validation summary, above the controls, and one beside the text field.

6. Click the **Back to List** link to return to the **Index** view.
7. Click the **Create** link below the video list.
8. Try to add a video with an empty title. Pay attention to the URL; it should not refresh. The same type of error displayed for the **Edit** view should be displayed.

Summary

In this chapter, you used Bower to add JQuery libraries to enforce client-side validation, and Bootstrap to style the **Index** view with CSS classes.

Next, you will start implementing the video course website.

Part 2:
MVC
How to Build a Video Course Website

9. The Use Case

Introduction

In the remainder of this book you will learn how to build an ASP.NET Core 2.0 Web Application with MVC and one with Razor Pages, Entity Framework Core 2.0, custom Tag Helpers, HTML, CSS, AutoMapper, and JW Player.

The Use Case

The customer has ordered a Video on Demand (VOD) application and has requested that the newest technologies be used when developing the solution. The application should be able to run in the cloud, be web based, and run on any device. They have specifically asked that Microsoft technologies be used as the core of the solution. Any deviations from that path should be kept to a minimum.

As a first step, they would like a demo version using dummy data to get a feel for the application. The dummy data source must be interchangeable with the final SQL database storage, with minimal extra cost.

YouTube should be used to store the videos, to keep costs down. No API or functionality for uploading videos is necessary in the final application. It is sufficient for the administrator to be able to paste in a link to a video stored in a YouTube account when adding a new video with the admin user interface.

The solution should contain three applications: The first is called **VideoOnDemand.Data**, and will contain all entity classes as well as a couple of services for interacting with the database that it creates. The second is a user interface for regular users called **VideoOnDemand.UI**; this application has a reference to the **Data** project to get access to the database through the services. The third application is for administrators and is called **VideoOnDemand. Admin**; with it, admins can perform CRUD operations on the tables in the database.

The User Interface (MVC)

This web application should be created using the MVC project template. Users should be able to register and log in to the web application. Upon successful login or registration, the user should be automatically redirected to the membership site.

The first view after login should be a dashboard, displaying the courses available to the user. When clicking on a course, the course curriculum should be displayed in a list below a marquee and some information about the course. Each course can have multiple modules, which can have multiple videos and downloadable content. Downloadable content should open in a separate browser tab.

When the user clicks on a video listing, a new view is opened, where a video player is preloaded with the video but displays an image (no auto play). Information about the course, and a description of the video, should be displayed below the video player. To the right of the video player, a thumbnail image for the next video in the module should be displayed, as well as buttons to the previous and next video. The buttons should be disabled if no video is available.

An instructor bio should be displayed in the **Course**, **Detail**, and **Video** views.

The menu should have a logo on the far left and a settings menu to the far right.

The database entity classes should not be used as view models; instead, each view should use a view model, which contains the necessary Data Transfer Objects (DTOs) and other properties. Auto Mapper should be used to convert entities to DTO objects, which are sent to the views.

Login and Register User

When an anonymous user visits the site, the **Login** view should be displayed. From that view, the visitor will be able to register with the site by clicking on a **Register as a new user** link. The link opens a **Register** view where a new user account can be created.

When these views are displayed, a menu with the standard options should be available, like **Home** (takes the visitor to the login view), **About**, and **Contact**. The two latter views don't have to be implemented since the company will do that themselves; just leave them with their default content.

The Administrator Interface (Razor Pages)

This web application should be created with Razor Pages. Each table should have four Razor Pages for adding and modifying data: **Index**, **Create**, **Edit**, **Delete**. To display data in a drop-down, a collection of **SelectList** items will be sent to the Razor Page from its code-behind file using the dynamic **ViewData** object, and displayed with a <select> element and the **ViewBag** object in the Razor Page. Data stored using the **ViewData** object in C# can be retrieved and displayed in HTML with the **ViewBag** object.

If the logged in user is an administrator, a drop-down menu should appear to the right of the logo, containing links to views for CRUD operations on the database connected to the site. There should also be a dashboard on the main **Index** page where the admin can click to open the **Index** pages associated with the different tables in the database and perform CRUD operations.

Conclusion

After careful consideration, these are the views and controls necessary for the application to work properly.

Login and Register

It is clear that the default views can be reused; they only need some styling. The default links for registering and logging in a user in the navigation bar has to be removed, and the **Home** controller's **Index** action will reroute to the **Login** view instead of displaying the **Index** view. This will ensure that the login panel is displayed when the application starts.

Below is a mock-up image of the **Login** and **Create** views. Note the icons in the textboxes; they will be represented by Glyphicons.

The application will collect the user's email and password when registering with the site, and that information will be requested of the visitor when logging in. There will also be a checkbox asking if the user wants to remain logged in when visiting the site the next time.

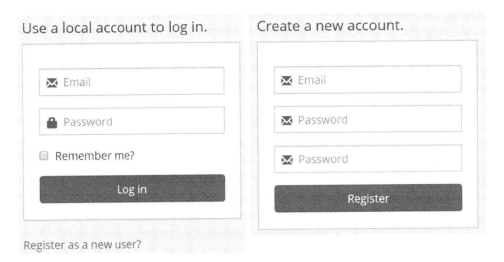

The User Dashboard View

By analyzing the use case you can surmise that the dashboard's course panels should be loaded dynamically, based on the number of courses the user has access to. The courses will be displayed three to a row, to make them large enough. This means that the view model has to contain a collection of collections, defined by a course DTO.

Each course DTO should contain properties for the course id, course title, description, a course image, and a marquee image. Each course should be displayed as a panel with the course image, title, description, and a button leading to the course view.

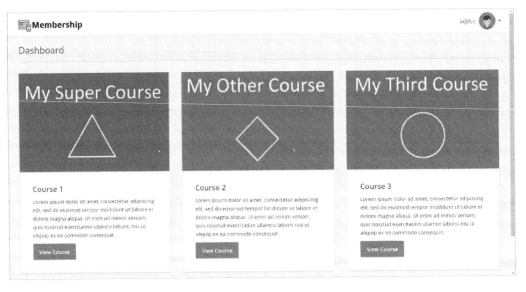

The Course View

The course view should have a button at the top, leading back to the dashboard. Below the button, there should be three sections: an overview, the course modules, and an instructor bio.

The marquee image, the course image (as a thumbnail in the marquee), the title, and description should be in the top panel.

Below the top panel to the left, the course modules and their content should be listed. Note that there are two possible types of content in a module: videos and downloads. Each video should display a thumbnail, title, description, and the length of the video (duration). Downloads are listed as links with a descriptive title.

To the right of the module list is the instructor bio, which contains a thumbnail, name, and description of the instructor.

To pull this off, the course view model needs to have a Course DTO, an Instructor DTO, and a list of Module DTOs. Each Instructor DTO should contain the avatar, name, and description of the instructor teaching a course. The Module DTO should contain the module id, title, and lists of Video DTOs and Download DTOs.

A Video DTO should contain the video id, title, description, duration, a thumbnail, and the URL to the video. When a video is clicked, the video should be loaded into, and displayed by, the **Video** view. Auto play should be disabled.

A Download DTO should contain a title and the URL to the content. When the link is clicked, the content should open in a new browser tab.

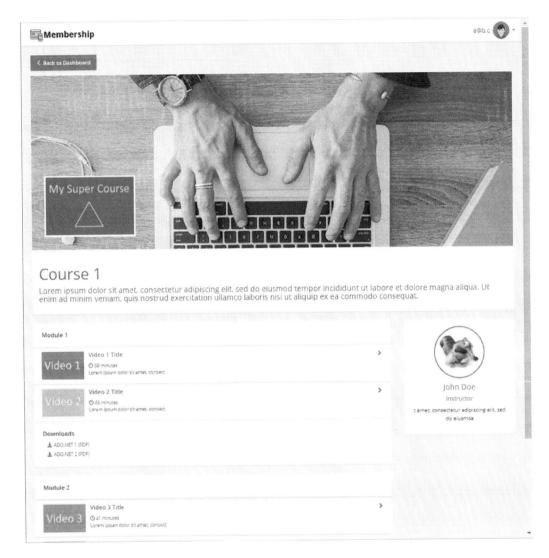

The Video View

There should be three sections in the **Video** view, below the button leading back to the **Course** view. To the left, a large video panel containing the video, course, and video information is displayed. To the top right is a panel displaying the image and title of the next video in the current module, along with **Previous** and **Next** buttons.

Below the *next video* panel is the *Instructor* panel.

To pull this off, the video view model must contain a Video DTO, an Instructor DTO, a Course DTO, and a LessonInfo DTO. The LessonInfo DTO contains properties for lesson number, number of lessons, video id, title, and thumbnail properties for the previous and next videos in the module.

The Administrator Dashboard Razor Page

The administrator dashboard page should have links, displayed as cards, to the different **Index** Razor Pages representing the tables in the database. A menu should also be available for navigating the Razor Pages.

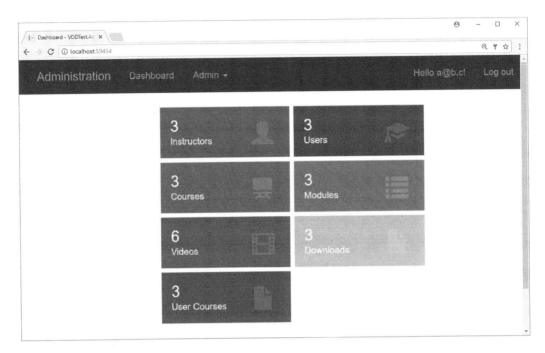

A Typical Administrator Index Razor Page

A typical **Index** page contains a title and two buttons at the top – **Create** and **Dashboard** – a table with information about the entity, and two buttons for editing and deleting information about the entity. A custom Tag Helper will be used to render the buttons.

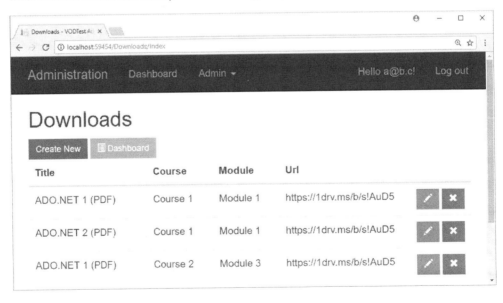

A Typical Administrator Create Razor Page

A typical **Create** Razor Page has labels and input fields for data needed to create a new record in the database.

The Razor Page should have a **Create** button that posts the data to the server, a **Back to List** button that takes the user back to the **Index** page, and a **Dashboard** button that takes the user back to the main **Index** page.

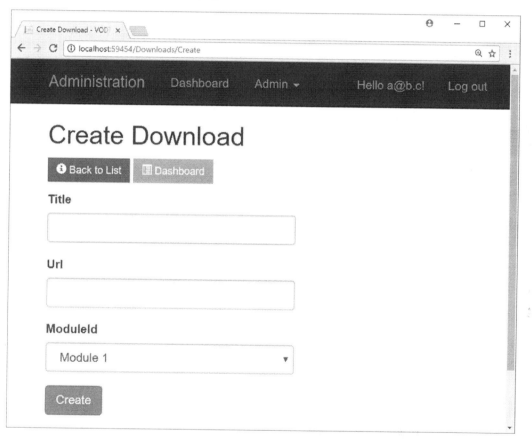

A Typical Administrator Edit Razor Page

A typical **Edit** Razor Page has labels and input fields for the data needed to update a record in the database.

The Razor Page also has a **Save** button that posts the data to the server, a **Back to List** button that takes the user back to the **Index** page, and a **Dashboard** button that takes the user back to the main **Index** page.

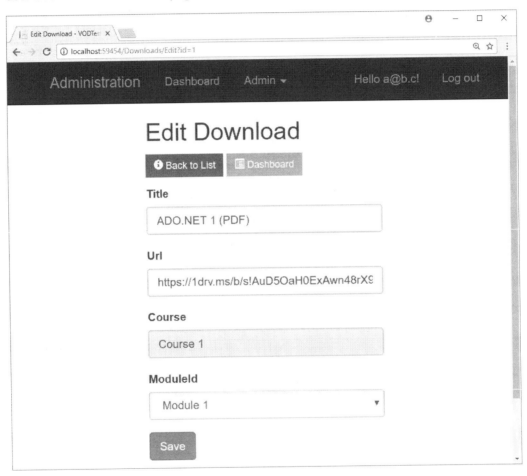

A Typical Administrator Delete Razor Page

A typical **Delete** Razor Page has labels for the entity data, a **Delete** button prompting the server to delete the entity from the database, a **Back to List** button that takes the user back to the **Index** page, an **Edit** button that takes the user to the **Edit** page, and a **Dashboard** button that takes the user back to the main **Index** page.

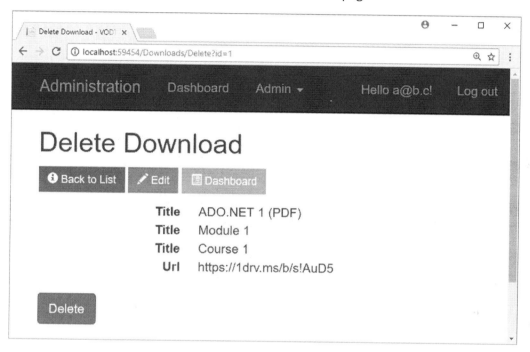

10. Setting Up the Solution

Introduction

In this chapter, you will create the solution and install the necessary NuGet packages for it in Visual Studio 2017.

Technologies Used in This Chapter

- **ASP.NET Core Web Application** – The template used to create the applications.
- **MVC** – To structure the UI application.
- **AutoMapper** – A NuGet package that, when installed, will map objects from one type to another. Will be used to map entity objects to DTOs.

Overview

The customer wants you to build the web applications using Visual Studio 2017, ASP.NET Core 2.0, and the **ASP.NET Core Web Application** template. The first step will be to create the solution and install all the necessary NuGet packages that aren't installed with the default UI project template. The template will install the basic MVC plumbing and a **Home** controller with **Index**, **About**, and **Contact** action methods, and their corresponding views.

Creating the Solution

If you haven't already installed Visual Studio 2017 version 15.3.5 version or later, you can download a free copy here: www.visualstudio.com/downloads.

1. Open Visual Studio 2017 and select **File-New-Project** in the main menu to create a new solution.
2. Click on the **Web** tab and then select **ASP.NET Core Web Application** in the template list (see image below).
3. Name the project *VideoOnDemand.UI* in the **Name** field.
4. Name the solution *VideoOnDemand* in the **Solution name** field. It should not end with *.UI*.
5. Click the **OK** button.
6. Make sure that **.NET Core** and **ASP.NET Core 2.0** are selected in the drop-downs.
7. Select **Web Application (Model-View-Controller)** in the template list.

8. Click the **Change Authentication** button and select **Individual User Accounts** in the pop-up dialog. This will make it possible for visitors to register and log in with your site using an email and a password (see image below).

   a. Select the **Individual User Accounts** radio button.

   b. Select **Store user account in-app** in the drop-down.

   c. Click the **OK** button in the pop-up dialog.

9. Click the **OK** button in the wizard dialog.

10. Open *appsettings.json* and add the following connection string. It's important that the connection string is added as a single line of code.

```
"ConnectionStrings": {
    "DefaultConnection": "Server=(localdb)\\mssqllocaldb;
        Database=VideoOnDemand2;Trusted_Connection=True;
        MultipleActiveResultSets=true"
}
```

It is no longer possible to manage NuGet packages with a *project.json* file. Instead, the NuGet packages are listed in the *.csproj* file, which can be edited directly from the IDE.

It is also important to understand the concept of Dependency Injection, since it is used to make object instances available throughout the application. If a resource is needed, it can be injected into the constructor and saved to a private class-level variable. No objects are created in the class itself; any objects needed can be requested through DI.

Installing AutoMapper

AutoMapper will be used to map entity (database table) objects to Data Transfer Objects (DTOs), which are used to transport data to the views. You can either add the following row to the <ItemGroup> node in the *.csproj* file manually and save the file or use the NuGet manager to add AutoMapper.

```
<PackageReference Include="AutoMapper" Version="6.1.1" />
```

The following listing shows you how to use the NuGet manager to install packages.

1. Right click on the **Dependencies** node in the Solution Explorer and select **Manage NuGet Packages** in the context menu.

2. Click on the **Browse** link at the top of the dialog.
3. Select **nuget.org** in the drop-down to the far right in the dialog.
4. Type *AutoMapper* in the textbox.
5. Select the **AutoMapper** package in the list; it will probably be the first package in the list.
6. Make sure that you use the latest stable version (6.1.1).
7. Click the **Install** button.

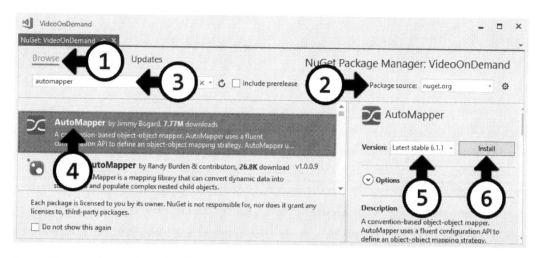

To verify that the package has been installed, you can open the *.csproj* file by right clicking on the project node and selecting **Edit VideoOnDemand.csproj**, or you can expand the *Dependencies-NuGet* folder in the Solution Explorer.

Creating the Database

There are only a few steps to creating the database that will enable users to register and log in. In a later chapter, you will expand the database by adding tables to store application data.

To create the database, you have to create an initial migration to tell Entity Framework how the database should be set up. You do this by executing the **add-migration** command in the *Package Manager Console*.

After the migration has been successfully created, you execute the **update-database** command in the same console to create the database. After the database has been created, you can view it in the *SQL Server Object Explorer*, which can be opened from the **View** menu.

Because the entities and the database context will be shared between the administration UI and the user UI, you will add a separate project called **VideoOnDemand.Data** for the database classes. This project will then be referenced from the other projects.

Adding the Database Project

1. Right click on the **VideoOnDemand** solution in the Solution Explorer and select **Add-New Project** in the menu.
2. Click on the **Web** tab and select **ASP.NET Core Web Application** in the template list.
3. Name the project **VideoOnDemand.Data** and click the **OK** button.
4. Make sure that **.NET Core** and **ASP.NET Core 2.0** are selected in the drop-downs.
5. Select **Empty** in the template list.
6. Click the **OK** button.
7. Right click on the **VideoOnDemand.Data** project and select **Set as StartUp project**.

Adding the User Class

1. Add a folder named *Data* to the **VideoOnDemand.Data** project.
2. Add a folder named *Entities* in the *Data* folder.
3. Add a class called **User** to the *Entities* folder. This will be the user identity class that will be used to handle users for both the administration and user websites.
4. Inherit the **IdentityUser** class in the **User** class to add the basic user functionality to it. The **User** class will now be able to handle users in the database and will be used when the database is created. You need to resolve the **Microsoft.AspNetCore.Identity** namespace.

```
public class User : IdentityUser
{
}
```

Adding the Database Context

1. Add a class called **VODContext** to the *Data* folder. This database context will be used to add entity classes that represent tables in the database, and to call the database from the other projects. You need to resolve the **VideoOnDemand. Data.Data.Entities** and **Microsoft.AspNetCore.Identity.EntityFrameworkCore** namespaces.

```
public class VODContext : IdentityDbContext<User>
{
}
```

2. Add a constructor that has a parameter of type **DbContextOptions** called **options**. You need to resolve the **Microsoft.EntityFrameworkCore** namespace.

```
public VODContext(DbContextOptions<VODContext> options)
: base(options)
{
}
```

3. Override the method called **OnModelCreating** and have it call the same method on the base class. You will later use this method to configure certain features of the database.

```
protected override void OnModelCreating(ModelBuilder builder)
{
    base.OnModelCreating(builder);
}
```

4. Add a file of type **ASP.NET Configuration File** called *application.json* to the project.

5. Open the *application.json* file to change the database name in the connection string to *VideoOnDemand2*; the same name you used in the **UI** project.

```
"DefaultConnection":
    "Server=(localdb)\\mssqllocaldb;Database=VideoOnDemand2;
    Trusted_Connection=True;MultipleActiveResultSets=true"
```

6. Open the *Startup.cs* file.

7. Add a constructor to the class and inject the **IConfiguration** interface to it. Store the injected object in a private read-only class-level property called **Configuration**. This will make it possible to read from the *application.json* configuration file, where the connection string is stored.

```
public IConfiguration Configuration { get; }

public Startup(IConfiguration configuration)
{
    Configuration = configuration;
}
```

8. Locate the **ConfigureServices** method and add the **SqlServer** provider to be able to create and call databases. Call the **AddDBContext** method on the **service** object and specify the **VODContext** as the context to use. Use the **options** action to specify the database provider and connection string.

```
services.AddDbContext<VODContext>(options => options.UseSqlServer(
Configuration.GetConnectionString("DefaultConnection")));
```

181

9. Call the **AddIdentity** method on the **service** object to use the **User** entity class when creating the **AspNetUsers** table in the database.

```
services.AddIdentity<User, IdentityRole>()
    .AddEntityFrameworkStores<VODContext>()
    .AddDefaultTokenProviders();
```

10. Open the *Package Manager Console* by selecting **View-Other Windows-Package Manager Console** in the main menu.

11. Select **VideoOnDemand.Data** in the right drop-down to select the correct project.

12. Type in *add-migration Initial* and press **Enter** on the keyboard to create a first migration called *Initial* for the database.

13. Type in *update-database* and press **Enter** to create the database.

14. Open the *SQL Server Object Explorer* from the **View** menu and make sure that the database was successfully created (see image on the next page).

15. Open the **AspNetRoles** table and add a role named **Admin** that can be used to distinguish regular users from administrators. Assign *1* to the record's **Id** column, *Admin* to its **Name** column, and *ADMIN* to its **NormalizedName** column. Right click on the table node and select **View Data** to open the table.

16. Open the *VideoOnDemand.UI* project in the Solution Explorer.

17. Right click on the **Dependencies** node in the Solution Explorer and select **Add Reference** to add a reference to the *VideoOnDemand.Data* project.

18. Delete the *Data* folder and all its content in the *VideoOnDemand.UI* project. It won't be needed since the database is located in a separate project.

19. Delete the *ApplicationUser.cs* file in the *Models* folder. It won't be needed since the database is located in a separate project.

20. Replace all occurrences of **ApplicationUser** with **User** and resolve the namespace **VideoOnDemand.Data.Data.Entities** in the **User** class.

21. Remove all references to the **VideoOnDemand.UI.Data** namespace.

22. Open the **Startup** class and add a reference to the **VideoOnDemand.Data.Data** namespace.

23. Replace all occurences of **ApplicationDbContext** with **VODContext**.

24. Save all files.

25. Right click on the **VideoOnDemand.UI** project and select **Set as StartUp project**.

It may take a second or two for the SQL Server node to populate in the SQL Server Object Explorer. When it has, expand the server named **MSSQLLocalDB** and then the **VideoOn-Demand** database. Several tables should have been added to the database. The tables prefixed with **AspNet** stores user account information, and are used when a user registers and logs in. In this course, you will use the **AspNetUsers**, **AspNetRoles**, and **AspNetUser-Roles** tables when implementing registration and login for your users, and to determine if a user is an administrator.

Summary

In this chapter, you created the project that will be used throughout the remainder of this book to create a user interface (UI). You also installed the AutoMapper NuGet package, which later will be used to map database entity objects to Data Transfer Objects (DTOs), which provide the views with data.

Next, you will redirect the **Home/Index** action to display the **Account/Login** view. This will display the login form when the application starts. Then you will style the login form, making it look more professional.

11. Login

Introduction

In this chapter, you will make the login view available as soon as a visitor navigates to the web application. To achieve this, you will redirect from the **Home/Index** action to the **Account/Login** action.

Because the login view only should be displayed to visitors who haven't already logged in, you will use Dependency Injection to make the **SignInManager** available from the controller, making it possible to check if the user is logged in.

To enable visitors to register and log in, you have to use the same connection string you used in the **VideoOnDemand.Data** project.

Technologies Used in This Chapter

1. **Dependency Injection** – To inject objects into a controller's constructor.
2. **C#** – For writing code in the controller's actions and constructor.
3. **Razor** – To incorporate C# in the views where necessary.
4. **HTML 5** – To build the views.
5. **Bootstrap and CSS** – To style the HTML 5 elements.
6. **TagHelpers** – To add HTML 5 elements and their attributes.

Redirecting to the Login View

ASP.NET Core is designed from the ground up to support and leverage Dependency Injection (DI). Dependency Injection is a way to let the framework automatically create instances of services (classes) and inject them into constructors. Why is this important? Well, it creates loose couplings between objects and their collaborators. This mean that no hardcoded instances need to be created in the collaborator itself; they are sent into it.

Not only can built-in framework services be injected, but objects from your own classes can also be configured for DI in the **Startup** class.

Now, you will use DI to pass in the **SignInManager** to a constructor in the **HomeController** class and store it in a private variable. The **SignInManager** and its **User** type need two **using** statements: **Microsoft.AspNetCore.Identity** and **VideoOnDemand.Data.Data. Entities**.

1. Open the **HomeController** class located in the *Controllers* folder in the **UI** project.

2. Add the following **using** statements.
   ```
   using Microsoft.AspNetCore.Identity;
   using VideoOnDemand.Data.Data.Entities;
   using VideoOnDemand.UI.Models;
   ```

3. Add a constructor that receives the **SignInManager** through dependency injection and stores it in a private class-level variable.
   ```
   private SignInManager<User> _signInManager;

   public HomeController(SignInManager<User> signInMgr)
   {
       _signInManager = signInMgr;
   }
   ```

4. Check if the user is signed in using the class-level variable you just added, and redirect to the **Login** action in the **AccountController** class if it's an anonymous user. Otherwise open the default **Index** view, for now. You will change this in a later chapter.
   ```
   public IActionResult Index()
   {
       if (!_signInManager.IsSignedIn(User))
           return RedirectToAction("Login", "Account");

       return View();
   }
   ```

5. Run the application by pressing F5 or Ctrl+F5 (without debugging) on the keyboard.

6. The login view should be displayed. If you look at the URL, it should point to /Account/login on the localhost (your local IIS server) because of the **RedirectToAction** method call.

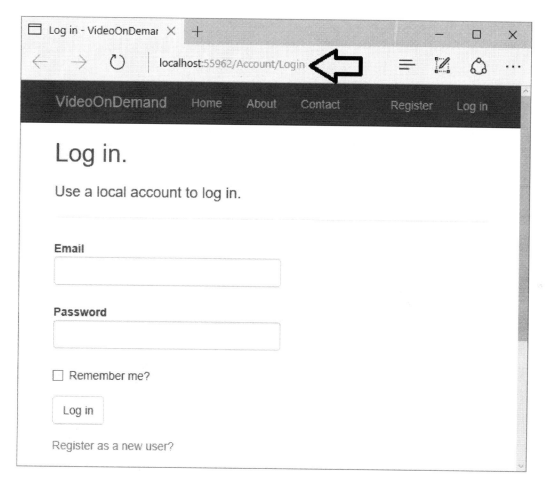

Styling the Login View

As you can see in the image above, the **Login** view isn't very pleasing to the eye. Let's change that by styling it with CSS, Bootstrap, and Glyphicons. After it has been styled, the view should look something like this.

Adding the login.css Stylesheet

1. Stop the application in Visual Studio.
2. Add a new style sheet file called *login.css* to the *wwwroot/css* folder in the Solution Explorer. Right click on the folder and select **Add-New Item**.
3. Select the **Style Sheet** template in the list, name it *login.css*, and click the **Add** button.
4. Remove the **Body** selector from the file.
5. Open the **_Layout** view in the *Views/Shared* folder.
6. Add a link to the *login.css* file in the **Development** <environment> tag. You can copy an existing link and alter it, or drag the file from the Solution Explorer and drop it in the **_Layout** view.
```
<environment include="Development">
    . . .
    <link rel="stylesheet" href="~/css/login.css" />
</environment>
```
7. Add the *login.css* file path to the **inputFiles** array in the *bundleconfig.json* file to minify the CSS. By minifying the files, you make them as small as possible for transfer from server to client.
```
"outputFileName": "wwwroot/css/site.min.css",
"inputFiles": [
    "wwwroot/css/site.css",
    "wwwroot/css/login.css"
]
```
8. Save all files.

Changing the Layout of the Login View

These changes will prepare the form for its much-needed styling.

1. Open the **Login** view in the *Views/Account* folder.
2. Remove the <h2> title element.
3. Remove the <div> with the **col-md-6 col-md-offset-2** classes and all its content.
4. Add the class **col-md-offset-4** to the <div> with the **col-md-4**.
5. Remove the horizontal rule <hr/> element from the form.
6. Cut out the <h4> heading at the top of the <form> element and paste it in above the <section> element. Add the id **login-panel-heading** to the <h4> element.

```
<div class="col-md-4 col-md-offset-4">
    <h4 id="login-panel-heading">Use a local account to Login.
    </h4>
```

7. Add two <div> elements below the <h4> heading and use Bootstrap classes to turn them into a panel and a panel body. This will make it easier to style the login form and to give it the nice border. Don't forget to add the ending </div> tags outside the </section> end tag.

```
<div class="panel login-panel">
    <div class="panel-body login-panel-body">
        <section>
```

8. Add the class **login-form** to the <form> element.
9. Remove the <label> and <span> elements from the email **form-group**.
10. Surround the **Email** <input> element with a <div> decorated with the **icon-addon** Bootstrap class. This selector will be used when styling the Glyphicon.
11. Add a new <label> element targeting the **Email** model property below the email <input> element, and add the **envelope** Glyphicon.
12. Add the **placeholder** attribute with the text *Email* to the email <input> element. The placeholder is instructional text displayed inside the textbox that is removed when the user types in the control.

```
<div class="form-group">
    <div class="icon-addon">
        <input asp-for="Email" placeholder="Email"
            class="form-control" />
        <label for="Email" class="glyphicon glyphicon-envelope" />
    </div>
</div>
```

13. Repeat steps 9-12 for the **Password** model property, but use the **glyphicon-lock** class instead.

14. Add the class **login-form-checkbox** to the <div> decorated with the **form-group** class surrounding the checkbox. You will use this class later to style the checkbox with CSS.

```
<div class="form-group login-form-checkbox">
    <div class="checkbox">
        <label asp-for="RememberMe">
            <input asp-for="RememberMe" />
            @Html.DisplayNameFor(m => m.RememberMe)
        </label>
    </div>
</div>
```

15. Add the class **login-form-submit** to the submit **form-group**.

16. Surround the **submit** <button> element with a <div> decorated with the **row** Bootstrap class.

17. Surround the **submit** <button> element with a <div> decorated with the **col-md-12** Bootstrap class.

18. Change the Bootstrap button type from **default** to **primary**.

```
<div class="form-group login-form-submit">
    <div class="row">
        <div class="col-md-12">
            <button type="submit" class="btn btn-primary">
                Login
            </button>
        </div>
    </div>
</div>
```

19. Move the two *Register a new user* and *Forgot your Password?* <p> elements immediately above the closing column </div>.

The form should look like this after the layout change.

Use a local account to log in.

Email

✉

Password

🔒

☐ Remember me?

Log in

The complete code for the **Login** View:

```
@model LoginViewModel
@inject SignInManager<User> SignInManager

@{
    ViewData["Title"] = "Log in";
}

<div class="row">
    <div class="col-md-4 col-md-offset-4">
        <h4 id="login-panel-heading">Use a local account to log in.</h4>
        <div class="panel login-panel">
            <div class="panel-body login-panel-body">
                <section>
                    <form asp-route-returnurl="@ViewData["ReturnUrl"]"
                        class="login-form" method="post">
                        <div asp-validation-summary="All"
                            class="text-danger"></div>
                        <div class="form-group">
                            <div class="icon-addon">
                                <input asp-for="Email" placeholder="Email"
                                    class="form-control" />
                                <label for="Email" class="glyphicon
                                    glyphicon-envelope" />
                            </div>
                        </div>
```

```html
                    <div class="form-group">
                        <div class="icon-addon">
                            <input asp-for="Password"
                                placeholder="Password"
                                class="form-control" />
                            <label for="Password" class="glyphicon
                                glyphicon-lock" />
                        </div>
                    </div>
                    <div class="form-group login-form-checkbox">
                        <div class="checkbox">
                            <label asp-for="RememberMe">
                                <input asp-for="RememberMe" />
                                @Html.DisplayNameFor(m => m.RememberMe)
                            </label>
                        </div>
                    </div>

                    <div class="form-group login-form-submit">
                        <div class="row">
                            <div class="col-md-12">
                                <button type="submit" class="btn
                                    btn-primary">Log in</button>
                            </div>
                        </div>
                    </div>
                </form>
            </section>
        </div>
    </div>
    <p><a asp-action="ForgotPassword">Forgot your password?</a></p>
    <p><a asp-action="Register" asp-route-returnurl=
        "@ViewData["ReturnUrl"]">Register as a new user?</a></p>
    </div>
</div>

@section Scripts {
    @await Html.PartialAsync("_ValidationScriptsPartial")
}
```

Styling the Login View

Now that you have altered the Login view's layout, it's time to style it using CSS. Add the CSS selector one at a time to the *login.css* file, save the file, and observe the changes in the browser.

Add a 40px top margin to the heading, pushing it down a little from the navigation bar.

```
#login-panel-heading {
    margin-top: 40px;
}
```

Next, make the panel width 280px, and remove the border.

```
.login-panel {
    width: 280px;
    border: none;
}
```

Next, add a darker gray color to the panel border and make it 1px wide, and add 20px padding to the panel body.

```
.login-panel-body {
    border: 1px solid #cecece !important;
    padding: 20px;
}
```

The form has bottom padding and margin that needs to be removed.

```
.login-form-submit {
    margin-bottom: 0px;
    padding-bottom: 0px;
}
```

The Glyphicons should be displayed inside the textboxes.

```
.icon-addon {
    position: relative;
    color: #555;
    display: block;
}
```

```
.icon-addon .glyphicon {
    position: absolute;
    left: 10px;
    padding: 10px 0;
}

.icon-addon .form-control {
    Padding-left: 30px;
    border-radius: 0;
}

.icon-addon:hover .glyphicon {
    color: #2580db;
}
```

The **submit** button should be aligned with the textboxes and have the same width as them.

```
.login-form button {
    width: 100%;
}
```

The last thing to style is the padding around the error messages to align them with the textboxes, and make them the same width.

```
.login-form .validation-summary-errors ul {
    padding-left: 20px;
}
```

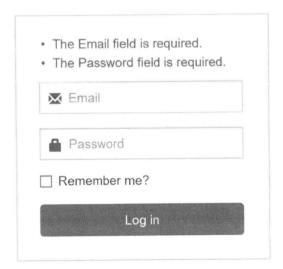

Summary

In this chapter, you changed the layout of the **Login** view, and applied CSS and Bootstrap classes to its elements, to make it look nicer to the user.

Next, you will change the layout of the **Account/Register** view and apply CSS and Bootstrap classes to its elements.

12. Register User

Introduction

In this chapter, you will alter the layout of the **Account/Register** view and style it using CSS and Bootstrap. The view can be reached from a link on the **Account/Login** view, which is available as soon as a visitor navigates to the web application.

Technologies Used in This Chapter

1. **Razor** – To incorporate C# in the views where necessary.
2. **HTML 5** – To build the views.
3. **Bootstrap and CSS** – To style the HTML 5 elements.

Overview

The task appointed to you by the company is to make sure that visitors have a nice user experience when registering with the site, using the **Account/register** view. The finished **Register** view should look like the image below.

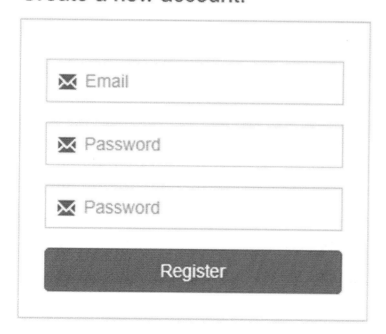

Changing the Layout of the Register View

These changes will prepare the form for its much-needed styling.

1. Add the Bootstrap class **col-md-offset-4** to the <div> decorated with the **col-md-4** class to push the login form four columns to the right.

2. Remove the <h2> heading.

3. Create a panel above the <form> element by adding a <div> element and decorate it with the **panel** class. Add another class called **register-panel**; it will be used to style the panel and its intrinsic elements.

4. Add another <div> below the panel <div> and decorate it with the **panel-body** class. Add another class called **register-panel-body**; it will be used to style its intrinsic elements.

   ```
   <div class="panel register-panel">
       <div class="panel-body register-panel-body">
   ```

5. Add a class called **register-form** to the <form> element.

6. Remove the <hr/> element from the form.

7. Move the <h4> heading above the panel <div> you just added and add the id **register-panel-heading** to it.

   ```
   <h4 id="register-panel-heading">Create a new account.</h4>
   ```

8. Remove the <label> and <span> elements from the email **form-group**.

9. Surround the **Email** <input> element with a <div> decorated with the **icon-addon** Bootstrap class.

10. Add a new <label> element targeting the **Email** model property below the email <input> element, and add the **envelope** Glyphicon.

11. Add the **placeholder** attribute with the text *Email* to the email <input> element.

    ```
    <div class="form-group">
        <div class="icon-addon">
            <input asp-for="Email" placeholder="Email"
                class="form-control" />
            <label for="Email" class="glyphicon glyphicon-envelope"/>
        </div>
    </div>
    ```

12. Repeat steps 8-11 for the **Password** model property. Use the **glyphicon-lock** class.

13. Repeat steps 8-11 for the **ConfirmPassword** model property. Use the **glyphicon-lock** class.

14. Surround the **submit** <button> element with a <div> decorated with the **row** Bootstrap class.

15. Add the class **register-form-submit** to the submit <button> element.

16. Change the Bootstrap button type from **default** to **primary**.

```
<button type="submit" class="register-form-submit btn
    btn-primary">
    Register
</button>
```

The complete markup for the **Register** view:

```
@model RegisterViewModel
@{
    ViewData["Title"] = "Register";
}

<div class="row">
    <div class="col-md-4 col-md-offset-4">
        <h4 id="register-panel-heading">Create a new account.</h4>
        <div class="panel register-panel">
            <div class="panel-body register-panel-body">
                <form asp-route-returnUrl="@ViewData["ReturnUrl"]"
                    class="register-form" method="post">
                    <div asp-validation-summary="All"
                        class="text-danger"></div>
                    <div class="form-group">
                        <div class="icon-addon">
                            <input asp-for="Email" placeholder="Email"
                                class="form-control" />
                            <label for="Email" class="glyphicon
                                glyphicon-envelope" />
                        </div>
                    </div>
                    <div class="form-group">
                        <div class="icon-addon">
                            <input asp-for="Password"
                                placeholder="Password"
                                class="form-control" />
                            <label for="Password" class="glyphicon
                                glyphicon-envelope" />
                        </div>
                    </div>
```

199

```
            </div>
            <div class="form-group">
                <div class="icon-addon">
                    <input asp-for="ConfirmPassword"
                        placeholder="Password"
                        class="form-control" />
                    <label for="Password" class="glyphicon
                        glyphicon-envelope" />
                </div>
            </div>
            <button type="submit" class="register-form-submit
                btn btn-primary">Register</button>
        </form>
        </div>
      </div>
    </div>
</div>

@section Scripts {
    @await Html.PartialAsync("_ValidationScriptsPartial")
}
```

Styling the Register View

Because the same styles already have been applied to elements in the **Login** view, the selectors and properties in the *login.css* file can be reused. Instead of adding a new style sheet for the **Register** view, you can add its CSS selectors to the existing selectors in the *login.css* file.

Add a 40px top margin to the panel by appending the **.register-panel** selector to the **.login-panel-heading** selector in the *login.css* file.

```
#login-panel-heading, #register-panel-heading {
    margin-top: 40px;
}
```

Next, add 20px padding, add a 1px dark gray border to the panel, and give the panel a fixed width of 280px.

```
.login-panel-body, .register-panel-body {
    border: 1px solid #cecece !important;
    padding: 20px;
}
```

```
.login-panel, .register-panel {
    width: 280px;
    border: none;
}
```

Make the button the same width as the textboxes.

```
.login-form button, .register-form button {
    margin-bottom: 5px;
    margin-left: 5px;
    max-width: 225px;
    width: 100%;
}
```

The last thing to alter is the error message element. Align it with the textboxes.

```
.login-form .validation-summary-errors ul,
.register-form .validation-summary-errors ul {
    padding-left: 20px;
}
```

The styled **Register** view should look like the image below.

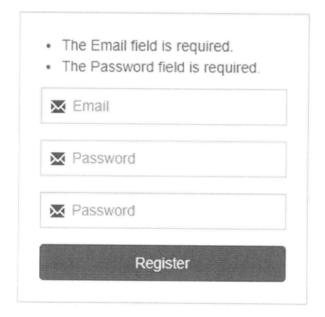

Changing the Register Action

This change will set the user's **EmailConfirmed** flag. You do this to tell the application that the user has verified the registration. This might not be necessary in all cases, but it shows you how to do it if you should need to modify user data when a user is created.

1. Open the **AccountController** class.
2. Locate the **Register** action.
3. Add the **EmailConfirmed** property to the **User** object and assign **true** to it.
   ```
   var user = new User { UserName = model.Email, Email = model.Email,
   EmailConfirmed = true };
   ```
4. Save the file.

Testing the Registration Form

1. Start the application.
2. Click the **Register as new user?** link below the login form.
3. Fill in an email address and a password and click the **Register** button. It can be a fake email address if you like. I usually use an easy-to-remember email address, like *a@b.c* when testing.
4. If the registration succeeded, the **Home/Index** view should be displayed, and the email should be visible to the right in the navigation bar.
5. Click the **Logout** link to the far right in the navigation bar. The login form should be displayed.
6. Try to log in to the site with the email you just registered with. This should take you back to the **Home/Index** view.
7. Close the application from Visual Studio.
8. Open the *SQL Server Object Explorer* from the **View** menu.
9. Expand the **MSSQLLocalDB** node, and then your database.
10. Expand the **Tables** node and right click on the **AspNetUsers** table. See image below.
11. Right click on the table and select **View Data** to open the table in Visual Studio.
12. The table should contain the user you added. See image below.

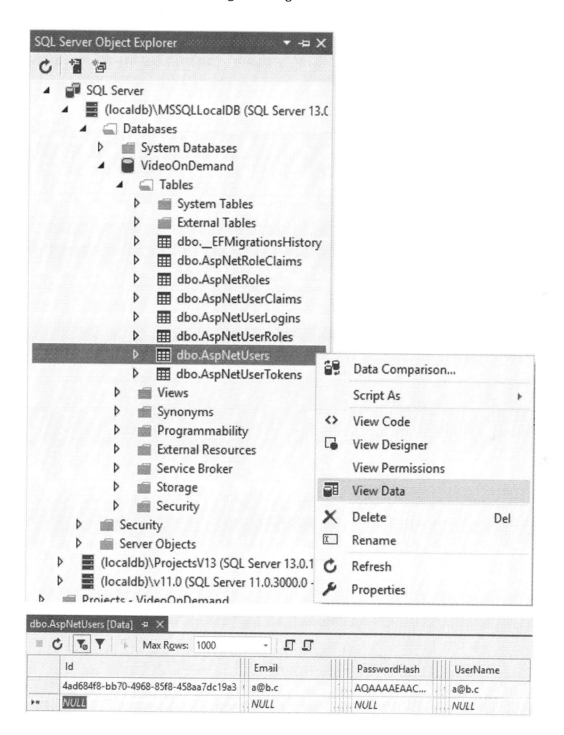

Summary

In this chapter, you changed the layout of the **Register** view and applied CSS and Bootstrap classes to spruce up its elements. You also registered a user and logged in using the account.

Next, you will change the layout of the navigation bar, and style it with CSS and Bootstrap classes. You will also create a drop-down menu for the logout and settings options, and remove their links from the navigation bar.

Then you will hide the **Home**, **About**, and **Contact** links whenever the user is logged in.

Lastly you will add a logotype to the navigation bar.

13. Modifying the Navigation Bar

Introduction

The default layout and styling of the navigation bar leaves a bit to be desired. In this chapter, you will alter the layout of the navigation bar, only displaying certain links when the user is logged out, and creating a drop-down menu for the **Logout** and **Settings** options. You will also add a logo to the navigation bar, making it look more professional.

Technologies Used in This Chapter

1. **Razor** – To incorporate C# in the views where necessary.
2. **HTML 5** – To build the views.
3. **Bootstrap and CSS** – To style the HTML 5 elements.

Overview

Your task is to change the appearance of the navigation bar. It should be white with a logo to the far left. The **Home, About**, and **Contact** links should only be visible to users before they have logged in to the site. No other links should be visible in the navigation bar, except for a drop-down menu at the far right, which should be visible when the user has logged in.

To control when the links are displayed you need to inject the **SignInManager** and **User-Manager** to the **_Layout** view.

```
@inject SignInManager<User> SignInManager
@inject UserManager<User> UserManager
```

To achieve this you will have to alter the **_Layout** and **_LoginPartial** views.

Current navigation bar when logged out

Current navigation bar when logged in

Altered navigation bar when logged out

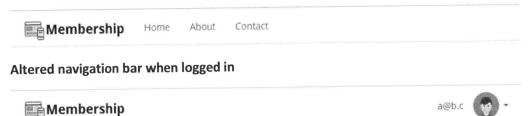

Altered navigation bar when logged in

Styling the Navigation Bar

You will change the navigation bar color to white, add a style sheet called *menu.css*, add a logo to the navigation bar, position the links, and hide them when logged in.

1. Right click on the *wwwroot/css* folder and select **Add-New Item** in the context menu.
2. Select the **Style Sheet** template and name the file *menu.css*.
3. Remove the **body** selector.
4. Add a reference to the *menu.css* file in the *bundleconfig.json* file to minify the styles for use when not in the development environment.

```
{
    "outputFileName": "wwwroot/css/site.min.css",
    "inputFiles": [
        "wwwroot/css/site.css",
        "wwwroot/css/login.css",
        "wwwroot/css/menu.css"
    ]
}
```

5. Open the **_Layout** view in the *Views/Shared* folder.
6. Add a <link> to the *menu.css* file in the **_Layout** view.
7. Locate the <nav> element inside the <body> element. Remove the **navbar-inverse** class. This should make the navigation bar white.
8. Add a **using** statement to the **VideoOnDemand.Data.Data.Entities** namespace.
9. To control when the links are displayed, you need to inject the **SignInManager** and **UserManager** into the **_Layout** view.

```
@inject SignInManager<User> SignInManager
@inject UserManager<User> UserManager
```

10. Use the **SignInManager** and the logged in user to hide the **Home**, **About**, and
    Contact links when the user is logged in.

```
@if (!SignInManager.IsSignedIn(User))
{
    <ul class="nav navbar-nav">
        <li><a asp-area="" asp-controller="Home"
            asp-action="Index">Home</a></li>
        <li><a asp-area="" asp-controller="Home"
            asp-action="About">About</a></li>
        <li><a asp-area="" asp-controller="Home"
            asp-action="Contact">Contact</a></li>
    </ul>
}
```

11. Add the logo image to the *wwwroot/images* folder. You can find all the images
    used in this book in the GitHub repository for this book, or use your own images.

12. To replace the brand text (*VideoOnDemand*) with a logo, you delete the text in
    the <a> tag decorated with the **navbar-brand** class, and add the logo image in its
    place. You can drag the image from the *wwwroot/images* folder.

13. Add the **alt** tag with the text *Brand* to the <img> element you added to the <a>
    tag.

```
<a asp-area="" asp-controller="Home" asp-action="Index"
class="navbar-brand">
    <img alt="Brand" src="~/images/Logos/membership-logo.png" />
</a>
```

14. Add a light gray horizontal bottom border to the navigation bar, and make the
    background color white. Add the CSS selector to the *menu.css* file.

```
.navbar {
    border-bottom: 1px solid #dadada;
    background-color: #fff;
}
```

15. Run the application and log out to verify that the **Home**, **About**, and **Contact**
    links are visible. Log in to the application and verify that the links no longer are
    visible.

Remove the Register and Login Links

The **Register** and **Login** links are redundant since the **Login** form is visible, and a register link is available below the **Login** form. Remove the links from the **_LoginPartial** view.

1. Open the **_LoginPartial** view located in the *Views/Shared* folder.
2. Delete the else-block from the view.
3. Save the file and run the application.
4. Verify that the links no longer appear when logged out.
5. Stop the application in Visual Studio.

Add the Drop-Down Menu

To give the navigation bar a cleaner look, you will remove the **Logout** and **Manage** links (the email greeting link) and add a drop-down link with an avatar and the email address.

1. Open the **_LoginPartial** view located in the *Views/Shared* folder.
2. Remove the **navbar-right** class from the <form> element.
3. Add an <li> element displaying the user's name (which by default is the email address) immediately inside the <ul> element decorated with the **navbar-right** class.
   ```
   <li>@User.Identity.Name</li>
   ```
4. Add another <li> element below the one you just added, and decorate it with the **drop-down** and **pull-right** Bootstrap classes. This will create the drop-down menu item, to which you will add options.
   ```
   <li class="dropdown pull-right">
   ```
5. Add an <a> element inside the previous <li> element. This will be the link to open the menu. Decorate it with the **drop-down-toggle** and **user-drop-down** classes, and give it the id **user-drop-down**. Also add the **data-toggle** attribute set to **drop-down**, the attribute **role** set to **button**, and the **aria-expanded** attribute set to **false**. These settings will ensure that the anchor tag will act as the menu's open/close button, and that the menu is closed by default.
   a. Add the avatar image inside the <a> tag and decorate the <img> element with the classes **img-circle** and **avatar**. Set the image height to 40.
   b. Add a caret symbol by decorating a <span> element with the **caret**, **text-light**, and **hidden-xs** Bootstrap classes. The second class gives the caret a

lighter gray color, and the last class hides the caret on portable devices, or when the browser has a very small size.

```
<a href="#" id="user-dropdown"
    class="dropdown-toggle user-dropdown"
    data-toggle="dropdown" role="button" aria-expanded="false">
    <img src="~/images/avatar.png" class="img-circle avatar"
        alt="" height="40">
    <span class="caret text-light hidden-xs"></span>
</a>
```

6. Add a <ul> element around the two original <li> elements and assign the **drop-down-menu** class and the **role="menu"** attribute to it.

   a. Replace the text and the method call in the <a> element in the first <li> with the text *Settings*.

   b. Replace the <button> element in the second <li> element with an <a> element calling the **submit** method.

   c. Move the <ul> and its <li> elements into the previously added <li> element below the <a> element.

```
<ul class="dropdown-menu" role="menu">
    <li>
        <a asp-area="" asp-controller="Manage" asp-action="Index"
            title="Manage">Settings</a>
    </li>
    <li>
        <a href="javascript:document.getElementById('logoutForm')
            .submit()">Log off</a>
    </li>
</ul>
```

The complete code in the **_LoginPartial** view:

```
@using Microsoft.AspNetCore.Identity
@using VideoOnDemand.Data.Data.Entities

@inject SignInManager<User> SignInManager
@inject UserManager<User> UserManager

@if (SignInManager.IsSignedIn(User))
{
    <form asp-area="" asp-controller="Account" asp-action="Logout"
        method="post" id="logoutForm">
        <ul class="nav navbar-nav navbar-right">
```

```
        <li>@User.Identity.Name</li>
        <li class="dropdown pull-right">
            <a href="#" id="user-dropdown" class="dropdown-toggle
                user-dropdown" data-toggle="dropdown"
                role="button" aria-expanded="false">
                <img src="~/images/avatar.png" class="img-circle
                    avatar" alt="" height="40">
                <span class="caret text-light hidden-xs"></span>
            </a>
            <ul class="dropdown-menu" role="menu">
                <li>
                    <a asp-area="" asp-controller="Manage"
                        asp-action="Index" title="Manage">Settings
                    </a>
                </li>
                <li>
                    <a href="javascript:document.getElementById(
                        'logoutForm').submit()">Log off</a>
                </li>
            </ul>
        </li>
    </ul>
</form>
}
```

Style the Drop-Down Menu

As it stands right now, the drop-down menu leaves a lot to be desired when it comes to styling. You will therefore apply CSS to its elements, to make it look crisp to the user. Add the CSS styling to the *menu.css* file.

When you have finished styling the drop-down menu, it should look like this.

To make the drop-down fit in better with the navigation bar, it has to be positioned 7px from the top and bottom, using padding. Note that the id has to be used for specificity.

```
.dropdown.pull-right {
    padding-top: 0px;
}

#user-dropdown {
    padding: 7px;
}
```

The email has to be pushed down to be aligned to the avatar. Add a 20px top padding and make the text gray.

```
.navbar-right > li {
    padding-top: 18px;
    color: #555;
}
```

Make the drop-down menu's corners more square and give it a more defined border without a drop shadow and padding.

```
.dropdown-menu {
    padding: 0;
    border: 1px solid #dadada;
    border-radius: 2px;
    box-shadow: none;
}
```

The menu items could be a bit larger. Add some padding and change the text color.

```
.dropdown-menu li > a {
    color: #666c74;
    padding: 15px 40px 15px 20px;
}
```

Summary

In this chapter, you modified the navigation bar and added a drop-down menu, all in an effort to make it look more professional and appealing to the user.

Next, you will figure out what Data Transfer Objects are needed to display the data in the *Membership* views.

14. Data Transfer Objects

Introduction

In this chapter, you will begin the creation of the *Membership* views, by figuring out what objects are needed to transfer the necessary data from the server to the client. These objects are referred to as Data Transfer Objects, or DTOs.

In some solutions the DTOs are the same as the entities used to create the database. In this solution you will create DTOs for data transfer only, and entities for database CRUD (Create, Read, Update, Delete) operations. The objects are then transformed from one to the other using AutoMapper that you installed earlier.

Technologies Used in This Chapter
1. **C#** – To create the DTOs.

Overview

Your task is to figure out what DTOs are needed to display the necessary data in the three *Membership* views: **Dashboard**, **Course**, and **Video**.

The DTOs

The best way to figure out what data is needed is to go back and review the use case and look at the mock-view images. Here they are again for easy reference.

Dashboard view

Course View

Video View

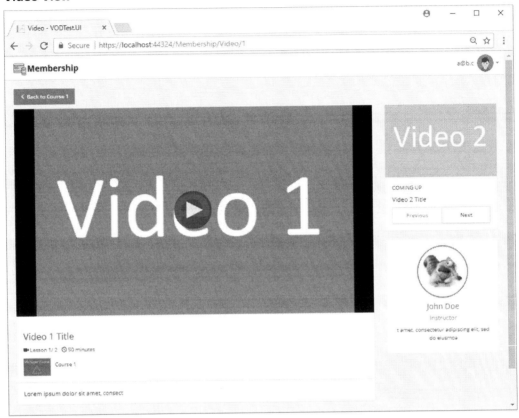

By studying the **Dashboard** view image you can surmise that the following data is needed for a single course panel: course image, title, description, and a button leading to the course view (course id). But if you examine the **Course** view image, you can see that the course also has a marquee image.

How do you translate this into a class? Let's do it together, property by property.

Looking at the **Course** and **Video** view images, you can see that they are more complex. They both have three distinct areas. The **Course** view has a description area with a marquee image, a list of modules, and an instructor bio. Each module also has lists of videos and downloads. The **Video** view has a video area with a description and video information, an area for navigating to previous and next videos, and an instructor bio.

The class will be called **CourseDTO**, and have the following properties:

Property name	Type
CourseId	int
CourseTitle	string
CourseDescription	string
MarqueeImageUrl	string
CourseImageUrl	string

The second class is the **DownloadDTO**, which has the following properties:

Property name	Type
DownloadUrl	string
DownloadTitle	string

The third class is the **VideoDTO**, which has the following properties:

Property name	Type
Id	int
Title	string
Description	string
Duration	string (how long the video is)
Thumbnail	string
Url	string (link to the video)

The fourth class is the **InstructorDTO**, which has the following properties:

Property name	Type
InstructorName	string
InstructorDescription	string
InstructorAvatar	string

The fifth class is the **ModuleDTO**, which has the following properties:

Property name	Type
Id	int
ModuleTitle	string
Videos	List<VideoDto>
Downloads	List<DownloadDto>

The sixth class is the **LessonInfoDTO**, which is used in the *Coming Up* section of the **Video** view.

Property name	Type
LessonNumber	int
NumberOfLessons	int
PreviousVideoId	int (used for the **Previous** button link)
NextVideoId	int (used for the **Next** button link)
NextVideoTitle	string
NextVideoThumbnail	string (the next video's image)

But there's one more DTO, the **UserCourseDTO**, which is used when matching a user with a course. Note that the **DisplayName** attribute is used to change the descriptive text displayed in the form labels for this model.

Property name	Type
UserId	string
CourseId	int
Email	string
CourseTitle	string

Adding the DTOs

Now it's time to add all the DTOs to the project. Let's do it together for one of them, then you can add the rest yourself.

1. Open the project in Visual Studio.
2. Right click on the *Modules* folder in the Solution Explorer and select **Add-New Folder**. Name the folder *DTOModels*.
3. Right click on the *DTOModels* folder and select **Add-Class**.
4. Select the **Class** template.
5. Name the class *CourseDTO* and click the **Add** button.
6. Add the properties from the **CourseDTO** list above.
7. Repeat the steps 3-6 for all other DTOs.

The complete code in the **CourseDTO** class:

```
public class CourseDTO
{
    public int CourseId { get; set; }
    public string CourseTitle { get; set; }
    public string CourseDescription { get; set; }
    public string MarqueeImageUrl { get; set; }
    public string CourseImageUrl { get; set; }
}
```

The complete code in the **DownloadDTO** class:

```
public class DownloadDTO
{
    public string DownloadUrl { get; set; }
    public string DownloadTitle { get; set; }
}
```

The complete code in the **VideoDTO** class:

```
public class VideoDTO
{
    public int Id { get; set; }
    public string Title { get; set; }
    public string Description { get; set; }
    public string Duration { get; set; }
    public string Thumbnail { get; set; }
    public string Url { get; set; }
}
```

The complete code in the **InstructorDTO** class:

```
public class InstructorDTO
{
    public string InstructorName { get; set; }
    public string InstructorDescription { get; set; }
    public string InstructorAvatar { get; set; }
}
```

The complete code in the **ModuleDTO** class:

```
public class ModuleDTO
{
    public int Id { get; set; }
    public string ModuleTitle { get; set; }
    public List<VideoDTO> Videos { get; set; }
    public List<DownloadDTO> Downloads { get; set; }
}
```

The complete code in the **LessonInfoDTO** class:

```
public class LessonInfoDTO
{
    public int LessonNumber { get; set; }
    public int NumberOfLessons { get; set; }
    public int PreviousVideoId { get; set; }
    public int NextVideoId { get; set; }
    public string NextVideoTitle { get; set; }
    public string NextVideoThumbnail { get; set; }
}
```

The complete code in the **UserCourseDTO** class:

Note that the **DisplayName** attribute is used to change the descriptive text displayed in the form labels for this model.

```
public class UserCourseDTO
{
    [DisplayName("User Id")]
    public string UserId { get; set; }
    [DisplayName("Course Id")]
    public int CourseId { get; set; }
    [DisplayName("Email")]
    public string UserEmail { get; set; }
```

```
    [DisplayName("Title")]
    public string CourseTitle { get; set; }
}
```

The View Models

That's great – now you know what the individual DTOs contain – but how do you get the information to the views? With the more complex views, there's no easy way to pass multiple DTOs at the same time. You could use Tuples, but that is hard to implement. A better choice is to use a view model.

A view model is exactly what it sounds like, a model that can contain other objects, and is sent to the view.

There will be three view models, although you could argue that the first one isn't strictly necessary, because it contains only one property. I beg to differ, however, because it will be easier to update the view with more data, if the need should arise.

The first view model is the **DashboardViewModel**, which has only one property. The property data type is somewhat complex; it is a list containing a list. The reason for using a list in a list is that you want to display three course panels on each row. An easy way to make sure that is possible is to add a list containing a maximum of three **CourseDTOs**, one for each row, to the outer list.

Property name	Type
Courses	List<List<CourseDTO>>

The second view model is the **CourseViewModel**, which contains a **CourseDTO**, an **InstructorDTO**, and a list of **ModuleDTOs**.

Property name	Type
Course	CourseDTO
Instructor	InstructorDTO
Modules	IEnumerable<ModuleDTO>

The third view model is the **VideoViewModel**, which contains a **VideoDTO**, an **Instructor-DTO**, a **CourseDTO**, and a **LessonInfoDTO**.

221

Property name	Type
Video	VideoDTO
Instructor	InstructorDTO
Course	CourseDTO
LessonInfo	LessonInfoDTO

Adding the View Models

Now, it's time to add all the view models to the project. Let's do it together for one of them, then you can add the rest yourself.

1. Open the **UI** project in Visual Studio.
2. Right click on the *Modules* folder in the Solution Explorer and select **Add-New Folder**. Name the folder *MembershipViewModels*.
3. Right click on the *MembershipViewModels* folder and select **Add-Class**.
4. Select the **Class** template.
5. Name the class *CourseViewModel* and click the **Add** button.
6. Add the properties from the **CourseViewModel** list above. Don't forget to add a using statement to the **DTOModels** namespace.
7. Repeat steps 3-6 for all the other view models.

The complete **CourseViewModel** class:

```
public class CourseViewModel
{
    public CourseDTO Course { get; set; }
    public InstructorDTO Instructor { get; set; }
    public IEnumerable<ModuleDTO> Modules { get; set; }
}
```

The complete **DashboardViewModel** class:

```
public class DashboardViewModel
{
    public List<List<CourseDTO>> Courses { get; set; }
}
```

The complete **VideoViewModel** class:

```
public class VideoViewModel
{
    public VideoDTO Video { get; set; }
    public InstructorDTO Instructor { get; set; }
    public CourseDTO Course { get; set; }
    public LessonInfoDTO LessonInfo { get; set; }
}
```

Summary

In this chapter, you figured out the Data Transfer Objects (DTOs) needed to display the data in the views. You also figured out how to transport multiple DTOs to the view with one model, a view model.

Next, you will figure out how the data will be stored in a data source using entity classes.

15. Entity Classes

Introduction

In this chapter, you will add the entity classes needed to store data in the data sources. In the next chapter you will implement a mock data repository using the entities you define in this chapter, and later on you will create database tables from the entities.

Now that you have defined the DTOs, you can figure out what the data objects, the entities, should contain. There will not always be a 1-1 match between a DTO and an entity; that's where an object mapper comes into the picture. In a later chapter you will use AutoMapper to convert an entity to a DTO.

Technologies Used in This Chapter

1. **C#** – Creating entity classes.
2. **Attributes** – To define behaviors of entity properties.

Overview

Your task is to use your knowledge about the DTOs to create a set of entity classes that will make up the data sources. Remember that an entity doesn't have to contain all properties of a DTO, and that sometimes it will contain more properties.

The Entities

Let's go back and review the DTOs one at a time, and decide which of their properties should be duplicated in the entities. Some of the entity properties need restrictions, like: maximum length, required, and if it's a primary key in the table.

The Video Entity

Properties of the **VideoDTO**: Id, Title, Description, Duration, Thumbnail, and Url.

The **Video** entity needs the same properties that the DTO has, but it could use a few more. You might want to keep track of a record's position relative to other records, so a **Position** property could be added to the class. Then the **Video** entity needs to know what module it belongs to, which can be solved by adding a **ModuleId** navigation property, as well as a property for the actual module. You will also add navigation properties for the **courseId** and the course. Navigation properties can be used to avoid complex LINQ joins.

225

A video can only belong to one module in this scenario. If you want a video to be used in multiple modules, you need to implement a many-to-many relationship entity between the **Video** and **Module** entities. In this application it is sufficient that a video only can belong to one module and that a module can have multiple videos associated with it.

You could also add a **CourseId** navigation property, to avoid lengthy joins.

Properties in the **Video** entity class:

Property	Type	Attribute/Comment
Id	int	Key (primary key in Entity Framework table)
Title	string	MaxLength(80) and Required
Description	string	MaxLength(1024)
Thumbnail	string	MaxLength(1024)
Url	string	MaxLength(1024)
Position	int	
Duration	int	
ModuleId	int	Navigation property
Module	Module	Navigation property
CourseId	int	Navigation property
Course	Course	Navigation property

The Download Entity

Properties in the **DownloadDTO**: DownloadUrl and DownloadTitle.

Looking back at the **Video** entity, you can surmise that more properties are needed in the **Download** entity than are defined in its DTO class. It needs a unique id, and the same navigation properties as the **Video** entity, as they are listed with the modules.

Note that the property names don't have to be the same in the DTO and the entity. Auto-Mapper can be configured to map between properties with different names. By default it uses auto-mapping between properties with identical names.

Properties in the **Download** entity class:

Property	Type	Attribute/Comment
Id	int	Key (will make it the primary key)
Title	string	MaxLength(80) and Required
Url	string	MaxLength(1024)
ModuleId	int	Navigation property
Module	Module	Navigation property
CourseId	int	Navigation property
Course	Course	Navigation property

The Instructor Entity

Properties in the **InstructorDTO**: InstructorName, InstructorDescription, and Instructor-Avatar.

Apart from the name, description, and avatar properties, the **Instructor** entity needs a unique id and a property that ties it to the **Course** entity. This makes it possible to assign the same instructor to many courses, but each course can only have one instructor. This is implemented by a 1-many relationship, where the many-part is located in the **Instructor** entity. Entity framework knows that it should implement a 1-many relationship if one entity has a collection of the other entity, and the other has a corresponding id.

Properties in the **Instructor** entity class:

Property	Type	Attribute/Comment
Id	int	Key (will make it the primary key)
Name	string	MaxLength(80) and Required
Description	string	MaxLength(1024)
Thumbnail	string	MaxLength(1024)
Courses	List<Course>	Navigation property

The Course Entity

Properties in the **CourseDTO**: CourseId, CourseTitle, CourseDescription, CourseImageUrl, and MarqueeImageUrl.

Apart from the DTO properties, the **Course** entity needs a unique id, an instructor id and a single **Instructor** entity, and a list of **Module** entities.

The single **Instructor** property is the 1 in the 1-many relationship between the **Course** and **Instructor** entities.

The list of **Module** entities is the many in a 1-many relationship between the **Course** entity and the **Module** entities. A course can have many modules, but a module can only belong to one course.

You could change this behavior by implementing another entity that connects the **Course** and the **Module** entities, creating a many-many relationship. Here you'll implement the 1-many relationship.

Property	Type	Attribute/Comment
Id	int	Key (will make it the primary key)
Title	string	MaxLength(80) and Required
Description	string	MaxLength(1024)
ImageUrl	string	MaxLength(255)
MarqueeImageUrl	string	MaxLength(255)
InstructorId	int	Navigation property
Instructor	Instructor	Navigation property
Modules	List<Module>	Navigation property

The Module Entity

Properties in the **ModuleDTO**: Id, ModuleTitle, Videos, and Downloads.

Apart from the DTO properties, the **Module** entity needs a unique id, and needs a navigation property to the **Course** entity it belongs to.

The single **Course** entity is the 1 in a 1-many relationship between the **Course** entity and the **Module** entity. A module can only belong to one course, but a course can have many modules.

The lists of **Video** and **Download** entities are the many part of the 1-many relationships between them and a **Module** entity; in other words, a collection property in an entity class signifies that many records of that type can be associated with the entity. For instance, an order has a 1-many relationship with its order rows, where one order can have many order rows. A module can have many videos and downloads, and a download and a video can only belong to one module.

Property	Type	Attribute/Comment
Id	int	Key (will make it the primary key)
Title	string	MaxLength(80) and Required
CourseId	int	Navigation property
Course	Course	Navigation property
Videos	List<Video>	Navigation property
Downloads	List<Download>	Navigation property

The UserCourse Entity

Properties in the **UserCourseDTO**: UserId, CourseId, CourseTitle, and UserEmail.

Apart from the DTO properties, the **UserCourse** entity needs a navigation property to the **Course** entity. Note that the **UserEmail** property in the DTO isn't persisted to the database; you get that info from the logged in user information.

In earlier versions of Entity Framework, a composite primary key – a primary key made up of more than one property – could be defined using attributes in the entity class. In Entity Framework Core, they are defined in the **DbContext** class, which you will do in a later chapter.

Property	Type	Attribute/Comment
UserId	string	Key (part of primary key)
User	User	Navigation property
CourseId	int	Key (part of primary key)
Course	Course	Navigation property

Adding the Entity Classes

With the entity properties defined, you can create their classes. Let's implement one to-gether, then you can add the rest yourself.

Depending on the order you implement the entity classes, you might end up with proper-ties that aren't fully implemented until other entity classes have been added. For instance, the **Instructor** entity has a property called **Courses**, which is dependent on the **Course** class.

1. Open the **VideoOnDemand.Data** project in the Solution Explorer.
2. Right click on the *Entities* folder and select **Add-Class**.
3. Name the class *Video* and click the **Add** button.
4. Add a public property named **Id** of type **int**.
5. Add the **[Key]** attribute to it, to make it the primary key. You will have to resolve the namespace **System.ComponentModel.DataAnnotations**. Note that the primary key properties in the **UserCourse** class shouldn't have the **[Key]** attribute because they make up a composite key.

   ```
   public class Video
   {
       [Key]
       public int Id { get; set; }
   }
   ```

6. Add another property named **Title** and restrict it to 80 characters. The title should also be required, because the video needs a title.

   ```
   [MaxLength(80), Required]
   public string Title { get; set; }
   ```

7. Add a property of type **string** named **Description** and restrict it to 1024 characters.
8. Add a property of type **string** named **Thumbnail** and restrict it to 1024 characters.
9. Add a property of type **string** named **Url** and restrict it to 1024 characters.
10. Add a property of type **int** named **Duration**.
11. Add a property of type **int** named **Position**.
12. Add a property of type **int** named **ModuleId**.
13. Add a property of type **int** named **CourseId**.

14. Repeat steps 4-7 to add the necessary properties for the other entity classes listed above.

15. Repeat steps 2-5 for the other entities and add the appropriate properties as described earlier.

The complete code for the **Video** entity class:

```
public class Video
{
    [Key]
    public int Id { get; set; }
    [MaxLength(80), Required]
    public string Title { get; set; }
    [MaxLength(1024)]
    public string Description { get; set; }
    public int Duration { get; set; }
    [MaxLength(1024)]
    public string Thumbnail { get; set; }
    [MaxLength(1024)]
    public string Url { get; set; }
    public int Position { get; set; }

    public int ModuleId { get; set; }
    public Module Module { get; set; }
    // Side-step from 3rd normal form for easier
    // access to a video's course
    public int CourseId { get; set; }
    public Course Course { get; set; }
}
```

The complete code for the **Download** entity class:

```
public class Download
{
    [Key]
    public int Id { get; set; }
    [MaxLength(80), Required]
    public string Title { get; set; }
    [MaxLength(1024)]
    public string Url { get; set; }

    public Module Module { get; set; }
    public int ModuleId { get; set; }
```

```
    // Side-step from 3rd normal form for easier
    // access to a video's course
    public Course Course { get; set; }
    public int CourseId { get; set; }
}
```

The complete code for the **Instructor** entity class:

```
public class Instructor
{
    [Key]
    public int Id { get; set; }
    [MaxLength(80), Required]
    public string Name { get; set; }
    [MaxLength(1024)]
    public string Description { get; set; }
    [MaxLength(1024)]
    public string Thumbnail { get; set; }

    public List<Course> Courses { get; set; }
}
```

The complete code for the **Course** entity class:

```
public class Course
{
    [Key]
    public int Id { get; set; }
    [MaxLength(255)]
    public string ImageUrl { get; set; }
    [MaxLength(255)]
    public string MarqueeImageUrl { get; set; }
    [MaxLength(80), Required]
    public string Title { get; set; }
    [MaxLength(1024)]
    public string Description { get; set; }

    public int InstructorId { get; set; }
    public Instructor Instructor { get; set; }
    public List<Module> Modules { get; set; }
}
```

The complete code for the **Module** entity class:

```
public class Module
{
    [Key]
    public int Id { get; set; }
    [MaxLength(80), Required]
    public string Title { get; set; }

    public int CourseId { get; set; }
    public Course Course { get; set; }
    public List<Video> Videos { get; set; }
    public List<Download> Downloads { get; set; }
}
```

The complete code for the **UserCourse** entity class:

```
public class UserCourse
{
    public string UserId { get; set; }
    public User User { get; set; }
    public int CourseId { get; set; }
    public Course Course { get; set; }
}
```

Summary

In this chapter, you discovered and implemented the entity classes, and their properties and restrictions.

Next, you will create a repository interface, and implement it in a class with mock data.

16. Mock Data Repository

Introduction

In this chapter, you will create an interface called **IReadRepository**, which will be a contract that any data source repository can implement for easy reuse. It will also be used whendependency injection is used to inject objects into constructors. This is crucial because it makes it possible to switch one repository for another without breaking the application; it is also a requirement from the customer.

You will implement the interface in a class called **MockReadRepository**, which will be used when building the user interface. Once the UI is working, you will switch to another repository called **SQLReadRepository**, which targets the database you will create in a later chapter.

You will add some dummy data in the **MockReadRepository** class that will act as an in-memory database, containing the same "tables" as the finished database implemented as collections. The collections use the same entity classes as the real database will do when storing the data.

Technologies Used in This Chapter
1. **C#** – To create the interface, repository class, and dummy data.
2. **LINQ** – To query the data in the in-memory database.

Overview

You will create a reusable interface, which will be used by all repositories that communicate with the user interface. You will also create an in-memory database, and fill it with data. Then you will call the repository methods from a controller to make sure that the correct data is returned.

Add the IReadRepository Interface and MockReadRepository Class

First you will add the **IReadRepository** interface, and then implement it in the **MockRead-Repository** class. The interface will be empty to start with, but you will add methods to it throughout this chapter. Once it has been completed, it can be reused by the **SQLRead-Repository** later in the book.

1. Right click on the **Dependencies** node in the **VideoOnDemand.UI** project in the Solution Explorer and select **Add-Add Reference**.
2. Select the **VideoOnDemand.Data** project in the list and click the **OK** button.
3. Right click on the project node in the Solution Explorer and select **Add-New Folder**.
4. Name the folder *Repositories*.
5. Right click on the *Repositories* folder and select **Add-New Item**.
6. Select the **Interface** template.
7. Name it *IReadRepository* and click the **Add** button.
8. Add the **public** access modifier to the class, to make it accessible in the whole solution.
9. Right click on the *Repositories* folder and select **Add-Class**.
10. Name the class *MockReadRepository* and click the **Add** button.
11. Implement the interface in the class.
    ```
    public class MockReadRepository : IReadRepository
    ```
12. Add a region called **Mock Data** to the class.
13. Save the files.

Add Data to the MockReadRepository Class

To build the UI, you need to add dummy data to the **MockReadRepository** class. The data can then be queried from the methods implemented through the **IReadRepository** interface, and used in the views. Add the following data in the **Mock Data** region. You can of course modify the data as you see fit.

The Course List

```
List<Course> _courses = new List<Course> {
    new Course { Id = 1, InstructorId = 1,
        MarqueeImageUrl = "/images/laptop.jpg",
        ImageUrl = "/images/course.jpg", Title = "C# For Beginners",
        Description = "Course 1 Description: A very very long description."
    },
    new Course { Id = 2, InstructorId = 1,
        MarqueeImageUrl = "/images/laptop.jpg",
        ImageUrl = "/images/course2.jpg", Title = "Programming C#",
```

```
            Description = "Course 2 Description: A very very long description."
        },
        new Course { Id = 3, InstructorId = 2,
            MarqueeImageUrl = "/images/laptop.jpg",
            ImageUrl = "/images/course3.jpg", Title = "MVC 5 For Beginners",
            Description = "Course 3 Description: A very very long description."
        }
    };
```

The UserCourses List

You can copy the user id from the **AspNetUsers** table and use it as the user id in the data.

```
List<UserCourse> _userCourses = new List<UserCourse>
{
    new UserCourse { UserId = "4ad684f8-bb70-4968-85f8-458aa7dc19a3",
        CourseId = 1 },
    new UserCourse { UserId = "00000000-0000-0000-0000-000000000000",
        CourseId = 2 },
    new UserCourse { UserId = "4ad684f8-bb70-4968-85f8-458aa7dc19a3",
        CourseId = 3 },
    new UserCourse { UserId = "00000000-0000-0000-0000-000000000000",
        CourseId = 1 }
};
```

The Modules List

```
List<Module> _modules = new List<Module>
{
    new Module { Id = 1, Title = "Module 1", CourseId = 1 },
    new Module { Id = 2, Title = "Module 2", CourseId = 1 },
    new Module { Id = 3, Title = "Module 3", CourseId = 2 }
};
```

The Downloads List

```
List<Download> _downloads = new List<Download>
{
    new Download{Id = 1, ModuleId = 1, CourseId = 1,
        Title = "ADO.NET 1 (PDF)",
        Url = "https://1drv.ms/b/s!AuD5OaH0ExAwn48rX9TZZ3kAOX6Peg" },
    new Download{Id = 2, ModuleId = 1, CourseId = 1,
        Title = "ADO.NET 2 (PDF)",
        Url = "https://1drv.ms/b/s!AuD5OaH0ExAwn48rX9TZZ3kAOX6Peg" },
```

```
        new Download{Id = 3, ModuleId = 3, CourseId = 2,
            Title = "ADO.NET 1 (PDF)",
            Url = "https://1drv.ms/b/s!AuD5OaH0ExAwn48rX9TZZ3kAOX6Peg" }
};
```

The Instructors List

```
List<Instructor> _instructors = new List<Instructor>
{
    new Instructor{ Id = 1, Name = "John Doe",
        Thumbnail = "/images/Ice-Age-Scrat-icon.png",
        Description = "Lorem ipsum dolor sit amet, consectetur elit."
    },
     new Instructor{ Id = 2, Name = "Jane Doe",
         Thumbnail = "/images/Ice-Age-Scrat-icon.png",
         Description = "Lorem ipsum dolor sit, consectetur adipiscing."
     }
};
```

The Videos List

```
List<Video> _videos = new List<Video>
{
    new Video { Id = 1, ModuleId = 1, CourseId = 1, Position = 1,
        Title = "Video 1 Title", Description = "Video 1 Description:
        A very very long description.", Duration = 50,
        Thumbnail = "/images/video1.jpg", Url = "http://some_url/manifest"
    },
    new Video { Id = 2, ModuleId = 1, CourseId = 1, Position = 2,
        Title = "Video 2 Title", Description = "Video 2 Description:
        A very very long description.", Duration = 45,
        Thumbnail = "/images/video2.jpg", Url = "http://some_url/manifest"
    },
    new Video { Id = 3, ModuleId = 3, CourseId = 2, Position = 1,
        Title = "Video 3 Title", Description = "Video 3 Description:
        A very very long description.", Duration = 41,
        Thumbnail = "/images/video3.jpg", Url = "http://some_url/manifest"
    },
    new Video { Id = 4, ModuleId = 2, CourseId = 1, Position = 1,
        Title = "Video 4 Title", Description = "Video 4 Description:
        A very very long description.", Duration = 42,
        Thumbnail = "/images/video4.jpg", Url = "http://some_url/manifest"
    }
};
```

The GetCourses Method

The first method you will add to the **IReadRepository** interface and implement in the **MockReadRepository** class is called **GetCourses**. It takes the user id as a parameter and returns an **IEnumerable** of **Course** objects.

The purpose of this method is to return a list with all courses available to the logged in user.

1. Open the **IReadRepository** interface.
2. Add a method description for the **GetCourses** method. It should return an **IEnumerable** of **Customer** entities. Resolve any missing **using** statements.
   ```
   IEnumerable<Course> GetCourses(string userId);
   ```
3. Open the **MockReadRepository** class and add the method. You can do it manually, or point to the squiggly line under the interface name and add it by clicking on the **Quick Actions** button; select **Implement interface**. Resolve any missing **using** statements.
   ```
   public IEnumerable<Course> GetCourses(string userId) { }
   ```
4. Now you need to write a LINQ query that targets the **_userCourses** list for the logged in user, and join in the **_courses** list to get to the courses.
   ```
   var courses = _userCourses.Where(uc => uc.UserId.Equals(userId))
       .Join(_courses, uc => uc.CourseId, c => c.Id,
           (uc, c) => new { Course = c })
       .Select(s => s.Course);
   ```
5. With the user's courses in a list, you can add the instructor and modules by looping through it and using LINQ to fetch the appropriate data. The course objects have an instructor id, and the modules have a course id assigned to them.
   ```
   foreach (var course in courses)
   {
       course.Instructor = _instructors.SingleOrDefault(
           s => s.Id.Equals(course.InstructorId));
       course.Modules = _modules.Where(
           m => m.CourseId.Equals(course.Id)).ToList();
   }
   ```
6. Return the courses list from the method.
   ```
   return courses;
   ```

The complete code in the **GetCourses** method:

```
public IEnumerable<Course> GetCourses(string userId)
{
    var courses = _userCourses.Where(uc => uc.UserId.Equals(userId))
        .Join(_courses, uc => uc.CourseId, c => c.Id,
            (uc, c) => new { Course = c })
        .Select(s => s.Course);

    foreach (var course in courses)
    {
        course.Instructor = _instructors.SingleOrDefault(
            s => s.Id.Equals(course.InstructorId));
        course.Modules = _modules.Where(
            m => m.CourseId.Equals(course.Id)).ToList();
    }

    return courses;
}
```

Testing the GetCourses Method

1. Open the **HomeController** class and find the **Index** action method. This is the action that is executed when a user navigates to the site.

2. Create an instance of the **MockReadRepository** class called **rep** before any other code inside the **Index** method. Resolve any missing **using** statements.
   ```
   var rep = new MockReadRepository();
   ```

3. Call the **GetCourses** method on the **rep** instance variable and store the result in a variable called **courses**. Don't forget to pass in a valid user id from the **_userCourses** list in the mock data. If you are unsure about which user id to use, you can copy it from the **AspNetUsers** table and paste it in here and in the **_userCourses** collection in the **MockReadRepository** class.
   ```
   var courses = rep.GetCourses(
       "4ad684f8-bb70-4968-85f8-458aa7dc19a3");
   ```

4. Place a breakpoint on the next code line in the **Index** action.

5. Press F5 on the keyboard to debug the application. When the breakpoint is hit, examine the content of the **courses** variable. It should contain a list of all courses available to the logged in user.

6. Stop the application in Visual Studio.

The complete code in the **Index** action:

```
public IActionResult Index()
{
    var rep = new MockReadRepository();
    var courses = rep.GetCourses(
        "4ad684f8-bb70-4968-85f8-458aa7dc19a3");

    if (!_signInManager.IsSignedIn(User))
        return RedirectToAction("Login", "Account");

    return View();
}
```

The GetCourse Method

The next method you will add to the **IReadRepository** interface and implement in the **MockReadRepository** class is called **GetCourse**. It takes a user id and a course id as parameters, and returns a **Course** object.

The purpose of this method is to return a specific course to a user when the button in one of the course panels is clicked.

1. Open the **IReadRepository** interface.
2. Add a method description for the **GetCourse** method. It should return an instance of the **Customer** entity. Resolve any missing **using** statements.
   ```
   Course GetCourse(string userId, int courseId);
   ```
3. Open the **MockReadRepository** class and add the method. Resolve any missing **using** statements.
   ```
   public Course GetCourse(string userId, int courseId) { }
   ```
4. Now you need to write a LINQ query that fetches a single course, using the **_userCourses** and **_courses** lists. Store the result in a variable called **course**.
   ```
   var course = _userCourses.Where(uc => uc.UserId.Equals(userId))
       .Join(_courses, uc => uc.CourseId, c => c.Id,
           (uc, c) => new { Course = c })
       .SingleOrDefault(s => s.Course.Id.Equals(courseId)).Course;
   ```
5. You need to fetch the instructor and assign the result to the **Instructor** property. Use the **InstructorId** property in the **course** object.
   ```
   course.Instructor = _instructors.SingleOrDefault(
       s => s.Id.Equals(course.InstructorId));
   ```

6. You need to fetch the course modules and assign the result to the **Modules** property.

```
course.Modules = _modules.Where(
    m => m.CourseId.Equals(course.Id)).ToList();
```

7. Next, you'll need to fetch the downloads and videos for each module, and assign the results to the **Downloads** and **Videos** properties respectively on each module instance.

```
foreach (var module in course.Modules)
{
    module.Downloads = _downloads.Where(
        d => d.ModuleId.Equals(module.Id)).ToList();
    module.Videos = _videos.Where(
        v => v.ModuleId.Equals(module.Id)).ToList();
}
```

8. Return the course object.

The complete code in the **GetCourse** method:

```
public Course GetCourse(string userId, int courseId)
{
    var course = _userCourses.Where(uc => uc.UserId.Equals(userId))
        .Join(_courses, uc => uc.CourseId, c => c.Id,
            (uc, c) => new { Course = c })
        .SingleOrDefault(s => s.Course.Id.Equals(courseId)).Course;

    course.Instructor = _instructors.SingleOrDefault(
        s => s.Id.Equals(course.InstructorId));

    course.Modules = _modules.Where(
        m => m.CourseId.Equals(course.Id)).ToList();

    foreach (var module in course.Modules)
    {
        module.Downloads = _downloads.Where(
            d => d.ModuleId.Equals(module.Id)).ToList();
        module.Videos = _videos.Where(
            v => v.ModuleId.Equals(module.Id)).ToList();
    }

    return course;
}
```

Testing the GetCourse Method

1. Open the **HomeController** class and find the **Index** action method. This action is executed when a user navigates to the site.
2. Locate the call to the **GetCourses** method in the **Index** action.
3. Call the **GetCourse** method on the **rep** instance variable below the previous method call. Store the result in a variable called **course**. Don't forget to pass in a valid user id from the **_userCourses** list and a valid course id from the **_courses** list in the mock data.

```
var course = rep.GetCourse(
    "4ad684f8-bb70-4968-85f8-458aa7dc19a3", 1);
```

4. Place a breakpoint on the next code line in the **Index** action.
5. Press F5 on the keyboard to debug the application. When the breakpoint is hit, examine the content of the **course** variable. The **course** object's properties should have data, including the **Videos**, **Downloads**, and **Modules** collections.
6. Stop the application in Visual Studio.

The complete code in the **Index** action:

```
public IActionResult Index()
{
    var rep = new MockReadRepository();
    var courses = rep.GetCourses(
        "4ad684f8-bb70-4968-85f8-458aa7dc19a3");
    var course = rep.GetCourse(
        "4ad684f8-bb70-4968-85f8-458aa7dc19a3", 1);


    if (!_signInManager.IsSignedIn(User))
        return RedirectToAction("Login", "Account");

    return View();
}
```

The GetVideo Method

The next method you will add to the **IReadRepository** interface and implement in the **MockReadRepository** class is called **GetVideo**. It takes a user id and a video id as parameters, and returns a **Video** object.

The purpose of this method is to return a specific video that the user requests by clicking on a video in one of the **Course** view's module lists.

1. Open the **IReadRepository** interface.
2. Add a method description for the **GetVideo** method. It should return an instance of the **Video** entity. Resolve any missing **using** statements.
    ```
    Video GetVideo(string userId, int videoId);
    ```
3. Open the **MockReadRepository** class and add the method. Resolve any missing **using** statements.
    ```
    public Video GetVideo(string userId, int videoId) { ... }
    ```
4. Now you need to write a LINQ query that fetches a single video using the **_videos** and **_userCourses** lists. Store the result in a variable called **video**.
    ```
    var video = _videos
        .Where(v => v.Id.Equals(videoId))
        .Join(_userCourses, v => v.CourseId, uc => uc.CourseId,
            (v, uc) => new { Video = v, UserCourse = uc })
        .Where(vuc => vuc.UserCourse.UserId.Equals(userId))
        .FirstOrDefault().Video;
    ```
5. Return the video.
    ```
    return video;
    ```

The complete code in the **GetVideo** method:

```
public Video GetVideo(string userId, int videoId)
{
    var video = _videos
        .Where(v => v.Id.Equals(videoId))
        .Join(_userCourses, v => v.CourseId, uc => uc.CourseId,
            (v, uc) => new { Video = v, UserCourse = uc })
        .Where(vuc => vuc.UserCourse.UserId.Equals(userId))
        .FirstOrDefault().Video;

    return video;
}
```

Testing the GetVideo Method

1. Open the **HomeController** class and find the **Index** action method.
2. Locate the call to the **GetCourse** method in the **Index** action.

3. Call the **GetVideo** method on the **rep** instance variable below the previous method call. Store the result in a variable called **video**. Don't forget to pass in a valid user id from the **_userCourses** list and a valid video id from the **_videos** list in the mock data.

```
var video = rep.GetVideo(
    "4ad684f8-bb70-4968-85f8-458aa7dc19a3", 1);
```

4. Place a breakpoint on the next code line in the **Index** action.
5. Press F5 on the keyboard to debug the application. When the breakpoint is hit, examine the content of the **video** variable.
6. Stop the application in Visual Studio.

The complete code in the **Index** action:

```
public IActionResult Index()
{
    var rep = new MockReadRepository();
    var courses = rep.GetCourses(
        "4ad684f8-bb70-4968-85f8-458aa7dc19a3");
    var course = rep.GetCourse(
        "4ad684f8-bb70-4968-85f8-458aa7dc19a3", 1);
    var video = rep.GetVideo(
        "4ad684f8-bb70-4968-85f8-458aa7dc19a3", 1);

    if (!_signInManager.IsSignedIn(User))
        return RedirectToAction("Login", "Account");

    return View();
}
```

The GetVideos Method

The next method you will add to the **IReadRepository** interface and implement in the **MockReadRepository** class is called **GetVideos**. It takes a user id and an optional module id as parameters, and returns a list of **Video** objects.

The purpose of this method is to return all videos for the logged in user, and display them in the **Course** view. If a module id is passed in, only the videos for that module will be returned.

1. Open the **IReadRepository** Interface.

2. Add a method description for the **GetVideos** class. It should return an **IEnumerable** of the **Video** entity and take a **userId** (**string**) and a **moduleId** (**int**) as parameters. The module id should be assigned the default value for the **int** data type. Resolve any missing **using** statements.

```
IEnumerable<Video> GetVideos(string userId, int moduleId =
default(int));
```

3. Open the **MockReadRepository** class and add the method. Resolve any missing **using** statements.

```
public IEnumerable<Video> GetVideos(string userId,
int moduleId = default(int)) { ... }
```

4. Now you need to write a LINQ query that fetches all videos for the logged in user, using the **_videos** and **_userCourses** lists. Store the result in a variable called **videos**.

```
var videos = _videos
    .Join(_userCourses, v => v.CourseId, uc => uc.CourseId,
        (v, uc) => new { Video = v, UserCourse = uc })
    .Where(vuc => vuc.UserCourse.UserId.Equals(userId));
```

5. Return all the videos in the **videos** collection if the module id is 0 (which is the default value for the **int** data type), otherwise return only the videos in the **videos** collection that match the module id.

```
return moduleId.Equals(0) ?
    videos.Select(s => s.Video) :
    videos.Where(v => v.Video.ModuleId.Equals(moduleId))
        .Select(s => s.Video);
```

The complete code in the **GetVideos** method:

```
public IEnumerable<Video> GetVideos(string userId, int moduleId = 0)
{
    var videos = _videos
        .Join(_userCourses, v => v.CourseId, uc => uc.CourseId,
            (v, uc) => new { Video = v, UserCourse = uc })
        .Where(vuc => vuc.UserCourse.UserId.Equals(userId));

    return moduleId.Equals(0) ?
        videos.Select(s => s.Video) :
        videos.Where(v => v.Video.ModuleId.Equals(moduleId))
            .Select(s => s.Video);
}
```

Testing the GetVideos Method

1. Open the **HomeController** class and find the **Index** action method.
2. Locate the call to the **GetVideo** method in the **Index** action.
3. Call the **GetVideos** method on the **rep** instance variable below the previous method call. Store the result in a variable called **videos**. Don't forget to pass in a valid user id from the **_userCourses** list in the mock data.

   ```
   var videos = rep.GetVideos(
       "4ad684f8-bb70-4968-85f8-458aa7dc19a3");
   ```

4. Call the **GetVideos** method on the **rep** instance variable below the previous method call. Store the result in a variable called **videosForModule**. Don't forget to pass in a valid user id from the **_userCourses** list and a valid module id from the **_modules** list in the mock data.

   ```
   var videosForModule = rep.GetVideos(
       "4ad684f8-bb70-4968-85f8-458aa7dc19a3", 1);
   ```

5. Place a breakpoint on the next code line in the **Index** action.
6. Press F5 on the keyboard to debug the application. When the breakpoint is hit, examine the content of the **videos** and **videosForModule** variables.
7. Stop the application in Visual Studio.
8. Delete all the test variables and the **rep** instance from the **Index** action when you have verified that the correct data is returned.

The complete code in the **Index** action before deleting the variables:

```
public IActionResult Index()
{
    var rep = new MockReadRepository();
    var courses = rep.GetCourses(
        "4ad684f8-bb70-4968-85f8-458aa7dc19a3");
    var course = rep.GetCourse(
        "4ad684f8-bb70-4968-85f8-458aa7dc19a3", 1);
    var video = rep.GetVideo("4ad684f8-bb70-4968-85f8-458aa7dc19a3", 1);
    var videos = rep.GetVideos("4ad684f8-bb70-4968-85f8-458aa7dc19a3");
    var videosForModule = rep.GetVideos(
        "4ad684f8-bb70-4968-85f8-458aa7dc19a3", 1);

    if (!_signInManager.IsSignedIn(User))
        return RedirectToAction("login", "Account");
```

```
        return View();
}
```

The complete code in the **Index** action after deleting the variables:

```
public IActionResult Index()
{
    if (!_signInManager.IsSignedIn(User))
        return RedirectToAction("Login", "Account");

    return View();
}
```

The complete code in the **IReadRepository** interface:

```
public interface IReadRepository
{
    IEnumerable<Course> GetCourses(string userId);
    Course GetCourse(string userId, int courseId);

    Video GetVideo(string userId, int videoId);
    IEnumerable<Video> GetVideos(string userId,
        int moduleId = default(int));
}
```

Summary

In this chapter, you added mock test data to a repository class, created the **IReadReposi-tory** interface, and implemented it in the **MockReadRepository** class. Then you tested the repository class from the **Index** action in the **Home** controller.

Next, you will create the **Membership** controller and add three actions: **Dashboard**, **Course**, and **Video**. These actions will be used when serving up the view to the user. Auto-Mapper and **IReadRepository** instances will be injected into the **Membership** controller. AutoMapper will be used to convert entity objects into DTO objects that can be sent to the UI views, when you add the views in later chapters.

17. The Membership Controller and AutoMapper

Introduction

In this chapter you will create a new **Membership** controller and add its three actions: **Dashboard**, **Course**, and **Video**. For now, they won't be serving up any views. You will use them to implement the mapping between entity objects and DTO objects with Auto-Mapper, and to fetch the data for each action from the **MockReadRepository** you implemented in the previous chapter.

AutoMapper and **IReadRepository** will be injected into the constructor you add to the **Membership** controller. Two other objects are injected into the constructor with Dependency Injection. The first is the **UserManager**, which is used to get the user id from the logged in user, and the second is the **IHttpContextAccessor**, which contains information about the logged in user.

Using AutoMapper removes tedious and boring work, code that you otherwise would have to implement manually to convert one object to another, with the risk of writing errouneous conversion code.

Technologies Used in This Chapter

1. **C#** – Creating controller actions, view models, and mapping objects.
2. **AutoMapper** – To map entity objects to DTO objects.

Overview

You will begin by adding the **Membership** controller and its action methods. Then you will use dependency injection to inject the four previously mentioned objects into the controller's constructor and save them in private class-level variables.

Then you will set up AutoMapper's configuration in the *Startup.cs* file. With that setup complete, you can proceed with the actual mappings in the action methods.

Adding the Membership Controller

You want to keep the membership actions separate from the **HomeController**, which handles the login and registration. To achieve this, you create the **MembershipController** class, and add the membership actions to it.

Three action methods are needed to serve up the views. The first is the **Dashboard** action, which displays the courses the user has access to. From each course panel in the **Dashboard** view, the user can click a button to open the course, using the second action method called **Course**. The **Course** view lists the content for that course. When a user clicks a video item, the video is opened in the **Video** view, which is generated by the **Video** action method.

Adding the Controller

1. Open the **VideoOnDemand.UI** project.
2. Right click on the *Controllers* folder in the Solution Explorer and select **Add-Controller**.
3. Select the **MVC Controller – Empty** template, and click the **Add** button.
4. Name the controller *MembershipController* and click the **Add** button.
5. Rename the **Index** action **Dashboard** and add the **[HttpGet]** attribute to it.
   ```
   [HttpGet]
   public IActionResult Dashboard()
   {
       return View();
   }
   ```
6. Copy the **Dashboard** action method and the attribute.
7. Paste it in twice and rename the methods **Course** and **Video**. Also add an **int** parameter called **id** to them.
   ```
   [HttpGet]
   public IActionResult Course(int id)
   {
       return View();
   }

   [HttpGet]
   public IActionResult Video(int id)
   {
       return View();
   }
   ```

8. Add a constructor to the controller.
```
public MembershipController() { }
```

9. Inject **IHttpContextAccesor** into the constructor and save the user from it to a variable called **user**. Resolve any missing **using** statements.
```
public MembershipController(IHttpContextAccessor
httpContextAccessor) {
    var user = httpContextAccessor.HttpContext.User;
}
```

10. Inject the **UserManager** into the constructor and call its **GetUserId** method. Save the user id in a private class-level variable called **_userId**. Resolve any missing **using** statements.
```
private string _userId;
public MembershipController(IHttpContextAccessor
httpContextAccessor,  UserManager<User> userManager)
{
    var user = httpContextAccessor.HttpContext.User;
    _userId = userManager.GetUserId(user);
}
```

11. Inject **IMapper** into the constructor to get access to AutoMapper in the controller. Save the instance to a private, read-only, class-level variable called **_mapper**.

12. To be able to inject objects from classes that you create, you have to add a service mapping to the **ConfigureServices** method in the *Startup.cs* file. Because you are injecting the **IReadRepository** interface into the constructor, you have to specify what class will be used to serve up the objects. Without the mapping an exception will be thrown.

    a. Open the *Startup.cs* file, and locate the **ConfigureServices** method and go to the end of the method.

    b. Use the **AddSingleton** method to add the connection between **IReadRepository** and **MockReadRepository**. This will ensure that only one instance of the class will be created when the interface is injected into constructors. It will also be very easy to switch the object class in the future. In a later chapter, you will switch the **MockReadRepsitory** class for the **SQLReadRepository** class, which also implements the **IReadRepository** interface.

```
        services.AddSingleton<IReadRepository, MockReadRepository>();
```

13. Inject the **IReadRepository** interface into the constructor and save the instance
to a private class-level variable called **_db**.

```
private IReadRepository _db;
public MembershipController(
IHttpContextAccessor httpContextAccessor,
UserManager<User> userManager,
IMapper mapper, IReadRepository db)
{
    ...
    _db = db;
}
```

The complete **MembershipController** class so far:

```
public class MembershipController : Controller
{
    private string _userId;
    private IReadRepository _db;
    private readonly IMapper _mapper;
    public MembershipController(
    IHttpContextAccessor httpContextAccessor,
    UserManager<User> userManager,
    IMapper mapper, IReadRepository db) {
        // Get Logged in user's UserId
        var user = httpContextAccessor.HttpContext.User;
        _userId = userManager.GetUserId(user);
        _mapper = mapper;
        _db = db;
    }

    [HttpGet]
    public IActionResult Dashboard()
    {
        return View();
    }

    [HttpGet]
    public IActionResult Course(int id)
    {
        return View();
    }
```

```
    [HttpGet]
    public IActionResult Video(int id)
    {
        return View();
    }
}
```

Configuring AutoMapper

For AutoMapper to work properly, you have to add configuration to the **ConfigureServices** method in the *Startup.cs* file. The configuration tells AutoMapper how to map between objects, in this case between entities and DTOs. Default mapping can be achieved by specifying the class names of the objects to be mapped, without naming specific properties. With default matching, only properties with the same name in both classes will be matched.

A more granular mapping can be made by specifying exactly which properties that match. In this scenario the property names can be different in the classes.

1. Open the *Startup.cs* file and locate the **ConfigureServices** method.
2. Go to the end of the method and assign a call to AutoMapper's
   MapperConfiguration method to a variable called **config**.
   ```
   var config = new AutoMapper.MapperConfiguration(cfg =>
   {
   });
   ```
3. Add a mapping for the **Video** entity and **VideoDTO** classes inside the **config** block. Since the properties of interest are named the same in both classes, no specific configuration is necessary.
   ```
   cfg.CreateMap<Video, VideoDTO>();
   ```
4. Add a mapping for the **Download** entity and the **DownloadDTO** classes inside the **config** block. Here specific configuration is necessary since the properties are named differently in the two classes.
   ```
   cfg.CreateMap<Download, DownloadDTO>()
       .ForMember(dest => dest.DownloadUrl,
           src => src.MapFrom(s => s.Url))
       .ForMember(dest => dest.DownloadTitle,
           src => src.MapFrom(s => s.Title));
   ```

5. Now do the same for the **Instructor**, **Course**, and **Module** entities and their DTOs. Note that there are no mappings for the **UserCourseDTO** and **LessonInfoDTO** because we don't need any.

6. Create a variable called **mapper** below the **config** block. Assign the result from a call to the **CreateMapper** method on the previously created **config** object to it.
   ```
   var mapper = config.CreateMapper();
   ```

7. Add the **mapper** object as a singleton instance to the **services** collection, like you did with the **IReadRepository**.
   ```
   services.AddSingleton(mapper);
   ```

8. Place a breakpoint at the end of the **Membership** constructor and start the application. Navigate to *http://localhost:xxxxx/Membership/Dashboard* to hit the constructor, where *xxxxx* is the port used by localhost (IIS) to serve up your application. You can assign a specific port under the **Debug** tab in the project properties dialog.

9. Inspect the class-level variables and verify that the **_db** variable has correct data for all entities.

10. Stop the application and remove the breakpoint.

The complete AutoMapper configuration in the **ConfigurationServices** method:

```
var config = new AutoMapper.MapperConfiguration(cfg =>
{
    cfg.CreateMap<Video, VideoDTO>();

    cfg.CreateMap<Instructor, InstructorDTO>()
        .ForMember(dest => dest.InstructorName,
            src => src.MapFrom(s => s.Name))
        .ForMember(dest => dest.InstructorDescription,
            src => src.MapFrom(s => s.Description))
        .ForMember(dest => dest.InstructorAvatar,
            src => src.MapFrom(s => s.Thumbnail));

    cfg.CreateMap<Download, DownloadDTO>()
        .ForMember(dest => dest.DownloadUrl,
            src => src.MapFrom(s => s.Url))
        .ForMember(dest => dest.DownloadTitle,
            src => src.MapFrom(s => s.Title));
```

```
    cfg.CreateMap<Course, CourseDTO>()
        .ForMember(dest => dest.CourseId, src =>
            src.MapFrom(s => s.Id))
        .ForMember(dest => dest.CourseTitle,
            src => src.MapFrom(s => s.Title))
        .ForMember(dest => dest.CourseDescription,
            src => src.MapFrom(s => s.Description))
        .ForMember(dest => dest.MarqueeImageUrl,
            src => src.MapFrom(s => s.MarqueeImageUrl))
        .ForMember(dest => dest.CourseImageUrl,
            src => src.MapFrom(s => s.ImageUrl));

    cfg.CreateMap<Module, ModuleDTO>()
        .ForMember(dest => dest.ModuleTitle,
            src => src.MapFrom(s => s.Title));
});

var mapper = config.CreateMapper();
services.AddSingleton(mapper);
```

Implementing the Action Methods

Now that you have set everything up for object mapping with AutoMapper, it's time to utilize that functionality in the three action methods you added to the **Membership-Controller** class earlier.

The Dashboard Action Method

This action will serve data to the **Dashboard** view, which you will add in a later chapter. The view will be served an instance of the **DashboardViewModel** class that you created in an earlier chapter.

The purpose of the **Dashboard** action method is to fill the **DashboardViewModel** with the appropriate data, using the **_db** in-mamory database that you added to the **MockRead-Repository** class. The **MockReadRepository** object was injected into the **Membership** constructor through the **IReadRepository** parameter, using dependency injection that you configured in the **ConfigureServices** method in the **Startup** class.

Your next task will be to fill the view model using AutoMapper, mapping data from the **_db** database to DTO objects that can be used in views that you will add in coming chapters.

The view will be able to display as many courses as the user has access to, but only three to a row. This means that you will have to divide the list of courses into a list of lists, with three **CourseDTO** objects each. This will make it easy to loop out the panels in the view when it is implemented.

To refresh your memory, this is the view that this action method will be serving up.

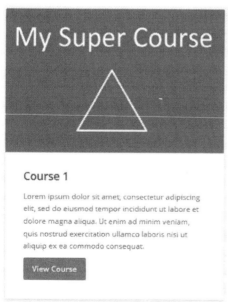

1. Open the **MembershipController** class and locate the **Dashboard** action method.
2. Call the **Map** method on the **_mapper** variable in the **Dashboard** action method to convert the result from a call to the **GetCourses** method on the **_db** variable; don't forget to pass in the logged in user's id, not a hardcoded value. This should fetch all the courses for the user and convert them into **CourseDTO** objects. Store the result in a variable named **courseDtoObjects**.

```
var courseDtoObjects = _mapper.Map<List<CourseDTO>>(
    _db.GetCourses(_userId));
```

3. Clear all breakpoints in the controller class.
4. Place a breakpoint on the return statement at the end of the **Dashboard** action method.
5. Run the application with debugging (F5).
6. Navigate to *http://localhost:xxxxx/Membership/Dashboard* to hit the breakpoint.
7. Inspect the **courseDtoObjects** variable to verify that it contains **CourseDTO** objects with data. If no courses are returned, then log in as a user represented in the **_userCourses** list in the **MockReadRepository** class or replace one of the user ids in the list with one for the logged in user from the **AspNetUsers** table.

```
[HttpGet]
public IActionResult Dashboard()
{
    var courseDtoObjects = _mapper.Map<List<CourseDTO>>(_db.GetCourse
                      ◢ ● courseDtoObjects  Count = 2  ◖
    return View();            ▷ ● [0]      {VideoOnDemand.Models.DTOModels.CourseDTO}
                              ▷ ● [1]      {VideoOnDemand.Models.DTOModels.CourseDTO}  ◀
}                             ▷ ● Raw View
```

8. Stop the application in Visual Studio.
9. Create an instance of the **DashboardViewModel** and the **Courses** property on the model below the **courseDtoObjects** variable. Note that the **Courses** property is a list of lists, where each of the inner lists will contain a maximum of three **CourseDTO** objects, to satisfy the view's needs.

```
var dashboardModel = new DashboardViewModel();
dashboardModel.Courses = new List<List<CourseDTO>>();
```

10. Divide the **CourseDTOs** in the **courseDtoObjects** collection into sets of three, and add them to new **List<CourseDTO>** instances.

```
var noOfRows - courseDtoObjects.Count <= 3 ? 1 :
    courseDtoObjects.Count / 3;
```

```
for (var i = 0; i < noOfRows; i++) {
    dashboardModel.Courses.Add(courseDtoObjects.Take(3).ToList());
}
```

11. Return the **DashboardViewModel** instance in the **View** method.

    ```
    return View(dashboardModel);
    ```

12. Make sure that the breakpoint is still on the return statement, and start the application with debugging (F5).

13. Navigate to *http://localhost:xxxxx/Membership/Dashboard* to hit the breakpoint.

14. Inspect the **dashboardModel** variable and verify that its **Courses** property contains at least one list of **CourseDTO** objects.

15. Stop the application in Visual Studio and remove the breakpoint.

The complete code for the **Dashboard** action:

```
[HttpGet]
public IActionResult Dashboard()
{
    var courseDtoObjects = _mapper.Map<List<CourseDTO>>(
        _db.GetCourses(_userId));

    var dashboardModel = new DashboardViewModel();
    dashboardModel.Courses = new List<List<CourseDTO>>();

    var noOfRows = courseDtoObjects.Count <= 3 ? 1 :
        courseDtoObjects.Count / 3;
    for (var i = 0; i < noOfRows; i++)
    {
        dashboardModel.Courses.Add(courseDtoObjects.Take(3).ToList());
    }

    return View(dashboardModel);
}
```

The Course Action Method

This action will serve data to the **Course** view, which you will add in a later chapter. The view will be served an instance of the **CourseViewModel** class that you created in a previous chapter.

The purpose of the **Course** action method is to fill that view model with the appropriate data using the **_db** in-mamory database that you added to the **MockReadRepository**. The **MockReadRepository** was injected into the **Membership** constructor through the **IRead-Repository** parameter using dependency injection, which you configured in the **Configure-Services** method in the **Startup** class.

Your next task will be to fill the view model using AutoMapper, to map data from the **_db** entities to DTO objects that can be used in views that you will add in coming chapters.

The view will display the selected course and its associated modules. Each module will list the videos and downloadables associated with it. The instructor bio will also be displayed beside the module list.

To refresh your memory, this is the view that this action method will be serving up.

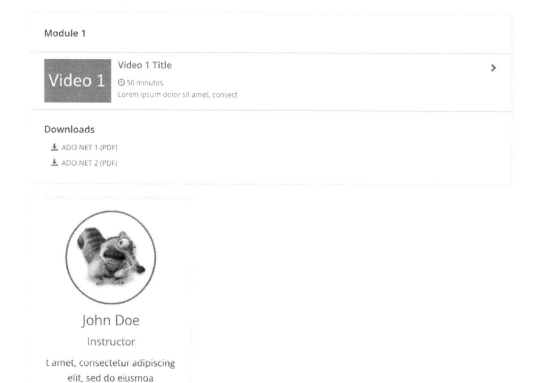

1. Open the **MembershipController** class and locate the **Course** action method.
2. Fetch the course matching the id passed in to the **Course** action and the logged in user's user id, by calling the **GetCourse** method on the **_db** variable. Store the result in a variable called **course**.

```
var course = _db.GetCourse(_userId, id);
```

3. Call the **Map** method on the **_mapper** variable to convert the course you just fetched into a **CourseDTO** object. Store the result in a variable named **mappedCourseDTOs**.

```
var mappedCourseDTOs = _mapper.Map<CourseDTO>(course);
```

4. Call the **Map** method on the **_mapper** variable to convert the **Instructor** object in the **course** object into an **InstructorDTO** object. Store the result in a variable named **mappedInstructorDTO**.

```
var mappedInstructorDTO =
_mapper.Map<InstructorDTO>(course.Instructor);
```

5. Call the **Map** method on the **_mapper** variable to convert the **Modules** collection in the **course** object into a **List<ModuleDTO>**. Store the result in a variable named **mappedModuleDTOs**.

```
var mappedModuleDTOs =
_mapper.Map<List<ModuleDTO>>(course.Modules);
```

6. Loop over the **mappedModuleDTOs** collection to fetch the videos and downloads associated with the modules. Use AutoMapper to convert videos and downloads in the **course** object's **Modules** collection to **List<VideoDTO>** and **List<DownloadDTO>** collections. Assign the collections to their respective properties in the loop's current **ModuleDTO**.

```
for (var i = 0; i < mappedModuleDTOs.Count; i++)
{
    mappedModuleDTOs[i].Downloads =
        course.Modules[i].Downloads.Count.Equals(0) ? null :
            _mapper.Map<List<DownloadDTO>>(
                course.Modules[i].Downloads);

    mappedModuleDTOs[i].Videos =
        course.Modules[i].Videos.Count.Equals(0) ? null :
            _mapper.Map<List<VideoDTO>>(course.Modules[i].Videos);
}
```

7. Create an instance of the **CourseViewModel** class named **courseModel**.

8. Assign the three mapped collections: **mappedCourseDTOs**, **mappedInstructorDTO**, and **mappedModuleDTOs** to the **courseModel** object's **Course**, **Instructor**, and **Modules** properties.

```
var courseModel = new CourseViewModel
{
    Course = mappedCourseDTOs,
    Instructor = mappedInstructorDTO,
    Modules = mappedModuleDTOs
};
```

9. Return the **courseModel** object with the **View** method.

```
return View(courseModel);
```

10. Place a breakpoint on the **return** statement at the end of the **Course** action.

11. Run the application with debugging (F5).

12. Navigate to *http://localhost:xxxxx/Membership/Course/1* to hit the breakpoint.

13. Inspect the **courseModel** variable to verify that it contains a course, an instructor, and modules with videos and downloads.
14. Stop the application in Visual Studio and remove the breakpoint.

The complete code for the **Course** action:

```
[HttpGet]
public IActionResult Course(int id)
{
    var course = _db.GetCourse(_userId, id);
    var mappedCourseDTOs = _mapper.Map<CourseDTO>(course);
    var mappedInstructorDTO =
        _mapper.Map<InstructorDTO>(course.Instructor);
    var mappedModuleDTOs =
        _mapper.Map<List<ModuleDTO>>(course.Modules);

    for (var i = 0; i < mappedModuleDTOs.Count; i++)
    {
        mappedModuleDTOs[i].Downloads =
            course.Modules[i].Downloads.Count.Equals(0) ? null :
            _mapper.Map<List<DownloadDTO>>(
                course.Modules[i].Downloads);

        mappedModuleDTOs[i].Videos =
            course.Modules[i].Videos.Count.Equals(0) ? null :
            _mapper.Map<List<VideoDTO>>(course.Modules[i].Videos);
    }

    var courseModel = new CourseViewModel
    {
        Course = mappedCourseDTOs,
        Instructor = mappedInstructorDTO,
        Modules = mappedModuleDTOs
    };

    return View(courseModel);
}
```

The Video Action Method

In this action, you will create an instance of the **VideoViewModel** class you added earlier. This model will then be sent to a **Video** view that you will add in an upcoming chapter.

The model will be filled with appropriate data, using the **_db** in-memory database that you added to the **MockReadRepository** class. The **MockReadRepository** was injected into the **Membership** controller's constructor through the **IReadRepository** parameter, using dependency injection. You configured the DI in the **ConfigureServices** method in the **Startup** class.

Your next task will be to fill the view model using AutoMapper, mapping data from the **_db** database to DTO objects that can be used in views in coming chapters.

The **Video** view will display the selected video, information about the video, buttons to select the next and previous videos, and an instructor bio.

To refresh your memory, this is the view the **Video** action will display.

Video 1 Title

 Lesson 1/ 2 🕐 50 minutes

 Course 1

Lorem ipsum dolor sit amet, consect

COMING UP

Video 2 Title

Previous	Next

John Doe

Instructor

t amet, consectetur adipiscing elit, sed do eiusmoa

1. Open the **MembershipController** class and locate the **Video** action method.
2. Call the **_db.GetVideo** method to fetch the video matching the id passed in to the **Video** action, and the logged in user's id. Store the result in a variable called **video**.

```
var video = _db.GetVideo(_userId, id);
```

3. Call the **_db.GetCourse** method to fetch the course matching the **CourseId** property in the **video** object, and the logged in user's id. Store the result in a variable called **course**.

    ```
    var course = _db.GetCourse(_userId, video.CourseId);
    ```

4. Call the **_mapper.Map** method to convert the **Video** object into a **VideoDTO** object. Store the result in a variable named **mappedVideoDTO**.

    ```
    var mappedVideoDTO = _mapper.Map<VideoDTO>(video);
    ```

5. Call the **_mapper.Map** method to convert the **course** object into a **CourseDTO** object. Store the result in a variable named **mappedCourseDTOs**.

    ```
    var mappedCourseDTO = _mapper.Map<CourseDTO>(course);
    ```

6. Call the **_mapper.Map** method to convert the **Instructor** object in the **course** object into an **InstructorDTO** object. Store the result in a variable named **mappedInstructorDTO**.

    ```
    var mappedInstructorDTO =
    _mapper.Map<InstructorDTO>(course.Instructor);
    ```

7. Call the **_db.GetVideos** method to fetch all the videos matching the current module id. You need this data to get the number of videos in the module, and to get the index of the current video. Store the videos in a variable called **videos**.

    ```
    var videos = _db.GetVideos(_userId, video.ModuleId).ToList();
    ```

8. Store the number of videos in a variable called **count**.

    ```
    var count = videos.Count();
    ```

9. Find the index of the current video in the module video list. You will display the index and the video count to the user, in the view. Store the value in a variable called **index**.

    ```
    var index = videos.IndexOf(video);
    ```

10. Fetch the id for the previous video in the module by calling the **ElementAtOrDefault** method on the **videos** collection. Store its id in a variable called **previousId**.

    ```
    var previous = videos.ElementAtOrDefault(index - 1);
    var previousId = previous == null ? 0 : previous.Id;
    ```

11. Fetch the id, title, and thumbnail for the next video in the module by calling the **ElementAtOrDefault** method on the **videos** collection. Store the values in variables called **nextId**, **nextTitle**, and **nextThumb**.

```
var next = videos.ElementAtOrDefault(index + 1);
var nextId = next == null ? 0 : next.Id;
var nextTitle = next == null ? string.Empty : next.Title;
var nextThumb = next == null ? string.Empty : next.Thumbnail;
```

12. Create an instance of the **VideoViewModel** class named **videoModel**.

```
var videoModel = new VideoViewModel
{
};
```

13. Assign the three mapped collections: **mappedCourseDTOs**, **mappedInstructorDTO**, and **mappedVideoDTOs** to the **videoModel** object's **Course**, **Instructor**, and **Video** properties. Create an instance of the **LessonInfoDTO** for the **LessonInfo** property in the **videoModel** object and assign the variable values to its properties. The **LessonInfoDTO** will be used with the previous and next buttons, and to display the index of the current video.

```
var videoModel = new VideoViewModel
{
    Video = mappedVideoDTO,
    Instructor = mappedInstructorDTO,
    Course = mappedCourseDTO,
    LessonInfo = new LessonInfoDTO
    {
        LessonNumber = index + 1,
        NumberOfLessons = count,
        NextVideoId = nextId,
        PreviousVideoId = previousId,
        NextVideoTitle = nextTitle,
        NextVideoThumbnail = nextThumb
    }
};
```

14. Return the **videoModel** object with the **View** method.

```
return View(videoModel);
```

15. Place a breakpoint on the return statement at the end of the **Video** action.

16. Run the application with debugging (F5).

17. Navigate to *http://localhost:xxxxx/Membership/Video/1* to hit the breakpoint.

18. Inspect the **videoModel** object to verify that it contains a video, a course, an instructor, and a lesson info object.

19. Stop the application in Visual Studio and remove the breakpoint.

The complete code for the **Video** action:

```
[HttpGet]
public IActionResult Video(int id)
{
    var video = _db.GetVideo(_userId, id);
    var course = _db.GetCourse(_userId, video.CourseId);
    var mappedVideoDTO = _mapper.Map<VideoDTO>(video);
    var mappedCourseDTO = _mapper.Map<CourseDTO>(course);
    var mappedInstructorDTO =
        _mapper.Map<InstructorDTO>(course.Instructor);

    // Create a LessonInfoDto object
    var videos = _db.GetVideos(_userId, video.ModuleId).ToList();
    var count = videos.Count();
    var index = videos.IndexOf(video);
    var previous = videos.ElementAtOrDefault(index - 1);
    var previousId = previous == null ? 0 : previous.Id;
    var next = videos.ElementAtOrDefault(index + 1);
    var nextId = next == null ? 0 : next.Id;
    var nextTitle = next == null ? string.Empty : next.Title;
    var nextThumb = next == null ? string.Empty : next.Thumbnail;

    var videoModel = new VideoViewModel
    {
        Video = mappedVideoDTO,
        Instructor = mappedInstructorDTO,
        Course = mappedCourseDTO,
        LessonInfo = new LessonInfoDTO
        {
            LessonNumber = index + 1,
            NumberOfLessons = count,
            NextVideoId = nextId,
            PreviousVideoId = previousId,
            NextVideoTitle = nextTitle,
            NextVideoThumbnail = nextThumb
        }
    };
    return View(videoModel);
}
```

Summary

In this chapter, you added configuration for the entity and DTO classes to AutoMapper in the **Startup** class. You also implemented the **Membership** controller and injected the necessary objects into its constructor. Then you implemented the three actions (**Dashboard**, **Course**, and **Video**) that will be used when rendering their corresponding views in coming chapters.

Next, you will implement the **Dashboard** view, and render it from the **Dashboard** action.

18. The Dashboard View

Introduction

In this chapter, you will add a **Dashboard** view to the *Views/Membership* folder. It will be rendered by the **Dashboard** action in the **Membership** controller. This is the first view the user sees after logging in; it lists all the courses the user has access to.

The courses are displayed three to a row, to make them the optimal size.

Technologies Used in This Chapter

1. **HTML** – To create the view's layout.
2. **CSS** – To style the view.
3. **Razor** – To use C# in the view.

Overview

Your task is to use the view model in the **Dashboard** action to render a view that displays the user's courses in a list. Each course should be displayed as a panel with the course image, title, description, and a button that opens the **Course** view for that course.

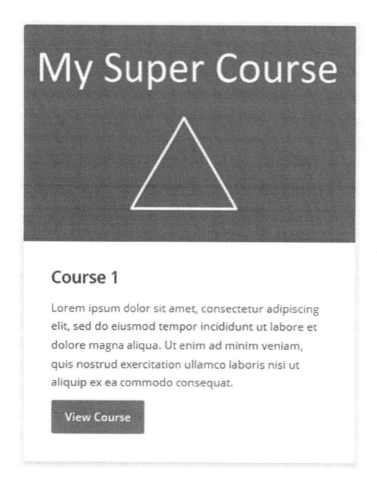

Implementing the Dashboard View

First, you will add the **Dashboard** view to the *Views/Membership* folder. Then you will add markup to the view, displaying the courses as panels. Looping over the courses in the view model, each panel will be rendered using a partial view called **_CoursePanelPartial**.

Adding the Dashboard View

To follow convention, the **Dashboard** view must reside in a folder named *Membership* located inside the *Views* folder. The convention states that a view must have the same name as the action displaying it, and it must be placed in a folder with the same name as the controller, inside the *Views* folder.

1. Open the **Membership** controller.
2. Right click on, or in, the **Dashboard** action and select **Add View** in the context menu.
3. You can keep the preselected values and click the **Add** button. This will add the necessary *Membership* folder to the *Views* folder, and scaffold the **Dashboard** view.

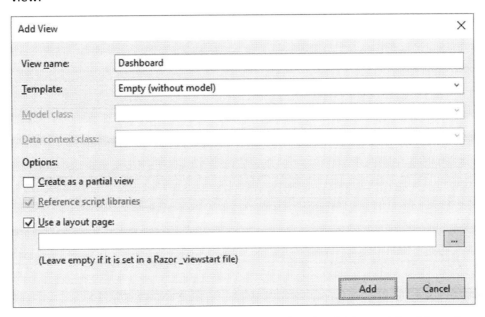

4. Open the *Views* folder and verify that the *Membership* folder and **Dashboard** view have been created.
5. Visual Studio can get confused when a view is scaffolded, and display errors that aren't real. Close the view and open it again to get rid of those errors.
6. Open the **_ViewImports** view and add a **using** statement for the **VideoOnDemand.UI.Models.MembershipViewModels** namespace, to get access to the **DashboardViewModel** class.
   `@using VideoOnDemand.UI.Models.MembershipViewModels`

7. Add an **@model** directive for the **DashboardViewModel** class at the beginning of the view.
   `@model DashboardViewModel`

8. Open the **HomeController** class and locate the **Index** action.

9. Remove the **View** method call from the **return** statement and add a redirect to the **Dashboard** action in the **Membership** controller.

```
return RedirectToAction("Dashboard", "Membership");
```

10. Start the application without debugging (Ctrl+F5) and log in if necessary. The text *Dashboard* should be displayed in the browser if the **Dashboard** view was rendered correctly.

The markup in the **Dashboard** view:

```
@model DashboardViewModel

@{
    ViewData["Title"] = "Dashboard";
}

<h2>Dashboard</h2>
```

The complete code for the **Index** action in the **Home** controller:

```
public IActionResult Index()
{
    if (!_signInManager.IsSignedIn(User))
        return RedirectToAction("Login", "Account");

    return RedirectToAction("Dashboard", "Membership");
}
```

Iterating Over the Courses in the Dashboard View

To display the courses three to a row, you have to add two **foreach** loops to the view. The outer loop iterates over the **Courses** collection (the parent collection) to create the rows, and the inner loop iterates over the (three) courses on that row.

For now, the view will only display a view title and the course titles; later the courses will be displayed here as panels.

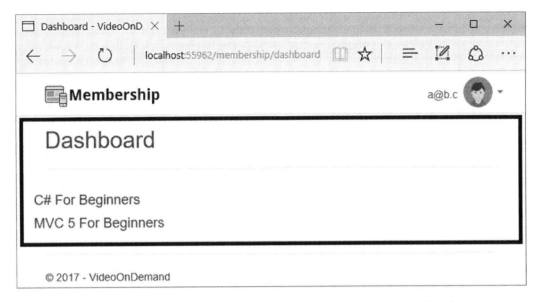

1. Add a CSS class called **text-dark** to the <h2>. You will use this class later to change the text color to a dark gray. Note that the class name isn't **dark-gray** or **gray**; If you name it text-dark, you don't have to remove or rename the class if the color or font weight is changed.
   ```
   <h2 class="text-dark">Dashboard</h2>
   ```

2. Add a <div> element around the <h2> element. Add two CSS classes called **membership** and **top-margin** to the <div>. The **membership** class is the main class for all *membership* views. The **top-margin** class will be used to add a top margin to all *membership* views.
   ```
   <div class="membership top-margin">
       <h2 class="text-dark">Dashboard</h2>
   </div>
   ```

3. Add a horizontal line below the <h2> element. Add two CSS classes called **thick** and **margin** to the <hr> element. These classes will be used to make the line thicker and give it a margin.
   ```
   <hr class="thick margin">
   ```

4. Add a **foreach** loop, below the <hr> element, that iterates over the **Course** collection in the view model. This loop represents the rows containing the course panels, where each row should have at most tree courses.
   ```
   @foreach (var dashboardRow in Model.Courses) { }
   ```

5. Add a <div> inside the loop and decorate it with the **row** Bootstrap class. The **row** class will style the <div> as a new row in the browser.
```
<div class="row">
</div>
```

6. Add a **foreach** loop inside the <div> that iterates over the (three) courses on that row. For now, add an <h4> element displaying the course title.
```
@foreach (var course in dashboardRow)
{
    <h4>@course.CourseTitle</h4>
}
```

7. Switch to the browser and refresh the **Dashboard** view (/*membership/dashboard*). The course titles should be displayed below the view's title.

The markup in the **Dashboard** view, so far:

```
@model DashboardViewModel

@{
    ViewData["Title"] = "Dashboard";
}

<div class="membership top-margin">
    <h2 class="text-dark">Dashboard</h2>
    <hr class="thick margin">
    @foreach (var dashboardRow in Model.Courses)
    {
        <div class="row">
            @foreach (var course in dashboardRow)
            {
                <h4>@course.CourseTitle</h4>
            }
        </div>
    }
</div>
```

Creating the _CoursePanelPartial Partial View

Instead of cluttering the **Dashboard** view with the course panel markup, you will create a partial view called **_CoursePanelPartial** that will be rendered for each course. A Bootstrap **panel** will be used to display the course information.

1. Right click on the *Views/Membership* folder and select **Add-View**.

2. Name the view **_CoursePanelPartial** and check the **Create as partial view** checkbox before clicking the **Add** button.

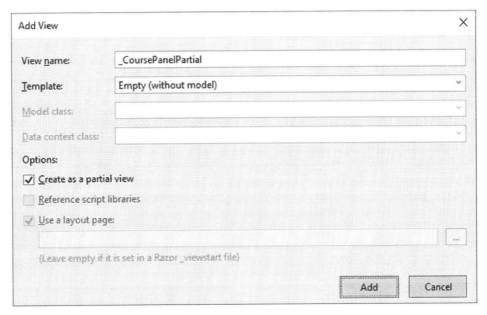

3. Delete all code in the view.

4. Open the **_ViewImports** view and add a **using** statement for the **VideoOnDemand.UI.Models.DTOModels** namespace. Save the file and close it.
    ```
    @using VideoOnDemand.UI.Models.DTOModels
    ```

5. Add an **@model** directive for the **CourseDTO** class to the partial view.
    ```
    @model CourseDTO
    ```

6. Add a <div> element and decorate it with the **col-sm-4** Bootstrap class, to give it 1/3 of the row space. The **col-sm-** classes have to add up to 12 on a row, and since 3 courses are added to each row, that is fulfilled.
    ```
    <div class="col-sm-4">
    </div>
    ```

7. Add a <div> inside the previous <div> and decorate it with the Bootstrap **panel** class to style it as a panel, the outer most container for the course information. Also add a CSS class called **course-listing**. It will act as a main selector, for specificity, and to keep the styles separate from other styles.

```
<div class="panel course-listing">
</div>
```

8. Add an <img> element decorated with a CSS class called **thumb** to the previous <div>. The class will be used when styling the image. Add the **CourseImageUrl** property in the view model as the image source.
```
<img class="thumb" src="@Model.CourseImageUrl">
```

9. Add a <div> element below the image and decorate it with the **panel-body** Bootstrap class. This is the area where the video information is displayed.
```
<div class="panel-body">
</div>
```

10. Add an <h3> element in the previous <div> and decorate it with a CSS class named **text-dark**. Add the **CourseTitle** property in the view model to it.
```
<h3 class="text-dark">@Model.CourseTitle</h3>
```

11. Add a <p> element for the **CourseDescription** view model property below the <h3> element.
```
<p>@Model.CourseDescription</p>
```

12. Add an <a> element below the description and style it as a blue button with the **btn btn-primary** Bootstrap classes. Use the **CourseId** view model property in the **href** URL to determine which course will be fetched by the **Course** action, and displayed by the **Course** view. Add the text *View Course* to the button.
```
<a class="btn btn-primary"
href="~/Membership/Course/@Model.CourseId">View Course</a>
```

13. Open the **Dashboard** view.

14. Replace the <h4> element with a call to the **PartialAsync** method that will render the **_CoursePanelPartial** partial view for each course.
```
@foreach (var course in dashboardRow)
{
    @await Html.PartialAsync("_CoursePanelPartial", course)
}
```

15. Save all files and refresh the **Dashboard** view in the browser. As you can see, the view needs styling, which will be your next task.

The complete markup for the **_CoursePanelPartial** partial view:

```
@model CourseDTO

<div class="col-sm-4">
    <div class="panel course-listing">
        <img class="thumb" src="@Model.CourseImageUrl">
        <div class="panel-body">
            <h3 class="text-dark">@Model.CourseTitle</h3>
            <p>@Model.CourseDescription</p>
            <a class="btn btn-primary"
              href="~/Membership/Course/@Model.CourseId">View Course</a>
        </div>
    </div>
</div>
```

Styling the Dashboard View and the _CoursePanelPartial Partial View

Now, you will use the CSS classes you added to the **Dashboard** view and the **_CoursePanel-Partial** partial view to style them with CSS. To do that, you will add two CSS style sheets called *membership.css* and *course-panel.css*. The *membership.css* file will contain CSS selectors that are reused in all the *Membership* views.

1. Right click on the *wwwroot/css* folder and select **Add-New Item**.
2. Select the **Style Sheet** template.
3. Name the style sheet *membership.css* and click the **Add** button.
4. Repeat steps 1-3 for the *course-panel.css* style sheet.
5. Open the **_Layout** view and add links to the files in the **Development** <environment> element inside the <head> element.
   ```
   <link rel="stylesheet" href="~/css/membership.css" />
   <link rel="stylesheet" href="~/css/course-panel.css" />
   ```
6. Open the *bundleconfig.json* file and add references to the CSS files.
   ```
   "wwwroot/css/membership.css",
   "wwwroot/css/course-panel.css"
   ```

Add the following CSS selectors one at a time to the *membership.css* file and save it. Refresh the browser and observe the changes.

Add a 25px top margin to the main <div> in the **Dashboard** view.

```
.membership.top-margin {
    margin-top: 25px;
}
```

Change the <h2> header color to a dark gray and make the font size smaller.

```
.membership h2 {
    font-size: 1.5em;
}

.membership .text-dark {
    color: #454c56 !important;
}
```

Change the color of the horizontal line to a light gray and make it thicker. Set its top margin to 15px and its bottom margin to 25px.

```
.membership hr {
    border-top: 1px solid #dadada;
}

    .membership hr.thick {
        border-top-width: 2px;
    }

    .membership hr.margin {
        margin: 15px 0 25px;
    }
```

Make the font size smaller and the font bold for all <h3> elements. This will affect the course title in the **Dashboard** view.

```
.membership h3 {
    font-size: 1.25em;
    font-weight: 600;
}
```

Make the font size smaller and the line height larger for all <p> and <a> elements. This will affect the course description and the buttons in the *Membership* views.

```
.membership p, .membership a {
    font-size: 0.875em;
    font-weight: 400;
    line-height: 1.6;
}
```

Style the **btn-primary** Bootstrap buttons in the *Membership* views to have a lighter blue color, more padding, smaller border radius, larger font-weight, and no border or outline.

```
.membership a.btn {
    font-weight: 800;
    padding: 9px 15px;
    border-radius: 2px;
}

    .membership a.btn.btn-primary {
        background-color: #2d91fb;
        outline: none;
        border: none;
    }

        .membership a.btn.btn-primary:hover {
            background-color: #0577f0;
            border-color: #0577f0;
        }
```

Change the font to Google's Open Sans for the entire application. If you want other font settings, you can create your own CSS link at Google.

Add a link to the Google font in the **_Layout** view's <head> element.

1. Open the **_Layout** view.
2. Add the font link to the <head> element.
   ```
   <link href="https://fonts.googleapis.com/css?
       family=Open+Sans:400,400i,600,600i" rel="stylesheet">
   ```
3. Open the *membership.css* file in the *wwwroot/css* folder.
4. Add the **Open Sans** font family to the **body** selector.
   ```
   body {
       font-family: "Open Sans", sans-serif;
   }
   ```

5. Add the **background-color** property to the **body** selector and change the background color to light gray.
    ```
    background-color: #f2f2f2;
    ```

6. Save the files.

Add the following CSS selectors one at a time to the *course-panel.css* file and save it. Refresh the browser and observe the changes.

Change the size of the course thumbnails in the **_CoursePanelPartial** partial view so that they fit in the panel.

```
.course-listing.panel .thumb {
    width: 100%;
    height: auto;
}
```

Add padding to the panel to make the text area look more uniform.

```
.course-listing.panel .panel-body {
    padding: 10px 30px 30px 30px;
}
```

Style the panel with a small border radius to make it look more square, and add a box shadow to lift it from the background. Remove the border to avoid displaying a thin white border around the panel.

```
.course-listing.panel {
    border: none;
    border-radius: 2px;
    box-shadow: 0 2px 5px 0 rgba(0, 0, 0, 0.1);
}
```

Summary

In this chapter, you added the **Dashboard** view and the **_CoursePanelPartial** partial view, and styled them with CSS and Bootstrap.

Next, you will add the **Course** view and the **_ModuleVideosPartial** and **_InstructorBio-Partial** partial views that are part of the **Course** view. Then you will style them with CSS and Bootstrap.

19. The Course View

Introduction

In this chapter, you will add the **Course** view and three partial views called **_Module-VideosPartial**, **_ModuleDownloadsPartial**, and **_InstructorBioPartial** that are part of the **Course** view. As you add view and partial view content, you style it with CSS and Bootstrap. The **Course** view is displayed when the user clicks one of the **Dashboard** view's course panel buttons. The view contains information about the selected course and has module lists containing all the videos belonging to that course. The instructor's bio is displayed beside the module lists. You will also add a button at the top of the view that takes the user back to the **Dashboard** view.

Technologies Used in This Chapter

1. **HTML** – To create the view's layout.
2. **CSS** – To style the view.
3. **Razor** – To use C# in the view.

Overview

Your task is to use the view model in the **Course** action and render a view that displays a marquee, course image, title, and description as a separate row below the *Back to Dashboard* button at the top of the view. Below that row, a second row divided into two columns should be displayed. Add rows in the left column for each module in the course, and list the videos for each module. Display the instructor's bio in the right column.

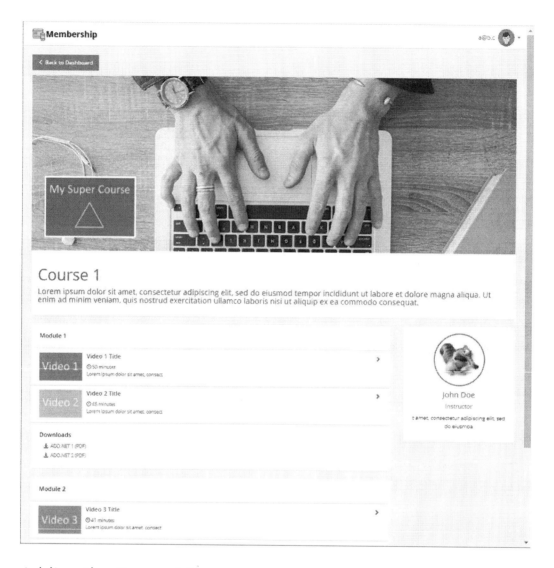

Adding the Course View

First, you will add the **Course** view to the *Views/Membership* folder.

Then, you will add a button that navigates to the **Dashboard** view, a marquee with a course image, course information, an instructor bio, and modules with videos and downloads. You will create three partial views, one called **_InstructorBioPartial** for the instructor bio, one called **_ModuleVideosPartial** for the videos, and one called **_ModuleDownloads-Partial** for downloads. The three areas will then be styled with Bootstrap and CSS.

1. Open the **Membership** controller.
2. Right click on the **Course** action and select **Add-View**.
3. Make sure that the **Create as partial view** checkbox is unchecked.
4. Click the **Add** button to create the view.

5. Close the **Course** view and open it again to get rid of any errors.
6. Add an **@model** directive for the **CourseViewModel** class at the beginning of the view.

   ```
   @model CourseViewModel
   ```

7. Save all the files.
8. Start the application without debugging (Ctrl+F5) and navigate to *Membership/Dashboard*. Open a course by clicking on one of the panel buttons, or navigate to the *Membership/Course/1* URL. The text *Course* should be displayed in the browser if the **Course** view was rendered correctly.

The markup in the **Course** view, so far:

```
@model CourseViewModel

@{
    ViewData["Title"] = "Course";
}
```

```
<h2>Course</h2>
```

Adding the Back to Dashboard Button

Now, you will add the button that takes the user back to the **Dashboard** view. The button should be placed inside a <div> decorated with three CSS classes called **membership, top-margin**, and **course-content**, which will be used later for styling.

The button should be placed on a separate row that takes up the full page width. Add the **row** and **col-sm-12** Bootstrap classes to two nested <div> elements to add the row and the column.

1. Open the **Course** view.
2. Remove the <h2> heading.
3. Add a <div> element and decorate it with the three CSS classes: **membership, top-margin**, and **course-content**.
    ```
    <div class="membership top-margin course-content">
    </div>
    ```
4. Add the row with a <div> element, place it inside the previous <div>, and decorate it with the **row** Bootstrap class and a CSS class called **navigation-bar**. The latter class will be used to add margin to the row.
    ```
    <div class="row navigation-bar">
    </div>
    ```
5. Add the column with a <div> element, place it inside the previous <div>, and decorate it with the **col-sm-12** Bootstrap class to make it as wide as possible.
    ```
    <div class="col-sm-12">
    </div>
    ```
6. Add a blue button using an <a> element, place it inside the previous <div>, and decorate it with the **btn** and **btn-primary** Bootstrap classes. Add the path to the **Dashboard** view in the **href** attribute.
    ```
    <a class="btn btn-primary" href="~/Membership/Dashboard"></a>
    ```
7. Add a <span> inside the <a> element and decorate it with the Glyphicon classes to add an arrow (<) icon. Add the text *Back to Dashboard* after the <span> in the <a> element.
    ```
    <a class="btn btn-primary" href="~/Membership/Dashboard">
    ```

```
        <span class="glyphicon glyphicon-menu-left"></span>
        Back to Dashboard
    </a>
```

8. Save the view and refresh it in the browser. A blue button with the text < *Back to Dashboard* should be visible at the top of the view.

9. Click the button to navigate to the **Dashboard** view.

10. Click the button in one of the panels in the **Dashboard** view to get back to the **Course** view.

The markup in the **Course** view, so far:

```
@model CourseViewModel

@{
    ViewData["Title"] = "Course";
}

<div class="membership top-margin course-content">
    <div class="row navigation-bar">
        <div class="col-sm-12">
            <a class="btn btn-primary" href="~/Membership/Dashboard">
                <span class="glyphicon glyphicon-menu-left"></span>
                Back to Dashboard
            </a>
        </div>
    </div>
</div>
```

Adding the Course.css Style Sheet

To style the **Course** view and its partial views, you need to add a CSS style sheet called *course.css* to the *wwwroot/css* folder and a link to the file in the **_Layout** view and the *bundleconfig.json* file.

1. Right click on the *wwwroot/css* folder and select **Add-New Item**.
2. Select the Style Sheet template and name the file *course.css*.
3. Click the **Add** button to create the file.
4. Open the **_Layout** view and add links to the file in the **Development** <environment> element.

    ```
    <link rel="stylesheet" href="~/css/course.css" />
    ```

5. Open the *bundleconfig.json* file and add a reference to the CSS file. `"wwwroot/css/course.css"`

6. Remove the **body** selector in the *course.css* file.

7. Save the files.

Adding the Course Information to the View

Now, you will add markup for the course information panel and style it with Bootstrap and CSS.

The panel should be placed on a separate row that takes up the full page width. Add the Bootstrap **row** and **col-sm-12** classes to two nested <div> elements. This will create a row and a column. Use the **panel** and **panel-body** Bootstrap classes to style the panel <div> elements.

Use a <div> to display the marquee image as a background image inside the panel.

Add the course title as an <h1> element and the course description as an <h4> element inside the **panel-body** <div>.

Course 1

Lorem ipsum dolor sit amet, consectetur adipiscing elit, sed do eiusmod tempor incididunt ut labore et dolore magna aliqua. Ut enim ad minim veniam, quis nostrud exercitation ullamco laboris nisi ut aliquip ex ea commodo consequat.

1. Open the **Course** view.

2. Add three nested <div> elements below the previous **row** <div> inside the *membership* <div>. Decorate the first with the Bootstrap **row** class, the second with the **col-sm-12** class, and the third with the **panel** class.

```
<div class="row">
    <div class="col-sm-12">
        <div class="panel">
        </div>
    </div>
</div>
```

3. Add a <div> inside the **panel** <div> and decorate it with a CSS class called **marquee**. Add the **background-image** style to it and use the **Course.MarqueeImageUrl** property to get the course's marquee image. Call the **url** method to ensure a correctly formatted URL.

```
<div class="marquee" style="background-image:
    url('@Model.Course.MarqueeImageUrl');">
</div>
```

4. Add an <img> element for the **Course.CourseImageUrl** property inside the **marquee** <div>; decorate it with a CSS class called **cover-image**.

```
<div class="marquee" style="background-image:
    url('@Model.Course.MarqueeImageUrl');">
    <img src="@Model.Course.CourseImageUrl" class="cover-image">
</div>
```

5. Add a <div> below the **marquee** <div> inside the **panel** <div>. Decorate it with the **panel-body** Bootstrap class. This is the area where the course title and description are displayed.

```
<div class="panel-body">
</div>
```

6. Add an <h1> element for the **Course.CourseTitle** property and an <h4> element for the **Course.CourseDescription** property inside the **panel-body** <div>.

7. Save all files and switch to the browser and refresh the view.

The markup for the course information row in the **Course** view:

```
<div class="row">
    <div class="col-sm-12">
        <div class="panel">
            <div class="marquee" style="background-image:
                url('@Model.Course.MarqueeImageUrl');">
                <img src="@Model.Course.CourseImageUrl"
                    class="cover-image">
            </div>
            <div class="panel-body">
```

```
            <h1>@Model.Course.CourseTitle</h1>
            <h4 class="product-desc">
                @Model.Course.CourseDescription</h4>
        </div>
      </div>
   </div>
</div>
```

Styling the Course Information Section

Now, you will style the course information panel with Bootstrap and CSS. Save the CSS file after adding each selector and refresh the browser to see the changes.

Open the *course.css* file and add a 10px bottom margin to the button row, using the **navigation-bar** class that you added to it.

```
.navigation-bar {
    margin-bottom: 10px;
}
```

Now, style the marquee. Make it cover the entire width of its container, give it a height of 400px, and hide any overflow. The marquee position has to be relative for the course image to be positioned correctly. Make the background image cover the entire available space.

```
.course-content .marquee {
    width: 100%;
    height: 400px;
    overflow: hidden;
    background-size: cover;
    /* Relative positioning of the marquee is needed for the cover
        image's absolute position */
    position: relative;
}
```

Now, style the cover image by making its width automatic and the height 140px. Use absolute positioning to place the image at the bottom of the marquee. Add a 30px margin to move the image away from the marquee borders. Add a 4px solid white border around the image and give it a subtle border radius of 2px.

```
.course-content .marquee .cover-image {
    width: auto;
    height: 140px;
```

```
    position: absolute;
    bottom: 0;
    margin: 30px;
    border: 4px solid #FFF;
    border-radius: 2px;
}
```

Open the *membership.css* file and add the following style to override the color for the <h1> and <h4> elements in the *Membership* views.

Change the color to a light gray for the <h1> and <h4> elements in the *Membership* views.

```
.membership h1, .membership h4 {
    color: #666c74;
}
```

Adding Columns for the Modules and the Instructor Bio

Before you can add the modules and the instructor bio, you need to create a new row divided into two columns, below the marquee. Add the **row**, **col-sm-9**, and **col-sm-3** Bootstrap classes to nested <div> elements, to create the row and columns.

1. Open the **Course** view and add a <div> element decorated with the **row** Bootstrap class below the previous **row** <div> containing the marquee.
   ```
   <div class="row"></div>
   ```

2. Add two <div> elements inside the **row** <div>. Decorate the first <div> with the **col-sm-9** Bootstrap class, and the second with the **col-sm-3** class. This will make the first column take up ¾ of the row width and the second column ¼ of the row width.
   ```
   <div class="col-md-9">
       @*Add modules here*@
   </div>
   <div class="col-md-3">
       @*Add instructor bio here*@
   </div>
   ```

The markup for the row and columns in the **Course** view:

```
<div class="row">
    <div class="col-sm-9">@*Add modules here*@</div>
    <div class="col-sm-3">@*Add instructor bio here*@</div>
</div>
```

Adding the Modules

To display the videos and downloads, you first have to add the modules they are associated with. The modules should be displayed below the marquee and take up ¾ of the row width. Use Razor to add a **foreach** loop that iterates over the **Modules** collection in the view model, and adds a Bootstrap panel for each module. Display the **ModuleTitle** for each module in the **panel-body** section.

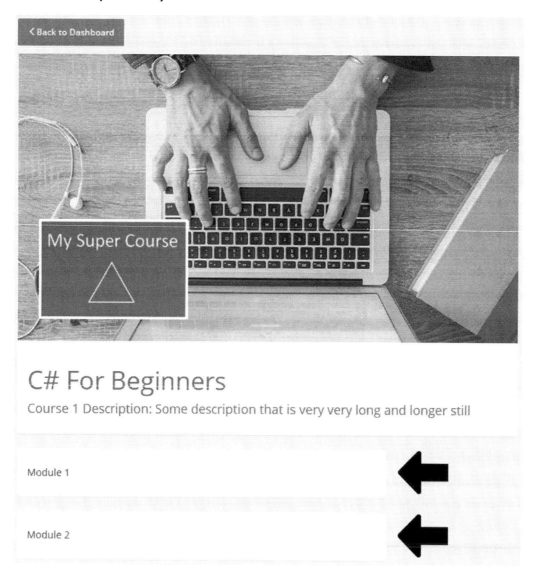

1. Open the **Course** view.

2. Locate the <div> decorated with the **col-sm-9** Bootstrap class and add a **foreach** loop, which iterates over the view model's **Modules** collection.
   ```
   @foreach (var module in Model.Modules)
   {
   }
   ```

3. Add a <div> decorated with the Bootstrap **panel** class inside the loop to create a module container for each module in the collection. Add another CSS class called **module**; it will be the parent selector for the panel's intrinsic elements.
   ```
   <div class="panel module">
   </div>
   ```

4. Add a <div> inside the **panel** <div> and decorate it with the **panel-body** Bootstrap class. Add an <h5> element containing the **ModuleTitle** property.
   ```
   <div class="panel-body">
       <h5>@module.ModuleTitle</h5>
   </div>
   ```

5. Save the files and refresh the browser. The module titles for the course you selected should be listed below the marquee.

The markup for the module panels:

```
<div class="col-sm-9">
    @foreach (var module in Model.Modules)
    {
        <div class="panel module">
            <div class="panel-body">
                <h5>@module.ModuleTitle</h5>
            </div>
        </div>
    }
</div>
```

Adding the Videos

To display the video items for the modules, you will create a partial view called **_Module-VideosPartial** that will be rendered for each video. Pass in the **Video** collection from the current module in the **Course** view's **foreach** loop, to the partial view.

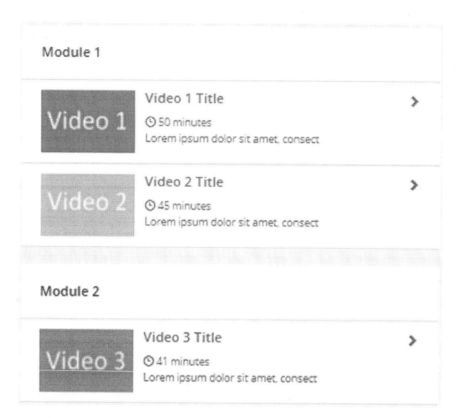

Use the Bootstrap **media** classes to display the video information in a uniform way.

1. Add a partial view called **_ModuleVideosPartial** to the *Views/Membership* folder.

2. Open the **Course** view.

3. Add an if-block that checks that the current module's **Videos** collection isn't **null**, below the previously added **panel-body** <div>. Pass in the **Video** collection from the current module to the **PartialAsync** method that renders the partial view, and displays the videos.

```
@if (module.Videos != null)
{
    @await Html.PartialAsync("_ModuleVideosPartial", module.Videos)
}
```

4. Open the **_ModuleVideosPartial** view.

5. Add an **@model** directive to an **IEnumerable<VideoDTO>**.
```
@model IEnumerable<VideoDTO>
```

6. Add a **foreach** loop that iterates over the view model.
   ```
   @foreach (var video in Model)
   {
   }
   ```

7. Add a <div> element decorated with the **panel-body** Bootstrap class and a CSS class called **module-video**, inside the loop. The CSS class will be used for styling later. The <div> will be a container for a single video.
   ```
   <div class="panel-body module-video">
   </div>
   ```

8. Add an <a> element with an **href** attribute, inside the previously added <div>, that opens a specific video to the **Video** view that you will add later. Use the current video's **Id** property to target the correct video in the **href**. Add the current video's **Title** property to the <a> element.
   ```
   <a href="~/Membership/Video/@video.Id">
       @video.Title
   </a>
   ```

9. Save all files and refresh the **Course** view in the browser. Each module should now have its videos listed as links. The links will not work because you haven't added the **Video** view yet.

10. Replace the **Title** property with a <div> decorated with the **media** Bootstrap class. This will format the content in a specific way, displaying an image to the left and a block of information to the right.
    ```
    <div class="media">
    </div>
    ```

11. Add the left (image) area to the **media** <div> by adding a <div> decorated with the **media-left** Bootstrap class. Add an additional Bootstrap class called **hidden-xs**, which will hide this <div> if the site is viewed on a smartphone or a small handheld device. You typically don't want to send large images to smartphones because they tend to take a long time to load.
    ```
    <div class="media-left hidden-xs">
    </div>
    ```

12. Add the video thumbnail to a <div> decorated with a CSS class called **thumb-container**. Use the image URL in the current video's **Thumbnail** property for the <img> element's **src** property.

```
<div class="thumb-container">
    <img src="@video.Thumbnail" class="thumb">
</div>
```

13. Save the files and refresh the **Course** view in the browser. Large thumbnail images will be displayed for each video; you will change that with CSS styling later.

14. Add a <div> decorated with the **media-body** Bootstrap class below the **media-left** <div>. This will be the (right) video information area.
```
<div class="media-body">
</div>
```

15. Add an <h5> element for the video title inside the **media-body** <div>. Add the view model's **Title** property to the element.
```
<h5>@video.Title</h5>
```

16. Add a <p> element decorated with a CSS class called **text-light** below the title. The CSS class will be used to display the video's length with a muted font. Add an <i> element for a watch Glyphicon; use the **glyphicon-time** class. Add the duration from the current video's **Duration** property followed by the text *minutes* after the <i> element.
```
<p class="text-light">
    <i class="glyphicon glyphicon-time"></i>
    @video.Duration minutes
</p>
```

17. Add the video description in a <p> element below the duration; use the current video's **Description** property.
```
<p>@video.Description</p>
```

18. Add a chevron icon to the right of each video item, to show that it can be opened. Add a Glyphicon inside a <div> decorated with the **media-right** and **hidden-xs** Bootstrap classes below the video description. Make the chevron muted by adding the **text-light** CSS class to it.
```
<div class="media-right hidden-xs text-light">
    <i class="glyphicon glyphicon-chevron-right"></i>
</div>
```

19. If you refresh the **Course** view in the browser, the video items would still only display one gigantic thumbnail image.

Next, you will style the partial view.

The complete markup for the **_ModuleVideosPartial** view:

```
@model IEnumerable<VideoDTO>

@foreach (var video in Model)
{
    <div class="panel-body module-video">
        <a href="~/Membership/Video/@video.Id">
            <div class="media">
                <div class="media-left hidden-xs">
                    <div class="thumb-container">
                        <img src="@video.Thumbnail" class="thumb">
                    </div>
                </div>
                <div class="media-body">
                    <h5>@video.Title</h5>
                    <p class="text-light">
                        <i class="glyphicon glyphicon-time"></i>
                        @video.Duration minutes
                    </p>
                    <p>@video.Description</p>
                </div>
                <div class="media-right hidden-xs text-light">
                    <i class="glyphicon glyphicon-chevron-right"></i>
                </div>
            </div>
        </a>
    </div>
}
```

Styling the _ModuleVideosPartial View

Before you start styling the **_ModuleVideosPartial** view, you need to add a new CSS Style Sheet called *module.css*. It will be used when styling the module section of the **Course** view.

1. Add a style sheet called *module.css* to the *wwwroot/css* folder.
2. Add a link to it in the **Development** <environment> element in the **_Layout** view.
3. Add a reference to it in the *bundleconfig.json* file.
4. Add the following styles to the *module.css* file. Add the selectors one at a time and refresh the browser to see the changes.

Add 10px top and bottom padding and 20px left and right padding to the modules **panel-body** elements.

```
.panel.module .panel-body {
    padding: 10px 20px;
}
```

Change the font weight to 600 for the module titles.

```
.module .panel-body h5 {
    font-weight: 600;
}
```

Add a 1px solid top border to the **module-video** <div> to separate the video items in the list.

```
.module-video {
    border-top: 1px solid #dadada;
}
```

Hide any overflow in the thumbnail image container and make it 100px wide. This means that the image can't be any wider than its container.

```
.module-video .thumb-container {
    overflow: hidden;
    width: 100px;
}
```

Make the thumbnail image as wide as it can be in its container.

```
.module-video .thumb {
    width: 100%;
}
```

Remove the top margin from the video title.

```
.module-video h5 {
    margin-top: 0;
}
```

Change the link color to gray and remove the text decoration (underlining) from the video links.

```
.module-video a {
    color: #666c74;
    text-decoration: none;
}
```

Remove the bottom margin for all paragraphs in the **module-video** container.

```
.module-video p {
    margin-bottom: 0;
}
```

Adding the Downloads

To display the downloads in each module, you will create a partial view called **_Module-DownloadsPartial** that will be rendered for each download link. Pass in the **Downloads** collection from the current module in the **Course** view's **foreach** loop, to the partial view.

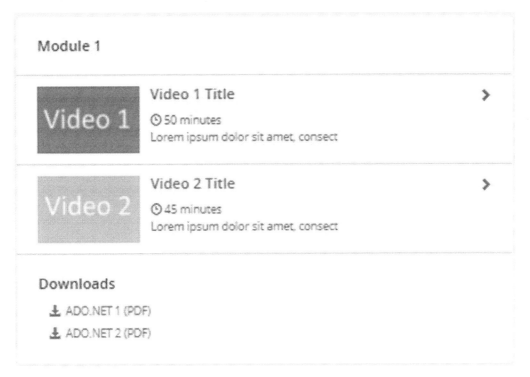

Use the Bootstrap **panel** classes to display the download information in a uniform way.

1. Add a partial view called **_ModuleDownloadsPartial** to the *Views/Membership* folder.

2. Open the **Course** view.

3. Add an if-block, checking that the current module's **Downloads** collection isn't null, below the *videos* if-block.
    ```
    @if (module.Downloads != null)
    {
    }
    ```

4. Add a horizontal line inside the if-block for the **Downloads** collection and decorate it with a CSS class called **no-margin** that will be used later to remove the element's margin.
    ```
    <hr class="no-margin">
    ```

5. Add a <div> decorated with the **panel-body** Bootstrap class below the <hr> element inside the if-block. Add a CSS class called **download-panel** to the <div>; this class will be used as a parent selector when styling the partial view.
    ```
    <div class="panel-body download-panel"></div>
    ```

6. Add an <h5> element with the text *Downloads* inside the previous <div>.
    ```
    <h5>Downloads</h5>
    ```

7. Render the partial view below the <h5> element. Pass in the **Downloads** collection from the current module to the **PartialAsync** method, which renders the **_ModuleDownloadsPartial** and displays the download links.
    ```
    @await Html.PartialAsync("_ModuleDownloadsPartial",
    module.Downloads)
    ```

8. Open the **_ModuleDownloadsPartial** view.

9. Add an **@model** directive to an **IEnumerable<DownloadDTO>**.
    ```
    @model IEnumerable<DownloadDTO>
    ```

10. Add an unordered list (<ul>) below the **@model** directive.

11. Add a **foreach** loop that iterates over the view model in the <ul> element.
    ```
    @foreach (var download in Model)
    {
    }
    ```

12. Add a listitem (<li>) inside the loop.

13. Add an <a> element inside the <li> element that uses the current download's **DownloadUrl** property in its **href** attribute, and opens the content in a separate browser tab. The <a> element should display a download Glyphicon and the text from the current download's **DownloadTitle** property.

```
<li>
    <a href="@download.DownloadUrl" target="_blank">
        <span class="glyphicon glyphicon-download-alt"></span>
         @download.DownloadTitle
    </a>
</li>
```

14. Save the files and refresh the **Course** view in the browser. A section with download links should be displayed in the module lists, where downloadable content is available.

Next, you will style the partial view.

The complete markup for the **_ModuleDownloadsPartial** view:

```
@model IEnumerable<DownloadDTO>

<ul>
    @foreach (var download in Model)
    {
        <li>
            <a href="@download.DownloadUrl" target="_blank">
                <span class="glyphicon glyphicon-download-alt"></span>
                 @download.DownloadTitle
            </a>
        </li>
    }
</ul>
```

The markup for rendering the **_ModuleDownloadsPartial** view in the **Course** view:

```
@if (module.Downloads != null)
{
    <hr class="no-margin">
    <div class="panel-body download-panel">
        <h5>Downloads</h5>
        @await Html.PartialAsync("_ModuleDownloadsPartial",
            module.Downloads)
    </div>
}
```

The complete code for the modules, videos, and downloads in the **Course** view:

```
<div class="col-sm-9">
@foreach (var module in Model.Modules)
{
    <div class="panel module">
        <div class="panel-body">
            <h5>@module.ModuleTitle</h5>
        </div>
        @if (module.Videos != null)
        {
            @await Html.PartialAsync("_ModuleVideosPartial",
                module.Videos)
        }
        @if (module.Downloads != null)
        {
            <hr class="no-margin">
            <div class="panel-body download-panel">
                <h5>Downloads</h5>
                @await Html.PartialAsync("_ModuleDownloadsPartial",
                    module.Downloads)
            </div>
        }
    </div>
}
</div>
```

Styling the _ModuleDownloadsPartial View

Open the *module.css* style sheet and add a selector for the **no-margin** class on <hr> elements. It should remove all margins.

```
.membership hr.no-margin {
    margin: 0;
}
```

Add a selector for <ul> elements in the <div> decorated with the **download-panel** class. Remove all bullet styles and add a 10px left padding.

```
.download-panel ul {
    list-style-type: none;
    padding-left: 10px;
}
```

Add a selector for <li> elements in the <div> decorated with the **download-panel** class. Add a 5px top margin and make the font size smaller.

```
.download-panel li {
    margin-top: 5px;
    font-size: 0.87em;
}
```

Adding the Instructor Bio

To display the instructor bio, you will create a partial view called **_InstructorBioPartial** that will be displayed to the right of the module lists in the **Course** view. Add the **PartialAsync** method inside the <div> decorated with the **col-sm-3** Bootstrap class in the **Course** View. Pass in the **Instructor** object from the view model to the method.

John Doe

Instructor

t amet, consectetur adipiscing
elit, sed do eiusmoa

1. Add a partial view called **_InstructorBioPartial** to the *Views/Membership* folder.
2. Open the **Course** view.
3. Add an if-block inside the <div> decorated with the **col-sm-3** Bootstrap class. Check that the **Instructor** object in the view model isn't **null**, and pass in the **Instructor** object to the **PartialAsync** method that will render the partial view.
    ```
    @if (Model.Instructor != null)
    {
        @await Html.PartialAsync("_InstructorBioPartial",
            Model.Instructor)
    }
    ```
4. Open the **_InstructorBioPartial** partial view.

5. Add an **@model** directive to the **InstructorDTO** class.
    ```
    @model InstructorDTO
    ```

6. Add a <div> decorated with the **panel** Bootstrap class and a CSS class called **instructor-bio**. It will be the parent selector for this panel.
    ```
    <div class="instructor-bio panel">
    </div>
    ```

7. Add a <div> decorated with the **panel-body** Bootstrap class inside the **panel** <div>.
    ```
    <div class="panel-body">
    </div>
    ```

8. Add an <img> element inside the **panel-body** <div> for the **InstructorThumbnail** property in the view model. Decorate the <div> with the **img-circle** Bootstrap class and a CSS class called **avatar**. The **avatar** class will style the instructor's thumbnail.
    ```
    <img src="@Model.InstructorAvatar" class="avatar img-circle">
    ```

9. Add an <h4> element for the **InstructorName** property in the view model.
    ```
    <h4>@Model.InstructorName</h4>
    ```

10. Add an <h5> element with the text *Instructor*. Decorate it with the **text-primary** Bootstrap class to make the text blue.
    ```
    <h5 class="text-primary">Instructor</h5>
    ```

11. Add a <p> element for the view model's **InstructorDescription** property.
    ```
    <p>@Model.InstructorDescription</p>
    ```

12. Save the files and refresh the browser to save the changes.

The complete code for the **_InstructorBioPartial** partial view:

```
@model InstructorDTO

<div class="instructor-bio panel">
    <div class="panel-body">
        <img src="@Model.InstructorAvatar" class="avatar img-circle">
        <h4>@Model.InstructorName</h4>
        <h5 class="text-primary">Instructor</h5>
        <p>@Model.InstructorDescription</p>
    </div>
</div>
```

Styling the _InstructorBioPartial Partial View

Before you start styling the **_InstructorBioPartial** view, you need to add a new CSS style sheet called *instructor-bio.css*. It will be used when styling the instructor bio section in the **Course** view.

1. Add a style sheet called *instructor-bio.css* to the *wwwroot/css* folder.
2. Add a link to it in the **Development** <environment> element in the **_Layout** view.
3. Add a reference to it in the *bundleconfig.json* file.
   ```
   "wwwroot/css/instructor-bio.css"
   ```

4. Add the following styles to the *instructor-bio.css* file. Add the selectors one at a time and refresh the browser to see the changes.

Open the *instructor-bio* style sheet and center the text in the **instructor-bio** container.

```
.instructor-bio {
    text-align: center;
}
```

Style the avatar to have a blue circle with 8px padding around it and make the image diameter 120px. The circle is created with the **img-circle** Bootstrap class, which styles the border of an element.

```
.instructor-bio .avatar {
    border: 2px solid #2d91fb;
    padding: 8px;
    height: 120px;
    width: 120px;
}
```

Summary

In this chapter, you created the **Course** view and its three partial views: **_ModuleVideos-Partial**, **_ModuleDownloadsPartial**, and **_InstructorBioPartial**. You also used Bootstrap to create rows and columns in a responsive design, and styled the views with Bootstrap and CSS.

Next, you will create the **Video** view, where the actual video can be viewed.

20. The Video View

Introduction

In this chapter, you will create the **Video** view and two partial views called **_VideoComing-UpPartial** and **_VideoPlayerPartial**. You will also reuse the already created **_InstructorBio-Partial** partial view. The content will be styled with CSS and Bootstrap as you add it. The **Video** view is displayed when the user clicks one of the video links in the **Course** view, and it contains a button that takes the user back to the **Course** view, a video player, information about the selected video, buttons to select the next and previous video, and the instructor's bio.

Technologies Used in This Chapter
1. **HTML** – To create the view's layout.
2. **CSS** – To style the view.
3. **Razor** – To use C# in the view.
4. **JavaScript** – To display the video player and load the selected video.

Overview

Your task is to use the view model in the **Video** action and render a view that displays a course image, video duration, title, and description as a separate column, on a new row, below the *Back to Course* button at the top of the view. Beside the video player column, a second column should be added. The upper part should contain the **_VideoComingUp-Partial** partial view, and the lower part the **_InstructorBioPartial** partial view.

In this exercise, the JWPlayer video player is used, but you can use any video player you like that can play YouTube videos.

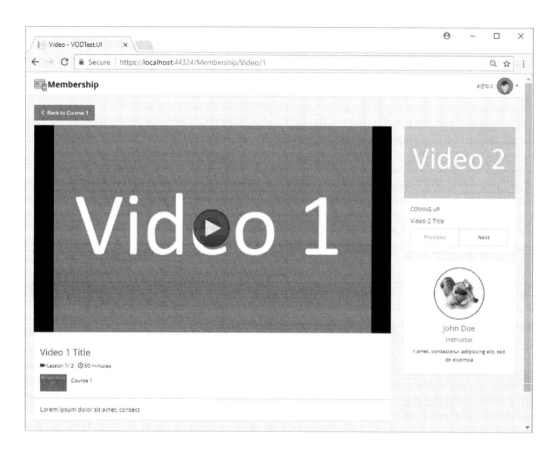

Video 1 Title

📹 Lesson 1/ 2   🕐 50 minutes

 Course 1

Lorem ipsum dolor sit amet, consect

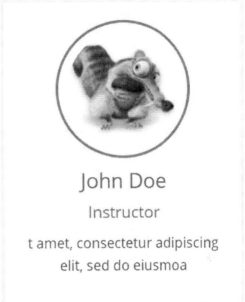

COMING UP

Video 2 Title

Previous	Next

John Doe

Instructor

t amet, consectetur adipiscing
elit, sed do eiusmoa

Adding the Video View

First, you will add the **Video** view to the *Views/Membership* folder.

Then, you will add a button that navigates to the **Course** view. The video player will be placed below the button, along with information about the video. To the right of the video player, in a separate column, the *Coming Up* section, with the **Previous** and **Next** buttons, will be displayed. Below that section, the instructor's bio will be displayed. You will create two partial views for the video player and the *Comin Up* section called **_VideoPlayerPartial** and **_VideoComingUpPartial**. Reuse the **_InstructorBioPartial** partial view to display the instructor's bio. The three areas will be styled with Bootstrap and CSS.

1. Open the **Membership** controller.
2. Right click on the **Video** action and select **Add-View**.
3. Make sure that the **Create as partial view** checkbox is unchecked.
4. Click the **Add** button to create the view.

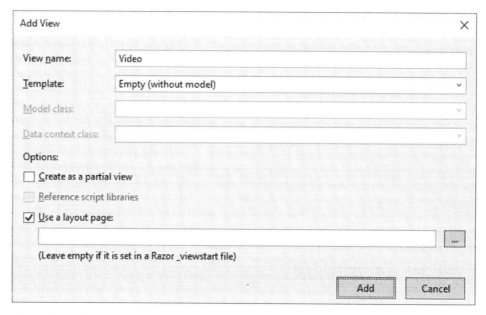

5. Close the **Video** view and open it again to get rid of any errors.

6. Add an **@model** directive for the **VideoViewModel** class at the beginning of the view.

```
@model VideoViewModel
```

7. Save all the files.

8. Start the application without debugging (Ctrl+F5). Click on one of the courses in the **Dashboard** view and then on one of the video links in the **Course** view. The text *Video* should be displayed in the browser if the **Video** view was rendered correctly.

The markup in the **Video** view, so far:

```
@model VideoViewModel

@{
    ViewData["Title"] = "Video";
}

<h2>Video</h2>
```

Adding the Back to Course Button

Now, you will add a button that takes the user back to the **Course** view, to display the course the video belongs to.

1. Open the **Video** view.
2. Remove the <h2> element.
3. Add a <div> element decorated with three CSS classes called **membership, top-margin**, and **video-content**. You have already added CSS for the two first classes. The last class will act as the parent selector when styling the **Video** view and its partial views. The <div> will act as the parent container for the content in the **Video** view.
   ```
   <div class="membership top-margin video-content">
   </div>
   ```
4. Add two nested <div> elements decorated with the **row** and **col-sm-12** Bootstrap classes respectively. Add the **navigation-bar** CSS class to the **row** <div>; you added a selector for this class earlier, to add a bottom margin to a button.
   ```
   <div class="row navigation-bar">
       <div class="col-sm-12">
       </div>
   </div>
   ```
5. Add an <a> element inside the *column* <div> and decorate it with the **btn** and **btn-primary** Bootstrap classes, to turn the anchor tag into a blue button. Use the **Course.CourseId** property from the view model when creating the **href** link back to the **Course** view. Note that the **href** must be added as a single line for the URL to work properly.
   ```
   <a class="btn btn-primary"
       href="~/Membership/Course/@Model.Course.CourseId">
   </a>
   ```
6. Add a <span> element for the **glyphicon-menu-left** Glyphicon inside the <a> element. Add the text *Back to* followed by the value from the **Course.CourseTitle** property from the view model after the <span>.
   ```
   <span class="glyphicon glyphicon-menu-left"></span>
   Back to @Model.Course.CourseTitle
   ```
7. Start the application without debugging (Ctrl+F5). Click on a course button in the **Dashboard** view, and then on a video link in the **Course** view.

8. A blue button with the text *Back to xxx* should be displayed at the top of the page. Click the button to get back to the **Course** View.

9. Click on a video link to get back to the **Video** view.

The complete code for the **Back to Course** button:

```
<div class="membership top-margin video-content">
    <div class="row navigation-bar">
        <div class="col-sm-12">
            <a class="btn btn-primary" href="~/Membership/Course/
                @Model.Course.CourseId">
                <span class="glyphicon glyphicon-menu-left"></span>
                Back to @Model.Course.CourseTitle
            </a>
        </div>
    </div>
</div>
```

Adding Row and Columns for the Video View Content

Now, you will use Bootstrap classes to add a row and columns that will hold the **Video** view's content.

1. Open the **Video** view.

2. Add a <div> element decorated with the **row** class, below the previous **row** <div>. Add two nested <div> elements decorated with the **col-sm-9** and **col-sm-3** classes respectively.

```
<div class="row">
    <div class="col-sm-9">
        @*Place the video player here*@
    </div>

    <div class="col-sm-3">
        @*Place the Coming Up and Instructor Bio sections here*@
    </div>
</div>
```

3. Save the file.

Adding the _VideoPlayerPartial Partial View

This partial view will display the panel containing the video player and its information.

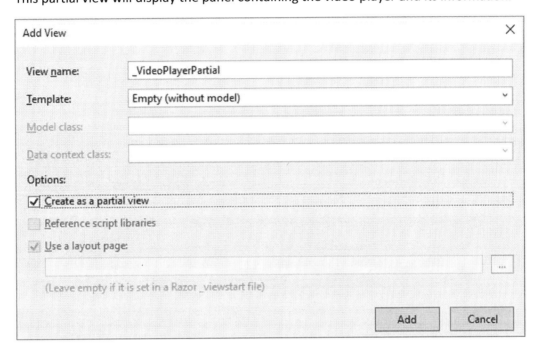

1. Add a partial view called **_VideoPlayerPartial** to the *Views/membership* folder.
2. Delete all code in the view and save it.
3. Close and open the view to get rid of any errors.
4. Add a **using** statement to the **MembershipViewModels** namespace.
   @using VideoOnDemand.UI.Models.MembershipViewModels

5. Add an **@model** directive to the **VideoViewModel** class. The view needs the view model to display all the information because the data is stored in several objects in the model.
   @model VideoViewModel

6. Add a <div> decorated with the **panel** Bootstrap class below the **@model** directive.
   ```
   <div class="panel">
   </div>
   ```

7. Add an if-block inside the **panel** <div> that checks that the **Video.Url** property in the view model isn't **null**.

```
@if (Model.Video.Url != null)
{
}
```

8. Add a <div> element inside the if-block with the **id** attribute set to **video**. This element will house the video player.

```
<div id="video" class="video-margin"> </div>
```

9. Add two hidden <div> elements named **hiddenUrl** and **hiddenImageUrl** below the previous <div>. Add the **Video.Url** property to the **hiddenUrl** <div> and the **Video.Thumbnail** property to the **hiddenImageUrl** <div>. The hidden values will be read from JavaScript when the player is rendered. It's important that the <div> elements are added as single lines of code and not split up on several rows, otherwise the URL might contain special characters.

```
<div id="hiddenUrl" hidden="hidden">@Model.Video.Url</div>
<div id="hiddenImageUrl" hidden="hidden">
    @Model.Video.Thumbnail</div>
```

10. Add a <div> decorated with the **panel-body** Bootstrap class below the if-block. This is the container for the video information.

```
<div class="panel-body"></div>
```

11. Add an <h2> element for the **Video.Title** property from the view model inside the previous <div>. Decorate the element with the **text-dark** CSS class to make the title dark gray.

```
<h2 class="text-dark">@Model.Video.Title</h2>
```

12. Add a <p> element for the lesson information; decorate it with the **text-light** CSS class to make the text a muted light gray. Add a video Glyphicon, display the video's position and the number of videos in the module, a time Glyphicon, and the video length followed by the text *minutes*. Use the **LessonInfo.LessonNumber** and **LessonInfo.NumberOfLessons** properties to display the video's position and the number of videos. Use the **Video.Duration** property to display how long the video is.

```
<p class="text-light">
    <i class="glyphicon glyphicon-facetime-video"></i>
    Lesson @Model.LessonInfo.LessonNumber/
        @Model.LessonInfo.NumberOfLessons  
```

312

```
      <i class="glyphicon glyphicon-time"></i>
      @Model.Video.Duration minutes
   </p>
```

13. Add a <div> decorated with the **media-object** Bootstrap class below the <p> element. This is the container for the video thumbnail and the video title.
```
<div class="media-object">
</div>
```

14. Add an <img> element inside a <div> decorated with the **media-left** Bootstrap class. This will display the thumbnail to the left in the container. Use the **Course.CourseImageUrl** property in the **src** attribute.
```
<div class="media-left">
    <img src="@Model.Course.CourseImageUrl">
</div>
```

15. Add a <div> element decorated with the **media-body** and **media-middle** Bootstrap classes below the **media-left** <div>. This will be the container for the title displayed beside the thumbnail. Add the **Course.CourseTitle** property from the view model to a <p> element inside the <div>.
```
<div class="media-body media-middle">
    <p>@Model.Course.CourseTitle</p>
</div>
```

16. Add a horizontal line below the **panel-body** <div> and decorate it with the **no-margin** CSS class that you added a selector for earlier.
```
<hr class="no-margin">
```

17. Add a <div> decorated with the **panel-body** Bootstrap class below the <hr> element. Add the **Video.Description** property from the view model to it.
```
<div class="panel-body">
    @Model.Video.Description
</div>
```

18. Open the **Video** view.

19. Add a call to the **PartialAsync** method to render the **_VideoPlayerPartial** partial view inside the <div> decorated with the **col-sm-9** Bootstrap class. Pass in the view model to the partial view. Surround the method call with an if-block that checks that the view model, **Video**, **LessonInfo**, and **Course** objects are not **null**, to ensure that the partial view only is rendered if there is sufficient data.

```
    <div class="col-sm-9">
        @if (Model != null && Model.Video != null &&
            Model.LessonInfo != null && Model.Course != null)
        {
            @await Html.PartialAsync("_VideoPlayerPartial", Model)
        }
    </div>
```

20. Save all the files and navigate to a video in the browser. You should see the video information and a huge thumbnail image.

Next, you will style the **_VideoPlayerPartial** partial view.

The complete code for the **_VideoPlayerPartial** partial view:

```
@model VideoViewModel

<div class="panel">
    @if (Model.Video.Url != null)
    {
        <div id="video" class="video-margin"> </div>
        <div id="hiddenUrl" hidden="hidden">@Model.Video.Url</div>
        <div id="hiddenImageUrl" hidden="hidden">
            @Model.Video.Thumbnail</div>
    }

    <div class="panel-body">
        <h2 class="text-dark">@Model.Video.Title</h2>
        <p class="text-light">
            <i class="glyphicon glyphicon-facetime-video"></i>
            Lesson @Model.LessonInfo.LessonNumber/
                @Model.LessonInfo.NumberOfLessons  
            <i class="glyphicon glyphicon-time"></i>
            @Model.Video.Duration minutes
        </p>
        <div class="media-object">
            <div class="media-left">
                <img src="@Model.Course.CourseImageUrl">
            </div>
            <div class="media-body media-middle">
                <p>@Model.Course.CourseTitle</p>
            </div>
        </div>
    </div>
    <hr class="no-margin">
```

```
<div class="panel-body">
    @Model.Video.Description
</div>
</div>
```

Styling the _VideoPlayerPartial Partial View

Before you start styling the **_VideoPlayerPartial** view, you need to add a new CSS style sheet called *video.css* that will be used when styling the **Video** view and its partial views.

1. Add a style sheet called *video.css* to the *wwwroot/css* folder.
2. Add links to it in the **Development** <environment> element in the **_Layout** view.
3. Add a reference to it in the *bundleconfig.json* file.
   "wwwroot/css/video.css"

Add the following styles to the *video.css* file. Add the selectors one at a time and refresh the browser to see the changes.

Open the *video.css* style sheet and make the video thumbnail's height 40px.

```
.video-content .media-left img {
    height: 40px;
}
```

Remove the video panel's border and border radius, to make it look more square.

```
.video-content .panel {
    border: none;
    border-radius: 0px;
}
```

Add JWPlayer

To play video with JWPlayer, you have to register with their site www.jwplayer.com and create a video player link that you add to the **_Layout** view. You also have to call the **jwplayer** JavaScript method in the view, to activate the video player.

315

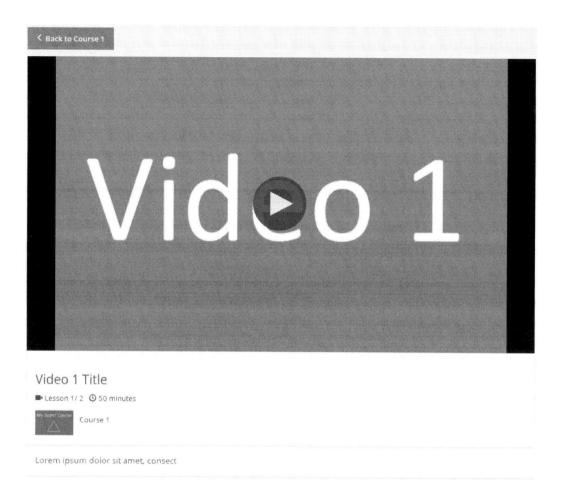

Video 1 Title

◼ Lesson 1/ 2 🕐 50 minutes

 Course 1

Lorem ipsum dolor sit amet, consect

Video 1 Title

◼ Lesson 1/ 2 🕐 50 minutes

My Super Course   Course 1

Lorem ipsum dolor sit amet, consect

Create a Video Player

1. Navigate to www.jwplayer.com and sign up for an account, and sign in.
2. Select the **Manage** link in the *Players* section of the menu.
3. Click the **Create New Player** button to create your video player.
4. Name the player in the text field; you can call it whatever you like.
5. Select the **Responsive** radio button in the *Basic Setup* section.
6. You can change other settings if you want, to customize the player more.
7. Click the **Save Changes** button.
8. Copy the link below the demo video player. This is the link that you will add to the **_Layout** view, to get access to the video player.

Add the Video Player to the Video View

1. Open the **_Layout** view.
2. Add the link you copied from the JWPlayer site to all the <environment> elements at the end of the <body> element.
3. Open the **Video** view.
4. Add a **Scripts** section at the bottom of the view where the **jwplayer** function is called as soon as the page has been loaded into the DOM. Note that the **jwplayer** function name must be written with lowercase characters.

```
@section Scripts
{
    <script type="text/javascript">
        $(function () {
            jwplayer("video").setup({
                file: $("#hiddenUrl").text(),
                image: $("#hiddenImageUrl").text()
            });
        });
    </script>
}
```

5. Save all files.
6. Refresh the **Video** view in the browser. The video image should be visible, and the video should start playing if you click on it.

Adding Properties to the LessonInfoDTO Class

There is one piece of information that you need to add to the **LessonInfoDTO** and the **Membership** controller. To avoid displaying an empty image container when the user navigates to the last video using the **Next** button in the *Coming Up* section, the current video's thumbnail should be displayed. You therefore have to include the current video's thumbnail and title in the **LessonInfoDTO** class and add that data to the view model in the **Video** action of the **Membership** controller.

1. Open the **LessonInfoDTO** class.
2. Add two **string** properties called **CurrentVideoTitle** and **CurrentVideoThumbnail**.
   ```
   public string CurrentVideoTitle { get; set; }
   public string CurrentVideoThumbnail { get; set; }
   ```
3. Open the **Membership** controller and locate the **Video** action.
4. Assign the thumbnail and title from the video object's **Thumbnail** and **Title** properties to the properties you just added to the **LessonInfoDTO** class.
   ```
   CurrentVideoTitle = video.Title,
   CurrentVideoThumbnail = video.Thumbnail
   ```
5. Add a video to the first module in the first course in the **MockReadRepository**. The first module should have at least three videos, so that you can use the **Previous** and **Next** buttons properly when you test the *Coming Up* section of the **Video** view.

The complete **LessonInfoDTO** class:

```
public class LessonInfoDTO {
    public int LessonNumber { get; set; }
    public int NumberOfLessons { get; set; }
    public int PreviousVideoId { get; set; }
    public int NextVideoId { get; set; }
    public string NextVideoTitle { get; set; }
    public string NextVideoThumbnail { get; set; }
    public string CurrentVideoTitle { get; set; }
    public string CurrentVideoThumbnail { get; set; }
}
```

The complete **LessonInfoDTO** object in the **Video** action:

```
LessonInfo = new LessonInfoDTO
{
    LessonNumber = index + 1,
    NumberOfLessons = count,
    NextVideoId = nextId,
    PreviousVideoId = previousId,
    NextVideoTitle = nextTitle,
    NextVideoThumbnail = nextThumb,
    CurrentVideoTitle = video.Title,
    CurrentVideoThumbnail = video.Thumbnail
}
```

Adding the _VideoComingUpPartial Partial View

This partial view will display the panel containing the thumbnail of the next video, its title, and the **Previous** and **Next** buttons. The **Previous** button should be disabled when information about the first video is displayed. The **Next** button should be disabled when information about the last video is displayed. The *Coming Up* panel should not be displayed if there are no videos.

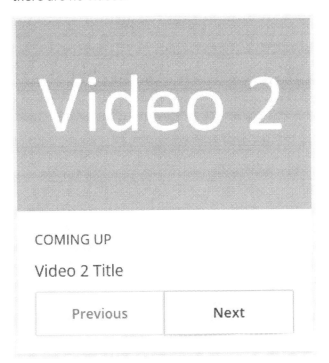

1. Add a partial view called **_VideoComingUpPartial** to the *Views/membership* folder.

2. Delete all code in the view and save it.

3. Close and open the view to get rid of any errors.

4. Add an **@model** directive to the **LessonInfoDTO** class.
   ```
   @model LessonInfoDTO
   ```

5. Add an if-block that checks that one of the **PreviousVideoId** or **NextVideoId** properties has a value greater than 0. If both are 0 then there are no other videos in the module, and the *Coming Up* section shouldn't be displayed.
   ```
   @if (Model.PreviousVideoId > 0 || Model.NextVideoId > 0)
   {
   }
   ```

6. Add a <div> element decorated with the **panel** Bootstrap class inside the if-block. Add a CSS class called **coming-up** to the <div> element; it will be the parent selector for this partial view.
   ```
   <div class="panel coming-up">
   </div>
   ```

7. Display a thumbnail for the current video, in the panel, if the **NextVideoId** property is 0, otherwise display the thumbnail for the next video. Use the **CurrentVideoThumbnail** and **NextVideoThumbnail** properties from the view model to display the correct image.
   ```
   @if (Model.NextVideoId == 0)
   {
       <img src="@Model.CurrentVideoThumbnail"
           class="img-responsive">
   }
   else
   {
       <img src="@Model.NextVideoThumbnail" class="img-responsive">
   }
   ```

8. Add a <div> decorated with the **panel-body** Bootstrap class below the previous if/else-blocks. This is the container for the *Coming Up* information.
   ```
   <div class="panel-body">
   </div>
   ```

9. Add a <p> element with the text *COURSE COMPLETED* and an <h5> element for the **CurrentVideoTitle** property from the view model in the **panel-body** <div> if

the **NextVideoId** property is 0. Otherwise, add a <p> element with the text *COMING UP* and an <h5> element for the **NextVideoTitle** property.

```
@if (Model.NextVideoId == 0)
{
    <p>COURSE COMPLETED</p>
    <h5>@Model.CurrentVideoTitle</h5>
}
else
{
    <p>COMING UP</p>
    <h5>@Model.NextVideoTitle</h5>
}
```

10. Add a <div> element for the **Previous** and **Next** buttons below the previous if/else-blocks. Decorate it with the **btn-group** Bootstrap class and add the **role** attribute set to **group**.

```
<div class="btn-group" role="group">
</div>
```

11. Add an if-block checking if the **PreviousVideoId** property in the view model is 0 inside the <div> element decorated with the **btn-group** Bootstrap class; if it is, then disable the **Previous** button. Use the **PreviousVideoId** in the <a> element's **href** attribute to target the correct video.

```
@if (Model.PreviousVideoId == 0)
{
    <a class="btn btn-default" disabled href="#">Previous</a>
}
else
{
    <a class="btn btn-default"
       href="~/Membership/Video/@Model.PreviousVideoId">
       Previous
    </a>
}
```

12. Add an if-block checking if the **NextVideoId** property in the view model is 0 below the previous if/else-blocks; if it is, then disable the **Next** button. Use the **NextVideoId** in the <a> element's **href** attribute to target the correct video.

```
@if (Model.NextVideoId == 0)
{
    <a class="btn btn-default" disabled href="#">Next</a>
}
```

```
    else
    {
        <a class="btn btn-default"
            href="~/Membership/Video/@Model.NextVideoId">Next</a>
    }
```

13. Open the **Video** view.

14. Add a call to the **PartialAsync** method to render the **_VideoComingUpPartial** partial view inside the <div> decorated with the **col-sm-3** Bootstrap class. Pass in the **LessonInfo** object from the view model to the partial view. Surround the method call with an if-block that checks that the view model and the **LessonInfo** object are not **null**.

```
<div class="col-sm-3">
    @if (Model != null && Model.LessonInfo != null)
    {
        @await Html.PartialAsync("_VideoComingUpPartial",
            Model.LessonInfo)
    }
</div>
```

15. Save all the files and navigate to a video in the browser. You should see the *Coming Up* section beside the video.

Next, you will style the **_VideoComingUpPartial** partial view.

The complete code for the **_VideoComingUpPartial** partial view:

```
@model LessonInfoDTO

@if (Model.PreviousVideoId > 0 || Model.NextVideoId > 0)
{
    <div class="panel coming-up">
        @if (Model.NextVideoId == 0)
        {
            <img src="@Model.CurrentVideoThumbnail"
                class="img-responsive">
        }
        else
        {
            <img src="@Model.NextVideoThumbnail"
                class="img-responsive">
        }
```

```
    <div class="panel-body">
        @if (Model.NextVideoId == 0)
        {
            <p>COURSE COMPLETED</p>
            <h5>@Model.CurrentVideoTitle</h5>
        }
        else
        {
            <p>COMING UP</p>
            <h5>@Model.NextVideoTitle</h5>
        }

        <div class="btn-group" role="group">
            @if (Model.PreviousVideoId == 0)
            {
                <a class="btn btn-default" disabled href="#">
                    Previous
                </a>
            }
            else
            {
                <a class="btn btn-default"
                    href="~/Membership/Video/@Model.PreviousVideoId">
                    Previous
                </a>
            }
            @if (Model.NextVideoId == 0)
            {
                <a class="btn btn-default" disabled href="#">
                    Next
                </a>
            }
            else
            {
                <a class="btn btn-default"
                    href="~/Membership/Video/@Model.NextVideoId">
                    Next
                </a>
            }
        </div>
    </div>
</div>
}
```

Styling the _VideoComingUpPartial Partial View

Open the *video.css* style sheet and make the button group as wide as possible.

```
.coming-up .btn-group {
    width: 100%;
}
```

Make each of the buttons take up 50% of the button group's width.

```
.coming-up .btn-group .btn {
    width: 50%;
}
```

Adding the _InstructorBioPartial Partial View

The last section you will add to the **Video** view is the **_InstructorBioPartial** partial view that displays information about the instructor.

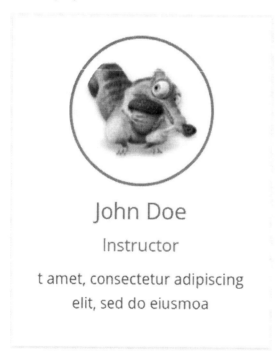

John Doe

Instructor

t amet, consectetur adipiscing
elit, sed do eiusmoa

1. Open the **Video** view.
2. Add a call to the **PartialAsync** method to render the **_InstructorBioPartial** partial view below the previous if-block inside the <div> decorated with the **col-sm-3**

Bootstrap class. Pass in the **instructor** object from the view model to the partial view. Surround the method call with an if-block that checks that the view model and the **Instructor** object are not **null**.

```
@if (Model != null && Model.Instructor != null)
{
    @await Html.PartialAsync("_InstructorBioPartial",
        Model.Instructor)
}
```

3. Save the file and refresh the **Video** view in the browser. The **_InstructorBioPartial** partial view should be displayed below the **_VideoComingUpPartial** partial view.

The complete code for the **Video** view:

```
@model VideoViewModel

@{
    ViewData["Title"] = "Video";
}

<div class="membership top-margin video-content">
    <div class="row navigation-bar">
        <div class="col-sm-12">
            <a class="btn btn-primary"
                href="~/Membership/Course/@Model.Course.CourseId">
                <span class="glyphicon glyphicon-menu-left"></span>
                Back to @Model.Course.CourseTitle
            </a>
        </div>
    </div>
    <div class="row">
        <div class="col-sm-9">
            @if (Model != null && Model.Video != null &&
                Model.LessonInfo != null && Model.Course != null)
            {
                @await Html.PartialAsync("_VideoPlayerPartial", Model)
            }
        </div>
```

```
        <div class="col-sm-3">
            @if (Model != null && Model.LessonInfo != null)
            {
                @await Html.PartialAsync("_VideoComingUpPartial",
                    Model.LessonInfo)
            }

            @if (Model != null && Model.Instructor != null)
            {
                @await Html.PartialAsync("_InstructorBioPartial",
                    Model.Instructor)
            }
        </div>
    </div>
</div>

@section Scripts
{
    <script type="text/javascript">
        $(function () {
            jwplayer("video").setup({
                file: $("#hiddenUrl").text(),
                image: $("#hiddenImageUrl").text()
            });
        });
    </script>
}
```

Summary

In this chapter, you added the **Video** view and its partial views. You also added JWPlayer to be able to play video content in the view.

In the next part of the book, you will add the entity classes to a SQL Server Database using Entity Framework migrations. You will also add a new data repository to interact with the database. When the repository is in place, you will create a user interface for administrators.

21. Creating the Database Tables

Introduction

In this chapter, you will create the database tables for storing the video data; you have already created the tables for user data in an earlier chapter. Although you could have several database contexts for interacting with the database, you will continue using the one that you already have created.

You will also seed the database with initial data after the tables have been created. This makes it a little easier for you to follow along as you create the various views, because then the views will already contain data that you are familiar with.

When the tables have been created and seeded, you will create a new data repository class called **SqlReadRepository**, using the same **IReadRepository** interface that you used when adding the **MockReadRepository** class. When it has been implemented, you will replace the **MockReadRepository** class with the **SqlReadRepository** class for the **IRead-Repository** service in the **ConfigureServices** method in the **Startup** class. This will make the application use the data from the database, instead of the mock data.

Technologies Used in This Chapter
1. **C#** – Used when seeding the database and creating the repository.
2. **Entity framework** – To create and interact with the new tables from the repository.
3. **LINQ** – To query the database tables.

Overview

Your first objective is to create the tables for storing video-related data in the database, and seed them with data. The second objective is to create a data repository that can communicate with the database tables, and use it instead of the existing mock data repository in the **Startup** class. After implementing these two steps, the application will work with live data from the database.

Adding the Tables

To tell Entity Framework that the entity classes should be added as tables in the database, you need to add them as **DbSet** properties in the **VODContext** class. Use the same entity classes you created for the mock data repository.

You can then inject the **VODContext** class into the constructor of the **SqlReadRepository** class to perform CRUD (Create, Read, Update, Delete) operations on the tables. When you replace the **MockReadRepository** class with the **SqlReadRepository** class in the **IReadRepository** service, the database data will be used instead of the mock data.

Adding the Entity Classes to the VODContext

1. Open the **VideoOnDemand.Data** project in the Solution Explorer.
2. Open the **VODContext** class located in the *Data* folder.
3. Add all the entity classes as **DbSet** properties to the class.
    ```
    public DbSet<Course> Courses { get; set; }
    public DbSet<Download> Downloads { get; set; }
    public DbSet<Instructor> Instructors { get; set; }
    public DbSet<Module> Modules { get; set; }
    public DbSet<UserCourse> UserCourses { get; set; }
    public DbSet<Video> Videos { get; set; }
    ```

4. Because the **UserCourses** table has a composite key (**UserId** and **CourseId**), you need to specify that in the **OnModelCreating** method in the **VODContext** class. In previous versions of ASP.NET you could do this in the entity class with attributes, but in ASP.NET Core 2.0 you pass it in as a Lambda expression to the **HasKey** method.
    ```
    builder.Entity<UserCourse>().HasKey(uc => new { uc.UserId,
    uc.CourseId });
    ```

5. To avoid cascading deletes when a parent record is deleted, you can add a delete behavior to the **OnModelCreating** method. A cascading delete will delete all related records to the one being deleted; for instance, if you delete an order, all its order rows will also be deleted.
    ```
    foreach (var relationship in
    builder.Model.GetEntityTypes().SelectMany(e =>
    e.GetForeignKeys()))
    {
        relationship.DeleteBehavior = DeleteBehavior.Restrict;
    }
    ```

The complete code in the **VODContext** class:

```
public class VODContext : IdentityDbContext<User>
{
    public DbSet<Course> Courses { get; set; }
    public DbSet<Download> Downloads { get; set; }
    public DbSet<Instructor> Instructors { get; set; }
    public DbSet<Module> Modules { get; set; }
    public DbSet<UserCourse> UserCourses { get; set; }
    public DbSet<Video> Videos { get; set; }

    public VODContext(DbContextOptions<VODContext> options)
    : base(options) { }

    protected override void OnModelCreating(ModelBuilder builder)
    {
        base.OnModelCreating(builder);

        // Composite key
        builder.Entity<UserCourse>().HasKey(uc =>
            new { uc.UserId, uc.CourseId });

        // Restrict cascading deletes
        foreach (var relationship in builder.Model.GetEntityTypes()
            .SelectMany(e => e.GetForeignKeys()))
        {
            relationship.DeleteBehavior = DeleteBehavior.Restrict;
        }
    }
}
```

Creating the Tables

To add the tables to the database, you have to create a new migration and update the database.

1. Open the Package Manager Console and select **VideoOnDemand.Data** in the right drop-down.
2. Execute the following command to create the migration data.
   ```
   add-migration CreateVideoRelatedTables
   ```
3. Execute the following command to make the migration changes in the database.
   ```
   update-database
   ```

Adding Seed Data

To have some data to work with when the tables have been created, you will add seed data to them when they have been created. You need to add a class called **DbInitializer** to the *Data* folder to add seed data.

The seed data is added using a **static** method called **Initialize**, which you will need to add to the class.

If you want the database to be recreated every time migrations are applied, you can add the following two code lines at the beginning of the **Initialize** method. This could be useful in certain test scenarios where you need a clean database. You will not add them in this exercise because you want to keep the data you add between migrations.

```
context.Database.EnsureDeleted();
context.Database.EnsureCreated();
```

To add data to a table, you create a list of the entity type and add instances to it. Then you add that list to the entity collection (the **DbSet** for that entity), in the **VODContext** class, using the **context** object passed into the **Initialize** method.

Note that the order in which you add the seed data is important because some tables may be related to other tables and need the primary keys from those tables.

1. Right click on the *VideoOnDemand.Data* project and select **Set as StartUp Project**.
2. Add a class called **DbInitializer** to the *Migrations* folder.
3. Add a **public static** method called **RecreateDatabase** to the class. It should take the **VODContext** as a parameter. This method can be called if the database needs to be recreated; all data in the entire database will be deleted when it is recreated.
   ```
   public static void RecreateDatabase(VODContext context)
   {
   }
   ```
4. Add calls to the **EnsureDeleted** and **EnsureCreated** methods on the **context** object to delete the database and create a new one.
   ```
   context.Database.EnsureDeleted();
   context.Database.EnsureCreated();
   ```

5. Add a **public static** method called **Initialize** to the class. It should take the **VODContext** as a parameter.

```
public static void Initialize(VODContext context)
{
}
```

6. To avoid repeating dummy data, you will add a variable with some Lorem Ipsum text that can be reused throughout the seeding process. You can generate Lorem Ipsum text at the following URL: http://loripsum.net/.

```
var description = "Lorem ipsum dolor sit amet, consectetur
adipiscing elit, sed do eiusmod tempor incididunt ut labore et
dolore magna aliqua. Ut enim ad minim veniam, quis nostrud
exercitation ullamco laboris nisi ut aliquip ex ea commodo
consequat.";
```

7. Add three variables that will hold the email, admin role id, and user id. These variables will be used throughout the **Initialize** method. The email address should be in the **AspNetUsers** table; if not, then add a user with that email address or change the variable value to an email address in the table. The user should be an administrator; if not, open the **AspNetUserRoles** table and add a record using the user id and *1* in the **RoleId** column.

```
var email = "a@b.c";
var adminRoleId = string.Empty;
var userId = string.Empty;
```

8. Try to fetch the user id from the **AspNetUsers** table using the **Users** entity.

```
if (context.Users.Any(r => r.Email.Equals(email)))
    userId = context.Users.First(r => r.Email.Equals(email)).Id;
```

9. Add an if-block that checks if the user id was successfully fetched. All the remaining code should be placed inside this if-block.

```
if (!userId.Equals(string.Empty))
{
}
```

10. Use the **Instructors** entity to add instructor data to the **Instructors** table in the database if no data has been added.

```
if (!context.Instructors.Any())
{
    var instructors = new List<Instructor>
    {
```

```
            new Instructor {
                Name = "John Doe",
                Description = description.Substring(20, 50),
                Thumbnail = "/images/Ice-Age-Scrat-icon.png"
            },
            new Instructor {
                Name = "Jane Doe",
                Description = description.Substring(30, 40),
                Thumbnail = "/images/Ice-Age-Scrat-icon.png"
            }
        };
        context.Instructors.AddRange(instructors);
        context.SaveChanges();
    }
```

11. Use the **Courses** entity to add course data to the **Courses** table in the database if no data has been added.

```
if (!context.Courses.Any())
{
    var instructorId1 = context.Instructors.First().Id;
    var instructorId2 = int.MinValue;
    var instructor = context.Instructors.Skip(1).FirstOrDefault();
    if (instructor != null) instructorId2 = instructor.Id;
    else instructorId2 = instructorId1;

    var courses = new List<Course>
    {
        new Course {
            InstructorId = instructorId1,
            Title = "Course 1",
            Description = description,
            ImageUrl = "/images/course.jpg",
            MarqueeImageUrl = "/images/laptop.jpg"
        },
        new Course {
            InstructorId = instructorId2,
            Title = "Course 2",
            Description = description,
            ImageUrl = "/images/course1.jpg",
            MarqueeImageUrl = "/images/laptop.jpg"
        },
        new Course {
            InstructorId = instructorId1,
            Title = "Course 3",
```

```
                Description = description,
                ImageUrl = "/images/course3.jpg",
                MarqueeImageUrl = "/images/laptop.jpg"
            }
        };
        context.Courses.AddRange(courses);
        context.SaveChanges();
    }
```

12. Try to fetch the course ids from the newly added courses. These ids will be used in other tables when referencing courses.

```
var courseId1 = int.MinValue;
var courseId2 = int.MinValue;
var courseId3 = int.MinValue;
if (context.Courses.Any())
{
    courseId1 = context.Courses.First().Id;

    var course = context.Courses.Skip(1).FirstOrDefault();
    if (course != null) courseId2 = course.Id;

    course = context.Courses.Skip(2).FirstOrDefault();
    if (course != null) courseId3 = course.Id;
}
```

13. Use the **UserCourses** entity to connect users and courses.

```
if (!context.UserCourses.Any())
{
    if (!courseId1.Equals(int.MinValue))
        context.UserCourses.Add(new UserCourse
            { UserId = userId, CourseId = courseId1 });

    if (!courseId2.Equals(int.MinValue))
        context.UserCourses.Add(new UserCourse
            { UserId = userId, CourseId = courseId2 });

    if (!courseId3.Equals(int.MinValue))
        context.UserCourses.Add(new UserCourse
            { UserId = userId, CourseId = courseId3 });

    context.SaveChanges();
}
```

14. Use the **Modules** entity to add module data to the **Modules** table in the database if no data has been added.

```
if (!context.Modules.Any())
{
    var modules = new List<Module>
    {
        new Module { CourseId = courseId1, Title = "Modeule 1" },
        new Module { CourseId = courseId1, Title = "Modeule 2" },
        new Module { CourseId = courseId2, Title = "Modeule 3" }
    };
    context.Modules.AddRange(modules);
    context.SaveChanges();
}
```

15. Try to fetch the module ids from the newly added modules. These ids will be used in other tables when referencing modules.

```
var moduleId1 = int.MinValue;
var moduleId2 = int.MinValue;
var moduleId3 = int.MinValue;
if (context.Modules.Any())
{
    moduleId1 = context.Modules.First().Id;

    var module = context.Modules.Skip(1).FirstOrDefault();
    if (module != null) moduleId2 = module.Id;
    else moduleId2 = moduleId1;

    module = context.Modules.Skip(2).FirstOrDefault();
    if (module != null) moduleId3 = module.Id;
    else moduleId3 = moduleId1;
}
```

16. Use the **Videos** entity to add video data to the **Videos** table in the database if no data has been added.

```
if (!context.Videos.Any())
{
    var videos = new List<Video>
    {
        new Video { ModuleId = moduleId1, CourseId = courseId1,
            Position = 1, Title = "Video 1 Title",
            Description = description.Substring(1, 35),
            Duration = 50, Thumbnail = "/images/video1.jpg",
            Url = "https://www.youtube.com/watch?v=BJFyzpBcaCY"
```

```
            },
            new Video { ModuleId = moduleId1, CourseId = courseId1,
                Position = 2, Title = "Video 2 Title",
                Description = description.Substring(5, 35),
                Duration = 45, Thumbnail = "/images/video2.jpg",
                Url = "https://www.youtube.com/watch?v=BJFyzpBcaCY"
            },
            new Video { ModuleId = moduleId1, CourseId = courseId1,
                Position = 3, Title = "Video 3 Title",
                Description = description.Substring(10, 35),
                Duration = 41, Thumbnail = "/images/video3.jpg",
                Url = "https://www.youtube.com/watch?v=BJFyzpBcaCY"
            },
            new Video { ModuleId = moduleId3, CourseId = courseId2,
                Position = 1, Title = "Video 4 Title",
                Description = description.Substring(15, 35),
                Duration = 41, Thumbnail = "/images/video4.jpg",
                Url = "https://www.youtube.com/watch?v=BJFyzpBcaCY"
            },
            new Video { ModuleId = moduleId2, CourseId = courseId1,
                Position = 1, Title = "Video 5 Title",
                Description = description.Substring(20, 35),
                Duration = 42, Thumbnail = "/images/video5.jpg",
                Url = "https://www.youtube.com/watch?v=BJFyzpBcaCY"
            }
        };
        context.Videos.AddRange(videos);
        context.SaveChanges();
    }
```

17. Use the **Downloads** entity to add download data to the **Downloads** table in the database if no data has been added.

```
if (!context.Downloads.Any())
{
    var downloads = new List<Download>
    {
        new Download{ModuleId = moduleId1, CourseId = courseId1,
            Title = "ADO.NET 1 (PDF)", Url = "https://some-url" },
        new Download{ModuleId = moduleId1, CourseId = courseId1,
            Title = "ADO.NET 2 (PDF)", Url = "https://some-url" },
        new Download{ModuleId = moduleId3, CourseId = courseId2,
            Title = "ADO.NET 1 (PDF)", Url = "https://some-url" }
    };
```

```
        context.Downloads.AddRange(downloads);
        context.SaveChanges();
    }
```

18. Inject the **VODContext** class into the **Configure** method in the **Startup** class.
    ```
    public void Configure(IApplicationBuilder app, IHostingEnvironment
    env, VODContext db) { ... }
    ```

19. Add a **using** statement to the **VideoOnDemand.Migrations** namespace.
    ```
    using VideoOnDemand.Data.Migrations
    ```

20. Call the **DbInitializer.Initialize** method with the **db** object, above the **App.Run**
    method call, to add the seed data when the application is started.
    ```
    DbInitializer.Initialize(db);
    ```

21. To fill the tables with the seed data, you have to start the application (Ctrl+F5).

22. Right click on the *VideoOnDemand.UI* project and select **Set as StartUp Project**.

23. Open the *SQL Server Object Explorer*.

24. Open the database and make sure that entity tables have been added.

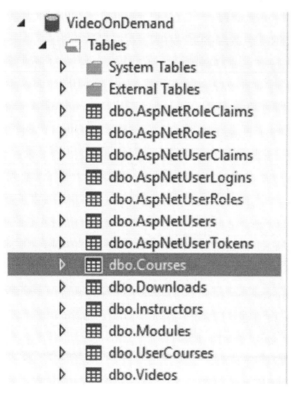

25. Right click on them and select **View Data** to verify that the seed data has been added.

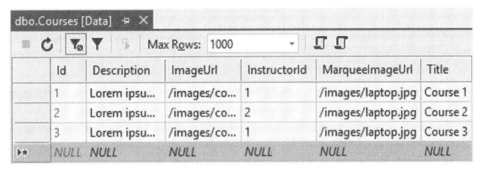

26. If for some reason the data hasn't been added, then recreate the database by calling the **RecreateDatabase** method you added earlier once from the **Configure** method in the **Startup** class. Remember to add a new user with the *a@b.c* email address and assign it the *Admin* role that you also have to add to the database, like you did in an earlier chapter.

The complete code for the **Configure** method in the **Startup** class:

```
public void Configure(IApplicationBuilder app, IHostingEnvironment env,
VODContext db)
{
    loggerFactory.AddConsole(Configuration.GetSection("Logging"));
    loggerFactory.AddDebug();

    if (env.IsDevelopment())
    {
        app.UseDeveloperExceptionPage();
    }

    DbInitializer.Initialize(db);

    app.Run(async (context) =>
    {
        await context.Response.WriteAsync("Hello World!");
    });
}
```

Summary

In this chapter, you created the application-related tables in the database and seeded them with data.

Next, you will create a data repository service that communicates with the database tables and use it instead of the existing mock data repository. After the repository swap, the application uses live data from the database.

22. The Database Read Service

Introduction

In this chapter, you will create a service called **DbReadService** in the **VideoOnDemand. Data** project. This service will be used from the **UI** and **Admin** projects to read data from the database. Since this is a service that will be injected with dependency injection, you need to create an interface for it.

The service will be called through a second service in the **UI** project called **SqlRead-Repository**, using the same **IReadRepository** interface that you used when adding the **MockReadRepository** class. You will replace the **MockReadRepository** class with the **SqlReadRepository** class for the **IReadRepository** service in the **ConfigureServices** method in the **Startup** class. This will make the application use the data from the database, instead of the mock data.

The **Admin** project doesn't have a service and will therefore use the **DbReadService** service directly.

Technologies Used in This Chapter

1. **C#** – Used to create the service.
2. **Entity framework** – To interact with the tables from the repository.
3. **LINQ** – To query the database tables.
4. **Reflection** – To fetch the names of intrinsic entities.

Overview

Your objective is to create a data service that communicates with the database tables. Some methods will use reflection to fetch intrinsic entities – properties in an entity that references other entities, essentially reading data from related tables.

Adding the DbReadService Service

You need to add an interface called **IDbReadService** that can be used from the two other projects with dependency injection to fetch data from the database. You then need to implement the interface in a class called **DbReadService** that contains the code to access the database.

The methods will be implemented as generic methods that can handle any entity and therefore fetch data from any table in the database.

Adding the Service Interface and Class

1. Open the **VideoOnDemand.Data** project.
2. Add a new folder to it called *Services*.
3. Right click on the folder, select **Add-New Item**, and select the **Interface** template. Add an interface called **IDbReadService** to the folder.
4. Add the **public** access modifier to the interface to make it accessible from any project.
   ```
   public interface IDbReadService { }
   ```
5. Add a class called **DbReadService** to the *Services* folder.
6. Add the interface to the class.
   ```
   public class DbReadService : IDbReadService
   {
   }
   ```
7. Add a constructor to the class and inject the **VODContext** to get access to the database from the service. Store the object in a class-level variable called **_db**.
   ```
   private VODContext _db;
   public DbReadService(VODContext db)
   {
       _db = db;
   }
   ```
8. Save the files.

The code for the **IDbReadService** interface, so far:

```
public interface IDbReadService { }
```

The code for the **DbReadService** class, so far:

```
public class DbReadService : IDbReadService
{
    private VODContext _db;
    public DbReadService(VODContext db)
    {
        _db = db;
    }
}
```

Fetching All Records in a Table (Get)

This overload (version) of the **Get** method will return all records in the specified table. Like all the other public methods you will add to this service, this one will be a generic method that can handle any entity. You choose the table to read from by defining the desired entity for the method when it is called.

Since the method will return all records in the table, no parameters are necessary.

The result will be returned as an **IQueryable<TEntity>**, which means that you can expand the query with LINQ without fetching any data.

1. Open the **IDbReadService** interface.
2. Add a method definition for a **Get** method that is defined by the entity type that substitutes the generic **TEntity** type when the method is called. You must limit the **TEntity** type to only classes since an entity only can be created using a class; if you don't do this a value type such as **int** or **double** can be used with the method, which would generate an exception.
    `IQueryable<TEntity> Get<TEntity>() where TEntity : class;`
3. Add the **Get** method to the **DbReadService** class, either manually or by using the **Quick Actions** light bulb button. If you auto generate the method with **Quick Actions**, you have to remove the **throw** statement.
4. Use the **Set** method on the **_db** context with the generic **TEntity** type to access the table associated with the defining entity.
    `return _db.Set<TEntity>();`
5. Save all files.

The code for the **IDbReadService** interface, so far:

```
public interface IDbReadService
{
    IQueryable<TEntity> Get<TEntity>() where TEntity : class;
}
```

The complete code for the **Get** method:

```
public IQueryable<TEntity> Get<TEntity>() where TEntity : class
{
    return _db.Set<TEntity>();
}
```

Finding an Entity's Intrinsic Entity Properties (GetEntityNames)

This method will return the names of all entity properties in an entity class. The names are then used to load these entities when the parent entity is loaded into memory. An example of intrinsic entity properties can be found in the **Course** class that has two. The first is the **Instructor** property and the second is the **Modules** collection.

If you have direct access to the **DbSets** in the database context class, you can use eager loading to load the data. But when working with generics and the methods in the **IRead-Repository** interface, the solution is a little bit more complex. One way to solve this is to use reflection to find the names of the intrinsic entities and load them using the combination of three methods: **Include**, which is available as an extension method on an entity loaded with the **Set** method on the database context, or the **Collection** and **Reference** extension methods available on the **Entry** method on the database context.

The private **GetEntityNames<TEntity>** method you will create will examine all properties in the entity defining the method and return the names of all properties that correspond to **DbSet** properties in the **VODContext** class, which are entities. It should not be added to the **IDbReadService** interface since it is a helper method only used internally in the **DbReadService** class.

To fetch the names, you first have to find the **DbSets** in the **VODContext** class by calling the **GetProperties** method on the type. You do this by reflecting over that class and fetching the names of all properties that are public and of instance type, and where the property type name contains *DbSet*.

Then you fetch all public instance properties in the entity defining the **GetEntityNames** method by calling the **GetProperties** method on the entity's type.

You then need to separate the collection properties from the reference (class) properties and return their names in two different collections from the **GetEntityNames** method; the easiest way to return two values from a method is to use tuples, which is built into C# 7 and later. Note that the **return** statement returns two collections called **collections** and **classes** by specifying the name of the tuple – defined by the method – followed by the name of the variable that holds the value.

```
private (IEnumerable<string> collections, IEnumerable<string>
references) GetEntityNames<TEntity>() where TEntity : class
{
    ...
    return (collections: collections, references: classes);
}
```

1. Open the **DbReadService** class.
2. Add a private method definition for a **GetEntityNames** method that is defined by the entity type that substitutes the generic **TEntity** type when the method is called. The method shouldn't have any parameters and it should return two **string** collections called **collections** and **references**. You must limit the **TEntity** type to classes since an entity only can be created using a class; if you don't do this a value type such as **int** or **double** can be used with the method, which would generate an exception.

    ```
    private (IEnumerable<string> collections, IEnumerable<string>
    references) GetEntityNames<TEntity>() where TEntity : class
    {
    }
    ```

3. Add the **DbSets** defined in the **VODContext** class. Use the **GetProperties** method on the class's type, and the property's **PropertyType.Name** property in a **Where** LINQ method to fetch only the properties whose type name contains *DbSet*. Store the **DbSets** in a variable called **dbsets**.

    ```
    var dbsets = typeof(VODContext)
        .GetProperties(BindingFlags.Public | BindingFlags.Instance)
        .Where(z => z.PropertyType.Name.Contains("DbSet"))
        .Select(z => z.Name);
    ```

4. Fetch the properties in the type defining the **GetEntityNames** method, the **TEntity** type. Use the **GetProperties** method on the type to fetch the properties.

    ```
    var properties = typeof(TEntity)
        .GetProperties(BindingFlags.Public | BindingFlags.Instance);
    ```

5. Fetch all intrinsic entity collection properties in the entity (**TEntity**). Use the entities stored in the **dbsets** collection that you fetched earlier to make sure that the property is defined as a **DbSet** in the **VODContext** class.

    ```
    var collections = properties
        .Where(l => dbsets.Contains(l.Name))
        .Select(s => s.Name);
    ```

6. Fetch all intrinsic entity reference properties (a class, not a collection) in the entity (**TEntity**). Use the entities stored in the **dbsets** collection that you fetched earlier to make sure that the property is defined as a **DbSet** in the **VODContext** class. You have to add an "s" at the end of the property name since a class property is declared without a plural "s" in the entity (i.e. **Instructor**), but the **DbSet** names are declared with the plural "s" in the **VODContext** class.

```
var classes = properties
    .Where(c => dbsets.Contains(c.Name + "s"))
    .Select(s => s.Name);
```

7. Return the name collections from the method as a tuple. Left of the colon is the name of the tuple variable defined by the **GetEntityNames** method, and to the right is the name of the collection containing the names you created with reflection in the method.

```
return (collections: collections, references: classes);
```

8. Save all files.

The complete code for the **GetEntityNames** method:

```
private (IEnumerable<string> collections, IEnumerable<string>
references) GetEntityNames<TEntity>() where TEntity : class
{
    var dbsets = typeof(VODContext)
        .GetProperties(BindingFlags.Public | BindingFlags.Instance)
        .Where(z => z.PropertyType.Name.Contains("DbSet"))
        .Select(z => z.Name);

    // Get the names of all the properties (tables) in the generic
    // type T that is represented by a DbSet
    var properties = typeof(TEntity)
        .GetProperties(BindingFlags.Public | BindingFlags.Instance);

    var collections = properties
        .Where(l => dbsets.Contains(l.Name))
        .Select(s => s.Name);

    var classes = properties
        .Where(c => dbsets.Contains(c.Name + "s"))
        .Select(s => s.Name);

    return (collections: collections, references: classes);
}
```

Fetching a Record by Id from a Table (Get)

This overload (version) of the **Get** method will return a single record from the specified table using the id passed-in through the **id** parameter. The returned record will contain related records if the method's **includeRelatedRecords** parameter is **true**.

Like all the other public methods, you will add it to the service. You choose the table to read from by defining the desired entity for the method when it is called.

The method's return data type is **TEntity**.

Begin by fetching the record from the table defined by the **TEntity** type and the passed-in id; this is easiest done by first calling the **Set** method for the **TEntity** type on the **context** object to get access to the table and then tag on the **Find** method on the **Set** method to get the record.

```
var record = _db.Set<TEntity>().Find(new object[] { id });
```

Then add an if-block that checks that the record variable isn't **null** and that the **includeRelatedRecords** parameter is **true**. If the criteria are met, the intrinsic **DbSet** properties should be loaded and filled with data.

Call the **GetEntityNames** method you added earlier inside the if-block to fetch the names of the **DbSet** properties in the **TEntity** type. Store the names in a variable called **entities**.

Iterate over the two name collections returned from the method – inside the if-block – and call the **Collection** and **Load** method on the **Entry** method to load the entities for the names in the **collections** collection. Do the same for the names in the **references** collection, but call the **Reference** method instead of the **Collection** method.

```
foreach (var entity in entities.collections)
    _db.Entry(record).Collection(entity).Load();
```

1. Open the **IDbReadService** interface.
2. Add a method definition for a **Get** method that is defined by the entity type that substitutes the generic **TEntity** type when the method is called. The method should have two parameters: **includeRelatedRecords (bool)**, which should have a default value of **false**, and **id (int)** for the record id. The method should return a record of the same type (**TEntity**) that defines the method. You must limit the **TEntity** type to only classes since an entity only can be created using a class; if

you don't do this a value type such as **int** or **double** can be used with the
method, which would generate an exception.

```
TEntity Get<TEntity>(int id, bool includeRelatedEntities = false)
where TEntity : class;
```

3. Add the **Get** method to the **DbReadService** class, either manually or by using the
    Quick Actions light bulb button. If you auto generate the method with **Quick
    Actions**, you have to remove the **throw** statement.

4. Use the **Set** method on the **_db** context with the generic **TEntity** type to access
    the table associated with the defining entity, and then tag on the **Find** method to
    fetch the record matching the passed-in id.

```
var record = _db.Set<TEntity>().Find(new object[] { id });
```

5. Add an if-block that checks that the record variable isn't **null** and that the
    includeRelatedRecords parameter is **true**.

```
if (record != null && includeRelatedEntities)
{
}
```

6. Fetch the names of the intrinsic entities by calling the **GetEntityNames** method
    inside the if-block. Store the returned collections in a variable called **entities**.

```
var entities = GetEntityNames<TEntity>();
```

7. Iterate over the names in the **collections** collection and load the entities for the
    names in the collection inside the if-block.

```
foreach (var entity in entities.collections)
    _db.Entry(record).Collection(entity).Load();
```

8. Iterate over the names in the **references** collection and load the entities for the
    names in the collection inside the if-block.

```
foreach (var entity in entities.references)
    _db.Entry(record).Reference(entity).Load();
```

9. Return the record below the if-block (with or without related records).

```
return record;
```

10. Save all files.

The code for the **IDbReadService** interface, so far:

```
public interface IDbReadService
{
    IQueryable<TEntity> Get<TEntity>() where TEntity : class;
    TEntity Get<TEntity>(int id, bool includeRelatedEntities = false)
        where TEntity : class;
}
```

The complete code for the **Get** method:

```
public TEntity Get<TEntity>(int id, bool includeRelatedEntities = false)
where TEntity : class
{
    var record = _db.Set<TEntity>().Find(new object[] { id });

    if (record != null && includeRelatedEntities)
    {
        var entities = GetEntityNames<TEntity>();

        // Eager load all the tables referenced by the generic type T
        foreach (var entity in entities.collections)
            _db.Entry(record).Collection(entity).Load();

        foreach (var entity in entities.references)
            _db.Entry(record).Reference(entity).Load();
    }

    return record;
}
```

Fetching a Record in a Table with a Composite Primary Key (Get)

This overload (version) of the **Get** method will return a single record with a composite primary key from the specified table. The method should return a record of the same generic type that defines the method (**TEntity**) and have two parameters: **userId** (**string**) and **id** (**int**).

Like all the other public methods you will add to this service, this one will be a generic method that can handle any entity with a composite primary key consisting of a **string** and an **int**. You choose the table to read from by defining the desired entity for the method when it is called.

Fetch the record from the table defined by the **TEntity** type and the passed-in ids; this is easiest done by first calling the **Set** method for the **TEntity** type on the context object to get access to the table and then tag on the **Find** method on the **Set** method to get the record.

```
var record = _db.Set<TEntity>().Find(new object[] { userId, id });
```

1. Open the **IDbReadService** interface.
2. Add a method definition for a **Get** method that is defined by the entity type that substitutes the generic **TEntity** type when the method is called. The method should have two parameters: **userId (string)** and **id (int)** for the record id. The method should return a record of the same type (**TEntity**) that defines the method. You must limit the **TEntity** type to only classes since an entity only can be created using a class; if you don't do this a value type such as **int** or **double** can be used with the method, which would generate an exception.
   ```
   TEntity Get<TEntity>(string userId, int id) where TEntity : class;
   ```
3. Add the **Get** method to the **DbReadService** class, either manually or by using the **Quick Actions** light bulb button. If you auto generate the method with **Quick Actions**, you have to remove the **throw** statement.
4. Use the **Set** method on the **_db** context with the generic **TEntity** type to access the table associated with the defining entity, and then tag on the **Find** method to fetch the record matching the passed-in ids.
   ```
   var record = _db.Set<TEntity>().Find(new object[] { userId, id });
   ```
5. Return the record.
   ```
   return record;
   ```
6. Save all files.

The code for the **IDbReadService** interface, so far:

```
public interface IDbReadService
{
    IQueryable<TEntity> Get<TEntity>() where TEntity : class;
    TEntity Get<TEntity>(int id, bool includeRelatedEntities = false)
        where TEntity : class;
    TEntity Get<TEntity>(string userId, int id) where TEntity : class;
}
```

The complete code for the **Get** method:

```
public TEntity Get<TEntity>(string userId, int id) where TEntity : class
{
    var record = _db.Set<TEntity>().Find(new object[] { userId, id });
    return record;
}
```

Fetch All Records and Related Records for an Entity (GetWithIncludes)

This method (**GetWithIncludes**) will return a collection of records for the entity defining the method along with their related records. The related records are fetched for the entity's intrinsic entity properties. The **Course** entity, for example, has two intrinsic entity properties: **Instructor** and **Modules**.

The **GetWithIncludes** method should return an **IEnumerable<TEntity>** to be able to return a collection of records for the entity defining the method. No parameters are necessary since the defining entity determines which records to fetch.

An example of when you would use this method is when you fetch all **UserCourse** entities and want to load the **User** and **Course** entity properties at the same time for all the **UserCourse** entities.

Like all the other public methods you will add to this service, this one will be a generic method that can handle any entity. You choose the table to read from by defining the desired entity for the method when it is called.

Start by calling the **GetEntityNames** method you created earlier and store the result in a variable called **entityNames**.

Create a **DbSet** for the entity (**TEntity**) by calling the **Set** method on the database context object. Store the **DbSet** in a variable called **dbset**.

Merge the entity names from the two collections (**collections** and **references**) in the **entityNames** variable. You can use the **Union** LINQ method and store the result in a variable called **entities**.

Iterate over the names in the **entities** variable and include each entity in the main entity by calling the **Include** method on the **Set** method, and then the **Load** method on the **Include** method.

```
foreach (var entity in entities)
```

```
_db.Set<TEntity>().Include(entity).Load();
```

1. Open the **IDbReadService** interface.
2. Add a method definition for the **GetWithIncludes** method that is defined by the entity type that substitutes the generic **TEntity** type when the method is called. The method should be parameterless and return an **IEnumerable<TEntity>**. You must limit the **TEntity** type to only classes since an entity only can be created using a class; if you don't do this a value type such as **int** or **double** can be used with the method, which would generate an exception.
   ```
   IEnumerable<TEntity> GetWithIncludes<TEntity>() where TEntity :
   class;
   ```
3. Add the **GetWithIncludes** method to the **DbReadService** class, either manually or by using the **Quick Actions** light bulb button. If you auto generate the method with **Quick Actions**, you have to remove the **throw** statement.
4. Call the **GetEntityNames** method you created earlier to fetch the names of all intrinsic entity properties.
   ```
   var entityNames = GetEntityNames<TEntity>();
   ```
5. Use the **Set** method on the **_db** context with the generic **TEntity** type to access the table associated with the defining entity.
   ```
   var dbset = _db.Set<TEntity>();
   ```
6. Merge the names from the **collections** and **references** collections returned from the **GetEntityNames** method. You can use the **Union** LINQ method.
   ```
   var entities = entityNames.collections.Union(
       entityNames.references);
   ```
7. Iterate over the names and load the entities corresponding to the names. Use the **Include** and **Load** methods on the **Set** method to load the entities.
   ```
   foreach (var entity in entities)
       _db.Set<TEntity>().Include(entity).Load();
   ```
8. Return the entities in the **dbset** variable.
   ```
   return dbset;
   ```
9. Save all files.

The code for the **IDbReadService** interface, so far:

```
public interface IDbReadService
{
    IQueryable<TEntity> Get<TEntity>() where TEntity : class;
    TEntity Get<TEntity>(int id, bool includeRelatedEntities = false)
        where TEntity : class;
    TEntity Get<TEntity>(string userId, int id) where TEntity : class;
    IEnumerable<TEntity> GetWithIncludes<TEntity>()
        where TEntity : class;
}
```

The complete code for the **GetWithIncludes** method:

```
public IEnumerable<TEntity> GetWithIncludes<TEntity>() where TEntity :
class
{
    var entityNames = GetEntityNames<TEntity>();
    var dbset = _db.Set<TEntity>();

    var entities = entityNames.collections.Union(
        entityNames.references);

    foreach (var entity in entities)
        _db.Set<TEntity>().Include(entity).Load();

    return dbset;
}
```

Converting an Entity List to a List of SelectList Items (GetSelectList)

This method (**GetSelectList**) will return a collection of **SelectList** items from the entity (table) defining the method. **SelectList** items are used when displaying data in drop-down controls in a Razor Page or a MVC view.

The **GetSelectList** method should have two parameters: **valueField (String)**, which holds the name of the property that will represent the value of each item in the drop-down (usually an id), and **textField (String)**, which holds the name of the property that will represent the text to display for each item in the drop-down.

Like all the other public methods you will add to this service, this one will be a generic method that can handle any entity. You choose the table to read from by defining the desired entity for the method when it is called.

Start by calling the **Get** method that returns an **IQueryable<TEntity>** and store the result in a variable called **items**. Then create an instance of the **SelectList** class and pass in the **items** collection and **valueField** and **textField** parameters.

```
return new SelectList(items, valueField, textField);
```

1. Open the **IDbReadService** interface.
2. Add a method definition for the **GetSelectList** method that is defined by the entity type that substitutes the generic **TEntity** type when the method is called. The method should have two parameters: **valueField (String)** and **textField (String)**. The method should return an instance of the **SelectList** class. You must limit the **TEntity** type to only classes since an entity only can be created using a class; if you don't do this a value type such as **int** or **double** can be used with the method, which would generate an exception.
   ```
   SelectList GetSelectList<TEntity>(string valueField, string textField) where TEntity : class;
   ```
3. Add the **GetSelectList** method to the **DbReadService** class, either manually or by using the **Quick Actions** light bulb button. If you auto generate the method with **Quick Actions**, you have to remove the **throw** statement.
4. Call the **Get** method that returns an **IQueryable<TEntity>** and store the result in a variable called **items**.
   ```
   var items = Get<TEntity>();
   ```
5. Return an instance of the **SelectList** class where you pass in the **items** variable, the **valueField**, and **textField** parameters to the constructor.
   ```
   return new SelectList(items, valueField, textField);
   ```
6. Save all files.

The complete code for the **IDbReadService** interface:

```
public interface IDbReadService
{
    IQueryable<TEntity> Get<TEntity>() where TEntity : class;
    TEntity Get<TEntity>(int id, bool includeRelatedEntities = false)
        where TEntity : class;
    TEntity Get<TEntity>(string userId, int id) where TEntity : class;
    IEnumerable<TEntity> GetWithIncludes<TEntity>()
        where TEntity : class;
```

```
    SelectList GetSelectList<TEntity>(string valueField,
        string textField) where TEntity : class;
}
```

The complete code for the **Get** method:

```
public SelectList GetSelectList<TEntity>(string valueField, string
textField) where TEntity : class
{
    var items = Get<TEntity>();
    return new SelectList(items, valueField, textField);
}
```

Summary

In this chapter, you created a service for reading data from the database. This service will be used from the **Admin** and **UI** projects to fetch data.

Next, you will add a SQL Server repository service in the **UI** project and replace the **MockReadRepository** with it to read from the database.

23. SQL Data Repository

Introduction

In this chapter, you will create a new data repository class called **SqlReadRepository**, using the same **IReadRepository** interface that you used when adding the **MockReadRepository** class. When it has been implemented, you will replace the **MockReadRepository** class with the **SqlReadRepository** class for the **IReadRepository** service in the **ConfigureServices** method in the **Startup** class. This will make the application use the data from the database, instead of the hard-coded data.

Technologies Used in This Chapter

1. **C#** – To create the repository.
2. **LINQ/Lambda** – To query the database tables.

Overview

Your objective is to create a data repository that can communicate with the database tables through the **IDbReadService** service, and use it instead of the existing mock data repository in the **Startup** class. Then the application will work with live data from the database.

Adding the SqlReadRepository Class

1. Use the **AddTransient** method on the services object to add the **IDbReadService** service from the **VideoOnDemand.Data** project to the **ConfigureServices** method in the **Startup** class in the **VideoOnDemand.UI** project.
   ```
   services.AddTransient<IDbReadService, DbReadService>();
   ```
2. Add a class called **SqlReadRepository** to the *Repositories* folder.
3. Add a constructor that is injected with the **IDbReadService**. Store the injected object in a private class-level variable called **_db**; this will give access to the database through the service in the class.
   ```
   public class SqlReadRepository
   {
       private IDbReadService _db;
   ```

```
        public SqlReadRepository(IDbReadService db)
        {
            _db = db;
        }
    }
```

4. Implement the **IReadRepository** interface in the class. This will add the methods that you need to implement. To add all the methods, you can point to the red squiggly line, click the light bulb button, and select **Implement Interface**.
```
public class SqlReadRepository : IReadRepository
{
    ...
}
```

5. Open the **Startup** class.

6. Copy the **MockReadRepository** service declaration in **ConfigureServices** method and paste in the copy below the one you copied. Comment out the original **MockReadRepository** service declaration.
```
//services.AddSingleton<IReadRepository, MockReadRepository>();
services.AddSingleton<IReadRepository, MockReadRepository>();
```

7. You need to change the **AddSingleton** method to **AddScoped** for it to work with the **VODContext** in the **VideoOnDemand.Data** project. Also change the **MockReadRepository** class to the **SqlReadRepository** class you just added.
```
//services.AddSingleton<IReadRepository, MockReadRepository>();
services.AddScoped<IReadRepository, SqlReadRepository>();
```

The code for the **SqlReadRepository** class:

```
public class SqlReadRepository : IReadRepository
{
    private IDbReadService _db;

    public SqlReadRepository(IDbReadService db) { _db = db; }

    public Course GetCourse(string userId, int courseId)
    {
        throw new NotImplementedException();
    }
```

```
public IEnumerable<Course> GetCourses(string userId)
{
    throw new NotImplementedException();
}

public Video GetVideo(string userId, int videoId)
{
    throw new NotImplementedException();
}

public IEnumerable<Video> GetVideos(string userId, int moduleId = 0)
{
    throw new NotImplementedException();
}
}
```

Implementing the GetCourses Method

1. Remove the **throw** statement from the **GetCourses** method in the **SqlReadRepository** class.

2. Use the **_db** service variable to fetch all courses for a specific user.

   a. Call the **GetWithIncludes** method for the **UserCourses** to fetch all the course id and user id combinations from the database.

   ```
   var courses = _db.GetWithIncludes<UserCourse>();
   ```

   b. Now select only the id combinations for the user id passed in to the **GetCourses** method by calling the **Where** LINQ method on the **GetWithIncludes** method.

   ```
   var courses = _db.GetWithIncludes<UserCourse>().Where(uc =>
   uc.UserId.Equals(userId));
   ```

   c. Next select the **Course** objects included with the **UserCourse** entities by calling the **Select** LINQ method on the **Where** method.

   ```
   var courses = _db.GetWithIncludes<UserCourse>().Where(uc =>
   uc.UserId.Equals(userId)).Select(c => c.Course);
   ```

   d. Return the courses from the **GetCourses** method.

   ```
   return courses;
   ```

3. Run the application and verify that the courses are displayed in the **Dashboard** view.

The complete code for the **GetCourses** method:

```
public IEnumerable<Course> GetCourses(string userId)
{
    var courses = _db.GetWithIncludes<UserCourse>()
        .Where(uc => uc.UserId.Equals(userId))
        .Select(c => c.Course);

    return courses;
}
```

Implementing the GetCourse Method

This method will fetch one course from the database.

1. Remove the **throw** statement from the **GetCourse** method in the **SqlReadRepository** class.

2. Check that the user is allowed to access the requested course by calling the **Get** method on the **_db** service variable. Use the **UserCourse** entity to define the method's type. Pass in the values of the **userId** and **courseId** parameters to the method and check that the result isn't **null**. Store the result in a variable called **hasAccess**.

   ```
   var hasAccess = _db.Get<UserCourse>(userId, courseId) != null;
   ```

3. Return the default value (**null**) for the **Course** entity if the user doesn't have access to the course.

   ```
   if (!hasAccess) return default(Course);
   ```

4. Fetch the course by calling the **Get** method on the **_db** service variable. Pass in the value form the **courseId** parameter and the value **true** to specify that related entities should be filled with data.

   ```
   var course = _db.Get<Course>(courseId, true);
   ```

5. Iterate over the modules in the **Modules** property of the course and add the downloads and videos.

   ```
   foreach (var module in course.Modules) {
       module.Downloads = _db.Get<Download>().Where(d =>
           d.ModuleId.Equals(module.Id)).ToList();
       module.Videos = _db.Get<Video>().Where(d =>
           d.ModuleId.Equals(module.Id)).ToList();
   }
   ```

6. Return the course from the method.

```
return course;
```

7. Run the application and click on one of the courses in the **Dashboard** view to verify that the correct course is displayed.

The complete code for the **GetCourse** method:

```
public Course GetCourse(string userId, int courseId)
{
    var hasAccess = _db.Get<UserCourse>(userId, courseId) != null;
    if (!hasAccess) return default(Course);

    var course = _db.Get<Course>(courseId, true);

    foreach (var module in course.Modules)
    {
        module.Downloads = _db.Get<Download>().Where(d =>
            d.ModuleId.Equals(module.Id)).ToList();

        module.Videos = _db.Get<Video>().Where(d =>
            d.ModuleId.Equals(module.Id)).ToList();
    }

    return course;
}
```

Implementing the GetVideo Method
This method will fetch one video from the database.

1. Remove the **throw** statement from the **GetVideo** method in the **SqlReadRepository** class.
2. Fetch the video matching the video id in the **videoId** parameter passed into the **GetVideo** method by calling the **Get** method on the **_db** service variable.
   ```
   var video = _db.Get<Video>(videoId);
   ```
3. Check that the user is allowed to view the video belonging to the course specified by the **CourseId** property of the video object. Return the default value for the **Video** entity if the user doesn't have access.
   ```
   var hasAccess =
       _db.Get<UserCourse>(userId, video.CourseId) != null;
   ```

```
if (!hasAccess) return default(Video);
```

4. Return the video in the **video** variable.

```
return video;
```

The complete code for the **GetVideo** method:

```
public Video GetVideo(string userId, int videoId)
{
    var video = _db.Get<Video>(videoId);

    var hasAccess = _db.Get<UserCourse>(userId, video.CourseId) != null;
    if (!hasAccess) return default(Video);

    return video;
}
```

Implementing the GetVideos Method

This method will fetch all videos associated with the logged in user.

1. Remove the **throw** statement from the **GetVideos** method in the **SqlReadRepository** class.
2. Fetch the module matching the module id in the **moduleId** parameter passed into the **GetVideos** method by calling the **Get** method on the **_db** service variable.

   ```
   var module = _db.Get<Module>(moduleId);
   ```

3. Check that the user is allowed to view the video belonging to the course specified by the **CourseId** property of the video object. Return the default value for a list of **Video** entities if the user doesn't have access.

   ```
   var hasAccess =
       _db.Get<UserCourse>(userId, module.CourseId) != null;
   if (!hasAccess) return default(IEnumerable<Video>);
   ```

4. Fetch the videos by calling the **Get** method on the **_db** service variable and filter on the **moduleId** parameter value with the **Where** LINQ method.

   ```
   var videos = _db.Get<Video>().Where(v =>
       v.ModuleId.Equals(moduleId));
   ```

5. Return the videos in the **videos** variable.

   ```
   return videos;
   ```

6. Run the application and click on one of the video items in the **Course** view to verify that the correct video is displayed.

The complete code for the **GetVideos** method:

```
public IEnumerable<Video> GetVideos(string userId, int moduleId)
{
    var module = _db.Get<Module>(moduleId);

    var hasAccess =
        _db.Get<UserCourse>(userId, module.CourseId) != null;
    if (!hasAccess) return default(IEnumerable<Video>);

    var videos = _db.Get<Video>().Where(v =>
        v.ModuleId.Equals(moduleId));

    return videos;
}
```

Summary

In this chapter, you created a data repository that communicates with the database tables through the **IDbReadService** service in the **Data** project and used it instead of the existing hard-coded data repository. After the repository swap, the application uses live data from the database.

Next, you will start building a user interface for administrators.

Part 3:
Razor Pages
How to Build the Administrator Website

24. Adding the Admin Project

Overview

In this chapter, you will add a **Web Application** project called **VideoOnDemand.Admin** to the solution. The application will be used by administrators to add, remove, update, and view data that then can be accessed by the regular users from the **VideoOnDemand.UI** project. To access the data, the application will share the same database context and data read service that you added earlier to the **VideoOnDemand.Data** project.

You will be using the **Web Application** project template when creating the **Admin** project; this is a new template that wasn't available in ASP.NET Core 1.1. It makes it possible to create a lightweight application using Razor Pages instead of creating a full-fledged MVC application with models, views, and controllers.

A good candidate for this type of application is a small company web page that contains a few pages of data with a navigation menu and maybe a few forms that the visitor can fill out.

Even though you are working with Razor Pages (and not views), they are still part of the same MVC framework. This means that you don't need to learn a whole new framework to create Razor Pages if you already know MVC.

Although it's possible to contain all code, C#, Razor syntax, and HTML in the same file, this is not the recommended practice. Instead, you create two files, one *.cshtml.cs* code-behind C# file and one *.cshtml* file for HTML and Razor syntax. The two files are presented as one node in the Solution Explorer inside the *Pages* folder.

The Razor Page looks and behaves much like a regular view; the difference is that it has a code-behind file that sort of acts as the page's model and controller in one.

One easy way to determine if a *.cshtml* file is a page (and not a view) is to look for the **@page** directive, which should be present in all Razor Pages.

Just like views, the Razor Pages have a **_Layout** view for shared HTML and imported JavaScripts and CSS style sheets. They also have a **_ViewImports** view where **using** statements, namepaces, and TagHelpers can be added that should be available in all pages.

Technologies Used in This Chapter

- **ASP.NET Core Web Application** – The project template used to create the MVC application.

Creating the Admin Solution

To make the implementation go a little bit smoother, you will use the **Web Application** template instead of the **Empty Template** that you used in the first part of the book. The benefit is that much of the plumbing already has been added to the project, so that you can be up-and-running quickly, doing the fun stuff – coding.

The template will install the basic Razor Pages plumbing and an **Account** controller that will be used when logging out from the **Admin** application.

Because the project template adds a lot of files that won't be needed in the **Admin** application, you will delete them before beginning the implementation. Most of the files you will remove handle database migrations, which you already have in place in the **Data** project, and Razor Pages that handle user scenarios that won't be covered in this book.

1. Open the **VideoOnDemand** solution in Visual Studio 2017.
2. Right click on the **VideoOnDemand** solution node in the Solution Explorer and select **File-New-Project** in the menu.
3. Click on the **Web** tab and then select **ASP.NET Core Web Application** in the template list (see image below).
4. Name the project *VideoOnDemand.Admin* in the **Name** field.
5. Click the **OK** button.
6. Make sure that **.NET Core** and **ASP.NET Core 2.0** are selected in the drop-downs.
7. Select **Web Application** in the template list.
8. Click the **Change Authentication** button and select **Individual User Accounts** in the pop-up dialog. This will make it possible for visitors to register and log in with your site using an email and a password (see image below).
   a. Select the **Individual User Accounts** radio button.
   b. Select **Store user account in-app** in the drop-down.
   c. Click the **OK** button in the pop-up dialog.
9. Click the **OK** button in the wizard dialog.

10. Open *appsettings.json* and add the following connection string. It's important that the string is added as a single line of code.

```
"ConnectionStrings": {
    "DefaultConnection": "Server=(localdb)\\mssqllocaldb;
        Database=VideoOnDemand2;Trusted_Connection=True;
        MultipleActiveResultSets=true"
}
```

11. Expand the *Pages-Account* folder. This folder contains the Razor Pages responsible for handling different user scenarios. In this application, you will only implement two of them, so you will remove the other pages to make it easier for you to find the relevant pages.

12. Delete the *Pages-Account-Manage* folder and all its content.

13. Delete all the pages in the *Pages-Account* folder except the **Login** and **Register** pages.

14. Delete the *Data* folder and all its content. This folder contains database-related files that already exist in the **Data** project.

15. Delete the *EmailSenderExtensions.cs* file from the *Extensions* folder.

16. Delete the *EmailSender.cs* and *IEmailSender.cs* files from the *Services* folder, but keep the folder.

17. Add a reference to the **VideoOnDemand.Data** project.

18. Open the **Startup** class and locate the **ConfigureServices** method.

19. Change the default **ApplicationDbContext** class defined for the **AddDbContext** and **AddEntityFrameworkStores** service methods to the **VODContext** class in the **Data** project. You need to resolve the **VideoOnDemand.Data.Data** namespace.

20. Change the default **ApplicationUser** class defined for the **AddIdentity** service method to the **User** class in the **Data** project. You need to resolve the **VideoOnDemand.Data.Data.Entities** namespace.

21. Remove the **AddRazorPagesOptions** from the **AddMvc** service method.

```
.AddRazorPagesOptions(options => {
    options.Conventions.AuthorizeFolder("/Account/Manage");
    options.Conventions.AuthorizePage("/Account/Logout");
})
```

22. Delete the **IEmailSender** service declaration.

```
services.AddSingleton<IEmailSender, EmailSender>();
```

23. Locate the **Configure** method in the **Startup** class.

24. Remove the database error page configuration.
app.UseDatabaseErrorPage();

25. Remove the **VideoOnDemand.Admin.Data** and **VideoOnDemand.Admin. Services using** statements and save all the files.

26. Open the **AccountController** class and remove all erroneous **using** statements and replace all occurrences of the **ApplicationUser** class with the **User** class from the **VideoOnDemand.Data** project. You have to resolve the **VideoOnDemand.Data.Data.Entities** namespace.

27. Repeat step 26 for the *Login.cshtml.cs* and *Register.cshtml.cs* files.

28. Remove the **IEmailService** field and DI from the *Register.cshtml.cs* file.

29. Open the **_ViewImports** view and replace the **VideoOnDemand.Admin.Data using** statement with the **VideoOnDemand.Data.Data.Entities using** statement.

30. Open the **_LoginPartial** view and remove the **VideoOnDemand.Admin.Data using** statement and replace all occurrences of the **ApplicationUser** class with the **User** class from the **VideoOnDemand.Data** project.

31. Save all files. Right click on the **Admin** project in the Solution Explorer and select **Set as StartUp Project** and then press F5 on the keyboard to run the application. Log in as one of the users you have previously added, and then log out.

The complete code in the **ConfigureServices** method:

```
public void ConfigureServices(IServiceCollection services)
{
    services.AddDbContext<VODContext>(options => options.UseSqlServer(
        Configuration.GetConnectionString("DefaultConnection")));

    services.AddIdentity<User, IdentityRole>()
        .AddEntityFrameworkStores<VODContext>()
        .AddDefaultTokenProviders();

    services.AddMvc();
}
```

The complete code in the **Configure** method:

```
public void Configure(IApplicationBuilder app, IHostingEnvironment env)
{
    if (env.IsDevelopment())
    {
        app.UseDeveloperExceptionPage();
        app.UseBrowserLink();
    }
    else
    {
        app.UseExceptionHandler("/Error");
    }

    app.UseStaticFiles();
    app.UseAuthentication();

    app.UseMvc(routes =>
    {
        routes.MapRoute(
            name: "default",
            template: "{controller}/{action=Index}/{id?}");
    });
}
```

Summary

In this chapter, you created the **VideoOnDemand.Admin** project that will enable administrators to update, delete, add and view data that will be available to regular users visiting the **VideoOnDemand.UI** website.

Next, you will start building a user interface for administrators by adding a dashboard and an **Admin** menu that will be used when navigating to the Razor Pages that will manipulate the data in the database.

25. The Administrator Dashboard

Introduction

In this chapter, you will create an **Admin** dashboard with links to all **Index** Razor Pages associated with the entities you have added. Since you know that a folder for pages should have the same name as its corresponding entity, all the dashboard items can be added before the actual folders and pages have been created.

You will create the dashboard using two partial views, one for the dashboard called **_DashboardPartial** and one for its items (cards) called **_CardPartial**. The dashboard partial view is rendered in the main **Index** page located in the *Pages* folder and will be restricted to logged in users. The partial views are loaded with the **PartialAsync** method located in the **Html** class.

You will also remove the **About** and **Contact** links and pages, and change the text to *Dashboard* for the **Home** link. Then you will move the menu into a partial view named **_MenuPartial** and render it from the **_Layout** view. Then you will restrict the menu to logged in users that belong to the **Admin** role.

Technologies Used in This Chapter

1. **C# and Razor** – To add authorization checks in the **_DashboardPartial** view.
2. **HTML** – To create the dashboard and its items.

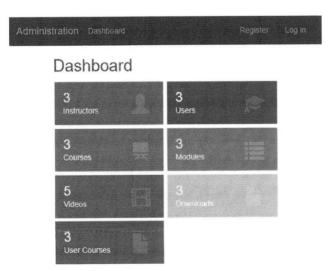

Modifying the Navigation Menu

The first thing you will modify is the menu in the navigation bar. By default, it has three links: **Home**, **About**, **Contact**, which are unnecessary since they won't be used in this administrator application. You will change the **Home** link to **Dashboard** and remove the other two. You will also remove the two **About** and **Contact** Razor Pages that the corresponding links open.

Then you will create a partial view named **_MenuPartial** to which you will move the remaining menu and then reference it from the **_Layout** partial view with the **PartialAsync** method.

1. Open the **_Layout** partial view in the **Admin** project.
2. Delete the two <li> elements for **About** and **Contact**.
3. Change the text to *Dashboard* for the **Home** <li> element.
4. Delete the **About** and **Contact** pages from the *Pages* folder.
5. Right click on the *Pages* folder and select **Add-New Item**.
6. Add a **MVC View Page** named **_MenuPartial** and remove all code in it. You use this template because a C# code-behind file is unnecessary.
7. Open the **_Layout** partial view and cut out the <ul> element containing the **Dashboard** <li> element and paste it into the **_MenuPartial** partial view.
    ```
    <ul class="nav navbar-nav">
        <li><a asp-page="/Index">Dashboard</a></li>
    </ul>
    ```
8. Open the **_Layout** view and use the **PartialAsync** method to render the **_MenuPartial** view above the **PartialAsync** method call that renders the **_LoginPartial** view.
    ```
    @await Html.PartialAsync("_MenuPartial")
    ```
9. Run the application. Log out if you are logged in. The navigation menu should now only have the **Dashboard**, **Register**, and **Login** links.
10. Now you will modify the menu to only be displayed when logged in. Add two **using** statements to the **Identity** and **Data.Entities** namespaces to the **_MenuPartial** view. The first one is needed to check if the user is signed in and the second is needed to gain access to the **User** entity that holds the logged in user's identity.
    ```
    @using Microsoft.AspNetCore.Identity
    @using VideoOnDemand.Data.Data.Entities
    ```

11. You need to inject the **SignInManager** for the current user to be able to check if the user is logged in.
    `@inject` `SignInManager<User> SignInManager`

12. Surround the <ul> element with an if-block that uses the **SignInManager's IsSignedIn** method to check that the user is logged in. Also call the **IsInRole** method on the **User** entity to check that the user belongs to the **Admin** role.
    `@if (SignInManager.IsSignedIn(User) && User.IsInRole("Admin")) { }`

13. Save all files.
14. Switch to the browser and refresh. The **Dashboard** link should disappear.
15. Open the **AspNetUserRoles** table in the database and make sure that the user id for the user you will log in with is in this table and has been assigned the admin role id.
16. Log in as an administrator. The **Dashboard** link should reappear.
17. Go back to the **_Layout** view in Visual Studio.
18. Change the text *VideoOnDemand.Admin* in the **navbar-brand** <a> element to *Administration*.
19. Save the file.
20. Switch to the browser and refresh. The brand to the far left in the navigation menu should now show *Administration*.
21. Refresh the browser to make sure that the text *Administration* is displayed to the far left in the navigation bar.

The complete code for the **_MenuPartial** view:

```
@using Microsoft.AspNetCore.Identity
@using VideoOnDemand.Data.Data.Entities
@inject SignInManager<User> SignInManager

@if (SignInManager.IsSignedIn(User) && User.IsInRole("Admin"))
{
    <ul class="nav navbar-nav">
        <li><a asp-page="/Index">Dashboard</a></li>
    </ul>
}
```

Creating the Dashboard

In this section, you will create a dashboard in the main **Index** page in the **Admin** project. This dashboard will act as a menu that displays statistics about the tables.

The first step is to add a method to the **DbReadService** in the **Data** project that returns the necessary statistics for the dashboard from the database.

The second step is to create a partial view called **_CardPartial** that will be used to render the dashboard items (cards).

The third step is to modify the **Index** view and its code-behind file to receive data from the database through the **DbReadService**.

Adding the Count Method to the DbReadService

To be able to display the number of records stored in the entity tables in the database on the cards, you will add a method called **Count** to the **DbReadService** class in the **Data** project. Instead of adding a model class with properties for the record count in each table and returning an object of that class from the method, you will make the method return a tuple containing the values.

Use the **Count** method on the entities in the method to return their number of records.

1. Open the **IDbReadService** interface in the **Data** project.
2. Add a method definition that returns an integer for each entity count. Use camel casing to name the tuple parameters the same as the entities. The **Count** method you add should not take any in-parameters.
   ```
   (int courses, int downloads, int instructors, int modules, int
   videos, int users, int userCourses) Count();
   ```

3. Open the **DbReadService** class and add the **Count** method.
4. Return the number of records in each entity and assign the values to the appropriate tuple parameter. Use the **Count** method on each entity in the **_db** context object to fetch the number of records.
   ```
   return (
   courses: _db.Courses.Count(),
   downloads: _db.Downloads.Count(),
   instructors: _db.Instructors.Count(),
   modules: _db.Modules.Count(),
   videos: _db.Videos.Count(),
   users: _db.Users.Count(),
   userCourses: _db.UserCourses.Count());
   ```

5. Open the **Startup** class in the **Admin** project.
6. Add the **IDbReadService** service to the **ConfigureServices** method.
   ```
   services.AddTransient<IDbReadService, DbReadService>();
   ```

7. Save all files.

The complete code in the **IDbReadService** interface:

```
public interface IDbReadService
{
    IQueryable<TEntity> Get<TEntity>() where TEntity : class;
    TEntity Get<TEntity>(int id, bool includeRelatedEntities = false)
        where TEntity : class;
    TEntity Get<TEntity>(string userId, int id) where TEntity : class;
    IEnumerable<TEntity> GetWithIncludes<TEntity>()
        where TEntity : class;
    SelectList GetSelectList<TEntity>(string valueField,
        string textField) where TEntity : class;
    (int courses, int downloads, int instructors, int modules,
        int videos, int users, int userCourses) Count();
}
```

The complete code in the **Count** method:

```
public (int courses, int downloads, int instructors, int modules, int
videos, int users, int userCourses) Count()
{
    return (
        courses: _db.Courses.Count(),
        downloads: _db.Downloads.Count(),
        instructors: _db.Instructors.Count(),
        modules: _db.Modules.Count(),
        videos: _db.Videos.Count(),
        users: _db.Users.Count(),
        userCourses: _db.UserCourses.Count());
}
```

Adding the CardViewModel Class

The **_CardPartial** partial view will take a view model that contains the number of records, the background color of the card, the name of the Glyphicon to display on the card, a description, and the URL to navigate to.

The view model will be implemented as a class called **CardViewModel** in a folder called *Models*.

1. Add a folder to the **Admin** project called *Models*.
2. Add a class called **CardViewModel** in the *Models* folder.

3. Add properties for the previously mentioned data named: **Count (int)**, **Description (string)**, **Icon (string)**, **Url (string)**, **BackgroundColor (string)**.
4. Save the file.

The complete code for the **CardViewModel** class:

```
public class CardViewModel
{
    public int Count { get; set; }
    public string Description { get; set; }
    public string Icon { get; set; }
    public string Url { get; set; }
    public string BackgroundColor { get; set; }
}
```

Adding the _CardPartial Partial View

To keep the code in the **Index** Razor Page as clean as possible, you will create a partial view called **_CardPartial** that will be rendered using the **PartialAsync** method located in the **Html** class.

The partial view will use the **CardViewModel** as a model to render the data from the database.

1. Right click on the *Pages* folder and select **Add-New Item**.
2. Add a **MVC View Page** named **_CardPartial** and remove all code in it.
3. Use the **@model** directive to add the **CardViewModel** class as a model to the view.
   ```
   @model VideoOnDemand.Admin.Models.CardViewModel
   ```
4. Because the dashboard cards should act as links to the other **Index** views, you will add it as an <a> element to the **_CardPartial** view. Use the model's **Url** property in the **href** attribute, add a CSS class called **card** that can be used for styling, and use the **BackgroundColor** property to add a style for the card's background color.
   ```
   <a href="@Model.Url" class="card" style="background-color:
   @Model.BackgroundColor"></a>
   ```
5. Add a <div> element decorated with a CSS class called **card-content** that can be used for styling elements inside the <a> element.

6. Add a <div> element decorated with a class called **card-data** that can be used for styling elements inside the previously added <div> element.

7. Add an <h3> element for the model's **Count** property inside the previously added <div> element.

8. Add a <p> element for the model's **Description** property below the <h3> element.

9. Add a <span> element below the innermost <div> element for the Glyphicon; use the model's **Icon** property to define which icon to display.

```
<span class="glyphicon glyphicon-@Model.Icon.ToLower()
    card-icon"></span>
```

10. Save the view.

The complete code for the **_CardPartial** view:

```
@model Slask.Admin.Models.CardViewModel

<a href="@Model.Url" class="card" style="background-color:
@Model.BackgroundColor">
    <div class="card-content">
        <div class="card-data">
            <h3>@Model.Count</h3>
            <p>@Model.Description</p>
        </div>
        <span class="glyphicon glyphicon-@Model.Icon.ToLower()
            card-icon"></span>
    </div>
</a>
```

Calling the Count Method from the Index Razor Page

Before the **_CardPartial** view can be added to the **Index** Razor Page, the data need to be fetched from the database and added to a property in the main **Index** Razor Page's code-behind file. Use the **Count** method you added to the **DbReadService** in the **Data** project to fetch the data and create instances from the **CardViewModel** and assign the fetched data to them. Also, assign values for the other properties as well.

1. Open the **Index** Razor Page in the *Pages* folder.

2. Use DI to inject the **IDbReadService** interface from the **Data** project into the constructor and store the injected instance in a private field called **_db** to make

it available from all methods in the code file. This will give access to the database throughout the file.

```
private IDbReadService _db;

IndexModel(IDbReadService db)
{
    _db = db;
}
```

3. Add a tuple variable called **Cards** to the class. It should contain parameters of the **CardViewModel** class for each value returned from the **Count** method in the **DbReadService** class.

```
public (CardViewModel instructors, CardViewModel users,
        CardViewModel courses, CardViewModel modules,
        CardViewModel videos, CardViewModel downloads,
        CardViewModel userCourses) Cards;
```

4. Call the **Count** method in the injected instance of the **DbReadService** class in the **OnGet** method.

```
var count = _db.Count();
```

5. Return a tuple with the **CardViewModel** instances for the cards.

```
Cards = (
    instructors: new CardViewModel { BackgroundColor = "#9c27b0",
        Count = count.instructors, Description = "Instructors",
        Icon = "user", Url = "./Instructors/Index" },
    users: new CardViewModel { BackgroundColor = "#414141",
        Count = count.users, Description = "Users",
        Icon = "education", Url = "./Users/Index" },
    courses: new CardViewModel { BackgroundColor = "#009688",
        Count = count.courses, Description = "Courses",
        Icon = "blackboard", Url = "./Courses/Index" },
    modules: new CardViewModel { BackgroundColor = "#f44336",
        Count = count.modules, Description = "Modules",
        Icon = "list", Url = "./Modules/Index" },
    videos: new CardViewModel { BackgroundColor = "#3f51b5",
        Count = count.videos, Description = "Videos",
        Icon = "film", Url = "./Videos/Index" },
    downloads: new CardViewModel { BackgroundColor = "#ffcc00",
        Count = count.downloads, Description = "Downloads",
        Icon = "file", Url = "./Downloads/Index" },
    userCourses: new CardViewModel { BackgroundColor = "#176c37",
        Count = count.userCourses, Description = "User Courses",
        Icon = "file", Url = "./UserCourses/Index" }
```

```
        );
```

6. Save all files.

The complete code for the **Index.cshtml.cs** file:

```
public class IndexModel : PageModel
{
    private IDbReadService _db;
    public (CardViewModel instructors, CardViewModel users,
            CardViewModel courses, CardViewModel modules,
            CardViewModel videos, CardViewModel downloads,
            CardViewModel userCourses) Cards;

    public IndexModel(IDbReadService db)
    {
        _db = db;
    }

    public void OnGet()
    {
        var count = _db.Count();
        Cards = (
            instructors: new CardViewModel { BackgroundColor = "#9c27b0",
                Count = count.instructors, Description = "Instructors",
                Icon = "user", Url = "./Instructors/Index" },
            users: new CardViewModel { BackgroundColor = "#414141",
                Count = count.users, Description = "Users",
                Icon = "education", Url = "./Users/Index" },
            courses: new CardViewModel { BackgroundColor = "#009688",
                Count = count.courses, Description = "Courses",
                Icon = "blackboard", Url = "./Courses/Index" },
            modules: new CardViewModel { BackgroundColor = "#f44336",
                Count = count.modules, Description = "Modules",
                Icon = "list", Url = "./Modules/Index" },
            videos: new CardViewModel { BackgroundColor = "#3f51b5",
                Count = count.videos, Description = "Videos",
                Icon = "film", Url = "./Videos/Index" },
            downloads: new CardViewModel { BackgroundColor = "#ffcc00",
                Count = count.downloads, Description = "Downloads",
                Icon = "file", Url = "./Downloads/Index" },
            userCourses: new CardViewModel { BackgroundColor = "#176c37",
                Count = count.userCourses, Description = "User Courses",
                Icon = "file", Url = "./UserCourses/Index" }
        );
```

```
        }
}
```

Styling the _CardPartial View

To style the **_CardPartial** view – the dashboard cards – you first have to render the view once in the **Index** Razor Page located in the *Pages* folder so that you can see it in the browser. Then you can use CSS to style the view by adding selectors to a new CSS file called *dashboard.css* that you will add to the *wwwroot/css* folder.

1. Open the **Index** Razor Page located in the *Pages* folder.
2. Remove all HTML from the page and change the title to *Dashboard*.
   ```
   @page
   @model IndexModel
   @{
       ViewData["Title"] = "Dashboard";
   }
   ```
3. Use the **PartialAsync** method located in the **Html** class to render the **_CardPartial** view once.
   ```
   @await Html.PartialAsync("_CardPartial", Model.Cards.instructors)
   ```
4. Add a new style sheet called *dashboard.css* to the *wwwroot/css* folder.
5. Remove the **body** selector.
6. Open the **_Layout** view and drag in a link to the CSS file inside the **Development** element below the already existing links.
   ```
   <link rel="stylesheet" href="~/css/dashboard.css" />
   ```
7. Open the *bundleconfig.json* file and add the path to the *dashboard.css* file.
   ```
   "inputFiles": [
       "wwwroot/css/site.css",
       "wwwroot/css/dashboard.css"
   ]
   ```
8. Save all files and open the *dashboard.css* file.
9. Run the application and see what the card looks like unstyled.

3

Instructors

The code for the **Index** Razor Page, so far:

```
@page
@model IndexModel
@{
    ViewData["Title"] = "Dashboard";
}

@await Html.PartialAsync("_CardPartial", Model.Cards.instructors)
```

I suggest that you refresh the browser after each change you make to the *dashboard.css* file.

Add a selector for the **card** class. Add a margin of 3.3333rem; rem is relative to the font size of the root element. Display the element as a block with relative positioning and float it to the left. Set the width to 24% of its container and its minimal width to 200px. Make the text color white and remove any text decoration from the links (the underlining).

```
.card {
    margin: .33333333rem;
    display: block;
    position: relative;
    float: left;
    width: 24%;
    min-width: 200px;
    color: #fff !important;
    text-decoration: none;
}
```

Next, add a hover effect to the card by adding the **:hover** selector to a new **card** selector. Remove all text decorations and dial down the opacity. This makes it look like the color changes when the mouse pointer is hovering over the card.

```
.card:hover {
    text-decoration: none;
    opacity: .8;
}
```

Add 15px padding between the card's border and its content.

```
.card-content {
    padding: 15px;
}
```

Remove the top and bottom margin for the <h3> element and the bottom margin for the <p> element.

```
.card-data h3 {
    margin-top: 0;
    margin-bottom: 0;
}

.card-data p {
    margin-bottom: 0;
}
```

Style the icon with absolute positioning inside its container. Place the icon 25px from the right side and 30% from the top. Change the font size to 35px and its opacity to 0.2.

```
.card-icon {
    position: absolute;
    right: 25px;
    top: 30%;
    font-size: 35px;
    opacity: .2;
}
```

Modifying the Index Razor Page

Now it's time to put it all together to create the dashboard in the **Index** view. You will use Bootstrap row, column, and offset classes to create the two-card wide list of clickable items. You will add different Bootstrap classes for varying browser sizes, making the dashboard look nice on different devices.

You will also restrict access to the dashboard to logged in users belonging to the **Admin** role.

1. Add a <br /> element below the **PartialAsync** method call.
2. Add a <div> element below the <br /> element and decorate it with the **row** Bootstrap class to create a new row.
   ```
   <div class="row"></div>
   ```

3. Add another <div> inside the previous <div> and decorate it with column and offset Bootstrap classes for extra small, small, and medium device sizes.
   ```
   <div class="col-xs-offset-2 col-sm-8 col-sm-offset-3 col-md-6
   col-md-offset-4"></div>
   ```

4. Move the **PartialAsync** method call inside the column <div> and copy it.
5. Paste in the copied code and change the model from **instructors** to **users**.
   ```
   <div class="row">
       <div class="col-xs-offset-2 col-sm-8 col-sm-offset-3 col-md-6
           col-md-offset-4">
           @await Html.PartialAsync("_CardPartial",
               Model.Cards.instructors)
           @await Html.PartialAsync("_CardPartial",
               Model.Cards.users)
       </div>
   </div>
   ```

6. Run the application. Two cards should be displayed, one for instructors and one for users. Clicking on them will display an empty page because the needed **Index** Razor Pages have not been added yet.

7. Copy the <div> elements decorated with the row class and all its content. Paste it in three more times so that you end up with four rows below one another. Remove the last **PartialAsync** method call to avoid displaying two identical cards.

8. Change the model parameter for the cards to reflect the remaining pages: **courses**, **modules**, **videos**, **downloads** and **userCourses**.

9. Run the application. All seven entity cards should be displayed.

10. Add two **using** statements to the **Identity** and **Data.Entities** namespaces below the **@page** directive in the **Index** Razor Page. This will give access to ASP.NET Core's identity framework and the **User** entity in the **VideoOnDemand.Data** project.
```
@using Microsoft.AspNetCore.Identity
@using VideoOnDemand.Data.Data.Entities
```

11. Use the **@inject** directive to Inject the **SignInManager** for the **User** entity below the **using** statements. This will give access to the **IsSignedIn** method in the **SignInManager** that checks if a user is logged in.
```
@inject SignInManager<User> SignInManager
```

12. Add an if-block around the HTML below the <br /> element. Call the **IsSignedIn** method and pass in the **User** entity to it, and check that the user belongs to the **Admin** role by calling the **IsInRole** method on the **User** entity.
```
@if (SignInManager.IsSignedIn(User) && User.IsInRole("Admin"))
{
}
```

13. Run the application. If you are logged out the dashboard shouldn't be visible. Log out and log in as a regular user; the dashboard shouldn't be visible.

14. Log in as an **Admin** user for the dashboard to be visible.

The complete code for the **Index** Razor Page:

```
@page
@using Microsoft.AspNetCore.Identity
@using VideoOnDemand.Data.Data.Entities
@inject SignInManager<User> SignInManager
@model IndexModel
@{
    ViewData["Title"] = "Dashboard";
}

<br />
```

```
@if (SignInManager.IsSignedIn(User) && User.IsInRole("Admin"))
{
    <div class="row">
        <div class="col-xs-offset-2 col-sm-8 col-sm-offset-3 col-md-6
        col-md-offset-4">
            @await Html.PartialAsync("_CardPartial",
                Model.Cards.instructors)
            @await Html.PartialAsync("_CardPartial", Model.Cards.users)
        </div>
    </div>
    <div class="row">
        <div class="col-xs-offset-2 col-sm-8 col-sm-offset-3 col-md-6
        col-md-offset-4">
            @await Html.PartialAsync("_CardPartial",
                Model.Cards.courses)
            @await Html.PartialAsync("_CardPartial",
                Model.Cards.modules)
        </div>
    </div>
    <div class="row">
        <div class="col-xs-offset-2 col-sm-8 col-sm-offset-3 col-md-6
        col-md-offset-4">
            @await Html.PartialAsync("_CardPartial", Model.Cards.videos)
            @await Html.PartialAsync("_CardPartial",
                Model.Cards.downloads)
        </div>
    </div>
    <div class="row">
        <div class="col-xs-offset-2 col-sm-8 col-sm-offset-3 col-md-6
        col-md-offset-4">
            @await Html.PartialAsync("_CardPartial",
                Model.Cards.userCourses)
        </div>
    </div>
}
```

Summary

In this chapter, you added a dashboard for administrators. The cards (items) displayed in the dashboard were added as links to enable navigation to the other **Index** Razor Pages you will add in an upcoming chapter.

In the next chapter, you will add a menu with links to the same entities that the dashboard cards link to.

26. The Admin Menu

Introduction

In this chapter, you will create an **Admin** menu with links to all **Index** Razor Pages associated with the entities in the **Data** project. Since you know that a Razor Page folder will have the same name as its corresponding entity, all the menu items can be added before the pages have been created.

You will create the menu in a partial view called **_AdminMenuPartial** that is rendered in the **_Layout** view, using the **PartialAsync** method in the **Html** class.

Technologies Used in This Chapter

3. **C#** – To add authorization checks in the **_AdminMenuPartial** partial view.
4. **HTML** – To create the drop-down menu and its items

Overview

Your task is to create a menu for all the **Index** Razor Pages, in a partial view called **_Admin-MenuPartial**, and then render it from the **_Layout** view.

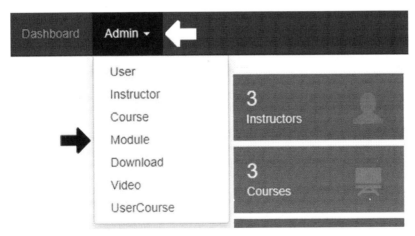

Adding the _AdminMenuPartial Partial View

Create a partial view called **_AdminMenuPartial** in the *Pages* folder. Add a <ul> element styled with the **nav navbar-nav** Bootstrap classes, to make it look nice in the navigation bar. Add an <li> element styled with the **drop-down** Bootstrap class to make it a drop-down button. Add an <a> element with the text *Admin* and a caret symbol, to the <li> element. Add a <ul> element styled with the **drop-down-menu** Bootstrap class that contains all the menu items as <li> elements. Use the **asp-page** Tag Helper to target the appropriate Razor Page.

1. Right click on the *Pages* folder and select **Add-New Item**.
2. Add a **MVC View Page** named **_ AdminMenuPartial** and delete all code in it.

3. Add two **using** statements to the **Identity** and **Data.Entities** namespaces below the **@page** directive in the **Index** Razor Page. This will give access to ASP.NET Core's identity framework and the **User** entity in the **VideoOnDemand.Data** project.
   ```
   @using Microsoft.AspNetCore.Identity
   @using VideoOnDemand.Data.Data.Entities
   ```

4. Use the **@inject** directive to Inject the **SignInManager** for the **User** entity below the **using** statements. This will give access to the **IsSignedIn** method in the **SignInManager** that checks if a user is logged in.
   ```
   @inject SignInManager<User> SignInManager
   ```

5. Add an if-block that checks if the user is signed in and belongs to the **Admin** role.
   ```
   @if (SignInManager.IsSignedIn(User) && User.IsInRole("Admin")) { }
   ```

6. Add a <ul> element decorated with the **nav** and **navbar-nav** Bootstrap classes inside the if-block. This is the main container for the *Admin* menu.

```
<ul class="nav navbar-nav">
</ul>
```

7. Add an <li> element inside the <ul> and decorate it with the **drop-down** Bootstrap class. This will be the container for the button that opens the menu.
```
<li class="dropdown">
</li>
```

8. Add an <a> element to the <li> element and assign # to its **href** attribute to stay on the current view when the menu item is clicked. To make it work as a toggle button for the menu, you must add the **drop-down-toggle** Bootstrap class, assign *drop-down* to the **data-toggle** attribute, and assign *button* to the **role** attribute. Assign *false* to the **aria-expanded** attribute to make the drop-down menu hidden by default.
```
<a href="#" class="dropdown-toggle" data-toggle="dropdown"
role="button" aria-expanded="false">
</a>
```

9. Add the text *Admin* and a <span> for the caret symbol to the <a> element; decorate the <span> with the **caret** and **text-light** classes.
```
Admin
<span class="caret text-light hidden-xs"></span>
```

10. Create the drop-down menu section of the menu by adding a <ul> element decorated with the **drop-down-menu** Bootstrap class and the **role** attribute set to *menu*, below the <a> element.
```
<ul class="dropdown-menu" role="menu">
</ul>
```

11. Add an <li> element containing an <a> element for each of the **Index** Razor Pages that you create. You can figure out all the folder names by looking at the entity class names; a folder should have the same name as the entity property in the **VODContext** class in the **Data** project. The URL path in the **asp-page** Tag Helper on the <a> element should contain the page folder followed by */Index*. Also, add a suitable description in the <a> element.
```
<li><a asp-page="/Instructors/Index">Instructor</a></li>
```

12. Open the **_Layout** view and use the **PartialAsync** method to render the partial view. Place the call to the **PartialAsync** method above the method call that renders the **_LoginPartial** partial view.

```
@await Html.PartialAsync("_AdminMenuPartial")
```

13. Save all the files and run the application (F5) and make sure that you are logged in as an administrator. Click the **Admin** menu to open it. Clicking any of the menu items will display an empty page because you haven't added the necessary **Index** Razor Pages yet.

The complete markup in the **_AdminMenuPartial** partial view:

```
@using Microsoft.AspNetCore.Identity
@using VideoOnDemand.Data.Data.Entities
@inject SignInManager<User> SignInManager

@if (SignInManager.IsSignedIn(User) && User.IsInRole("Admin"))
{
    <ul class="nav navbar-nav">
        <li class="dropdown">
            <a href="#" class="dropdown-toggle" data-toggle="dropdown"
                role="button" aria-expanded="false">
                Admin
                <span class="caret text-light hidden-xs"></span>
            </a>
            <ul class="dropdown-menu" role="menu">
                <li><a asp-page="/Instructors/Index">Instructor</a></li>
                <li><a asp-page="/Users/Index">User</a></li>
                <li><a asp-page="/Courses/Index">Course</a></li>
                <li><a asp-page="/Modules/Index">Module</a></li>
                <li><a asp-page="/Downloads/Index">Download</a></li>
                <li><a asp-page="/Videos/Index">Video</a></li>
                <li><a asp-page="/UserCourses/Index">UserCourse</a></li>
            </ul>
        </li>
    </ul>
}
```

Summary

In this chapter, you added the **Admin** menu and targeted the **Index** Razor Pages that you will add throughout the rest of the book.

In the next chapter, you will create a custom Tag Helper for the buttons you will add to the Razor Pages.

27. Custom Button Tag Helper

Introduction

In this chapter, you will create a configurable button Tag Helper that will be used instead of links in the Razor Pages. The Tag Helper will use attributes and attribute values to configure the finished HTML elements, such as the path, Bootstrap button style and size, what Glyphicon to display, if any, and the description on the button. The ids needed for some of the Razor Pages will be assigned dynamically, depending on the id attributes that have been added to the Tag Helper. All ids will begin with an *id* prefix, or just **id**, if that is the name of the action parameter.

For example, if the attribute **id-courseId="1"** is added to the Tag Helper, then a URL parameter with the name **courseId** will be added to the URL, with a value of 1. If you want to add a URL parameter named **id** with a value of 2, then the Tag Helper attribute should be **id="2"**.

<page-button path="Videos/Edit" **glyph**="pencil" id-courseId="1">
</page-button>

http://localhost:55962/Videos/Edit?courseId=1

<page-button path="Videos/Edit" **glyph**="pencil" id="2"></**page-button**>

http://localhost:55962/Videos/Edit?id=2

A Tag Helper is created with a C# class that builds the HTML element with C# code. It is then inserted into the views as HTML markup.

The class must inherit from the **TagHelper** class and implement a method called **Process**, which creates or modifies the HTML element. Tag Helper attributes can be added as properties in the class, or dynamically to a collection, by adding them to the HTML Tag Helper element.

Technologies Used in This Chapter
1. **C#** – to create the Tag Helper.
2. **HTML** – To create and add the Tag Helper to the Razor Pages.

Overview

Your task is to create a custom Tag Helper called **page-button**. You'll start with the more static approach using strings to pass in values, and then implement a more dynamic way of reading attributes and their values. The links should be displayed as Bootstrap-styled buttons with a description and/or a Glyphicon.

You should be able to configure the following with the Tag Helper: add a path, a description, use different Bootstrap button styles and sizes, and add a Glyphicon name. Each value should be represented by a string for easy use in the class.

For example, the following Tag Helpers would create two buttons. The first would have a pencil Glyphicon and the second the remove Glyphicon. The first button would be targeting the **Edit** Razor Page for altering a record in the database, and the other would target the **Delete** Razor Page that removes a record from the database. Both will use the **id** attribute to store the necessary record id. This id is then appended to the URL that the button targets, sending it to the code-behind page for that Razor Page. The **Bootstrap-style** attribute determines what color the button will have. The **@item.Id** fetches the values in the model's **Id** property and inserts it as a value for the **id** attribute.

```
<page-button path="Videos/Edit" Bootstrap-style="success" glyph="pencil"
id="@item.Id"></page-button>
```

```
<page-button path="Videos/Delete" Bootstrap-style="danger" glyph="remove"
id="@item.Id"></page-button>
```

The following Tag Helper would create a button without an id that targets the **Index** Razor Page, which lists all the records in the table. Note that it has both an information Glyphicon and a *Back to List* description (see image above).

```
<page-button path="Videos/Index" Bootstrap-style="primary"
glyph="info-sign" description="Back to List"></page-button>
```

The following Tag Helper would create a button without an id that targets the **Create** Razor Page, which is used to add a new record to the table. Note that it only has the description *Create New* and no Glyphicon.

```
<page-button path="Videos/Create" Bootstrap-style="primary"
description="Create New"></page-button>
```

Implementing the Page-Button Tag Helper

The Tag Helper should be created in a class called **PageButtonTagHelper** in a folder named *TagHelpers* located directly under the project node. Use the **New Item** dialog's **Razor Tag Helper** template.

You can use the **HtmlTargetElement** attribute to limit the scope of the Tag Helper to a specific HTML element type.

```
[HtmlTargetElement("my-tag-helper")]
public class MyTagHelperTagHelper : TagHelper
```

The Tag Helper will produce an <a> element styled as a Bootstrap button.

To make the Tag Helper available in Razor Pages, you need to add an **@addTagHelper** directive that includes all Tag Helpers in the project assembly, to the _ViewImports view.

```
@addTagHelper "*, VideoOnDemand.Admin"
```

When you add the Tag Helper to the view, it's very important that you use a closing tag, otherwise the Tag Helper won't work.

```
<page-button></page-button>
```

Creating the Tag Helper

1. Add an **@addTagHelper** directive that includes all Tag Helpers in the project assembly, to the _**ViewImports** view.
   ```
   @addTagHelper "*, VideoOnDemand.Admin"
   ```

2. Add a folder named *TagHelpers* to the project.

3. Add a **Razor Tag Helper** class called **PageButtonTagHelper** to the folder. Right click on the folder and select **Add-New Item**. Select the **Razor Tag Helper** template, name it, and click the **Add** button.
   ```
   [HtmlTargetElement("tag-name")]
   public class PageButtonTagHelper : TagHelper
   {
       public override void Process(TagHelperContext context,
       TagHelperOutput output) { }
   }
   ```

4. Change the **HtmlTargetElement** attribute to **page-button**. This will be the name of the Tag Helper's "element" name. It's not a real HTML element, but it looks like one, to blend in with the HTML markup. It will, however, generate a real HTML element when rendered.
```
[HtmlTargetElement("page-button")]
```

5. Add the properties that will hold the <page-button> element's attribute values to the class.

   a. **Path (string)**: The name of the folder containing the page to target and the name of the page to open. Should have an empty string as a default value. Example of a valid value for this element parameter: *Videos/Edit*.
   ```
   public string Path { get; set; } = string.Empty;
   ```

   b. **Description (string)**: The text to display on the button; don't add this attribute to the element if you want a button without a description. Should have an empty string as a default value.
   ```
   public string Description { get; set; } = string.Empty;
   ```

   c. **Glyph (string)**: The name of the Glyphicon to display on the button. You can skip the *glyphicon-* prefix; don't add this attribute to the element if you want a button without a Glyphicon. Should have an empty string as a default value. Example of two valid values for this element parameter that would display the same icon: *pencil* or *glyphicon-pencil*.
   ```
   public string Glyph { get; set; } = string.Empty;
   ```

   d. **BootstrapStyle (string)**: The name of the Bootstrap style to add to the button. Determines the button color; don't add this attribute to the element if you want the default button style. Should have the string *btn-default* as a default value. You can leave out the *btn-* prefix from the style. Example of two valid values for this element parameter that would display the same style: *success* or *btn-success*.
   ```
   public string BootstrapStyle { get; set; } = "btn-default";
   ```

   e. **BootstrapSize (string)**: The name of the Bootstrap size used to display the button. Determines the button size; don't add this attribute to the element if you want the small button size. Should have the string *btn-sm* as a default value. You can leave out the *btn-* prefix from the size.

Example of two valid values for this element parameter that would display button with the same size: *lg* or *btn-lg*.

```
public string BootstrapSize { get; set; } = "btn-sm";
```

6. Add exceptions to the **Process** method that are thrown if any of the parameters are **null**. Call the **Process** method in the base class below the if-statements.

```
if (context == null)
    throw new ArgumentNullException(nameof(context));
if (output == null)
    throw new ArgumentNullException(nameof(output));

base.Process(context, output);
```

7. Add a variable named **href** to hold the finished URL that will be added to the <a> element's **href** attribute.

```
var href = "";
```

8. Add an if-block that checks if the **Path** property has content.

```
if (Path.Trim().Length > 0)
{
}
```

9. Build the **href** inside the if-block using the **Path** property. If the **Path** property begins with a slash (/), you just add it to the **href** string, otherwise you add a slash and **Path** property.

```
if (Path.StartsWith('/'))
    href = $@"href='{Path.Trim()}'";
else
    href = $@"href='/{Path.Trim()}'";
```

10. Add the **href** variable to an <a> element, inside the if-block, by calling the **AppendHtml** method on the **output** object. Add the **Description** property to the <a> element.

```
output.Content.AppendHtml($@"<a {href}>{Description}</a>");
```

11. Open the **Index** Razor Page in the *Pages* folder and add the Tag Helper at the end of the page below all other content. Add a path to the **path** attribute and a description to the **description** attribute.

```
<page-button path="Videos/Create" description="Create New">
</page-button>
```

12. Run the application.

13. There should be a link with the text *Create New* below the cards in the dashboard.
14. Stop the application.

The code for the **page-button** Tag Helper, so far:

```
[HtmlTargetElement("page-button")]
public class PageButtonTagHelper : TagHelper
{
    #region Properties
    public string Path { get; set; } = string.Empty;
    public string Description { get; set; } = string.Empty;
    public string Glyph { get; set; } = string.Empty;
    public string BootstrapStyle { get; set; } = "btn-default";
    public string BootstrapSize { get; set; } = "btn-sm";
    #endregion

    public override void Process(TagHelperContext context,
    TagHelperOutput output)
    {
        if (context == null) throw new
            ArgumentNullException(nameof(context));
        if (output == null) throw new
            ArgumentNullException(nameof(output));

        base.Process(context, output);

        var href = "";

        if (Path.Trim().Length > 0)
        {
            // Assemble the value for the href parameter
            if (Path.StartsWith('/'))
                href = $@"href='{Path.Trim()}'";
            else
                href = $@"href='/{Path.Trim()}'";

            output.Content.AppendHtml($@"<a {href}>{Description}</a>");
        }
    }
}
```

URL Parameter Values

The next step will be to add ids to the URL's parameter list. You will implement this using the **TagHelperContext** object instead of adding properties to the class, because it makes more sense to do it dynamically. To implement this, you will check for attribute names beginning with *id* and fetch their values using the **AllAttributes** method on the **context** object.

1. Fetch the ids that begin with *id* from the **context** object and store them in a variable called **ids** below the **href** if/else statement.
   ```
   var ids = context.AllAttributes.Where(c =>
       c.Name.StartsWith("id"));
   ```

2. Add a **string** variable called **param** and a **foreach** loop that iterates over the **ids** array, below the code for the **ids** variable.
   ```
   var param = "";
   foreach (var id in ids)
   {
       ...
   }
   ```

3. Add a variable called **name** inside the loop, and assign the value from the **Name** property.
   ```
   var name = id.Name;
   ```

4. It's important to know if there are any characters after the dash, or if a dash exists; if it does, then the part after the dash becomes the name of the parameter. If the name is *id* without a dash, then the parameter name is **Id**. Add the code inside the loop.
   ```
   if (name.Contains("-"))
       name = name.Substring(name.IndexOf('-') + 1);
   ```

5. Assign the name in the **name** variable and the value in the **id.Value** property to the **param** variable to start building the parameter list. Add the code inside the loop.
   ```
   param += $"&{name}={id.Value}";
   ```

6. If the string begins with an ampersand (&) then remove it.
   ```
   if (param.StartsWith("&")) param = param.Substring(1);
   ```

7. If the **param** variable contains parameter values, then insert them into the URL in the **href** variable.

```
if (param.Length > 0) href = href.Insert(href.Length -
1,$"?{param}");
```

8. Open the **Index** Razor Page in the *Pages* folder and alter the Tag Helper to target the **Edit** action. Don't forget to add one or more ids.

```
<page-button path="Videos/Edit" description="Edit" id="1"
id-videoId="2"></page-button>
```

9. Run the application and inspect the URL when hovering over the link. The following URL should be displayed for the link.

http://localhost:55962/Videos/Edit?id=1&videoId=2

The code in the **Process** method, so far:

```
public override void Process(TagHelperContext context,

TagHelperOutput output)
{
    if (context == null)
        throw new ArgumentNullException(nameof(context));
    if (output == null)
        throw new ArgumentNullException(nameof(output));

    base.Process(context, output);

    var href = "";
    if (Path.Trim().Length > 0)
    {
        // Assemble the value for the href parameter
        if (Path.StartsWith('/')) href = $@"href='{Path.Trim()}'";
        else href = $@"href='/{Path.Trim()}'";

        var ids = context.AllAttributes.Where(c =>
            c.Name.StartsWith("id"));

        // Generate Id parameters
        var param = "";
        foreach (var id in ids)
        {
            var name = id.Name;
            if (name.Contains("-"))
```

```
            name = name.Substring(name.IndexOf('-') + 1);
            param += $"&{name}={id.Value}";
    }
    if (param.StartsWith("&")) param = param.Substring(1);
    if (param.Length > 0)
        href = href.Insert(href.Length - 1, $"?{param}");

    output.Content.AppendHtml($@"<a {href}>{Description}</a>");
    }
}
```

Glyphicons

The next step will be to display Glyphicons in the link. Let's use the **Glyph** property you added earlier to determine if an icon should be displayed, and use the value, if available, as the icon class name.

1. Add a **string** variable called **glyphClasses** below the param code and assign an empty string to it.
   ```
   var glyphClasses = string.Empty;
   ```

2. Trim the content in the **Glyph** property to remove any beginning or trailing spaces.
   ```
   Glyph = Glyph.Trim();
   ```

3. Remove the *glyphicon-* prefix if it has been added to the HTML attribute.
   ```
   if (Glyph.StartsWith("glyphicon-"))
       Glyph = Glyph.Substring(Glyph.IndexOf('-') + 1);
   ```

4. Add an if-block that checks that the **Glyph** property has content; you don't want to add the Glyphicon classes if no icon has been specified.
   ```
   if (Glyph.Length > 0)
   {
   }
   ```

5. Assign a string containing the Glyphicon classes to the **glyphClasses** variable inside the if-block.
   ```
   glyphClasses = $"class='glyphicon glyphicon-{Glyph}'";
   ```

6. Check if the **Description** property contains a value and add a space to the beginning of the description if that is the case. This will add some space between the icon and the descriptive text.

```
if (Description.Length > 0) Description = $" {Description}";
```

7. Add the value in the **glyphClasses** variable to a <span> before the **Description** property in the <a> element.

```
output.Content.AppendHtml($@"<a {href}>
    <span {glyphClasses}></span>{Description}</a>");
```

8. Open the **Index** Razor Page in the *Pages* folder and add a Glyphicon class name to the Tag Helper's **glyph** attribute.

```
<page-button path="Videos/Edit" description="Edit" id="1" id-
videoId="2" glyph="pencil"></page-button>
```

9. Run the application and navigate to the **Index** Razor Page in the *Pages* folder (the dashboard) and verify that the **pencil** Glyphicon is visible in the link.

The code in the **Process** method, so far:

```
public override void Process(TagHelperContext context,
TagHelperOutput output)
{
    if (context == null)
        throw new ArgumentNullException(nameof(context));
    if (output == null)
        throw new ArgumentNullException(nameof(output));

    base.Process(context, output);

    var href = "";
    if (Path.Trim().Length > 0)
    {
        // Assemble the value for the href parameter
        if (Path.StartsWith('/')) href = $@"href='{Path.Trim()}'";
        else href = $@"href='/{Path.Trim()}'";

        var ids = context.AllAttributes.Where(c =>
            c.Name.StartsWith("id"));

        // Generate Id parameters
        var param = "";
        foreach (var id in ids)
        {
            var name = id.Name;
            if (name.Contains("-"))
                name = name.Substring(name.IndexOf('-') + 1);
```

```
            param += $"&{name}={id.Value}";
        }

    if (param.StartsWith("&")) param = param.Substring(1);
    if (param.Length > 0)
        href = href.Insert(href.Length - 1, $"?{param}");

    // Display Glyph icons
    var glyphClasses = string.Empty;
    Glyph = Glyph.Trim();
    if (Glyph.StartsWith("glyphicon-"))
        Glyph = Glyph.Substring(Glyph.IndexOf('-') + 1);
    if (Glyph.Length > 0)
    {
        glyphClasses = $"class='glyphicon glyphicon-{Glyph}'";
        if (Description.Length > 0)
            Description = $" {Description}";
    }

    output.Content.AppendHtml($@"<a {href}>
        <span {glyphClasses}></span>{Description}</a>");
    }
}
```

Turning Links into Buttons

The next step will be to display the links as buttons, using Bootstrap classes and the **BootstrapStyle** and **BootstrapSize** properties.

1. Trim the content in the **BootstrapStyle** property and add the *btn-* Bootstrap prefix if it is missing.

```
BootstrapStyle = BootstrapStyle.Trim();
if (!BootstrapStyle.StartsWith("btn-"))
    BootstrapStyle = $"btn-{BootstrapStyle}";
```

2. Trim the content in the **BootstrapStyle** property and add the *btn-* Bootstrap prefix if it is missing.

```
BootstrapSize = BootstrapSize.Trim();
if (!BootstrapSize.StartsWith("btn-"))
    BootstrapSize = $"btn-{BootstrapSize}";
```

3. Add a **string** variable called **BootstrapClass** and assign an empty string to it.

```
var BootstrapClass = string.Empty;
```

4. Add the Bootstrap classes **btn-sm** and **btn-{*the fetched button type}** to the **BootstrapClass** variable if the **BootstrapStyle** and **BootstrapSize** properties have more than four characters, which means that they could have legitimate values.

```
if (BootstrapStyle.Length > 4 && BootstrapSize.Length > 4)
    BootstrapClass = $"class='{BootstrapSize} {BootstrapStyle}'";
```

5. Add the button style and size to the <a> element.

```
output.Content.AppendHtml($"<a {BootstrapClass} {href}><span
{glyphClasses}></span>{Description}</a>");
```

6. Add a **style** attribute to the <a> element and set the minimum width to 30px and display it as an inline block. Remember that the string must be on a single line.

```
output.Content.AppendHtml($"<a style='min-width:30px;
    display:inline-block;' {BootstrapClass} {href}>
    <span {glyphClasses}></span>{Description}</a>");
```

7. Add the **Bootstrap-style** and **Bootstrap-size** attributes to the <page-button> element. Add a description and verify that the text is displayed on the button.

```
<page-button path="Videos/Edit" Bootstrap-style="success"
    Bootstrap-size="lg" description="Edit" glyph="pencil"
    id="1"></page-button>
```

8. Run the application and navigate to the **Index** Razor Page in the *Pages* folder (the dashboard). Verify that the link is displayed as a Bootstrap button.

Styling the Buttons

You'll need to add a style sheet called *admin.css* where you can style the buttons and Razor Pages associated with the administrator user interface. The buttons text decoration (underlining) should be removed. The button column in the table that you will add to the **Index** Razor Pages needs to have a fixed minimum width, with enough room for the two small buttons (**btn-sm**).

1. Add a style sheet to the *wwwroot/css* folder called *admin.css*.
2. Add a link to it in the **Development** section of the _**Layout** view.
3. Add a link to it in the *bundleconfig.json* file.

```
"inputFiles": [
"wwwroot/css/site.css",
"wwwroot/css/dashboard.css",
"wwwroot/css/admin.css"
]
```

4. Add a selector for <a> elements decorated with the **btn-sm** Bootstrap class to the style sheet. It should remove their text decoration and border radius, to hide the link underlining and give the buttons sharp edges. If you use the **<page-button>** element with larger or smaller buttons, you should add them to this selector.
    ```
    a.btn-sm {
        text-decoration: none;
        border-radius: 0px;
    }
    ```

5. Make the button column at least 85px wide in all **Index** Razor Pages associated with the administrator UI; you will add the table and buttons in an upcoming chapter. Add a class selector called **button-col-width** to the <td> containing the buttons in the table you add to the pages. Add the same selector containing the styling to the style sheet.
    ```
    .button-col-width {
        min-width: 85px;
    }
    ```

6. Make sure that the Bootstrap size is assigned "sm" or "btn-sm" in the <page-button> element in the **Index** page, or is left out altogether. Save all files and run the application. The button should now have square edges.

7. Stop the application and delete the <page-button> element from the **Index** page.

8. Save all files.

Summary

In this chapter, you implemented a custom button Tag Helper and tested it in a Razor Page. You learned a more static approach using string values from Tag Helper attributes, and a more dynamic way to find out what attributes have been added, and read their values.

The purpose of the Tag Helper you created is to replace links with Bootstrap-styled buttons. You can, however, use Tag Helpers for so much more.

In the upcoming chapters, you will use the button Tag Helper to add buttons to the various Razor Pages you will create for the **Admin** UI.

In the next chapter, you will add a new service for writing data to the database.

28. The Database Write Service

Introduction

In this chapter, you will create a service called **DbWriteService** in the **VideoOn-Demand.Data** project. This service will be used from the **Admin** project to write data to the database. Since this is a service that will be injected with dependency injection, you need to create an interface for it.

The **Admin** project doesn't have an existing service for writing data and will therefore use the **DbWriteService** service you will create in the **Data** project directly.

Technologies Used in This Chapter

1. **C#** – Used to create the service.
2. **Entity framework** – To interact with the tables in the database.
3. **LINQ** – To query the database tables.

Overview

Your objective is to create a data service that adds, updates, and deletes data in the database tables.

Adding the DbWriteService Service

You need to add an interface called **IDbWriteService** that can be used from other projects with dependency injection to add and modify data in the database. You then need to implement the interface in a class called **DbWriteService** that contains the code to access the database.

The methods will be implemented as generic methods that can handle any entity and therefore add or modify data in any table in the database.

Adding the Service Interface and Class

1. Open the **VideoOnDemand.Data** project.
2. Open the *Services* folder.
3. Add an interface called **IDbWriteService** to the folder. Right click on the folder, select **Add-New Item**, and select the **Interface** template.

4. Add the **public** access modifier to the interface to make it accessible from any project.
```
public interface IDbWriteService
```

5. Add a class called **DbWriteService** to the *Services* folder.

6. Add the interface to the class.
```
public class DbWriteService : IDbWriteService
{
}
```

7. Add a constructor to the class and inject the **VODContext** to get access to the database from the service. Store the object in a class-level variable called **_db**.
```
private VODContext _db;
public DbWriteService(VODContext db)
{
    _db = db;
}
```

8. Open the **Startup** class in the **Admin** project.

9. Add the **IDbWriteService** service to the **ConfigureServices** method.
```
services.AddTransient<IDbWriteService, DbWriteService>();
```

8. Save the files.

The code for the **IDbWriteService** interface, so far:

```
public interface IDbWriteService { }
```

The code for the **DbWriteService** class, so far:

```
public class DbWriteService : IDbWriteService
{
    private VODContext _db;
    public DbWriteService(VODContext db)
    {
        _db = db;
    }
}
```

The Add Method

The **Add** method will add a new record in the specified table. Like all the other public methods you will add to this service, this one will be an asynchronous generic method that can handle any entity. You choose the table to add data to by defining the desired entity for the method when it is called.

Since the method adds a new record in a database table, the item to add has to be passed in as a parameter of the same type as the defining entity.

The result will be returned as a **bool** specifying if the changes were persisted in the table or not.

```
public async Task<bool> Add<TEntity>(TEntity item) where TEntity : class
{
}
```

1. Open the **IDbWriteService** interface.
2. Add a method definition for an **Add** method that is defined by the entity type that substitutes the generic **TEntity** type when the method is called. You must limit the **TEntity** type to only classes since an entity only can be created using a class; if you don't do this a value type such as **int** or **double** can be used with the method, which will generate an exception. The method should return a **Task<bool>** to denote that it is an asynchronous method returning a Boolean value.
   ```
   Task<bool> Add<TEntity>(TEntity item) where TEntity : class;
   ```
3. Add the **Add** method to the **DbWriteService** class, either manually or by using the **Quick Actions** light bulb button. If you auto generate the method with **Quick Actions**, you have to remove the **throw** statement.
4. Add a try/catch-block where the catch returns **false**, denoting that the data couldn't be persisted to the table.
5. Call the **AddAsync** method on the **_db** context with the generic **TEntity** type to access the table associated with the defining entity, and pass in the item to add from the try-block.
   ```
   await _db.AddAsync<TEntity>(item);
   ```
6. Return **true** or **false** depending on if the changes were persisted to the table.
   ```
   return await _db.SaveChangesAsync() >= 0;
   ```
7. Save all files.

The code for the **IDbWriteService** interface, so far:

```
public interface IDbWriteService
{
    Task<bool> Add<TEntity>(TEntity item) where TEntity : class;
}
```

The complete code for the **Add** method:

```
public async Task<bool> Add<TEntity>(TEntity item) where TEntity : class
{
    try
    {
        await _db.AddAsync<TEntity>(item);
        return await _db.SaveChangesAsync() >= 0;
    }
    catch
    {
        return false;
    }
}
```

The Delete Method

The **Delete** method will remove a record from the specified table. Like all the other public methods you will add to this service, this one will be an asynchronous generic method that can handle any entity. You choose the table to delete data from by defining the desired entity for the method when it is called.

Since the method removes a record in a database table, the item to delete has to be passed in as a parameter of the same type as the defining entity.

The result will be returned as a **bool** specifying if the changes were persisted in the table or not.

```
public async Task<bool> Delete<TEntity>(TEntity item) where TEntity :
class { }
```

1. Open the **IDbWriteService** interface.
2. Add a method definition for a **Delete** method that is defined by the entity type that substitutes the generic **TEntity** type when the method is called. You must limit the **TEntity** type to only classes since an entity only can be created using a

class; if you don't do this a value type such as **int** or **double** can be used with the method, which will generate an exception. The method should return a **Task<bool>** to denote that it is an asynchronous method returning a Boolean value.

```
Task<bool> Delete<TEntity>(TEntity item) where TEntity : class;
```

3. Add the **Delete** method to the **DbWriteService** class, either manually or by using the **Quick Actions** light bulb button. If you auto generate the method with **Quick Actions**, you have to remove the **throw** statement.

4. Add a try/catch-block where the catch returns **false**, denoting that the changes couldn't be persisted to the table.

5. Call the **Remove** method on the **Set<TEntity>** method on the **_db** context with the item to remove, from the try-block.
```
_db.Set<TEntity>().Remove(item);
```

6. Return **true** or **false** depending on if the changes were persisted to the table.
```
return await _db.SaveChangesAsync() >= 0;
```

7. Save all files.

The code for the **IDbWriteService** interface, so far:

```
public interface IDbWriteService
{
    Task<bool> Add<TEntity>(TEntity item) where TEntity : class;
    Task<bool> Delete<TEntity>(TEntity item) where TEntity : class;
}
```

The complete code for the **Delete** method:

```
public async Task<bool> Delete<TEntity>(TEntity item) where TEntity :
class
{
    try
    {
        _db.Set<TEntity>().Remove(item);
        return await _db.SaveChangesAsync() >= 0;
    }
    catch
    {
        return false;
    }
}
```

The Update Method

The **Update** method will update a record in the specified table. Like all the other public methods you will add to this service, this one will be an asynchronous generic method that can handle any entity. You choose the table to update data in by defining the desired entity for the method when it is called.

Since the method updates a record in a database table, the item to update has to be passed in as a parameter of the same type as the defining entity.

The result will be returned as a **bool** specifying if the changes were persisted in the table or not.

```
public async Task<bool> Update<TEntity>(TEntity item) where TEntity :
class { }
```

1. Open the **IDbWriteService** interface.
2. Copy the **Delete** method definition and paste it in. Rename the pasted-in method **Update**.
   ```
   Task<bool> Update<TEntity>(TEntity item) where TEntity : class;
   ```
3. Open the **DbWriteService** class and copy the **Delete** method and paste it in.
4. Change the name of the pasted-in method to **Update**.
5. Change the **Remove** method call to call the **Update** method.
   ```
   _db.Set<TEntity>().Update(item);
   ```
6. Save all files.

The code for the **IDbWriteService** interface, so far:

```
public interface IDbWriteService
{
    Task<bool> Add<TEntity>(TEntity item) where TEntity : class;
    Task<bool> Delete<TEntity>(TEntity item) where TEntity : class;
    Task<bool> Update<TEntity>(TEntity item) where TEntity : class;
}
```

The complete code for the **Update** method:

```
public async Task<bool> Update<TEntity>(TEntity item) where TEntity :
class
{
    try
    {
        _db.Set<TEntity>().Update(item);
        return await _db.SaveChangesAsync() >= 0;
    }
    catch
    {
        return false;
    }
}
```

The Update Method for Entities with a Combined Primary Key

This **Update** method will update a record from the specified table by removing the original record and adding the new record; this method is used with the **UserCourse** entity where a combined primary key is used. Like all the other public methods you will add to this service, this one will be an asynchronous generic method that can handle any entity. You choose the table to update data in by defining the desired entity for the method when it is called.

Since the method updates a record with a combined primary key, the **Update** method used in the previous section can't be used. The original item to update and the updated item must be passed in as parameters of the same type as the defining entity. Instead of calling the **Update** method, the **Remove** and **Add** methods will be called.

The result will be returned as a **bool** specifying if the changes were persisted in the table or not.

```
public async Task<bool> Update<TEntity>(TEntity originalItem, TEntity
updatedItem) where TEntity : class { }
```

1. Open the **IDbWriteService** interface.
2. Copy the **Update** method definition and paste it in. Add a new parameter called **updatedItem** and change the name of the **item** parameter to **originalItem.**
   ```
   Task<bool> Update<TEntity>(TEntity originalItem, TEntity
   updatedItem) where TEntity : class;
   ```

3. Open the **DbWriteService** class and copy the **Update** method and paste it in.
4. Change the **Update** method call to call the **Remove** method and pass in the **originalItem** parameter to it.
   ```
   _db.Set<TEntity>().Remove(originalItem);
   ```

5. Add a call to the **Add** method below the **Remove** method and pass in the **updatedItem** parameter to it.
   ```
   _db.Set<TEntity>().Add(updatedItem);
   ```

6. Save all files.

The code for the **IDbWriteService** interface, so far:

```
public interface IDbWriteService
{
    Task<bool> Add<TEntity>(TEntity item) where TEntity : class;
    Task<bool> Delete<TEntity>(TEntity item) where TEntity : class;
    Task<bool> Update<TEntity>(TEntity item) where TEntity : class;
    Task<bool> Update<TEntity>(TEntity originalItem,
        TEntity updatedItem) where TEntity : class;
}
```

The complete code for the **Update** method:

```
public async Task<bool> Update<TEntity>(TEntity originalItem, TEntity
updatedItem) where TEntity : class
{
    try
    {
        _db.Set<TEntity>().Remove(originalItem);
        _db.Set<TEntity>().Add(updatedItem);
        return await _db.SaveChangesAsync() >= 0;
    }
    catch
    {
        return false;
    }
}
```

Summary

In this chapter, you created a service for writing data to the database. This service will be used from the **Admin** project to fetch data.

Next, you will add a user service that will be used from the **Admin** project to manage users in the **AspNetUsers** table and their roles in the **AspNetUserRoles** table.

29. The User Service

Introduction

In this chapter, you will create a service called **UserService** in the **Admin** project. The service will be used to manage users in the **AspNetUsers** table and their roles in the **AspNetUserRoles** table. Since this is a service that will be injected with dependency injection, you need to create an interface for it.

Technologies Used in This Chapter

1. **C#** – Used to create the service.
2. **Entity framework** – To interact with the tables in the database.
3. **LINQ** – To query the database tables.

Overview

Your objective is to create a data service that adds, updates, and deletes data in the **AspNetUsers** and **AspNetUserRoles** database tables.

Adding the UserService Service

You need to add an interface called **IUserService** in a folder called *Services* in the **Admin** project. You then need to implement the interface in a class called **UserService** with code to access the database.

The methods will not be implemented as generic methods since they only will be used with the **AspNetUsers** and **AspNetUserRoles** database tables.

The UserPageModel Class

This class will transport the data fetched from the database to the **User** CRUD Razor Pages. It will contain three properties: the first is **Id (string)** representing the user id. It should be decorated with the **[Required]** and **[Display]** attributes; the first attribute will require an id to be entered, and the second will change the label text to *User Id*. The second property is **Email (string)**. It should be decorated with the **[Required]** and **[EmailAddress]** attributes; the first attribute will require an email address to be entered, and the second will perform checks on the entered data to ensure that it is a valid email address. The third property is **IsAdmin (bool)**, which will have the same attributes as the **Id** property. It will be displayed as a checkbox that shows if the user has been assigned the **Admin** role.

Adding the UserPageModel Class

1. Create a new folder called *Models* in the **Admin** project, if it doesn't already exist.
2. Add a class called **UserPageModel** to the *Models* folder.
3. Add a property named **Id (string)**.
4. Add the **[Required]** and **[Display]** attributes. The **[Display]** attribute should change the text to *User id*.
   ```
   [Required]
   [Display(Name = "User Id")]
   public string Id { get; set; }
   ```
5. Add a property named **Email (string)**.
6. Add the **[Required]** and **[EmailAddress]** attributes.
7. Add a property named **IsAdmin (bool)**.
8. Add the **[Required]** and **[Display]** attributes. The **[Display]** attribute should change the text to *Is Admin*.
9. Save the class.

The complete code for the **UserPageModel** class:

```
public class UserPageModel
{
    [Required]
    [Display(Name = "User Id")]
    public string Id { get; set; }
    [Required]
    [EmailAddress]
    public string Email { get; set; }
    [Required]
    [Display(Name = "Is Admin")]
    public bool IsAdmin { get; set; }
}
```

Adding the Service Interface and Class

1. Open the **VideoOnDemand.Admin** project.
2. Add a new folder called *Services*.

3. Add an interface called **IUserService** to the folder. Right click on the folder, select **Add-New Item**, and select the **Interface** template.

4. Add the **public** access modifier to the interface to make it accessible from any project.
```
public interface IUserService
```

5. Add a class called **UserService** to the *Services* folder.

6. Add the interface to the class.
```
public class UserService : IUserService
{
}
```

7. Add a constructor to the class and inject the **VODContext** to get access to the database from the service. Store the object in a class-level variable called **_db**. Also, inject the **UserManager** that is used when adding a new user and store it in a **readonly** variable called **_userManager**.
```
private VODContext _db;
private readonly UserManager<User> _userManager;
public UserService(VODContext db, UserManager<User> userManager)
{
    _db = db;
    _userManager = userManager;
}
```

8. Open the **Startup** class and add the **UserService** service to the **ConfigureServices** method.
```
services.AddTransient<IUserService, UserService>();
```

9. Save the files.

The code for the **IUserService** interface, so far:
```
public interface IUserService { }
```

The code for the **UserService** class, so far:
```
public class UserService : IUserService
{
    private VODContext _db;
    private readonly UserManager<User> _userManager;
```

```
    public UserService(VODContext db, UserManager<User> userManager)
    {
        _db = db;
        _userManager = userManager;
    }
}
```

The GetUsers Method

The **GetUsers** method will fetch all users in the **AspNetUsers** table ordered by email address and return them as an **IEnumerable<UserPageModel>** collection. The collection is then used to display the users in the **Index** Razor Page for the **User** entity.

```
IEnumerable<UserPageModel> GetUsers();
```

1. Open the **IUserService** interface.
2. Add a method definition for the **GetUsers** method that returns an **IEnumerable<UserPageModel>** collection.
   ```
   IEnumerable<UserPageModel> GetUsers();
   ```
3. Add a using statement to the **System.Linq** namespace to gain access to the **orderby** LINQ keyword to be able to sort the records by email.
4. Add the **GetUsers** method to the **UserService** class, either manually or by using the **Quick Actions** light bulb button. If you auto generate the method with **Quick Actions**, you have to remove the **throw** statement.
5. Return all users converted into **UserPageModel** objects ordered by the user's email addresses. Use the **Any** LINQ method on the **AspNetUserRoles** table to figure out if the user is an administrator.
   ```
   return from user in _db.Users
   orderby user.Email
   select new UserPageModel
   {
       Id = user.Id,
       Email = user.Email,
       IsAdmin = _db.UserRoles.Any(ur =>
           ur.UserId.Equals(user.Id) &&
           ur.RoleId.Equals(1.ToString())))
   };
   ```
6. Save all files.

The code for the **IUserService** interface, so far:

```
public interface IUserService
{
    IEnumerable<UserPageModel> GetUsers();
}
```

The complete code for the **GetUsers** method:

```
public IEnumerable<UserPageModel> GetUsers()
{
    return from user in _db.Users
        orderby user.Email
        select new UserPageModel
        {
            Id = user.Id,
            Email = user.Email,
            IsAdmin = _db.UserRoles.Any(ur =>
                ur.UserId.Equals(user.Id) &&
                ur.RoleId.Equals(1.ToString()))
        };
}
```

The GetUser Method

The **GetUser** method will fetch one user in the **AspNetUsers** table and return it as a **UserPageModel** object; the object is then used when displaying the user in the **Create, Edit**, and **Delete** Razor Pages for the **User** entity. The method should have a **userId (string)** parameter that is used when fetching the desired user from the database.

```
UserPageModel GetUser(string userId);
```

1. Open the **IUserService** interface.
2. Add a method definition for the **GetUser** method that returns a **UserPageModel** object. The method should have a **userId (string)** parameter.
   ```
   UserPageModel GetUser(string userId);
   ```
3. Add the **GetUser** method to the **UserService** class, either manually or by using the **Quick Actions** light bulb button. If you auto generate the method with **Quick Actions**, you have to remove the **throw** statement.

4. Return the user matching the passed-in user id converted into a **UserPageModel** object. Use the **Any** LINQ method on the **AspNetUserRoles** table to figure out if the user is an administrator.

```
return (from user in _db.Users
    where user.Id.Equals(userId)
    select new UserPageModel
    {
        Id = user.Id,
        Email = user.Email,
        IsAdmin = _db.UserRoles.Any(ur =>
            ur.UserId.Equals(user.Id) &&
            ur.RoleId.Equals(1.ToString())))
}).FirstOrDefault();
```

5. Save all files.

The code for the **IUserService** interface, so far:

```
public interface IUserService
{
    IEnumerable<UserPageModel> GetUsers();
    UserPageModel GetUser(string userId);
}
```

The complete code for the **GetUser** method:

```
public UserPageModel GetUser(string userId)
{
    return (from user in _db.Users
        where user.Id.Equals(userId)
        select new UserPageModel
        {
            Id = user.Id,
            Email = user.Email,
            IsAdmin = _db.UserRoles.Any(ur =>
                ur.UserId.Equals(user.Id) &&
                ur.RoleId.Equals(1.ToString())))
    }).FirstOrDefault();
}
```

The RegisterUserPageModel Class

The **RegisterUserPageModel** class is used in the **Create** Razor Page for the **AspNetUsers** table. The class should contain tree string properties called **Email**, **Password**, and **Confirm-Password**. The properties should be decorated with attributes that help with client-side validation.

The **Email** and **Password** properties should be decorated with the **[Required]** attribute.

The **Email** property should also be decorated with the **[EmailAddress]** attribute.

The **Password** property should also be formatted as a password and have a maximum length of 100 characters.

The **ConfirmPassword** property should be formatted as a password and be compared to the content in the **Password** property using the **[Compare]** attribute.

1. Add a class called **RegisterUserPageModel** to the *Models* folder.
2. Add an **Email** (**string**) property decorated with **[Required]** and **[EmailAddress]** attributes.
   ```
   [Required]
   [EmailAddress]
   public string Email { get; set; }
   ```
3. Add a **Password** (**string**) property decorated with **[Required]**, **[StringLength]**, and **[DataType]** attributes.
   ```
   [Required]
   [StringLength(100, ErrorMessage = "The {0} must be at least {2}
       and at max {1} characters long.", MinimumLength = 6)]
   [DataType(DataType.Password)]
   public string Password { get; set; }
   ```
4. Add a **ConfirmPassword** (**string**) property decorated with **[Display]**, **[Compare]**, and **[DataType]** attributes.
   ```
   [DataType(DataType.Password)]
   [Display(Name = "Confirm password")]
   [Compare("Password", ErrorMessage =
       "The password and confirmation password do not match.")]
   public string ConfirmPassword { get; set; }
   ```
5. Save all files.

The complete code for the **RegisterUserPageModel** class:

```
public class RegisterUserPageModel
{
    [Required]
    [EmailAddress]
    [Display(Name = "Email")]
    public string Email { get; set; }

    [Required]
    [StringLength(100, ErrorMessage = "The {0} must be at least {2}
        and at max {1} characters long.", MinimumLength = 6)]
    [DataType(DataType.Password)]
    [Display(Name = "Password")]
    public string Password { get; set; }

    [DataType(DataType.Password)]
    [Display(Name = "Confirm password")]
    [Compare("Password", ErrorMessage =
        "The password and confirmation password do not match.")]
    public string ConfirmPassword { get; set; }
}
```

The AddUser Method

The **AddUser** method will add a new user in the **AspNetUsers** table asynchronously and return an **IdentityResult** object returned from the **CreateAsync** method call on the **User-Manager** object. The method should take a **RegisterUserPageModel** instance as a parameter named **user**.

```
Task<IdentityResult> AddUser(RegisterUserPageModel user);
```

1. Open the **IUserService** interface.
2. Add a method definition for the **AddUser** method that returns **Task<IdentityResult>** and have a **User (RegisterUserPageModel)** parameter.
   ```
   Task<IdentityResult> AddUser(RegisterUserPageModel user);
   ```
3. Add the **AddUser** method to the **UserService** class, either manually or by using the **Quick Actions** light bulb button. If you auto generate the method with **Quick Actions**, you have to remove the **throw** statement.
4. Create an instance of the **User** class and assign the email from the passed-in user object to the newly created **User** instance. Also, assign **true** to the

EmailConfirmed property to signal that an email confirmation has been received. Although not strictly necessary in this scenario, it could be vital if you choose to implement email verification later.

```
var dbUser = new User { UserName = user.Email, Email = user.Email,
EmailConfirmed = true };
```

5. Call the **CreateAsync** method on the **_userManager** instance to try to add the new user. Store the returned result in a variable called **result**. You have to call the method with the **await** keyword since it is an asynchronous method.

```
var result = await _userManager.CreateAsync(dbUser,
user.Password);
```

6. Return the result in the **result** variable from the method.

```
return result;
```

7. Save all files.

The code for the **IUserService** interface, so far:

```
public interface IUserService
{
    IEnumerable<UserPageModel> GetUsers();
    UserPageModel GetUser(string userId);
    Task<IdentityResult> AddUser(RegisterUserPageModel user);
}
```

The complete code for the **AddUser** method:

```
public async Task<IdentityResult> AddUser(RegisterUserPageModel user)
{
    var dbUser = new User { UserName = user.Email, Email = user.Email,
        EmailConfirmed = true };
    var result = await _userManager.CreateAsync(dbUser, user.Password);
    return result;
}
```

The UpdateUser Method

The **UpdateUser** method will update a user in the **AspNetUsers** table asynchronously and return a **bool** value based on the result from the value returned from the **SaveChanges-Async** method call on the **_db** context object. The method should take a **UserPageModel** instance as a parameter named **user**.

```
Task<bool> UpdateUser(UserPageModel user);
```

The first thing the method should do is to fetch the user from the **AspNetUsers** table matching the value of the **Id** property in the passed-in object. Store the user in a variable called **dbUser**.

Then the **dbUser** needs to be checked to make sure that it isn't **null** and that the email in the passed-in object isn't an empty string. You could add more checks to see that the email is a valid email address, but I leave that as an extra exercise for you to solve on your own.

Then you assign the email address from the passed-in user to the **dbUser** fetched from the database to update it.

Next you need to find out if the user in the database — matching the passed-in user id in the **user** object — is an administrator. You do that by creating an instance of the **Identity-UserRole** class using the id for the **Admin** role in the **AspNetRoles** table and the user id from the **user** parameter. Then you use the **AnyAsync** LINQ method to check if the user-role combination is in the **AspNetUserRoles** table. Sort the result in a variable called **isAdmin**.

If the value in the **isAdmin** variable is **true** and the value in the **IsAdmin** property in the **user** object is **false**, then the admin role checkbox has been unchecked in the UI and the role should be removed from the **AspNetUserRoles** table by calling the **Remove** method on the **UserRoles** entity on the **_db** context object.

If the value in the **IsAdmin** property in the **user** parameter is **true** and the value in the **isAdmin** variable is **false**, then the admin role checkbox has been checked in the UI and the role should be added to the **AspNetUserRoles** table by awaiting a call to the **AddAsync** method on the **UserRoles** entity on the **_db** context object.

Then **await** the result from the **SaveChangesAsync** method and return **true** if the data was persisted to the database, otherwise return **false**.

1. Open the **IUserService** interface.
2. Add a method definition for the **UpdateUser** method that returns a **bool** value and has a **UserPageModel** parameter called **user**.
   ```
   Task<bool> UpdateUser(UserPageModel user);
   ```
3. Add the **UpdateUser** method to the **UserService** class, either manually or by using the **Quick Actions** light bulb button. If you auto generate the method with **Quick Actions**, you have to remove the **throw** statement.

4. Fetch the user matching the user id from the passed-in **user** parameter and store the user in a variable called **dbUser**.
    ```
    var dbUser = await _db.Users.FirstOrDefaultAsync(u =>
        u.Id.Equals(user.Id));
    ```

5. Return **false** if the **dbUser** is **null** (the user doesn't exist) or the email address in the passed-in **user** parameter is an empty string.
    ```
    if (dbUser == null) return false;
    if (string.IsNullOrEmpty(user.Email)) return false;
    ```

6. Assign the email address from the passed-in **user** parameter to the fetched user in the **dbUser** variable to update its email address.
    ```
    dbUser.Email = user.Email;
    ```

7. Create a new instance of the **IdentityUserRole<string>** class using the role id for the **Admin** role and the user id from the passed-in **user** parameter. Store the object in a variable called **userRole**. You will use this object to find out if the user already is an administrator and has an entry in the **AspNetUserRoles** table.
    ```
    var userRole = new IdentityUserRole<string>() {
        RoleId = "1",
        UserId = user.Id
    };
    ```

8. Query the **AspNetUserRoles** table with the **AnyAsync** method on the **UserRoles** entity by passing in the **userRole** object you created in the previous step to find out if the user is an administrator.
    ```
    var isAdmin = await _db.UserRoles.AnyAsync(ur =>
        ur.Equals(userRole));
    ```

9. Add an if/else if-block that removes the **Admin** role if the admin checkbox is unchecked in the UI, or adds the role if the checkbox is checked.
    ```
    if(isAdmin && !user.IsAdmin)
        _db.UserRoles.Remove(userRole);
    else if (!isAdmin && user.IsAdmin)
        await _db.UserRoles.AddAsync(userRole);
    ```

10. Call the **SaveChangesAsync** method to persist the changes in the database and **await** the result. Return **true** if the data was persisted, otherwise return **false**.
    ```
    var result = await _db.SaveChangesAsync();
    return result >= 0;
    ```

11. Save all files

The code for the **IUserService** interface, so far:

```
public interface IUserService
{
    IEnumerable<UserPageModel> GetUsers();
    UserPageModel GetUser(string userId);
    Task<IdentityResult> AddUser(RegisterUserPageModel user);
    Task<bool> UpdateUser(UserPageModel user);
}
```

The complete code for the **UpdateUser** method:

```
public async Task<bool> UpdateUser(UserPageModel user)
{
    var dbUser = await _db.Users.FirstOrDefaultAsync(u =>
        u.Id.Equals(user.Id));
    if (dbUser == null) return false;
    if (string.IsNullOrEmpty(user.Email)) return false;

    dbUser.Email = user.Email;

    var userRole = new IdentityUserRole<string>()
    {
        RoleId = "1",
        UserId = user.Id
    };

    var isAdmin = await _db.UserRoles.AnyAsync(ur =>
        ur.Equals(userRole));

    if(isAdmin && !user.IsAdmin)
        _db.UserRoles.Remove(userRole);
    else if (!isAdmin && user.IsAdmin)
        await _db.UserRoles.AddAsync(userRole);

    var result = await _db.SaveChangesAsync();
    return result >= 0;
}
```

The DeleteUser Method

The **DeleteUser** method will remove a user from the **AspNetUsers** table asynchronously and return a **bool** value based on the result returned from the **SaveChangesAsync** method call on the **_db** context sobject. The method should take a **string** parameter named **userId** representing the user to remove.

```
Task<bool> DeleteUser(string userId);
```

The first thing the method should do is to fetch the user from the **AspNetUsers** table matching the value of the **userId** parameter. Store the user in a variable called **dbUser**.

Then the **dbUser** needs to be checked to make sure that it isn't **null** to make sure that the user exists, and returns **false** if it doesn't exist.

Next, you remove the roles associated with the user id in the **AspNetUserRoles** table. Fetch the roles by using the **Where** LINQ method on the **UserRoles** entity, and remove any existing roles for the user by calling the **RemoveRange** method on the **UserRoles** entity.

Then you remove the user from the **AspNetUsers** table by calling the **Remove** method on the **User** entity.

Then **await** the result from the **SaveChangesAsync** method and return **true** if the changes were persisted to the database, otherwise return **false**.

1. Open the **IUserService** interface.
2. Add a method definition for the **DeleteUser** method that returns a **bool** value and has a **string** parameter called **userId**.
   ```
   Task<bool> DeleteUser(string userId);
   ```
3. Add the **DeleteUser** method to the **UserService** class, either manually or by using the **Quick Actions** light bulb button. If you auto generate the method with **Quick Actions**, you have to remove the **throw** statement.
4. Add a try/catch-block where the catch-block returns **false**.
5. Fetch the user matching the user id from the passed-in **userId** parameter in the try-block.
   ```
   var dbUser = await _db.Users.FirstOrDefaultAsync(d =>
       d.Id.Equals(userId));
   ```
6. Return **false** if the **dbUser** is **null** (the user doesn't exist).
   ```
   if (dbUser == null) return false;
   ```

7. Fetch the roles associated with the user id and remove them from the **AspNetUserRoles** table.

```
var userRoles = _db.UserRoles.Where(ur =>
    ur.UserId.Equals(dbUser.Id));

_db.UserRoles.RemoveRange(userRoles);
```

8. Remove the user from the **AspNetUsers** table.

```
_db.Users.Remove(dbUser);
```

9. Call the **SaveChangesAsync** method to persist the changes in the database and **await** the result. Return **true** if the data was persisted, otherwise return **false**.

```
var result = await _db.SaveChangesAsync();
return result >= 0;
```

10. Save all files.

The complete code for the **IUserService** interface:

```
public interface IUserService {
    IEnumerable<UserPageModel> GetUsers();
    UserPageModel GetUser(string userId);
    Task<IdentityResult> AddUser(RegisterUserPageModel user);
    Task<bool> UpdateUser(UserPageModel user);
    Task<bool> DeleteUser(string userId);
}
```

The complete code for the **DeleteUser** method:

```
public async Task<bool> DeleteUser(string userId)
{
    try
    {
        var dbUser = await _db.Users.FirstOrDefaultAsync(d =>
            d.Id.Equals(userId));
        if (dbUser == null) return false;

        var userRoles = _db.UserRoles.Where(ur =>
            ur.UserId.Equals(dbUser.Id));

        _db.UserRoles.RemoveRange(userRoles);
        _db.Users.Remove(dbUser);

        var result = await _db.SaveChangesAsync();
        if (result < 0) return false;
```

```
    }
    catch
    {
        return false;
    }

    return true;
}
```

Summary

In this chapter, you created a service for handling users and their roles in the **AspNetUsers** and **AspNetUserRoles** database tables. This service will be used from the **Admin** project to handle user data and assign administrator privileges to users.

Next, you will begin adding the Razor Pages that make up the administrator UI.

30. The User Razor Pages

In this chapter, you will create the **User** Razor Pages, which are used to perform CRUD operations against the **AspNetUsers** and the **AspNetUserRoles** tables in the database. These Razor Pages are a bit different, in that they use a page model instead of an entity class. The **AspNetUsers** table handles users and the **AspNetUserRoles** assigns roles to registered users.

You will use the **ViewBag** container to send collection data to the pages that contain drop-downs to provide them with data; this is to prevent the item indices being displayed as text boxes.

Technologies Used in This Chapter
1. **C#** – To write code in Razor Page code-behind methods.
2. **HTML** – To add content to the Razor Pages.
3. **Entity framework** – To perform CRUD operations.

Overview

In this chapter, you will create the **User** Razor Pages. This enables the administrator to display, add, update, and delete data in the **AspNetUsers** and the **AspNetUserRoles** tables.

In this scenario where the two tables aren't linked through the entity classes, you will use a view model class called **UserPageModel** to pass the data from the code-behind to the page with either a property of type **UserPageModel** or **IEnumerble<UserPageModel>** declared directly in the code-behind. Remember that the code-behind doubles as a model and controller.

All the Razor Page code-behind **PageModel** classes need access to the **IUserService** service in the **Admin** project to fetch and modify data in the **AspNetUsers** and **AspNetUserRoles** tables in the database. The easiest way to achieve this is to add a constructor to the class and use DI to inject the service into the class.

The code-behind file belonging to a Razor Page can be accessed by expanding the Razor Page node and opening the nested *.cshtml.cs* file.

Each Razor Page comes with a predefined **@page** directive signifying that it is a Razor Page and not a MVC view. It also has an **@model** directive defined that is linked directly to the code-behind class; through this model, you can access the public properties that you add to the class from the HTML in the page using Razor syntax.

The code-behind class comes with an empty **OnGet** method that can be used to fetch data that will be used in the Razor Page, much like an **HttpGet** action method in a controller.

You can also add an asynchronous **OnPostAsync** method that can be used to handle posts from the client to the server, for instance a form that is submitted. This method is similar to the **HttpPost** action method in a controller.

As you can see, the code-behind class works kind of like a combined controller and model. You can use controllers, if needed, to handle requests that don't require a Razor Page, such as logging out a user.

The [TempData] Attribute

The **[TempData]** attribute is new in ASP.NET Core 2.0 and can be used with properties in controllers and Razor Pages to store data until it is read. It is particularly useful for redirection, when data is needed for more than a single request. The **Keep** and **Peek** methods can be used to examine the data without deletion.

Since the **[TempData]** attribute is built on top of session state, it can be shared between Razor Pages. You will take advantage of this when sending a message from one Razor Page to another, and display it using the <status-message> Tag Helper that you will implement in the next chapter.

You will prepare for the Tag Helper by adding a **[TempData]** property called **Status-Message (string)** to the code-behind class for the Razor Pages you create. This property will hold the message assigned in one of the **Create, Edit**, or **Delete** Razor Pages and display it in the Tag Helper that you will add to the **Index** Razor Page. By adding the property to several code-behind classes, the message can be changed as needed because only one property is created in the session state.

The Users/Index Razor Page

The **Index** Razor Page in the *Users* folder can be viewed as a dashboard for users, listing them in a table with data about the users and buttons to edit and delete each user. It also has a **Create New** button above the HTML table for creating a new user in the **AspNetUsers** database table.

There will be four Razor Pages in the *Users* folder when you have added them all: **Index**, **Create**, **Edit**, and **Delete**.

To add, read, and modify user data, the **IUserService** service needs to be Injected into the Razor Page code-behind **IndexModel** class's constructor and stored in a private field called **_userService**.

Altering the IndexModel Class

The first thing you want to do is to restrict the usage to administrators only with the **[Authorize]** attribute.

Then you need to inject the **UserService** into the constructor that you will add to the class. Store the service instance in a private class-level variable called **_userService**.

Then fetch all users with the **GetUsers** method on the **_userService** object in the **OnGet** method and store them in an **IEnumerable<UserPageModel>** collection called **Users**; this collection will be part of the model that is used from the HTML Razor Page.

Add a **string** property called **StatusMessage** and decorate it with the **[TempData]** attribute. This property will get its value from the other Razor Pages when a successful result has been achieved, such as adding a new user.

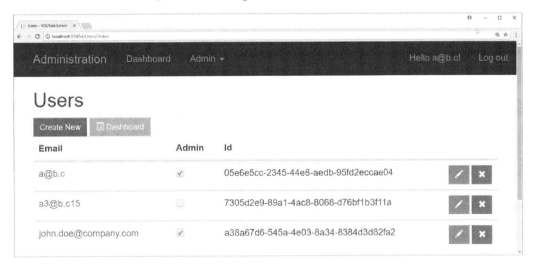

1. Create a folder named *Users* in the *Pages* folder.
2. Add a Razor Page, using the template with the same name, and name It **Index**.
3. Expand the **Index** node in the Solution Explorer and open the *Index.cshtml.cs* file.

4. Add the **[Authorize]** attribute to the class and specify that the **Admin** role is needed to access the page from the browser.
```
[Authorize(Roles = "Admin")]
public class IndexModel : PageModel
```

5. Inject **IUserService** into a constructor and save the injected object in a class-level variable called **_userService**. The variable will give you access to the service from any method in the class.
```
private IUserService _userService;
public IndexModel(IUserService userService)
{
    _userService = userService;
}
```

6. Add a public class-level **IEnumerable<UserPageModel>** collection variable called **Users**.
```
public IEnumerable<UserPageModel> Users = new List<UserPageModel>();
```

7. Call the **GetUsers** method on the **_userServices** object from the **OnGet** method and store the result in the **Users** property you just added.
```
public void OnGet()
{
    Users = _userService.GetUsers();
}
```

8. Add a public string property called **StatusMessage** and decorate it with the **[TempData]** attribute. This property will get its value from the other Razor Pages when a successful result has been achieved, such as adding a new user.
```
[TempData]
public string StatusMessage { get; set; }
```

9. Save all files.

The complete code in the **Index** code-behind file:
```
[Authorize(Roles = "Admin")]
public class IndexModel : PageModel
{
    private IUserService _userService;
    public IEnumerable<UserPageModel> Users = new List<UserPageModel>();

    [TempData]
    public string StatusMessage { get; set; }
```

```
    public IndexModel(IUserService userService)
    {
        _userService = userService;
    }

    public void OnGet()
    {
        Users = _userService.GetUsers();
    }
}
```

Altering the Index Razor Page

First add **using** statements to the **Identity** and **Entities** namespaces and inject the **SignIn-Manager** to be able to check that the user has the correct credentials.

Use the **ViewData** object to add a **Title** property with the text *Users* to it. This value will be displayed on the browser tab.

Add an if-block that checks that the user is signed in and belongs to the **Admin** role. All remaining code should be placed inside the if-block so that only administrators can view it.

```
@if (SignInManager.IsSignedIn(User) && User.IsInRole("Admin")) { }
```

Add a <div> decorated with the Bootstrap **row** class to create a new row of data on the page. Then add a <div> decorated with the Bootstrap **col-md-8** and **col-md-offset-2** classes to create a column that has been offset by two columns (pushed in from the left) inside the row.

Add a page title displaying the text *Users* using an <h2> element inside the column <div>.

Use the <page-button> Tag Helper to add a **Create New** button below the <h2> heading. Assign *Users/Create* to the **path** attribute to target the **Create** Razor Page you will add later, *primary* to the **Bootstrap-style** attribute and *Create New* to the **description** attribute.

```
<page-button path="Users/Create" Bootstrap style-"primary"
description="Create New"></page-button>
```

Add another <page-button> Tag Helper that targets the **Index** view in the *Pages* folder (not the one in the *Pages/Users* folder) to display the main dashboard. Assign *Index* without a folder path to the **path** attribute to target the main **Index** Razor Page, *warning* to the **Bootstrap-style** attribute, *list-alt* to the **glyph** attribute to add a Glyphicon to the button, and *Dashboard* to the **description** attribute.

```
<page-button path="Index" Bootstrap-style="warning" glyph="list-alt"
description="Dashboard"></page-button>
```

Add a table with four columns where the first three have the following headings: **Email**, **Admin**, and **Id**. The fourth heading should be empty. Decorate the <table> element with the Bootstrap **table** class. Also, add a table body to the table.

Iterate over the users in the **Model.Users** property – the **Users** property you added to the code-behind file – and display the data in the **Email**, **IsAdmin**, and **Id** properties in the first three columns. Add two buttons for the **Edit** and **Delete** Razor Pages to the fourth column, and don't forget to add the **id-userId** attribute containing the user id for the current user in the iteration; the id is needed to fetch the correct user for the Razor Page that is opened. Decorate the <td> column element with the **button-col-width** CSS class so that you later can assign a width to the column.

```
<td class="button-col-width">
    <page-button path="Users/Edit" Bootstrap-style="success"
    glyph="pencil" id-userId="@user.Id"></page-button>

    <page-button path="Users/Delete" Bootstrap-style="danger"
    glyph="remove" id-userId="@user.Id"></page-button>
</td>
```

Add an empty <div> decorated with the **col-md-2** Bootstrap class below the previous column <div> to fill the entire row with columns. A Bootstrap row should have 12 columns. Bootstrap is very forgiving if you forget to add up the columns on a row.

1. Open the *Index.cshtml* HTML Razor page.
2. Add **using** statements to the **Identity** and **Entities** namespaces and inject the **SignInManager** to be able to check that the user has the correct credentials.
   ```
   @using Microsoft.AspNetCore.Identity
   @using VideoOnDemand.Data.Data.Entities
   ```

```
@inject SignInManager<User> SignInManager
```

3. Add a **Title** property with the text *Users* to the **ViewData** object.
```
@{
    ViewData["Title"] = "Users";
}
```

4. Add an if-block that checks that the user is signed in and belongs to the **Admin** role.
```
@if (SignInManager.IsSignedIn(User) && User.IsInRole("Admin")) { }
```

5. Add a <div> decorated with the Bootstrap **row** class to create a new row of data on the page. Then add a <div> decorated with the Bootstrap **col-md-8** and **col-md-offset-2** classes to create a column that has been offset by two columns inside the row. Add a column for the remaining Bootstrap columns below the previous column. All remaining code and HTML will be added to the first column <div>.
```
<div class="row">
    <div class="col-md-8 col-md-offset-2">
    </div>
    <div class="col-md-2">
    </div>
</div>
```

6. Add an <h2> heading with the text *Users* inside the first column <div>.
```
<h2>Users</h2>
```

7. Use the <page-button> Tag Helper to add a **Create New** button. Assign *Users/Create* to the **path** attribute to target the **Create** Razor Page you will add to the *Users* folder later, *primary* to the **Bootstrap-style** attribute and *Create New* to the **description** attribute.
```
<page-button path="Users/Create" Bootstrap-style="primary"
description="Create New"></page-button>
```

8. Add another <page-button> Tag Helper that targets the **Index** view in the *Pages* folder (not the one in the *Pages/Users* folder) to display the main dashboard. Assign *Index* to the **path** attribute to target the main **Index** Razor Page, *warning* to the **Bootstrap-style** attribute, *list-alt* to the **glyph** attribute to add a Glyphicon to the button, and *Dashboard* to the **description** attribute (the button text).
```
<page-button path="Index" Bootstrap-style="warning" glyph="list-
alt" description="Dashboard"></page-button>
```

9. Add a table with four columns where the first three have the following headings: **Email**, **Admin**, and **Id**. The fourth heading should be empty. Decorate the <table> element with the Bootstrap **table** class. Also, add a table body to the table.

```
<table class="table">
    <thead>
        <tr>
            <th>Email</th>
            <th>Admin</th>
            <th>Id</th>
            <th></th>
        </tr>
    </thead>
    <tbody>
    </tbody>
</table>
```

10. Iterate over the users in the **Model.Users** property in the <tbody> element and display the data in the **Email**, **IsAdmin**, and **Id** properties in the first three columns. The **DisplayFor** method will add an appropriate HTML element for the property data type and display the property value in it.

```
<tbody>
    @foreach (var user in Model.Users)
    {
        <tr>
            <td>@Html.DisplayFor(modelItem => user.Email)</td>
            <td>@Html.DisplayFor(modelItem => user.IsAdmin)</td>
            <td>@Html.DisplayFor(modelItem => user.Id)</td>
        </tr>
    }
</tbody>
```

11. Add a fourth <td> decorated with the **button-col-width** CSS for the two buttons leading to the **Edit** and **Delete** Razor Pages. Don't forget to add the **id-userId** attribute containing the user id for the current user in the iteration.

```
<td class="button-col-width">
    <page-button path="Users/Edit" Bootstrap-style="success"
      glyph="pencil" id-userId="@user.Id"></page-button>

    <page-button path="Users/Delete" Bootstrap-style="danger"
      glyph="remove" id-userId="@user.Id"></page-button>
</td>
```

12. Run the application (Ctrl+F5) and click the **Users** card on the main dashboard, or select **User** in the **Admin** menu. Make sure the Razor Page is displaying the users in a table and that the buttons are present. You can't use the buttons since the **Create**, **Edit**, and **Delete** Razor Pages haven't been created yet.

The complete code in the **Index** Razor Page:

```
@page
@using Microsoft.AspNetCore.Identity
@using VideoOnDemand.Data.Data.Entities
@inject SignInManager<User> SignInManager
@model IndexModel
@{
    ViewData["Title"] = "Users";
}

@if (SignInManager.IsSignedIn(User) && User.IsInRole("Admin"))
{
    <div class="row">
        <div class="col-md-8 col-md-offset-2">
            <h2>Users</h2>
            <status-message message="@Model.StatusMessage"
                message-type="success"></status-message>
            <page-button path="Users/Create" Bootstrap-style="primary"
                description="Create New"></page-button>
            <page-button path="Index" Bootstrap-style="warning"
                glyph="list-alt" description="Dashboard"></page-button>
            <table class="table">
                <thead>
                    <tr>
                        <th>Email</th>
                        <th>Admin</th>
                        <th>Id</th>
                        <th></th>
                    </tr>
                </thead>
                <tbody>
                    @foreach (var user in Model.Users)
                    {
                        <tr>
                            <td>@Html.DisplayFor(modelItem =>
                                user.Email)</td>
                            <td>@Html.DisplayFor(modelItem =>
                                user.IsAdmin)</td>
```

443

```
                                    <td>@Html.DisplayFor(modelItem =>
                                        user.Id)</td>
                                    <td class="button-col-width">
                                        <page-button path="Users/Edit"
                                         Bootstrap-style="success"
                                         glyph="pencil" id-userId="@user.Id">
                                        </page-button>
                                        <page-button path="Users/Delete"
                                          Bootstrap-style="danger"
                                          glyph="remove" id-userId="@user.Id">
                                        </page-button>
                                    </td>
                                </tr>
                            }
                        </tbody>
                    </table>
                </div>
                <div class="col-md-2">
                </div>
            </div>
}
```

The Users/Create Razor Page

The **Create** Razor Page in the *Users* folder is used to add a new user to the **AspNetUsers** table in the database. It can be reached by clicking the **Create New** button above the table in the **Index** Razor Page, or by navigating to the */Users/Create* URI.

To add a new user, the **IUserService** service needs to be injected into the Razor Page code-behind **CreateModel** class's constructor and stored in a private field called **_userService**.

Altering the CreateModel Class

The first thing you want to do is to restrict the usage to administrators only with the **[Authorize]** attribute.

Then you need to inject the **UserService** into the constructor that you will add to the class. Store the service instance in a private class-level variable called **_userService** to add the user to the database.

No data is needed to display the **Create** Razor Page, but it needs a **RegisterUserPageModel** variable called **Input** that can pass the form data from the UI to the **OnPostAsync** code-behind method where the **AddUser** method is called on the **_userService** object.

Add a **string** property called **StatusMessage** and decorate it with the **[TempData]** attribute. This property will be assigned a message to be displayed in the **Index** Razor Page after the form data has been processed successfully in the **OnPostAsync** method and a redirect to the **Index** Razor Page is made.

In the **OnPostAsync** method, you need to check that the model state is valid before any other action is performed.

If the asynchronous **IUserService.AddUser** method returns **true** in the **Succeeded** property of the method's result, then assign a message to the **StatusMessage** property that is used in the **Index** Razor Page, and redirect to that page by returning a call to the **RedirectToPage** method.

Iterate over the errors in the **result.Errors** collection and add them to the **ModelState** object with the **AddModelError** method so that the errors can be used in the UI validation when the form is redisplayed to the user.

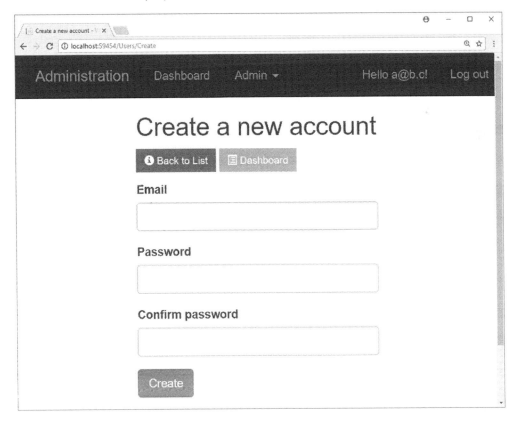

1. Add a Razor Page, using the template with the same name, and name it **Create**.

2. Expand the **Create** node in the Solution Explorer and open the *Create.cshtml.cs* file.

3. Add the **[Authorize]** attribute to the class and specify that the **Admin** role is needed to access the page from the browser.
```
[Authorize(Roles = "Admin")]
public class CreateModel : PageModel
```

4. Inject **IUserService** into a constructor and save the injected object in a class-level variable called **_userService**. The variable will give you access to the service from any method in the class.
```
private IUserService _userService;
public CreateModel(IUserService userService)
{
    _userService = userService;
}
```

5. Add a public class-level **RegisterUserPageModel** variable decorated with the **[BindProperty]** attribute called **Input**. This property will be bound to the form controls in the HTML Razor Page.
```
[BindProperty]
public RegisterUserPageModel Input { get; set; } =
    new RegisterUserPageModel();
```

6. Add a public string property called **StatusMessage** and decorate it with the **[TempData]** attribute. This property will get its value from the other Razor Pages when a successful result has been achieved, such as adding a new user.
```
[TempData]
public string StatusMessage { get; set; }
```

7. Leave the **OnGet** method empty and add a new asynchronous method called **OnPostAsync** that returns **Task<IActionResult>**, which essentially makes it the same as an **HttpPost** MVC action method.
```
public async Task<IActionResult> OnPostAsync() { }
```

8. Check that the model state is valid with an if-block in the **OnPostAsync** method.
```
if (ModelState.IsValid) { }
```

9. Call the **AddUser** method in the **UserService** service and pass in the **Input** object returned from the form inside the if-block to add the user. Store the returned object in a variable called **result**.
```
var result = await _userService.AddUser(Input);
```

10. Add an if-block that checks if the **result.Succeeded** property is **true**, which means that the user was successfully added to the database.
```
if (result.Succeeded) { }
```

11. Assign a success message to the **StatusMessage** property and redirect to the **Index** Razor Page inside the **Succeeded** if-block.
```
StatusMessage = $"Created a new account for {Input.Email}.";
return RedirectToPage("Index");
```

12. Add a **foreach** loop below the **Succeeded** if-block that iterates over any errors in the **result.Errors** collection and adds them to the **ModelState** with the **AddModelError** method for use in UI validation when the form is reposted.
```
foreach (var error in result.Errors)
{
    ModelState.AddModelError(string.Empty, error.Description);
}
```

13. Return the page using the **Page** method below the **ModeState.IsValid** if-block at the end of the method. This will return the **Create** Razor Page displaying any validation errors that have been detected.
```
return Page();
```

14. Save all files.

The complete code in the **Create** code-behind file:

```
[Authorize(Roles = "Admin")]
public class CreateModel : PageModel
{
    private IUserService _userService;

    [BindProperty]
    public RegisterUserPageModel Input { get; set; } =
        new RegisterUserPageModel();

    // Used to send a message back to the Index Razor Page.
    [TempData]
    public string StatusMessage { get; set; }

    public CreateModel(IUserService userService)
    {
        _userService = userService;
    }
```

```
    public void OnGet()
    {
    }

    public async Task<IActionResult> OnPostAsync()
    {
        if (ModelState.IsValid)
        {
            var result = await _userService.AddUserAsync(Input);

            if (result.Succeeded)
            {
                // Message sent back to the Index Razor Page.
                StatusMessage = $"Created a new account for
                    {Input.Email}.";

                return RedirectToPage("Index");
            }

            foreach (var error in result.Errors)
            {
                ModelState.AddModelError(string.Empty,
                    error.Description);
            }
        }

        // Something failed, redisplay the form.
        return Page();
    }
}
```

Altering the Create Razor Page

First add **using** statements to the **Identity** and **Entities** namespaces and inject the **SignIn-Manager** to be able to check that the user has the correct credentials.

Use the **ViewData** object to add a **Title** property with the text *Create a new account* to it. This value will be displayed on the browser tab.

Add an if-block that checks that the user is signed in and belongs to the **Admin** role. All remaining code should be placed inside the if-block so that only administrators can view it.

```
@if (SignInManager.IsSignedIn(User) && User.IsInRole("Admin")) { }
```

Add a <div> decorated with the Bootstrap **row** class to create a new row of data on the page. Then add a <div> decorated with the Bootstrap **col-md-4** and **col-md-offset-4** classes to create a column that has been offset by four columns (pushed in from the left) inside the row.

Add a page title displaying the text in the **ViewData** object's **Title** property using an <h2> element inside the column <div>.

Use the <page-button> Tag Helper to add a **Back to List** button below the <h2> heading. Assign *Users/Index* to the **path** attribute to target the **Index** Razor Page in the *Users* folder, *primary* to the **Bootstrap-style** attribute, *info-sign* to the **glyph** attribute to add an icon, and *Back to List* to the **description** attribute.

```
<page-button path="Users/Index" Bootstrap-style="primary" glyph="info-
sign" description="Back to List"></page-button>
```

Add another <page-button> Tag Helper that targets the **Index** Razor Page in the *Pages* folder (not the one in the *Pages/Users* folder) to display the main dashboard. Assign *Index* to the **path** attribute to target the main **Index** Razor Page, *warning* to the **Bootstrap-style** attribute, *list-alt* to the **glyph** attribute to add a Glyphicon to the button, and *Dashboard* to the **description** attribute.

```
<page-button path="Index" Bootstrap-style="warning" glyph="list-alt"
description="Dashboard"></page-button>
```

Add an empty <p></p> element to create some distance between the buttons and the form.

Add a form that validates on all errors using the <form> element and a <div> element with the **asp-validation-summary** Tag Helper.

```
<form method="post">
    <div asp-validation-summary="All" class="text-danger"></div>
</form>
```

Add a <div> decorated with the **form-group** class below the previous <div> inside the <form> element. Add a <label> element with its **asp-for** attribute assigned a value from the **Input.Email** model property, inside the previous <div> element.

```
<label asp-for="Input.Email"></label>
```

Add an <input> element with its **asp-for** attribute assigned a value from the **Input.Email** model property below the <label> element. Decorate the <input> element with the **form-control** class to denote that the element belongs to a form.

```
<input asp-for="Input.Email" class="form-control" />
```

Add a <span> element with its **asp-validation-for** attribute assigned a value from the **Input.Email** model property, below the <input> element. Decorate the <span> element with the **text-danger** class to make the text red.

```
<input asp-for="Input.Email" class="form-control" />
```

Copy the **form-group** decorated <div> you just finished and paste it in twice. Modify the pasted in code to target the **Password** and **ConfirmPassword** model properties.

Add a **submit** button above the closing </form> element and decorate it with the **btn** and **btn-success** Bootstrap classes to make it a styled green button.

Load the **_ValidationScriptsPartial** partial view inside a **@section** block named **Scripts** below the if-block to load the necessary UI validation scripts.

1. Open the *Create.cshtml* HTML Razor page.
2. Add **using** statements to the **Identity** and **Entities** namespaces and inject the **SignInManager** to be able to check that the user has the correct credentials.
   ```
   @using Microsoft.AspNetCore.Identity
   @using VideoOnDemand.Data.Data.Entities
   @inject SignInManager<User> SignInManager
   ```
3. Add a **Title** property with the text *Create a new account* to the **ViewData** object.
   ```
   @{
       ViewData["Title"] = "Create a new account";
   }
   ```
4. Add an if-block that checks that the user is signed in and belongs to the **Admin** role.
   ```
   @if (SignInManager.IsSignedIn(User) && User.IsInRole("Admin")) { }
   ```
5. Add a <div> decorated with the Bootstrap **row** class to create a new row of data on the page. Then add a <div> decorated with the Bootstrap **col-md-8** and **col-md-**

offset-2 classes to create a column that has been offset by two columns inside the row.

```
<div class="row">
    <div class="col-md-8 col-md-offset-2">
    </div>
</div>
```

6. Add an <h2> heading with the title from the **ViewData** object inside the <div>.

```
<h2>@ViewData["Title"]</h2>
```

7. Use the <page-button> Tag Helper to add a **Back to List** button below the <h2> heading. Assign *Users/Index* to the **path** attribute to target the **Index** Razor Page in the *Users* folder, *primary* to the **Bootstrap-style** attribute, *info-sign* to the **glyph** attribute to add an icon, and *Back to List* to the **description** attribute.

```
<page-button path="Users/Index" Bootstrap-style="primary"
glyph="info-sign" description="Back to List"></page-button>
```

8. Add another <page-button> Tag Helper that targets the **Index** view in the *Pages* folder (not the one in the *Pages/Users* folder) to display the main dashboard. Assign *Index* to the **path** attribute to target the main **Index** Razor Page, *warning* to the **Bootstrap-style** attribute, *list-alt* to the **glyph** attribute to add a Glyphicon to the button, and *Dashboard* to the **description** attribute.

```
<page-button path="Index" Bootstrap-style="warning" glyph="list-
alt" description="Dashboard"></page-button>
```

9. Add an empty <p></p> element to create some distance between the buttons and the form.

```
<p></p>
```

10. Add a form that validates on all errors using the <form> element and a <div> element with the **asp-validation-summary** Tag Helper. Decorate the <div> element with the **text-danger** Bootstrap class to give the text a red color.

```
<form method="post">
    <div asp-validation-summary="All" class="text-danger"></div>
</form>
```

11. Add a <div> decorated with the **form-group** class below the previous <div> inside the <form> element.
    a. Add a <label> element with its **asp-for** attribute assigned a value from the **Input.Email** model property, inside the previous <div> element.
    b. Add an <input> element with its **asp-for** attribute assigned a value from the **Input.Email** model property below the <label> element.

c. Add a <span> element with its **asp-validation-for** attribute assigned a
    value from the **Input.Email** model property below the <input> element.
    Decorate the <span> element with the **text-danger** class to give the text
    red color.

```
<div class="form-group">
    <label asp-for="Input.Email"></label>
    <input asp-for="Input.Email" class="form-control" />
    <span asp-validation-for="Input.Email"
        class="text-danger"></span>
</div>
```

12. Copy the **form-group** decorated <div> you just finished and paste it in twice.
    Modify the pasted in code to target the **Password** and **ConfirmPassword** model
    properties.

13. Add a submit button above the closing </form> element and decorate it with the
    btn and **btn-success** Bootstrap classes to make it a styled green button.
    ```
    <button type="submit" class="btn btn-success">Create</button>
    ```

14. Load the **_ValidationScriptsPartial** partial view inside a **@section** block named
    Scripts below the if-block, to load the necessary UI validation scripts.
    ```
    @section Scripts {
        @await Html.PartialAsync("_ValidationScriptsPartial")
    }
    ```

15. Run the application (Ctrl+F5) and click the **Users** card on the main dashboard, or
    select **User** in the **Admin** menu. Make sure the Razor Page is displaying the users
    in a table and that the buttons are present. Click the **Create New** button to open
    the **Create** Razor Page. Try to add a new user and check that it has been added
    to the **AspNetUsers** table in the database. Also, try the **Back to List** and
    Dashboard buttons to navigate to the *Users/Index* and *Pages/Index* Razor Pages
    respectively.

The complete code in the **Create** HTML Razor Page:

```
@page
@using Microsoft.AspNetCore.Identity
@using VideoOnDemand.Data.Data.Entities
@inject SignInManager<User> SignInManager

@model CreateModel
@{ ViewData["Title"] = "Create a new account"; }
```

```
@if (SignInManager.IsSignedIn(User) && User.IsInRole("Admin"))
{
    <div class="row">
        <div class="col-md-4 col-md-offset-4">
            <h2>@ViewData["Title"]</h2>
            <page-button path="Users/Index" Bootstrap-style="primary"
             glyph="info-sign" description="Back to List"></page-button>

            <page-button path="Index" Bootstrap-style="warning"
             glyph="list-alt" description="Dashboard"></page-button>
            <p></p>
            <form method="post">
                <div asp-validation-summary="All"
                 class="text-danger"></div>

                <div class="form-group">
                    <label asp-for="Input.Email"></label>
                    <input asp-for="Input.Email" class="form-control" />
                    <span asp-validation-for="Input.Email"
                     class="text-danger"></span>
                </div>
                <div class="form-group">
                    <label asp-for="Input.Password"></label>
                    <input asp-for="Input.Password"
                     class="form-control" />
                    <span asp-validation-for="Input.Password"
                     class="text-danger"></span>
                </div>
                <div class="form-group">
                    <label asp-for="Input.ConfirmPassword"></label>
                    <input asp-for="Input.ConfirmPassword"
                     class="form-control" />
                    <span asp-validation-for="Input.ConfirmPassword"
                     class="text-danger"></span>
                </div>
                <button type="submit" class="btn btn-success">Create
                </button>
            </form>
        </div>
    </div>
}

@section Scripts {
    @await Html.PartialAsync("_ValidationScriptsPartial") }
```

The Users/Edit Razor Page

Because the **Edit** Razor Page is almost identical to the **Create** Razor Page, you will copy the **Create** page and make changes to it.

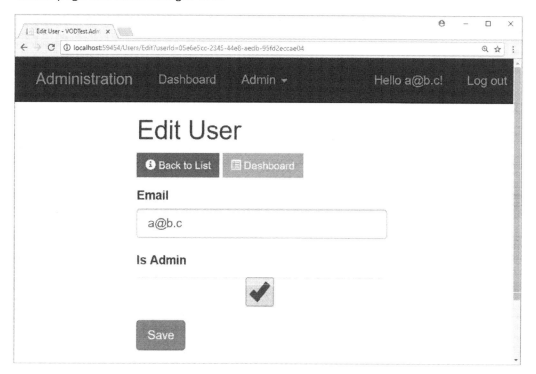

Altering the EditModel class

1. Copy the **Create** Razor Page and its code-behind file in the *Users* folder, paste them into the same folder, and change their names to **Edit**.
2. Open the *Edit.cshtml.cs* file.
3. Change the class name and constructor to **EditModel**.
4. Change the data type for the **Input** property to **UserPageModel**.
   ```
   public UserPageModel Input { get; set; } = new UserPageModel();
   ```
5. Locate the **OnGet** method and assign an empty string to the **StatusMessage** property to clear any residual message.
6. Call the **GetUser** method in the **_userService** service instance and assign the fetched user to the **Input** property. The **Input** property is part of the model sent to the **Edit** page and is bound to the form controls.

```
public void OnGet(string userId)
{
    StatusMessage = string.Empty;
    Input = _userService.GetUser(userId);
}
```

7. Replace the call to the **AddUser** method with a call to the **UpdateUser** method in the **OnPostAsync** method.
   ```
   var result = await _userService.UpdateUser(Input);
   ```

8. Since the result from the **UpdateUser** is a Boolean value, you have to remove the **IsSucceeded** property that doesn't exist.

9. Change the text assigned to the **SuccessMessage** to:
   ```
   if (result)
   {
       StatusMessage = $"User {Input.Email} was updated.";
       return RedirectToPage("Index");
   }
   ```

10. Remove the **foreach** loop and its contents.

The complete code for the **EditModel** class:

```
[Authorize(Roles = "Admin")]
public class EditModel : PageModel
{
    private IUserService _userService;

    [BindProperty]
    public UserPageModel Input { get; set; } = new UserPageModel();

    [TempData]
    public string StatusMessage { get; set; }

    public EditModel(IUserService userService)
    {
        _userService = userService;
    }

    public void OnGet(string userId)
    {
        Input = _userService.GetUser(userId);
        StatusMessage = string.Empty;
    }
}
```

```
    public async Task<IActionResult> OnPostAsync()
    {
        if (ModelState.IsValid)
        {
            var result = await _userService.UpdateUserAsync(Input);

            if (result)
            {
                StatusMessage = $"User {Input.Email} was updated.";
                return RedirectToPage("Index");
            }
        }

        return Page();
    }
}
```

Altering the Edit Razor Page

1. Open the *Edit.cshtml* file.
2. Change the name of the model class to **EditModel**.
3. Change the **ViewData** object's **Title** property to *Edit User*.
4. Add a hidden <input> element for the **Input.Id** property above the first **form-group** decorated <div>.
   ```
   <input type="hidden" asp-for="Input.Id" />
   ```
5. Change the second **form-group**'s intrinsic elements to target the **Input.IsAdmin** property.
   ```
   <div class="form-group">
       <label asp-for="Input.IsAdmin"></label>
       <input asp-for="Input.IsAdmin" class="form-control" />
       <span asp-validation-for="Input.IsAdmin"
        class="text-danger"></span>
   </div>
   ```
6. Remove the third **form-group** and all its content.
7. Change the text on the **submit** button to *Save*.

The complete code in the **Edit** Razor Page:

```
@page
@using Microsoft.AspNetCore.Identity
@using VideoOnDemand.Data.Data.Entities
@inject SignInManager<User> SignInManager
```

```
@model EditModel
@{
    ViewData["Title"] = "Edit User";
}

@if (SignInManager.IsSignedIn(User) && User.IsInRole("Admin"))
{
    <div class="row">
        <div class="col-md-4 col-md-offset-4">
            <h2>@ViewData["Title"]</h2>
            <page-button path="Users/Index" Bootstrap-style="primary"
             glyph="info-sign" description="Back to List"></page-button>
            <page-button path="Index" Bootstrap-style="warning"
             glyph="list-alt" description="Dashboard"></page-button>
            <p></p>
            <form method="post">
                <div asp-validation-summary="All"
                 class="text-danger"></div>
                <input type="hidden" asp-for="Input.Id" />
                <div class="form-group">
                    <label asp-for="Input.Email"></label>
                    <input asp-for="Input.Email" class="form-control" />
                    <span asp-validation-for="Input.Email"
                     class="text-danger"></span>
                </div>
                <div class="form-group">
                    <label asp-for="Input.IsAdmin"></label>
                    <input asp-for="Input.IsAdmin"
                     class="form-control" />
                    <span asp-validation-for="Input.IsAdmin"
                     class="text-danger"></span>
                </div>
                <button type="submit" class="btn btn-success">Save
                </button>
            </form>
        </div>
    </div>
}

@section Scripts {
    @await Html.PartialAsync("_ValidationScriptsPartial")
}
```

The Users/Delete Razor Page

This Razor Page will display information about the user and a button to delete the user. You will copy the **Edit** page and alter it.

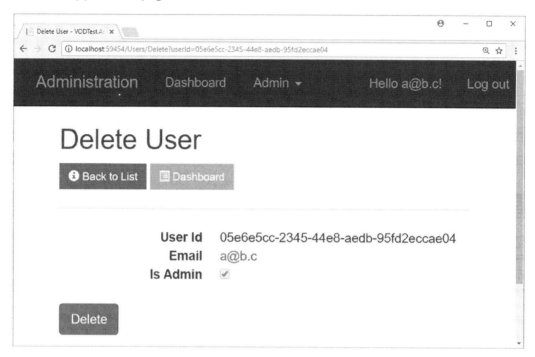

Altering the DeleteModel Class

1. Copy the **Edit** Razor Page and its code-behind file in the *Users* folder, paste them into the same folder, and change their names to **Delete**.
2. Open the *Delete.cshtml.cs* file.
3. Change the class and constructor name to **DeleteModel**.
4. Replace the call to the **UpdateUser** method with a call to the **DeleteUser** method in the **OnPostAsync** method. Pass in the **Id** property value of the **Input** object to the **DeleteUser** method to specify which user to delete.
   ```
   var result = await _userService.DeleteUser(Input.Id);
   ```
5. Change the text assigned to the **SuccessMessage** to:
   ```
   StatusMessage = $"User {Input.Email} was deleted.";
   ```

The complete code for the **DeleteModel** class:

```
public class DeleteModel : PageModel
{
    private IUserService _userService;

    [BindProperty]
    public UserPageModel Input { get; set; } = new UserPageModel();

    [TempData]
    public string StatusMessage { get; set; }

    public DeleteModel(IUserService userService)
    {
        _userService = userService;
    }

    public void OnGet(string userId)
    {
        Input = _userService.GetUser(userId);
        StatusMessage = string.Empty;
    }

    public async Task<IActionResult> OnPostAsync()
    {
        if (ModelState.IsValid)
        {
            var result = await _userService.DeleteUser(Input.Id);

            if (result)
            {
                StatusMessage = $"User {Input.Email} was deleted.";
                return RedirectToPage("Index");
            }
        }

        return Page();
    }
}
```

Altering the Delete Razor Page

1. Open the *Delete.cshtml* file.
2. Change the name of the model class to **DeleteModel**.

3. Change the **ViewData** object's **Title** property to *Delete User*.
4. The form needs to be a little wider since the user id is displayed on this page. Change the Bootstrap column classes on the second <div> to:
   ```
   <div class="col-md-6 col-md-offset-3">
   ```
5. Replace the <p></p> paragraph element with a horizontal rule.
   ```
   <hr />
   ```
6. Add a data list (not a table) below the horizontal rule above the <form> element. Add <dt> and <dd> elements for the **Id**, **Email**, and **IsAdmin** properties in the **Input** object. The <dt> element contains the label and the <dd> element contains the data. The **DisplayNameFor** method fetches the name of the property or the name in the **[Display]** attribute. The **DisplayFor** method fetches the value stored in the property.
   ```
   <dl class="dl-horizontal">
       <dt>@Html.DisplayNameFor(model => model.Input.Id)</dt>
       <dd>@Html.DisplayFor(model => model.Input.Id)</dd>
       <dt>@Html.DisplayNameFor(model => model.Input.Email)</dt>
       <dd>@Html.DisplayFor(model => model.Input.Email)</dd>
       <dt>@Html.DisplayNameFor(model => model.Input.IsAdmin)</dt>
       <dd>@Html.DisplayFor(model => model.Input.IsAdmin)</dd>
   </dl>
   ```
7. Remove all the **form-group** decorated <div> elements and their contents. The controls are no longer needed, since no data is altered with the form.
8. Add hidden <input> elements for the **Input.Email** and **Input.IsAdmin** properties below the existing hidden <input> element.
   ```
   <input type="hidden" asp-for="Input.Id" />
   <input type="hidden" asp-for="Input.Email" />
   <input type="hidden" asp-for="Input.IsAdmin" />
   ```
9. Change the text to *Delete* and the Bootstrap button style to **btn-danger** on the **submit** button.
   ```
   <button type="submit" class="btn btn-danger">Delete</button>
   ```
10. Save all files.

The complete code in the **Delete** Razor Page:

```
@page
@using Microsoft.AspNetCore.Identity
@using VideoOnDemand.Data.Data.Entities
@inject SignInManager<User> SignInManager
```

```
@model DeleteModel
@{
    ViewData["Title"] = "Delete User";
}


@if (SignInManager.IsSignedIn(User) && User.IsInRole("Admin"))
{
    <div class="row">
        <div class="col-md-6 col-md-offset-3">
            <h2>@ViewData["Title"]</h2>

            <page-button path="Users/Index" Bootstrap-style="primary"
             glyph="info-sign" description="Back to List"></page-button>

            <page-button path="Index" Bootstrap-style="warning"
             glyph="list-alt" description="Dashboard"></page-button>

            <hr />

            <dl class="dl-horizontal">
                <dt>@Html.DisplayNameFor(model => model.Input.Id)</dt>
                <dd>@Html.DisplayFor(model => model.Input.Id)</dd>
                <dt>@Html.DisplayNameFor(model =>
                    model.Input.Email)</dt>
                <dd>@Html.DisplayFor(model => model.Input.Email)</dd>
                <dt>@Html.DisplayNameFor(model =>
                    model.Input.IsAdmin)</dt>
                <dd>@Html.DisplayFor(model => model.Input.IsAdmin)</dd>
            </dl>

            <form method="post">
                <div asp-validation-summary="All" class="text-danger">
                </div>
                <input type="hidden" asp-for="Input.Id" />
                <input type="hidden" asp-for="Input.Email" />
                <input type="hidden" asp-for="Input.IsAdmin" />
                <button type="submit" class="btn btn-danger">Delete
                </button>
            </form>
        </div>
    </div>
}
```

Summary

In this chapter, you used the **UserService** service for handling users and user roles in the **AspNetUsers** and **AspNetUserRoles** database tables from the Razor Pages you added to the *Users* folder. The pages you added perform CRUD operations on the previously mentioned tables.

Next, you will create a new Tag Helper that displays the text in the **StatusMesage** property you added to the code-behind of the Razor Pages.

31. The StatusMessage Tag Helper

Introduction

In this chapter, you will create a Tag Helper that displays a success message sent from another page when data has been successfully added, updated, or deleted. The Tag Helper will use attributes and attribute values to configure the finished HTML elements, such as the message and the message type.

The **StatusMessage** property you added earlier to the Razor Pages will be used to store the message that is assigned in the **OnPostAsync** method when the data has been modified. You can see an example of the **alert** message under the heading in the image below. The message element is a <div> decorated with the Bootstrap **alert** classes.

The **[TempData]** attribute is new in ASP.NET Core 2.0 and can be used with properties in controllers and Razor Pages to store data until it is read. It is particularly useful for redirection, when data is needed for more than a single request. The **Keep** and **Peek** methods can be used to examine the data without deletion.

Since the **[TempData]** attribute is built on top of session state, it can be shared between Razor Pages. You will use this to send a message from one Razor Page to another and display it using the <status-message> Tag Helper that you will implement in this chapter.

Technologies Used in This Chapter

1. **C#** – To create the Tag Helper.
2. **HTML** – To create the Tag Helper and add it to the Razor Pages.

Adding the Tag Helper Class

1. Add a **Razor Tag Helper** class called **StatusMessageTagHelper** to the *TagHelpers* folder.
   ```
   [HtmlTargetElement("tag-name")]
   public class StatusMessageTagHelper : TagHelper
   {
       public override void Process(TagHelperContext context,
       TagHelperOutput output) { }
   }
   ```

2. Change the **HtmlTargetElement** attribute to **status-message**. This will be the Tag Helper's "element" name. It's not a real HTML element, but it looks like one, to blend in with the HTML markup. It will, however, generate a real HTML element when rendered.
   ```
   [HtmlTargetElement("status-message")]
   ```

3. Add two **string** properties called **Message** and **MessageType** to the class and assign *success* to the **MessageType** property. These properties will be the Tag Helper attributes you will use with the <status-message> element.
   ```
   public string Message { get; set; }
   // Possible Bootstrap classes: success, danger, warning, ...
   public string MessageType { get; set; } = "success";
   ```

4. Return from the **Process** method if the **Message** property is **null** or empty.
   ```
   if (string.IsNullOrEmpty(Message)) return;
   ```

5. Throw an **ArgumentNullException** if either of the **context** or **output** method parameters are **null**. If they are **null**, the Tag Helper element can't be rendered.
   ```
   if (context == null)
       throw new ArgumentNullException(nameof(context));
   if (output == null)
       throw new ArgumentNullException(nameof(output));
   ```

6. Call the **base** class's **Process** method with the two method parameters.
   ```
   base.Process(context, output);
   ```

7. Tell the **Process** method the element type that it should output. Use the **TagName** property on the **output** object to specify the Tag Helper's main element container.
   ```
   output.TagName = "div";
   ```

8. Add the **alert** element and style it. Use the two properties to assign the text to be displayed and to style the background color of the <div>. Only append the message if the **Message** property isn't **null** or empty. You can see examples of alerts on the Bootstrap website:
   https://getbootstrapbootstrap.com/docs/3.3/components/#alerts
   ```
   var content = $"<div class='alert alert-{MessageType} " +
       "alert-dismissible' role='alert'><button type='button' " +
       "class='close' data-dismiss='alert' aria-label='Close'>" +
       "<span aria-hidden='true'>&times;</span></button>";

   if (!string.IsNullOrEmpty(Message)) content += Message;
   ```

9. Add the element in the **content** variable to the **output** object's **Content** property. Also, append a closing </div> to the **output** object.
   ```
   output.Content.AppendHtml(content);
   output.Content.AppendHtml("</div>");
   ```

10. Save the file and open the **Index** Razor Page in the *Users* folder.

11. Add a <status-message> element above the two <page-button> Tag Helpers you added previously and below the <h2> heading. Assign the **@Model.StatusMessage** property to the **message** attribute and *success* to the **message-type** attribute (you can skip this attribute if you want the default *success* type).
    ```
    <h2>Users</h2>
    <status-message message="@Model.StatusMessage"
     message-type="success"></status-message>
    ```
    Or you can leave out the message-type attribute.
    ```
    <h2>Users</h2>
    <status-message message="@Model.StatusMessage"></status-message>
    ```

12. Save all files and start the application.

13. Open the *Users/Index* page and add a new user. A success message should be displayed with the Tag Helper when you have been redirected to the **Index** page.

14. Edit the user you just added. A success message should be displayed with the Tag Helper when you have been redirected to the **Index** page.
15. Delete the user you added. A success message should be displayed with the Tag Helper when the user has been removed and you have been redirected to the **Index** page.

Summary

In this chapter, you created a Tag Helper that displays the text from the **StatusMesage** property you added to the code-behind of the Razor Pages in the previous chapter.

Next, you will use the Razor Pages you added in this chapter to create new Razor Pages for the other entities.

32. The Remaining Razor Pages

Overview

In this chapter, you will create the Razor Pages for the other entities by copying and modifying the Razor Pages in the *Users* folder. In most cases only small changes have to be made to the HTML and code-behind files. Depending on the what the page is used for, you must add or remove the services injected into the constructor.

Some of the pages have drop-down elements that you have to add since the *User* pages don't have any. You add a drop-down to the form by adding a <select> element and assigning a collection of **SelectList** items to it; you can fetch such a list by calling the **GetSelectList** in the **DbReadService** you added earlier to the **Data** project. You can send the collection to the page with the **ViewData** object and use the **ViewBag** object to assign it to the <select> element.

```
public void OnGet()
{
    ViewData["Modules"] = _dbReadService.GetSelectList<Module>(
        "Id", "Title");
}
```

```
<div class="form-group">
    <label asp-for="Input.ModuleId" class="control-label"></label>
    <select asp-for="Input.ModuleId" class="form-control"
        asp-items="ViewBag.Modules"></select>
</div>
```

Technologies Used in This Chapter
1. **C#** – To write code in the Razor Pages code-behind methods.
2. **HTML** – To add content to the Razor Pages.
3. **Entity framework** – To perform CRUD operations.

The Video Razor Pages
1. Copy the *Users* folder and all its contents.
2. Paste in the copied folder in the *Pages* folder and rename it *Videos*.

The typical **Index** Razor Page

The typical **Delete** Razor Page

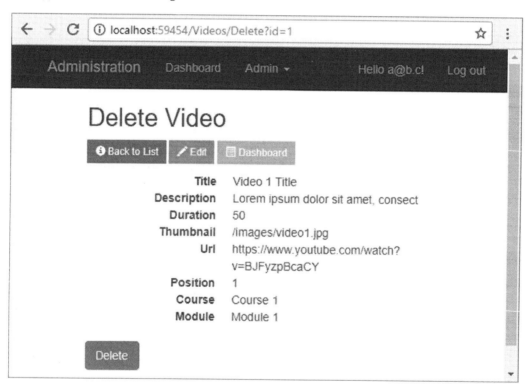

The typical **Create** Razor Page

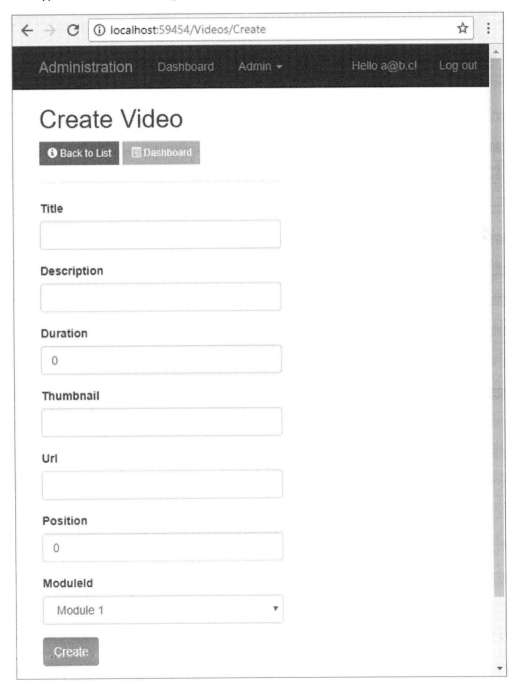

The typical **Edit** Razor Page

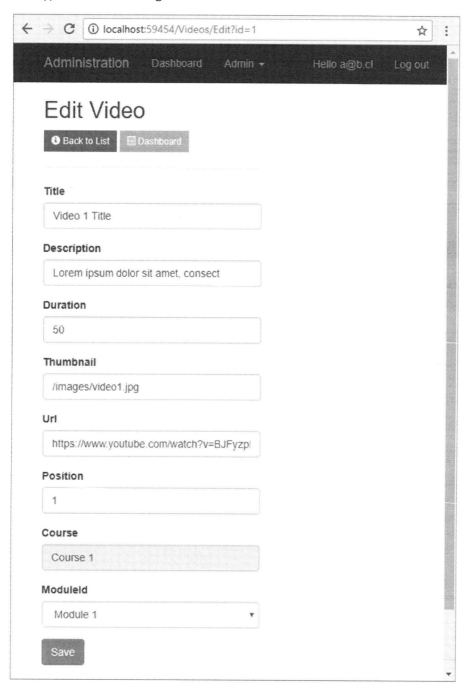

The IndexModel Class

1. Open the **IndexModel** class in the *Videos* folder (the *.cshtml.cs* file).
2. Change the namespace to **Videos**.
   ```
   namespace VideoOnDemand.Admin.Pages.Videos
   ```

3. Change the injected service to **IDbReadService**.
   ```
   private IDbReadService _dbReadService;
    public IndexModel(IDbReadService dbReadService)
    {
        _dbReadService = dbReadService;
    }
   ```

4. Change the **IEnumerable** collection to store **Video** objects and rename it **Items**.
   ```
   public IEnumerable<Video> Items = new List<Video>();
   ```

5. Replace the code in the **OnGet** method with a call to the **GetWithIncludes** method in the read service and specify the **Video** entity as the method's type.
   ```
   public void OnGet()
   {
        Items = _dbReadService.GetWithIncludes<Video>();
   }
   ```

6. Save all files.

The complete code for the **IndexModel** class:

```
[Authorize(Roles = "Admin")]
public class IndexModel : PageModel
{
    private IDbReadService _dbReadService;
    public IEnumerable<Video> Items = new List<Video>();
    [TempData] public string StatusMessage { get; set; }

    public IndexModel(IDbReadService dbReadService)
    {
        _dbReadService = dbReadService;
    }

    public void OnGet()
    {
        Items = _dbReadService.GetWithIncludes<Video>();
    }
}
```

The Index Razor Page

1. Open the **Index** Razor Page in the *Videos* folder (the *.cshtml* file).
2. Change the **ViewData** title to *Videos*.
3. Change the column from **col-md-8 col-md-offset-2** to **col-md-12** to make the column fill the entire row.
4. Change the **path** attribute of the first <page-button> element to *Videos/Create*.
5. Change the **foreach** loop to iterate over the **Items** collection, and name the loop variable **item**.

   ```
   @foreach (var item in Model.Items)
   ```

6. Change the <td> elements to display the values from the properties in the **item** loop variable. Add and remove <td> elements as needed.
7. Change the *User* folder in the **path** properties to *Video* in the **Edit** and **Delete** <page-button> elements.
8. Replace the **id-userId** attribute with an **id** attribute for the **Edit** and **Delete** <page-button> elements.

   ```
   <page-button path="Videos/Edit" Bootstrap-style="success"
       glyph="pencil" id="@item.Id"></page-button>
   ```

9. Remove the <div> that is decorated with **col-md-2**; it's no longer needed since the previous column takes up the entire width of the row.
10. Save all files.

The complete code for the **Index** Razor Page:

```
@page
@using Microsoft.AspNetCore.Identity
@using VideoOnDemand.Data.Data.Entities
@inject SignInManager<User> SignInManager
@model IndexModel
@{
    ViewData["Title"] = "Videos";
}

@if (SignInManager.IsSignedIn(User) && User.IsInRole("Admin"))
{
    <div class="row">
        <div class="col-md-12">
            <h2>@ViewData["Title"]</h2>
            <status-message message="@Model.StatusMessage"
             message-type="success"></status-message>
```

```html
<page-button path="Videos/Create" Bootstrap-style="primary"
 description="Create New"></page-button>
<page-button path="Index" Bootstrap-style="warning"
 glyph="list-alt" description="Dashboard"></page-button>

<table class="table">
    <thead>
        <tr>
            <td>Title</td>
            <td>Description</td>
            <th>Url</th>
            <th>Course</th>
            <th>Module</th>
            <th></th>
        </tr>
    </thead>
    <tbody>
        @foreach (var item in Model.Items)
        {
            <tr>
                <td>@Html.DisplayFor(modelItem =>
                    item.Title)</td>
                <td>@Html.DisplayFor(modelItem =>
                    item.Description)</td>
                <td>@Html.DisplayFor(modelItem =>
                    item.Url)</td>
                <td>@Html.DisplayFor(modelItem =>
                    item.Course.Title)</td>
                <td>@Html.DisplayFor(modelItem =>
                    item.Module.Title)</td>
                <td class="button-col-width">
                    <page-button path="Videos/Edit"
                        Bootstrap-style="success"
                        glyph="pencil" id="@item.Id">
                    </page-button>
                    <page-button path="Videos/Delete"
                        Bootstrap-style="danger"
                        glyph="remove" id="@item.Id">
                    </page-button>
                </td>
            </tr>
        }
    </tbody>
</table>
```

```
        </div>
    </div>
}
```

The CreateModel Class

1. Open the **CreateModel** class in the *Videos* folder (the *.cshtml.cs* file).
2. Change the namespace to **Videos**.
   ```
   namespace VideoOnDemand.Admin.Pages.Videos
   ```

3. Remove the injected service and inject the two **IDbReadService** and **IDbWriteService** services.
   ```
   private IDbReadService _dbReadService;
   private IDbWriteService _dbWriteService;
   public CreateModel(IDbReadService dbReadService, IDbWriteService
   dbWriteService)
   {
       _dbReadService = dbReadService;
       _dbWriteService = dbWriteService;
   }
   ```

4. Replace the **IEnumerable Input** property with one for the **Video** entity.
   ```
   public Video Input { get; set; } = new Video();
   ```

5. Add a call to the **GetSelectList** method for the **Modules** entity on the read service in the **OnGet** method. Specify that the **Id** property should provide the value and the **Title** property the text to be displayed for the items in the drop-down.
   ```
   public void OnGet()
   {
       ViewData["Modules"] =
           _dbReadService.GetSelectList<Module>("Id", "Title");
   }
   ```

6. Replace the code line with the **AddUser** method call with a call to the **Get** method in the **DbReadService** service for the **Module** entity and store the course id from that call in the **Input** object's **CourseId** property. Use the **ModuleId** property in the **Input** object when fetching the course id.
   ```
   Input.CourseId =
       _dbReadService.Get<Module>(Input.ModuleId).CourseId;
   ```

7. Call the asynchronous **Add** method in the **DbWriteService** service with the **Input** object as a parameter below the previous method call. Store the returned value in a variable called **success**.
```
var success = await _dbWriteService.Add(Input);
```

8. Replace **result.Succeeded** with **success** in the if statement. Assign the text *Created a new video:* followed by the video title to the **SuccessMessage** property; use the **Title** property from the **Input** object to get the video title.
```
if (success)
{
    StatusMessage = $"Created a new Video: {Input.Title}.";
    return RedirectToPage("Index");
}
```

9. Remove the **foreach** loop and its content.

10. Save all files.

The complete code for the **CreateModel** class:
```
[Authorize(Roles = "Admin")]
public class CreateModel : PageModel
{
    private IDbReadService _dbReadService;
    private IDbWriteService _dbWriteService;

    [BindProperty] public Video Input { get; set; } = new Video();
    [TempData] public string StatusMessage { get; set; }

    public CreateModel(IDbReadService dbReadService,
    IDbWriteService dbWriteService)
    {
        _dbReadService = dbReadService;
        _dbWriteService = dbWriteService;
    }

    public void OnGet()
    {
        ViewData["Modules"] = _dbReadService.GetSelectList<Module>(
            "Id", "Title");
    }
}
```

```
public async Task<IActionResult> OnPostAsync()
{
    if (ModelState.IsValid)
    {
        Input.CourseId = _dbReadService.Get<Module>(
            Input.ModuleId).CourseId;
        var success = await _dbWriteService.Add(Input);

        if (success)
        {
            StatusMessage = $"Created a new Video: {Input.Title}.";
            return RedirectToPage("Index");
        }
    }

    // If we got this far, something failed, redisplay form
    return Page();
}
}
```

The Create Razor Page

1. Open the **Create** Razor Page in the *Videos* folder (the *.cshtml* file).
2. Change the **ViewData** title to *Create Video*.
3. Add an offset to the column <div> to push the form to the right **col-md-offset-4**.
   ```
   <div class="col-md-4 col-md-offset-4">
   ```

4. Change the folder path from *Users* to *Videos/Create* in the first <page-button> element.
5. Change the content in the **form-group** <div> elements to display the values from the properties in the **Input** variable. Add and remove **form-group** <div> elements as needed.
6. Add a drop-down for the **Module** entity using the **ViewBag.Modules** property. Store the module id for the selected drop-down item in the **Input.ModuleId** property.
   ```
   <div class="form-group">
       <label asp-for="Input.ModuleId" class="control-label"></label>
       <select asp-for="Input.ModuleId" class="form-control"
           asp-items="ViewBag.Modules"></select>
   </div>
   ```

The complete code for the **Create** Razor Page:

```
@page
@using Microsoft.AspNetCore.Identity
@using VideoOnDemand.Data.Data.Entities
@inject SignInManager<User> SignInManager

@model CreateModel
@{
    ViewData["Title"] = "Create Video";
}

@if (SignInManager.IsSignedIn(User) && User.IsInRole("Admin"))
{
    <div class="row">
        <div class="col-md-4 col-md-offset-4">
            <h2>@ViewData["Title"]</h2>
            <page-button path="Videos/Index" Bootstrap-style="primary"
             glyph="info-sign" description="Back to List"></page-button>
            <page-button path="Index" Bootstrap-style="warning"
             glyph="list-alt" description="Dashboard"></page-button>
            <p></p>
            <form method="post">
                <div asp-validation-summary="ModelOnly"
                    class="text-danger"></div>
                <div class="form-group">
                    <label asp-for="Input.Title" class="control-label">
                    </label>
                    <input asp-for="Input.Title" class="form-control" />
                    <span asp-validation-for="Input.Title"
                        class="text-danger"></span>
                </div>
                <div class="form-group">
                    <label asp-for="Input.Description"
                        class="control-label"></label>
                    <input asp-for="Input.Description"
                        class="form-control" />
                    <span asp-validation-for="Input.Description"
                        class="text-danger"></span>
                </div>
                <div class="form-group">
                    <label asp-for="Input.Duration"
                        class="control-label"></label>
                    <input asp-for="Input.Duration"
```

```
                            class="form-control" />
                    <span asp-validation-for="Input.Duration"
                        class="text-danger"></span>
                </div>
                <div class="form-group">
                    <label asp-for="Input.Thumbnail"
                        class="control-label"></label>
                    <input asp-for="Input.Thumbnail"
                        class="form-control" />
                    <span asp-validation-for="Input.Thumbnail"
                        class="text-danger"></span>
                </div>
                <div class="form-group">
                    <label asp-for="Input.Url" class="control-label">
                    </label>
                    <input asp-for="Input.Url" class="form-control" />
                    <span asp-validation-for="Input.Url"
                        class="text-danger"></span>
                </div>
                <div class="form-group">
                    <label asp-for="Input.Position"
                        class="control-label"></label>
                    <input asp-for="Input.Position"
                        class="form-control" />
                    <span asp-validation-for="Input.Position"
                        class="text-danger"></span>
                </div>
                <div class="form-group">
                    <label asp-for="Input.ModuleId"
                        class="control-label"></label>
                    <select asp-for="Input.ModuleId"
                        class="form-control"
                        asp-items="ViewBag.Modules"></select>
                </div>
                <button type="submit" class="btn btn-success">Create
                </button>
            </form>
        </div>
    </div>
}

@section Scripts {
    @{await Html.RenderPartialAsync("_ValidationScriptsPartial");}
}
```

The EditModel Class

1. Delete both the **Edit** Razor Page files in the *Videos* folder (*.cshtml* and *.cshtml.cs*).

2. Copy both the **Create** Razor Page files in the *Videos* folder and paste them into the *Videos* folder. Rename the files *Edit.cshtml* and *Edit.cshtml.cs*.

3. Open the *Edit.cshtml.cs* file in the *Videos* folder and rename the class and constructor **EditModel**.

4. Add an **int** parameter called **id** to the **OnGet** method.

5. Use the **Get** method in read service to fetch the **Video** entity matching the id in the **id** parameter you just added. Save the video in the **Input** property.

```
public void OnGet(int id)
{
    ViewData["Modules"] =
        _dbReadService.GetSelectList<Module>("Id", "Title");
    Input = _dbReadService.Get<Video>(id, true);
}
```

6. Because a course object isn't needed in the **Input** object to update the **Video** entity, you should assign **null** to it. Place the code below the code that assigns the course id.

```
Input.Course = null;
```

7. Replace the asynchronous **Add** method call in the write service with a call to the **Update** method in the same service. Store the returned value in a variable called **success**.

```
var success = await _dbWriteService.Update(Input);
```

8. Replace the text in the **SuccessMessage** property to *Updated Video:* followed by the title of the video.

```
StatusMessage = $"Updated Video: {Input.Title}.";
```

9. Save all files.

The complete code for the **EditModel** class:

```
[Authorize(Roles = "Admin")]
public class EditModel : PageModel
{
    private IDbWriteService _dbWriteService;
    private IDbReadService _dbReadService;

    [BindProperty] public Video Input { get; set; } = new Video();
    [TempData] public string StatusMessage { get; set; }
```

```
    public EditModel(IDbReadService dbReadService,
    IDbWriteService dbWriteService)
    {
        _dbWriteService = dbWriteService;
        _dbReadService = dbReadService;
    }

    public void OnGet(int id)
    {
        ViewData["Modules"] = _dbReadService.GetSelectList<Module>(
            "Id", "Title");
        Input = _dbReadService.Get<Video>(id, true);
    }

    public async Task<IActionResult> OnPostAsync()
    {
        if (ModelState.IsValid)
        {
            Input.CourseId =
                _dbReadService.Get<Module>(Input.ModuleId).CourseId;
            Input.Course = null;
            var success = await _dbWriteService.Update(Input);

            if (success)
            {
                StatusMessage = $"Updated Video: {Input.Title}.";
                return RedirectToPage("Index");
            }
        }
        // If we got this far, something failed, redisplay form
        return Page();
    }
}
```

The Edit Razor Page

1. Open the **Edit** Razor Page in the *Videos* folder (the *.cshtml* file).
2. Change the **@model** directive to use the **EditModel** class.
3. Change the **ViewData** title to *Edit Video*.
4. Add a hidden <input> element for the **Input.Id** property value above the first **form-group** <div>. The hidden element is needed to keep track of the id for the entity being edited.
   ```
   <input type="hidden" asp-for="Input.Id" />
   ```

5. Add a **form-group** <div> with a label and a **readonly** <input> element for the course title in the **Input.Course.Title** property above the **form-group** <div> containing the drop-down.

```
<div class="form-group">
    <label class="control-label">Course</label>
    <input asp-for="Input.Course.Title" readonly
        class="form-control" />
</div>
```

6. Change the **submit** button's text to *Save*.

```
<button type="submit" class="btn btn-success">Save</button>
```

7. Save all files.

The complete code for the **Edit** Razor Page:

```
@page
@using Microsoft.AspNetCore.Identity
@using VideoOnDemand.Data.Data.Entities
@inject SignInManager<User> SignInManager

@model EditModel
@{
    ViewData["Title"] = "Edit Video";
}

@if (SignInManager.IsSignedIn(User) && User.IsInRole("Admin"))
{
    <div class="row">
        <div class="col-md-4 col-md-offset-4">
            <h2>@ViewData["Title"]</h2>
            <page-button path="Videos/Index" Bootstrap-style="primary"
             glyph="info-sign" description="Back to List"></page-button>
            <page-button path="Index" Bootstrap-style="warning"
             glyph="list-alt" description="Dashboard"></page-button>
            <p></p>
            <form method="post">
                <div asp-validation-summary="ModelOnly"
                    class="text-danger"></div>
                <input type="hidden" asp-for="Input.Id" />
                <div class="form-group">
                    <label asp-for="Input.Title" class="control-label">
                    </label>
                    <input asp-for="Input.Title" class="form-control" />
```

```
            <span asp-validation-for="Input.Title"
                class="text-danger"></span>
        </div>
        <div class="form-group">
            <label asp-for="Input.Description"
                class="control-label"></label>
            <input asp-for="Input.Description"
                class="form-control" />
            <span asp-validation-for="Input.Description"
                class="text-danger"></span>
        </div>
        <div class="form-group">
            <label asp-for="Input.Duration"
                class="control-label"></label>
            <input asp-for="Input.Duration"
                class="form-control" />
            <span asp-validation-for="Input.Duration"
                class="text-danger"></span>
        </div>
        <div class="form-group">
            <label asp-for="Input.Thumbnail"
                class="control-label"></label>
            <input asp-for="Input.Thumbnail"
                class="form-control" />
            <span asp-validation-for="Input.Thumbnail"
                class="text-danger"></span>
        </div>
        <div class="form-group">
            <label asp-for="Input.Url" class="control-label">
            </label>
            <input asp-for="Input.Url" class="form-control" />
            <span asp-validation-for="Input.Url"
                class="text-danger"></span>
        </div>
        <div class="form-group">
            <label asp-for="Input.Position"
                class="control-label"></label>
            <input asp-for="Input.Position"
                class="form-control" />
            <span asp-validation-for="Input.Position"
                class="text-danger"></span>
        </div>
        <div class="form-group">
            <label class="control-label">Course</label>
```

```
                    <input asp-for="Input.Course.Title" readonly
                        class="form-control" />
                </div>
                <div class="form-group">
                    <label asp-for="Input.ModuleId"
                        class="control-label"></label>
                    <select asp-for="Input.ModuleId"
                        class="form-control"
                        asp-items="ViewBag.Modules"></select>
                </div>
                <button type="submit" class="btn btn-success">Save
                </button>
            </form>
        </div>
    </div>
}
@section Scripts {
    @{await Html.RenderPartialAsync("_ValidationScriptsPartial");}
}
```

The DeleteModel Class

1. Delete both the **Delete** Razor Page files in the *Videos* folder (*.cshtml* and *.cshtml.cs*).
2. Copy both the **Edit** Razor Page files in the *Videos* folder and paste them into the *Videos* folder. Rename the files *Delete.cshtml* and *Delete.cshtml.cs*.
3. Open the *Delete.cshtml.cs* file in the *Videos* folder and rename the class and the constructor **DeleteModel**.
4. Remove the row with the call to the **GetSelectList** method from the **OnGet** method.
5. Remove the rows with the **Input.CourseId** and **Input.Course** assignments from the **OnPostAsync** method.
6. Replace the asynchronous write service **Update** method call with a call to the **Delete** method in the same service. Store the returned value in a variable called **success**.
    ```
    var success = await _dbWriteService.Delete(Input);
    ```
7. Replace the text in the **SuccessMessage** property to *Deleted Video:* followed by the title of the video.
    ```
    StatusMessage = $"Deleted Video: {Input.Title}.";
    ```
8. Save all files.

The complete code for the **DeleteModel** class:

```
[Authorize(Roles = "Admin")]
public class DeleteModel : PageModel
{
    private IDbWriteService _dbWriteService;
    private IDbReadService _dbReadService;

    [BindProperty] public Video Input { get; set; } = new Video();
    [TempData] public string StatusMessage { get; set; }

    public DeleteModel(IDbReadService dbReadService,
    IDbWriteService dbWriteService)
    {
        _dbWriteService = dbWriteService;
        _dbReadService = dbReadService;
    }

    public void OnGet(int id)
    {
        Input = _dbReadService.Get<Video>(id, true);
    }

    public async Task<IActionResult> OnPostAsync()
    {
        if (ModelState.IsValid)
        {
            var success = await _dbWriteService.Delete(Input);

            if (success)
            {
                StatusMessage = $"Deleted Video: {Input.Title}.";
                return RedirectToPage("Index");
            }
        }

        // If we got this far, something failed, redisplay form
        return Page();
    }
}
```

The Delete Razor Page

1. Open the **Delete** Razor Page in the *Videos* folder (the *.cshtml* file).
2. Change the **@model** directive to use the **DeleteModel** class.

3. Change the **ViewData** title to *Delete Video*.

4. Add a <page-button> element for a button leading to the **Edit** Razor Page. Don't forget to add the video id to an attribute called **id**.

```
<page-button path="Videos/Edit" Bootstrap-style="success"
    glyph="pencil" description="Edit" id="@Model.Input.Id">
</page-button>
```

5. Add a data list using <dl>, <dt>, and <dd> elements for the properties in the **Input** object.

6. Remove all the **form-group** <div> elements and their contents from the form.

7. Add a hidden <input> element for the **Input.Title** property value below the existing hidden <input> element.

```
<input type="hidden" asp-for="Input.Title" />
```

8. Change the **submit** button's text to *Delete* and change the button type to **btn-danger**.

```
<button type="submit" class="btn btn-danger">Delete</button>
```

9. Save all files.

The complete code for the **Delete** Razor Page:

```
@page
@using Microsoft.AspNetCore.Identity
@using VideoOnDemand.Data.Data.Entities
@inject SignInManager<User> SignInManager

@model DeleteModel
@{
    ViewData["Title"] = "Delete Video";
}

@if (SignInManager.IsSignedIn(User) && User.IsInRole("Admin"))
{
    <div class="row">
        <div class="col-md-6 col-md-offset-2">
            <h2>@ViewData["Title"]</h2>
            <page-button path="Videos/Index" Bootstrap-style="primary"
                glyph="info-sign" description="Back to List">
            </page-button>
            <page-button path="Videos/Edit" Bootstrap-style="success"
                glyph-"pencil" description="Edit" id="@Model.Input.Id">
            </page-button>
```

```
            <page-button path="Index" Bootstrap-style="warning"
                glyph="list-alt" description="Dashboard">
            </page-button>
            <p></p>
            <dl class="dl-horizontal">
                <dt>@Html.DisplayNameFor(model =>
                    model.Input.Title)</dt>
                <dd>@Html.DisplayFor(model => model.Input.Title)</dd>
                <dt>@Html.DisplayNameFor(model =>
                    model.Input.Description)</dt>
                <dd>@Html.DisplayFor(model =>
                    model.Input.Description)</dd>
                <dt>@Html.DisplayNameFor(model =>
                    model.Input.Duration)</dt>
                <dd>@Html.DisplayFor(model => model.Input.Duration)</dd>
                <dt>@Html.DisplayNameFor(model =>
                    model.Input.Thumbnail)</dt>
                <dd>@Html.DisplayFor(model =>
                    model.Input.Thumbnail)</dd>
                <dt>@Html.DisplayNameFor(model => model.Input.Url)</dt>
                <dd>@Html.DisplayFor(model => model.Input.Url)</dd>
                <dt>@Html.DisplayNameFor(model =>
                    model.Input.Position)</dt>
                <dd>@Html.DisplayFor(model => model.Input.Position)</dd>
                <dt>@Html.DisplayNameFor(model =>
                    model.Input.Course)</dt>
                <dd>@Html.DisplayFor(model =>
                    model.Input.Course.Title)</dd>
                <dt>@Html.DisplayNameFor(model =>
                    model.Input.Module)</dt>
                <dd>@Html.DisplayFor(model =>
                    model.Input.Module.Title)</dd>
            </dl>
            <form method="post">
                <div asp-validation-summary="All" class="text-danger">
                </div>
                <input type="hidden" asp-for="Input.Id" />
                <input type="hidden" asp-for="Input.Title" />
                <button type="submit" class="btn btn-danger">Delete
                </button>
            </form>
        </div>
    </div>
}
```

The Downloads Razor Pages

1. Copy the *Videos* folder and all its contents.
2. Paste in the copied folder in the *Pages* folder and rename it *Downloads*.

The IndexModel Class

1. Open the **IndexModel** class in the *Downloads* folder (the *.cshtml.cs* file).
2. Change the namespace to **Downloads**.
    ```
    namespace VideoOnDemand.Admin.Pages.Downloads
    ```
3. Change the **IEnumerable** collection to store **Download** objects and rename it **Items**.
    ```
    public IEnumerable<Download> Items = new List<Download>();
    ```
4. Replace the code in the **OnGet** method with a call to the **GetWithIncludes** method in the read service and specify the **Download** entity as the method's type.
    ```
    public void OnGet()
    {
        Items = _dbReadService.GetWithIncludes<Download>();
    }
    ```
5. Save all files.

The Index Razor Page

1. Open the **Index** Razor Page in the *Downloads* folder (the *.cshtml* file).
2. Change the **ViewData** title to *Downloads*.
3. Change the folder part of the **path** attribute of all the <page-button> elements from *Videos* to *Downloads*.
4. Change the headings in the <th> elements to match the property values of the entity. Add and remove <th> elements as needed.
5. Change the <td> elements to display the values from the properties in the **item** loop variable. Add and remove <td> elements as needed.
6. Save all files.

The CreateModel Class

1. Open the **CreateModel** class in the *Downloads* folder (the *.cshtml.cs* file).
2. Change the namespace to **Downloads**.
    ```
    namespace VideoOnDemand.Admin.Pages.Downloads
    ```

3. Replace the **IEnumerable Input** property with one for the **Download** entity.
   `public Download Input { get; set; } = new Download();`

4. Change the text in the **SuccessMessage** property to *Created a new Download:* followed by the title of the download.
   `StatusMessage = $"Created a new Download: {Input.Title}.";`

5. Save all files.

The Create Razor Page

1. Open the **Create** Razor Page in the *Downloads* folder (the *.cshtml* file).
2. Change the **ViewData** title to *Create Download*.
3. Change the *Video* folder in the **path** attribute to *Downloads* in the first <page-button> element.
4. Change the content in the **form-group** <div> elements to display the values from the properties in the **Input** variable. Add and remove **form-group** <div> elements as needed.
5. Save all files.

The EditModel Class

1. Open the **EditModel** class in the *Downloads* folder (the *.cshtml.cs* file).
2. Change the namespace to **Downloads**.
   `namespace VideoOnDemand.Admin.Pages.Downloads`

3. Change the data type to **Download** for the **Input** variable.
   `public Download Input { get; set; } = new Download();`

4. Change the data type to **Download** for the **Get** method call in the **OnGet** method.
   `Input = _dbReadService.Get<Download>(id, true);`

5. Replace the text in the **SuccessMessage** property to *Updated Download:* followed by the title of the download.
   `StatusMessage = $"Updated Download: {Input.Title}.";`

6. Save all files.

The Edit Razor Page

1. Open the **Edit** Razor Page in the *Downloads* folder (the *.cshtml* file).
2. Change the **ViewData** title to *Edit Download*.
3. Change the folder part of the **path** attribute of all the <page-button> element from *Videos* to *Downloads*.
4. Change the **form-group** <div> elements' contents to match the properties in the **Input** object.
5. Save all files.

The DeleteModel Class

1. Open the **DeleteModel** class in the *Downloads* folder (the *.cshtml.cs* file).
2. Change the namespace to **Downloads**.
   ```
   namespace VideoOnDemand.Admin.Pages.Downloads
   ```
3. Change the data type to **Download** for the **Input** variable.
   ```
   public Download Input { get; set; } = new Download();
   ```
4. Change the data type to **Download** for the **Get** method call in the **OnGet** method.
   ```
   Input = _dbReadService.Get<Download>(id, true);
   ```
5. Replace the text in the **SuccessMessage** property to *Deleted Download:* followed by the title of the download.
   ```
   StatusMessage = $"Deleted Download: {Input.Title}.";
   ```
6. Save all files.

The Delete Razor Page

1. Open the **Delete** Razor Page in the *Downloads* folder (the *.cshtml* file).
2. Change the **ViewData** title to *Delete Download*.
3. Change the folder part of the **path** attribute of all the <page-button> elements from *Videos* to *Downloads*.
4. Change the contents of the <dd> and <dt> elements to match the properties in the **Input** object.
5. Save all files.

The Instructors Razor Pages

1. Copy the *Videos* folder and all its contents.
2. Paste in the copied folder in the *Pages* folder and rename it *Instructors*.

The IndexModel Class

1. Open the **IndexModel** class in the *Instructors* folder (the *.cshtml.cs* file).
2. Change the namespace to **Instructors**.
   ```
   namespace VideoOnDemand.Admin.Pages.Instructors
   ```

3. Change the **IEnumerable** collection to store **Instructor** objects and rename it **Items**.
   ```
   public IEnumerable<Instructor> Items = new List<Instructor>();
   ```

4. Replace the call to the **GetWithIncludes** method with a call to the **Get** method in the **OnGet** method and specify the **Instructor** entity as the method's type. You call the **Get** method because the data in the related tables are not needed.
   ```
   public void OnGet()
   {
       Items = _dbReadService.Get<Instructor>();
   }
   ```

5. Save all files.

The Index Razor Page

1. Open the **Index** Razor Page in the *Instructors* folder (the *.cshtml* file).
2. Change the **ViewData** title to *Instructor*.
3. Change the folder part of the **path** attribute of all the <page-button> elements from *Videos* to *Instructors*.
4. Change the headings in the <th> elements to match the property values of the entity. Add and remove <th> elements as needed.
5. Change the <td> elements to display the values from the properties in the **item** loop variable. Add and remove <td> elements as needed.
6. Save all files.

The CreateModel Class

1. Open the **CreateModel** class in the *Instructors* folder (the *.cshtml.cs* file).
2. Change the namespace to **Instructors**.
   ```
   namespace VideoOnDemand.Admin.Pages.Instructors
   ```

3. Replace the **IEnumerable Input** property with one for the **Instructor** entity.
   ```
   public Instructor Input { get; set; } = new Instructor();
   ```

4. Remove the **IDbReadService** constructor injection and the **_dbReadService** variable.
5. Remove all code from the **OnGet** method.
6. Remove the **Input.CourseId** property code from the **OnPostAsync** method.
7. Change the text in the **SuccessMessage** property to *Created a new Instructor:* followed by the name of the instructor.
   ```
   StatusMessage = $"Created a new Instructor: {Input.Name}.";
   ```

8. Save all files.

The Create Razor Page

1. Open the **Create** Razor Page in the *Instructors* folder (the *.cshtml* file).
2. Change the **ViewData** title to *Create Instructor*.
3. Change the *Video* folder in the **path** attribute to *Instructors* in the first <page-button> element.
4. Change the content in the **form-group** <div> elements to display the values from the properties in the **Input** variable. Add and remove **form-group** <div> elements as needed.
5. Save all files.

The EditModel Class

1. Open the **EditModel** class in the *Instructors* folder (the *.cshtml.cs* file).
2. Change the namespace to **Instructors**.
   ```
   namespace VideoOnDemand.Admin.Pages.Instructors
   ```

3. Change the data type to **Instructor** for the **Input** variable.
   ```
   public Instructor Input { get; set; } = new Instructor();
   ```

4. Change the data type to **Instructor** and remove the **true** parameter for the **Get** method call in the **OnGet** method. You remove the **true** parameter because related entities don't need to be loaded.

```
Input = _dbReadService.Get<Instructor>(id);
```

5. Remove the **GetSelectList** code from the **OnGet** method. The **Instructor** entity isn't related to the **Module** entity.

6. Remove the **Input.CourseId** and **Input.Course** code rows from the **OnPostAsync** method.

7. Replace the text in the **SuccessMessage** property to *Updated Instructor:* followed by the name of the instructor.
```
StatusMessage = $"Updated Instructor: {Input.Name}.";
```

8. Save all files.

The Edit Razor Page

1. Open the **Edit** Razor Page in the *Instructors* folder (the *.cshtml* file).

2. Change the **ViewData** title to *Edit Instructor*.

3. Change the folder part of the **path** attribute for all the <page-button> elements from *Videos* to *Instructors*.

4. Change the **form-group** <div> elements' contents to match the properties in the **Input** object.

5. Save all files.

The DeleteModel Class

1. Open the **DeleteModel** class in the *Instructors* folder (the *.cshtml.cs* file).

2. Change the namespace to **Instructors**.
```
namespace VideoOnDemand.Admin.Pages.Instructors
```

3. Change the data type to **Instructor** for the **Input** variable.
```
public Instructor Input { get; set; } = new Instructor();
```

4. Change the data type to **Instructor** and remove the **true** parameter for the **Get** method call in the **OnGet** method.
```
Input = _dbReadService.Get<Instructor>(id);
```

5. Replace the text in the **SuccessMessage** property to *Deleted Instructor:* followed by the name of the instructor.
```
StatusMessage = $"Deleted Instructor: {Input.Name}.";
```

6. Save all files.

The Delete Razor Page

1. Open the **Delete** Razor Page in the *Instructors* folder (the *.cshtml* file).
2. Change the **ViewData** title to *Delete Instructor*.
3. Change the folder part of the **path** attribute for all the <page-button> elements from *Videos* to *Instructors*.
4. Change the contents of the <dd> and <dt> elements to match the properties in the **Input** object.
5. Change the **Input.Title** to **Input.Name** for the second hidden <input> element.
   ```
   <input type="hidden" asp-for="Input.Name" />
   ```
6. Save all files.

The Courses Razor Pages

1. Copy the *Videos* folder and all its contents.
2. Paste in the copied folder in the *Pages* folder and rename it *Courses*.

The IndexModel Class

1. Open the **IndexModel** class in the *Courses* folder (the *.cshtml.cs* file).
2. Change the namespace to **Courses**.
   ```
   namespace VideoOnDemand.Admin.Pages.Courses
   ```
3. Change the **IEnumerable** collection to store **Course** objects and rename it **Items**.
   ```
   public IEnumerable<Course> Items = new List<Course>();
   ```
4. Replace the data type defining the **GetWithIncludes** method with **Course**.
   ```
   public void OnGet()
   {
       Items = _dbReadService.GetWithIncludes<Course>();
   }
   ```
5. Save all files.

The Index Razor Page

1. Open the **Index** Razor Page in the *Courses* folder (the *.cshtml* file).
2. Change the **ViewData** title to *Course*.
3. Change the folder part of the **path** attribute of all the <page-button> elements from *Videos* to *Courses*.

4. Change the headings in the <th> elements to match the property values of the table. Add and remove <th> elements as needed.
5. Change the <td> elements to display the values from the properties in the **item** loop variable. Add and remove <td> elements as needed.
6. Save all files.

The CreateModel Class

1. Open the **CreateModel** class in the *Courses* folder (the *.cshtml.cs* file).
2. Change the namespace to **Courses**.
   ```
   namespace VideoOnDemand.Admin.Pages.Courses
   ```

3. Replace the **IEnumerable Input** property with one for the **Course** entity.
   ```
   public Course Input { get; set; } = new Course();
   ```

4. Rename the dynamic **Modules** property **Instructors**, change the defining type of the method and the property specifying the text to be displayed in the drop-down in the **OnGet** method to **Instructor**.
   ```
   public void OnGet()
   {
       ViewData["Instructors"] =
           _dbReadService.GetSelectList<Instructor>("Id", "Name");
   }
   ```

5. Remove the **Input.CourseId** property code from the **OnPostAsync** method.
6. Change the text in the **SuccessMessage** property to *Created a new Course:* followed by the course title.
   ```
   StatusMessage = $"Created a new Course: {Input.Title}.";
   ```

7. Save all files.

The Create Razor Page

1. Open the **Create** Razor Page in the *Courses* folder (the *.cshtml* file).
2. Change the **ViewData** title to *Create Course*.
3. Change the *Video* folder in the **path** attribute to *Courses* in the first <page-button> element.
4. Change the content in the **form-group** <div> elements to display the values from the properties in the **Input** variable. Add and remove **form-group** <div> elements as needed.
5. Save all files.

The EditModel Class

1. Open the **EditModel** class in the *Courses* folder (the *.cshtml.cs* file).
2. Change the namespace to **Courses**.
   ```
   namespace VideoOnDemand.Admin.Pages.Courses
   ```
3. Change the data type to **Course** for the **Input** variable.
   ```
   public Course Input { get; set; } = new Course();
   ```
8. Rename the dynamic **Modules** property **Instructors**. Change the defining type of the method and the property specifying the text to be displayed in the drop-down in the **OnGet** method to **Instructor**.
   ```
   ViewData["Instructors"] =
       _dbReadService.GetSelectList<Instructor>("Id", "Name");
   ```
4. Change the data type to **Instructor** and remove the **true** parameter for the **Get** method call in the **OnGet** method. You remove the **true** parameter because related entities don't need to be loaded.
   ```
   Input = _dbReadService.Get<Course>(id);
   ```
5. Remove the **Input.CourseId** and **Input.Course** code rows from the **OnPostAsync** method.
6. Replace the text in the **SuccessMessage** property to *Updated Course:* followed by the course title.
   ```
   StatusMessage = $"Updated Course: {Input.Title}.";
   ```
7. Save all files.

The Edit Razor Page

1. Open the **Edit** Razor Page in the *Courses* folder (the *.cshtml* file).
2. Change the **ViewData** title to *Edit Course*.
3. Change the folder part of the **path** attribute of all the <page-button> elements from *Videos* to *Courses*.
4. Change the **form-group** <div> elements' contents to match the properties in the **Input** object.
5. Save all files.

The DeleteModel Class

1. Open the **DeleteModel** class in the *Courses* folder (the *.cshtml.cs* file).
2. Change the namespace to **Courses**.
   ```
   namespace VideoOnDemand.Admin.Pages.Courses
   ```

3. Change the data type to **Course** for the **Input** variable.
   ```
   public Course Input { get; set; } = new Course();
   ```

4. Change the data type to **Course** for the **Get** method call in the **OnGet** method.
   ```
   Input = _dbReadService.Get<Course>(id, true);
   ```

5. Change the text in the **SuccessMessage** property to *Deleted Course:* followed by the course title.
   ```
   StatusMessage = $"Deleted Course: {Input.Title}.";
   ```

6. Save all files.

The Delete Razor Page

1. Open the **Delete** Razor Page in the *Courses* folder (the *.cshtml* file).
2. Change the **ViewData** title to *Delete Course*.
3. Change the folder part of the **path** attribute of all the <page-button> elements from *Videos* to *Courses*.
4. Change the contents of the <dd> and <dt> elements to match the properties in the **Input** object.
5. Save all files.

The Modules Razor Pages

1. Copy the *Videos* folder and all its contents.
2. Paste in the copied folder in the *Pages* folder and rename it *Modules*.

The IndexModel Class

1. Open the **IndexModel** class in the *Modules* folder (the *.cshtml.cs* file).
2. Change the namespace to **Modules**.
   ```
   namespace VideoOnDemand.Admin.Pages.Modules
   ```

3. Change the **IEnumerable** collection to store **Module** objects and rename it **Items**.
   ```
   public IEnumerable<Module> Items = new List<Module>();
   ```

4. Replace the data type defining the **GetWithIncludes** method to **Module**.

```
public void OnGet()
{
    Items = _dbReadService.GetWithIncludes<Module>();
}
```

5. Save all files.

The Index Razor Page

1. Open the **Index** Razor Page in the *Modules* folder (the *.cshtml* file).
2. Change the **ViewData** title to *Module*.
3. Change the folder part of the **path** attribute of all the <page-button> elements from *Videos* to *Modules*.
4. Change the headings in the <th> elements to match the property values of the table. Add and remove <th> elements as needed.
5. Change the <td> elements to display the values from the properties in the **item** loop variable. Add and remove <td> elements as needed.
6. Save all files.

The CreateModel Class

1. Open the **CreateModel** class in the *Modules* folder (the *.cshtml.cs* file).
2. Change the namespace to **Modules**.

```
namespace VideoOnDemand.Admin.Pages.Modules
```

3. Replace the **IEnumerable Input** property with one for the **Module** entity.

```
public Module Input { get; set; } = new Module();
```

4. Rename the dynamic **Modules** property **Courses** and change the defining type of the method to **Course**.

```
public void OnGet()
{
    ViewData["Courses"] = _dbReadService.GetSelectList<Course>(
        "Id", "Title");
}
```

5. Remove the **Input.CourseId** property code from the **OnPostAsync** method.
6. Change the text in the **SuccessMessage** property to *Created a new Module:* followed by the course title.

```
StatusMessage = $"Created a new Module: {Input.Title}.";
```

7. Save all files.

The Create Razor Page

1. Open the **Create** Razor Page in the *Modules* folder (the *.cshtml* file).
2. Change the **ViewData** title to *Create Module*.
3. Change the *Video* folder in the **path** attribute to *Modules* in the first <page-button> element.
4. Change the content in the **form-group** <div> elements to display the values from the properties in the **Input** variable. Add and remove **form-group** <div> elements as needed.
5. Save all files.

The EditModel Class

1. Open the **EditModel** class in the *Modules* folder (the *.cshtml.cs* file).
2. Change the namespace to **Modules**.
   ```
   namespace VideoOnDemand.Admin.Pages.Modules
   ```

3. Change the data type to **Module** for the **Input** variable.
   ```
   public Module Input { get; set; } = new Module();
   ```

4. Rename the dynamic **Modules** property **Courses** and change the defining type of the method to **Course** in the **OnGet** method.
   ```
   ViewData["Courses"] = _dbReadService.GetSelectList<Course>(
       "Id", "Title");
   ```

5. Change the data type to **Module** and remove the **true** parameter for the **Get** method call in the **OnGet** method. You remove the **true** parameter because related entities don't need to be loaded.
   ```
   Input = _dbReadService.Get<Module>(id);
   ```

6. Remove the **Input.CourseId** and **Input.Course** code rows from the **OnPostAsync** method.
7. Replace the text in the **SuccessMessage** property to *Updated Module:* followed by the course title.
   ```
   StatusMessage = $"Updated Module: {Input.Title}.";
   ```

8. Save all files.

The Edit Razor Page

1. Open the **Edit** Razor Page in the *Modules* folder (the *.cshtml* file).
2. Change the **ViewData** title to *Edit Module*.
3. Change the folder part of the **path** attribute of all the <page-button> elements from *Videos* to *Modules*.
4. Change the **form-group** <div> elements' contents to match the properties in the **Input** object.
5. Save all files.

The DeleteModel Class

1. Open the **DeleteModel** class in the *Modules* folder (the *.cshtml.cs* file).
2. Change the namespace to **Modules**.
    ```
    namespace VideoOnDemand.Admin.Pages.Modules
    ```
3. Change the data type to **Module** for the **Input** variable.
    ```
    public Module Input { get; set; } = new Module();
    ```
4. Change the data type to **Module** for the **Get** method call in the **OnGet** method.
    ```
    Input = _dbReadService.Get<Module>(id, true);
    ```
5. Change the text in the **SuccessMessage** property to *Deleted Module:* followed by the module title.
    ```
    StatusMessage = $"Deleted Module: {Input.Title}.";
    ```
6. Save all files.

The Delete Razor Page

1. Open the **Delete** Razor Page in the *Modules* folder (the *.cshtml* file).
2. Change the **ViewData** title to *Delete Module*.
3. Change the folder part of the **path** attribute of all the <page-button> elements from *Videos* to *Modules*.
4. Change the contents of the <dd> and <dt> elements to match the properties in the **Input** object.
5. Save all files.

The UserCourses Razor Pages

1. Copy the *Videos* folder and all its contents.
2. Paste in the copied folder in the *Pages* folder and rename it *UserCourses*.

The IndexModel Class

1. Open the **IndexModel** class in the *UserCourses* folder (the *.cshtml.cs* file).
2. Change the namespace to **UserCourse**.
   ```
   namespace VideoOnDemand.Admin.Pages.UserCourses
   ```

3. Change the **IEnumerable** collection to store **UserCourse** objects and rename it **Items**.
   ```
   public IEnumerable<UserCourse> Items = new List<UserCourse>();
   ```

4. Replace the data type defining the **GetWithIncludes** method to **UserCourse**.
   ```
   public void OnGet()
   {
       Items = _dbReadService.GetWithIncludes<UserCourse>();
   }
   ```

5. Save all files.

The Index Razor Page

1. Open the **Index** Razor Page in the *UserCourses* folder (the *.cshtml* file).
2. Change the **ViewData** title to *Users and Courses*.
3. Change the folder part of the **path** attribute of all the <page-button> elements from *Videos* to *UserCourses*.
4. Change the headings in the <th> elements to match the property values of the entity. Add and remove <th> elements as needed.
5. Change the <td> elements to display the values from the properties in the **item** loop variable. Add and remove <td> elements as needed.
6. Remove the **id** attribute of the <page-button> element.
7. Add two id attributes called **id-UserId** and **id-CourseId** to the <page-button> elements and assign the appropriate properties to them from the **item** loop variable.
   ```
   <page-button path="UserCourses/Edit" Bootstrap-style="success"
       glyph="pencil" id-userId="@item.UserId"
       id-courseId="@item.CourseId"></page-button>
   ```

   ```
   <page-button path="UserCourses/Delete" Bootstrap-style="danger"
       glyph="remove" id-userId="@item.UserId"
       id-courseId="@item.CourseId"></page-button>
   ```

8. Save all files.

The CreateModel Class

1. Open the **CreateModel** class in the *UserCourses* folder (the *.cshtml.cs* file).
2. Change the namespace to **UserCourse**.
   ```
   namespace VideoOnDemand.Admin.Pages.UserCourses
   ```

3. Replace the **Input** property with one for the **UserCourse** entity.
   ```
   public UserCourse Input { get; set; } = new UserCourse();
   ```

4. Inject the **IUserService** service into the constructor and save the object in a private class-level variable called **_userService**.
   ```
   private IUserService _userService;

   public CreateModel(IDbReadService dbReadService, IDbWriteService
   dbWriteService, IUserService userService)
   {
       _dbReadService = dbReadService;
       _dbWriteService = dbWriteService;
       _userService = userService;
   }
   ```

5. Rename the dynamic **Modules** property in the **OnGet** method **Courses** and change the defining type of the method to **Course**.
   ```
   ViewData["Courses"] = _dbReadService.GetSelectList<Course>(
       "Id", "Title");
   ```

6. Add another dynamic property called **Users** with the defining type **User**. Specify that the user's email address should be displayed in the drop-down.
   ```
   ViewData["Users"] = _dbReadService.GetSelectList<User>(
       "Id", "Email");
   ```

7. Remove the **Input.CourseId** property code from the **OnPostAsync** method.
8. Fetch the course and user from the database in the **success** if-block and use the course title and user email in the **SuccessMessage** property.
   ```
   if (success)
   {
       var user = _userService.GetUser(Input.UserId);
       var course = _dbReadService.Get<Course>(Input.CourseId);
       StatusMessage = $"User-Course combination [{course.Title} |
           {user.Email}] was created.";
       return RedirectToPage("Index");
   }
   ```

9. Copy the two **ViewData** properties from the **OnGet** method and paste them in above the **return** statement at the end of the **OnPostAsync** method to fill the drop-downs again.

```
ViewData["Users"] = _dbReadService.GetSelectList<User>(
    "Id", "Email");
ViewData["Courses"] = _dbReadService.GetSelectList<Course>(
    "Id", "Title");
return Page();
```

10. Save all files.

The Create Razor Page

1. Open the **Create** Razor Page in the *UserCourses* folder (the *.cshtml* file).
2. Change the **ViewData** title to *Add User to Course*.
3. Change the *Video* folder in the **path** attribute to *UserCourses* in the first <page-button> element.
4. Delete all **form-group** <div> elements and add two <select> elements for the **Users** and **Courses** collections in the dynamic **ViewBag** object that was filled with the **ViewData** object in the code-behind file.

```
<div class="form-group">
    <label asp-for="Input.UserId" class="control-label"></label>
    <select asp-for="Input.UserId" class="form-control"
        asp-items="ViewBag.Users"></select>
</div>
<div class="form-group">
    <label asp-for="Input.CourseId" class="control-label"></label>
    <select asp-for="Input.CourseId" class="form-control"
        asp-items="ViewBag.Courses"></select>
</div>
```

5. Save all files.

The UserCoursePageModel Class

This class will be used to transfer data to and from the **Edit** Razor Page in the *UserCourses* folder. The model is necessary since the entity class doesn't have all the necessary properties needed in the page.

1. Add a class called **UserCoursePageModel** to the *Models* folder.
2. Add two **string** properties called **Email** and **CourseTitle**.

3. Add two properties declared with the **UserCourse** class called **UserCourse** and **UpdatedUserCourse**. These two properties will be used to keep track of the original **UserCourse** values and the values selected by the user in the UI.
4. Save the file.

The complete code for the **UserCoursePageModel** class:

```
public class UserCoursePageModel
{
    public string Email { get; set; }
    public string CourseTitle { get; set; }
    public UserCourse UserCourse { get; set; } = new UserCourse();
    public UserCourse UpdatedUserCourse { get; set; } =
        new UserCourse();
}
```

The EditModel Class

1. Open the **EditModel** class in the *UserCourses* folder (the *.cshtml.cs* file).
2. Change the namespace to **UserCourses**.
   ```
   namespace VideoOnDemand.Admin.Pages.UserCourses
   ```

3. Replace the **Input** property data type with the **UserCoursePageModel** class.
   ```
   public UserCoursePageModel Input { get; set; } =
       new UserCoursePageModel();
   ```

4. Inject the **IUserService** service into the constructor and save the object in a private class-level variable called **_userService**.
5. Rename the dynamic **Modules** property in the **OnGet** method **Courses** and change the defining method type to **Course**.
   ```
   ViewData["Courses"] = _dbReadService.GetSelectList<Course>(
       "Id", "Title");
   ```

6. Change the name of the **id** parameter sent in to the **OnGet** method to **courseId** and add a second parameter called **userId (string)**.
7. Remove the line of code that assigns a value to the **Input** object in the **OnGet** method.
8. Fetch the user-course combination from the **UserCourses** database table matching the user id and course id sent in to the **OnGet** method and store it in the **UserCourse** property of the **Input** object.
   ```
   Input.UserCourse = _dbReadService.Get<UserCourse>(
   ```

```
    userId, courseId);
```

9. Assign the value of the **UserCourse** property of the **Input** object to the
   UpdatedUserCourse property. The two values will initially be the same, but
   when the user selects values in the UI the values of the **UpdatedUserCourse**
   property will change.
   ```
   Input.UpdatedUserCourse = Input.UserCourse;
   ```

10. Fetch the course and user from the database and assign the course title and user
    email to the **CourseTitle** and **Email** properties of the **Input** object.
    ```
    public void OnGet(int courseId, string userId)
    {
        ViewData["Courses"] =
            _dbReadService.GetSelectList<Course>("Id", "Title");
        Input.UserCourse = _dbReadService.Get<UserCourse>(
            userId, courseId);
        Input.UpdatedUserCourse = Input.UserCourse;
        var course = _dbReadService.Get<Course>(courseId);
        var user = _userService.GetUser(userId);
        Input.CourseTitle = course.Title;
        Input.Email = user.Email;
    }
    ```

11. Remove the **Input.CourseId** and **Input.Course** assignments from the
    OnPostAsync method.

12. Pass in the **UserCourse** and **UpdatedUserCourse** properties from the **Input**
    object to the **Update** method in the **OnPostAsync** method.

13. Fetch the updated user-course combination from the database in the **success** if-
    block and use the values in the **SuccessMessage** property text.
    ```
    if (success)
    {
        var updatedCourse = _dbReadService.Get<Course>(
            Input.UpdatedUserCourse.CourseId);

        StatusMessage = $"The [{Input.CourseTitle} | {Input.Email}]
            combination was changed to [{updatedCourse.Title} |
            {Input.Email}].";

        return RedirectToPage("Index");
    }
    ```

14. Copy the **ViewData** property from the **OnGet** method and paste it in above the **return** statement at the end of the **OnPostAsync** method to fill the drop-down again.

```
ViewData["Courses"] = _dbReadService.GetSelectList<Course>(
    "Id", "Title");

return Page();
```

15. Save all files.

The complete code for the **EditModel** class:

```
[Authorize(Roles = "Admin")]
public class EditModel : PageModel {
    private IDbWriteService _dbWriteService;
    private IDbReadService _dbReadService;
    private IUserService _userService;

    [BindProperty]
    public UserCoursePageModel Input { get; set; } =
        new UserCoursePageModel();

    [TempData] public string StatusMessage { get; set; }

    public EditModel(IDbReadService dbReadService,
    IDbWriteService dbWriteService, IUserService userService)
    {
        _dbWriteService = dbWriteService;
        _dbReadService = dbReadService;
        _userService = userService;
    }

    public void OnGet(int courseId, string userId)
    {
        ViewData["Courses"] = _dbReadService.GetSelectList<Course>(
            "Id", "Title");
        Input.UserCourse = _dbReadService.Get<UserCourse>(
            userId, courseId);
        Input.UpdatedUserCourse = Input.UserCourse;
        var course = _dbReadService.Get<Course>(courseId);
        var user = _userService.GetUser(userId);
        Input.CourseTitle = course.Title;
        Input.Email = user.Email;
    }
```

```
public async Task<IActionResult> OnPostAsync()
{
    if (ModelState.IsValid)
    {
        var success = await _dbWriteService.Update(Input.UserCourse,
            Input.UpdatedUserCourse);

        if (success)
        {
            var updatedCourse = _dbReadService.Get<Course>(
                Input.UpdatedUserCourse.CourseId);
            StatusMessage = $"The [{Input.CourseTitle} |
                {Input.Email}] combination was changed to
                [{updatedCourse.Title} | {Input.Email}].";

            return RedirectToPage("Index");
        }
    }

    // If we got this far, something failed, redisplay form
    ViewData["Courses"] = _dbReadService.GetSelectList<Course>(
        "Id", "Title");
    return Page();
}
}
```

The Edit Razor Page

1. Open the **Edit** Razor Page in the *UserCourses* folder (the *.cshtml* file).
2. Change the **ViewData** title to *Change course for user*.
3. Change the folder part of the **path** attribute of all the <page-button> elements from *Videos* to *UserCourses*.
4. Replace the hidden <input> element with four hidden <input> elements for the following properties: **Input.UserCourse.UserId**, **Input.UserCourse.CourseId**, **Input.UpdatedUserCourse.UserId**, **Input.CourseTitle**.
   ```
   <input type="hidden" asp-for="Input.UserCourse.UserId" />
   <input type="hidden" asp-for="Input.UserCourse.CourseId" />
   <input type="hidden" asp-for="Input.UpdatedUserCourse.UserId" />
   <input type="hidden" asp-for="Input.CourseTitle" />
   ```
6. Delete all **form-group** <div> elements and add a <select> element for the **Courses** collection in the dynamic **ViewBag** object (that was filled with the **ViewData** object in the code-behind file). Also, add a **readonly** <input> element

506

for the user's email address; it should be read-only because the administrator should not be able change user.

```
<div class="form-group">
    <label asp-for="Input.Email" class="control-label"></label>
    <input asp-for="Input.Email" readonly class="form-control" />
    <span asp-validation-for="Input.Email"
        class="text-danger"></span>
</div>
<div class="form-group">
    <label asp-for="Input.UpdatedUserCourse.CourseId"
        class="control-label"></label>
    <select asp-for="Input.UpdatedUserCourse.CourseId"
        class="form-control" asp-items="ViewBag.Courses"></select>
</div>
```

5. Save all files.

The DeleteModel Class

1. Open the **DeleteModel** class in the *UserCourses* folder (the *.cshtml.cs* file).
2. Change the namespace to **UserCourses**.
   ```
   namespace VideoOnDemand.Admin.Pages.UserCourses
   ```

3. Change the data type to **UserCoursePageModel** for the **Input** variable.
   ```
   public UserCoursePageModel Input { get; set; } =
       new UserCoursePageModel();
   ```

4. Inject the **IUserService** service into the constructor and save the object in a private class-level variable called **_userService**.
5. Rename the **id** parameter **courseId** and add a second parameter called **userId** (**string**) to the **OnGet** method.
6. Delete the code in the **OnGet** method.
7. Fetch the course, user, and user-course from the database. Assign the course title and user email to the **CourseTitle** and **Email** properties and the user-course to the **UserCourse** property of the **Input** object.
   ```
   public void OnGet(int courseId, string userId) {
       var user = _userService.GetUser(userId);
       var course = _dbReadService.Get<Course>(courseId);
       Input.UserCourse = _dbReadService.Get<UserCourse>(
           userId, courseId);
       Input.Email = user.Email;
       Input.CourseTitle = course.Title;
   }
   ```

8. Change the parameter sent into the **Delete** method to **Input.UserCourse** in the **OnPostAsync** method.
```
var success = await _dbWriteService.Delete(Input.UserCourse);
```

9. Change the text in the **SuccessMessage** property.
```
StatusMessage = $"User-Course combination [{Input.CourseTitle} |
    {Input.Email}] was deleted.";
```

10. Save all files.

The Delete Razor Page

1. Open the **Delete** Razor Page in the *UserCourses* folder (the *.cshtml* file).
2. Change the **ViewData** title to *Remove user from course*.
3. Change the folder part of the **path** attribute of all the <page-button> elements from *Videos* to *UserCourses*.
4. Replace the **id** attribute of the **Edit** button with two new ids for user id and course id.
```
<page-button path="UserCourses/Edit" Bootstrap-style="success"
    glyph="pencil" description="Edit"
    id-userId="@Model.Input.UserCourse.UserId"
    id-courseId="@Model.Input.UserCourse.CourseId">
</page-button>
```

5. Change the contents of the <dd> and <dt> elements to match the properties in the **Input** object.
6. Replace the hidden <input> elements with four hidden <input> elements for the following properties: **Input.UserCourse.UserId**, **Input.UserCourse.CourseId**, **Input.Email**, **Input.CourseTitle**.
```
<input type="hidden" asp-for="Input.UserCourse.UserId" />
<input type="hidden" asp-for="Input.UserCourse.CourseId" />
<input type="hidden" asp-for="Input.Email" />
<input type="hidden" asp-for="Input.CourseTitle" />
```

7. Save all files.

Summary

In this chapter, you implemented the rest of the Razor Pages needed in the administration application by reusing already created Razor Pages.

Thank you for taking the time to read the book and implement the projects.

Other Books by the Author

ASP.NET Core 2.0 – MVC & Razor Pages

ASP.NET Core 1.1 – Building a Website

ASP.NET Core 1.1 – Building a Web API

ASP.NET MVC 5 – Building a Website

C# for Beginners

Video Courses by the Author

MVC 5 – How to Build a Membership Website (video course)

This is a comprehensive video course on how to build a membership site using ASP.NET MVC 5. The course has in excess of **24 hours** of video.

In this video course you will learn how to build a membership website from scratch. You will create the database using Entity Framework code-first, scaffold an Administrator UI, and build a front-end UI using HTML5, CSS3, Bootstrap, JavaScript, C#, and MVC 5. Prerequisites for this course are: a good knowledge of the C# language and basic knowledge of MVC 5, HTML5, CSS3, Bootstrap, and JavaScript.

You can watch this video course on Udemy at this URL:
www.udemy.com/building-a-mvc-5-membership-website

Store Secret Data in a .NET Core Web App with Azure Key Vault (video course)

In this Udemy course you will learn how to store sensitive data in a secure manner. First you will learn how to store data securely in a file called *secrets.json* with the User Manager. The file is stored locally on your machine, outside the project's folder structure, and is therefore not checked into your code repository. Then you will learn how to use Azure Web App Settings to store key-value pairs for a specific web application. The third and final way to secure your sensitive data is using Azure Key Vault, secured with Azure Active Directory in the cloud.

The course is taught using an ASP.NET Core 2.0 Web API solution in Visual Studio 2015.

You really need to know this if you are a serious developer.

You can watch this video course on Udemy at this URL:
www.udemy.com/store-secret-data-in-net-core-web-app-with-azure-key-vault

Made in the USA
Lexington, KY
30 May 2018